From

The Vermont Military Museum & Library
789 National Guard Road
Colchester, VT 05664
(802) 338-3360

Visit Us On Facebook:

https://www.facebook.com/people/Vermont-National-Guard-Library-Museum/100064516847172/

Battle ships
of World War I

Battle ships

of World War I

An Illustrated Encyclopedia of the
Battleships of all Nations 1914-1918

Antony Preston

GALAHAD BOOKS · NEW YORK CITY

Acknowledgements

I should like to extend my thanks to the Trustees and the Director of the National Maritime Museum for their help in making this book possible. As usual I have enjoyed the unstinted help of my colleagues at the Museum, George Osbon, David Lyon and Keith Thomas, who pointed out material and photographs I might otherwise have missed. Many people have helped at all stages in the production of this book, but I must mention specifically John Campbell, for allowing me to use material from his forthcoming book and for his invaluable comments on many hundreds of minor points.

The staffs of the Naval Historical Branch of the Ministry of Defence and the Imperial War Museum have helped to locate a great deal of obscure material, and I must thank Messrs. Vickers–Armstrong, whose Elswick records yielded so much useful information on weapons. The Musée de la Marine in Paris, the U.S. National Archives and the Austrian Staatsarchiv in Vienna provided many useful photographs and drawings. M. Philippe Masson of the French Ministry of Marine gave advice on French archive sources, while Phillip K. Lundeberg of the Smithsonian Institution provided much appreciated assistance on United States sources.

The line drawings have been prepared from official material wherever possible, with reference to photographs, and I must record my deep debt to John Roberts and John Dominy for their invaluable assistance. Photographs have been supplied by the National Maritime Museum (particularly the Richard Perkins Collection), Imperial War Museum, Musée de la Marine (France), B. Drüppel (Germany), P. A. Vicary, Aldo Fraccaroli, Naval Photograph Club, Wright and Logan, the Bundesarchiv, the U.S. Navy History Dept. and the Ministry of Defence.

*The half-title shows H.M.S. Colossus
at battle practice (Author's collection).*

*The frontispiece shows S.M.S. Baden
towards the end of the war
(Bundesarchiv).*

Library of Congress Catalog Card Number: 74-29816
ISBN: 0-88365-300-1
Manufactured in the United States of America.
Published by arrangement with Stackpole Books.

Contents

Abbreviations & Data Glossary

Dimensions shown are length × beam × draught. The length shown is always the length between perpendiculars, unless otherwise indicated as oa (overall) or wl (waterline). 'Between perpendiculars', commonly abbreviated as bp or pp, is a convenient method of expressing the length of the major portion of the hull, between a perpendicular through the forward hawsepipe and an after perpendicular through the rudderpost. Although only approximate it gives a useful standard of comparison without having to bother about the variation caused by different types of bow or stern. The beam shown is always maximum beam, whereas draught is mean unless otherwise stated.

Guns are described by calibre or diameter of bore (eg: 12in) and by length of barrel expressed in terms of calibres (eg: a 45cal 12in gun is 45 × 12in long, or 45ft). The number of guns in each mounting shown thus, 3 × 3, 2 × 2, means that the ship has three triple mountings of one calibre, and two twin mountings of the same calibre.

Armour thicknesses are the maximum and minimum; there were many variations in the distribution of armour in any individual class, and these are too numerous to describe in detail.

Machinery consists of either reciprocating, quadruple- or triple-expansion, or steam turbines. The power of reciprocating machinery is expressed as indicated horsepower (ihp) and that of turbines as shaft horsepower (shp). The boilers are distinguished by the manufacturer's name, and in all cases are of the water-tube type. Speeds shown are the designed speed, unless otherwise indicated.

Fuel capacity is shown as normal/maximum stowage, the maximum being very rarely carried unless a long voyage was undertaken. All endurance figures should be taken with reserve, as they are based on the consumption in tons per knot per hour on the original trials. As it is almost axiomatic that a ship will never reach her trial speed again, and that her normal condition in service will be with a foul bottom, the coal consumption would be higher. In addition coal-fired ships always had difficulty in maintaining speed indefinitely, as stokers and trimmers encountered increasing trouble in getting coal from the furthermost bunkers.

Complement figures are subject to variation, as wartime crews were larger than peacetime. They also varied from ship to ship, and all figures quoted are approximate.

Deck levels are described according to British rather than American practice, ie: upper deck (quarterdeck or fantail), forecastle deck (the weather deck running aft from the bow), main deck (the deck level below the upper deck).

Turrets are numbered in order to avoid confusion. Wing turrets are numbered from port to starboard, from the bow.

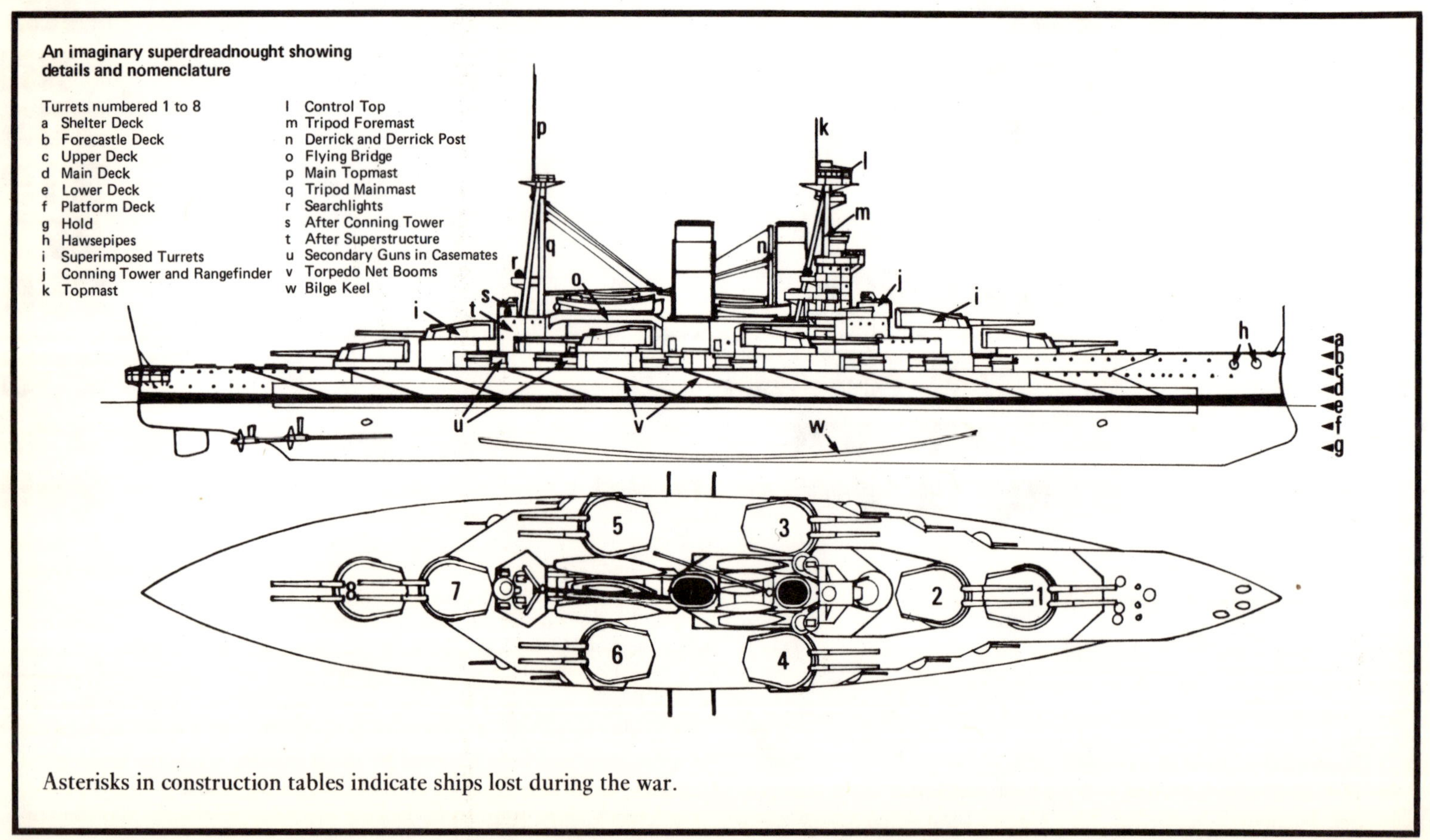

Asterisks in construction tables indicate ships lost during the war.

Introduction

The greatest unit of naval power in World War I, the battleship dominated naval and political thought in a way that we can only begin to understand, and was as much a symbol of national prestige as a weapon of war. For many reasons battleships were the most complex machines yet devised by man, and only the more advanced countries of the world could build them: they needed the heaviest hydraulic equipment to turn and elevate their enormous guns; the guns themselves could be made in only a dozen or so factories; and their propelling machinery comprised the most powerful units in existence.

The commitment of money was prodigious: for example the British battleships afloat in 1914 represented an investment of £100,000,000 ($400,000,000) at 1914 prices, without taking into account the hidden costs of providing docks, manning and coaling. It was estimated that the British Fleet at Scapa Flow used 100,000tons of coal each *week*, and the battleships alone absorbed nearly 50,000 men.

Although the origins of the capital ship can be traced back to the great ships of the Tudor Navy, the evolution of the modern battleship began in the Crimean War of 1854–6, when armour was first used to protect a series of floating batteries. The idea had been French, as an antidote to the menace of the explosive shell, which was capable of destroying wooden ships of the line in a matter of minutes. The French dutifully passed their ideas on to their British allies, who were able to use their superior ship-building resources to build very similar ships, but also taking the opportunity to build the last three with iron, instead of armoured wooden hulls.

Anglo-French concord did not survive for long, and by 1858 the French were so intoxicated by their discovery of armour that they decided to build a fleet of ironclads to challenge British supremacy. Although the Emperor kept a cool head, there were alarmists on both sides of the Channel who took some of the arguments seriously. The laying down of the ironclad frigates *Gloire*, *Invincible*, *Normandie* and *Couronne* in 1858 was the signal for a 'French invasion scare', but the British Admiralty kept calm, and took counsel of its architects and designers. When more was known of the French ironclads the British were able to reply with two ships which were superior in every respect, the *Warrior* and *Black Prince*. In the race which followed the French discovered that their industrial resources did not compare with the British in such vital matters as the rolling of iron armour plates and the manufacture of heavy engine castings.

The next landmark was in the field of gun mountings. The *Warrior* and *Gloire* were strictly orthodox in their layout, with single tiers of guns on the broadside, as in the old sailing frigates, but in 1855 Captain Cowper Coles of the Royal Navy had designed an armoured raft with a protected gun position, and by 1861 he built a revolving 'cupola' for heavy guns which was mounted on the floating battery *Trusty*. At the same time in the United States the Swedish-born engineer Ericsson was persuading the Navy Department in Washington to allow him to build a turreted ironclad to attack the Confederate ships in their harbours. On 9 March 1862 Ericsson's *Monitor* fought her action with the C.S.S. *Virginia* (ex-*Merrimac*) off Hampton Roads, and firmly established the turret as the most economical method of mounting guns.

In 1864 the British launched a ship which stands out as the true progenitor of the modern battleship. This was the coast defence turret-ship *Prince Albert*, which embodied in essence the future developments of twentieth-century designs: she was unrigged, and had her main armament in turrets on the centreline. In her time the importance of this little ship was overlooked, but had her design been developed into a larger seagoing battleship, the twentieth-century dreadnought might have taken shape much sooner. As it was, the next twenty-four years saw a weird series of variations on armour and layout of guns in all navies, and practical simplicity did not return until the closing years of the Victorian age.

Another important change in the design of the battleship was the introduction by the French of the 'barbette' mounting for heavy guns. This was basically a cylindrical tower built into a ship, with the gun or guns firing over the top, and revolving on a separate turntable inside the tower. In this respect it differed from the turret, where the deck and turret-base bore the combined weight of both turret and guns. Although the turret continued to hold its own right down to the late 1880s, it was finally displaced by the barbette, which was modified to include a shield protecting the guns and their crews from enemy gunfire. In modern terminology the shield to the barbette has become the turret, and will be referred to as such throughout this book; the term 'barbette' remained in use, but it came to be restricted to the base on which the 'turret' or barbette-shield rested. By 1914 these distinctions had become blurred, but the term 'turret-ship' indicated that a ship was armed with the old style of turret.

Other ships marked the evolution of the battleship: the *Devastation* of 1871 was the first seagoing battleship to dispense entirely with masts and yards, and in the *Collingwood* of 1882 the modern battleship finally took shape, with guns in barbettes forward and aft, separated by a secondary armament of 6in guns. These ships and all the experimental prototypes which had contributed to their evolution, had been built in ones and twos, but in the mid-1880s the British began to lay down homogeneous classes. With the passing of the Naval Defence Act in 1889 this trend was continued, partly to speed up the time of construction, but partly as a reflection of the growing confidence felt by British designers. Under Sir William White, the Royal Corps of Naval Constructors led the world in ideas, and their ships set new criteria of power and good looks.

After the Naval Defence Act battleship design stabilised for a decade, with a standard armament of four 12in guns, a displacement of 10–14,000tons, and speeds varying from 17 to 19knots. Within these broad limits the designers in each country turned out many variations, but for a time nobody was anxious to make any startling increases in size, armament or speed. However, at the turn of the century various designers, notably Brin in Italy and the Navy Department in Washington, reintroduced the medium gun of 7–9in calibre to bolster gunpower. As battle ranges were still limited to 3–4000yds, guns of this intermediate range could do almost as much damage as the main armament.

The testing ground for many of the theories of ship design which had been under development was the Russo-Japanese War of 1904–5. In this localised conflict the efficient Japanese Fleet utterly annihilated the poorly led and badly equipped Russians, but in essence the ideas and theories which were being tested were French versus British. French techniques of armouring had been adopted by the Russians, while the majority of Japanese ships have been built in British yards, and the results proved that French ships were badly lacking in ability to absorb punishment.

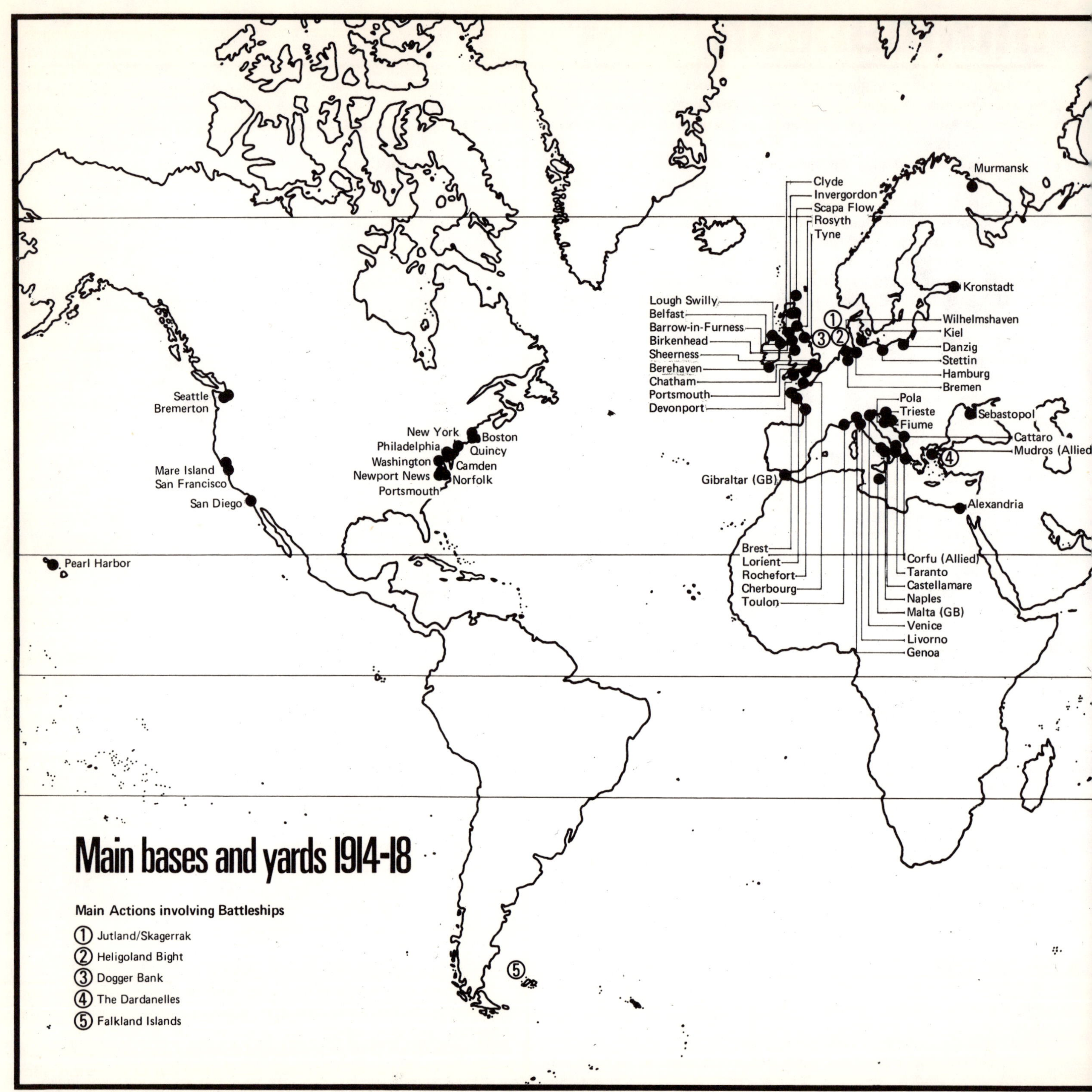

Main bases and yards 1914-18

Main Actions involving Battleships

1. Jutland/Skagerrak
2. Heligoland Bight
3. Dogger Bank
4. The Dardanelles
5. Falkland Islands

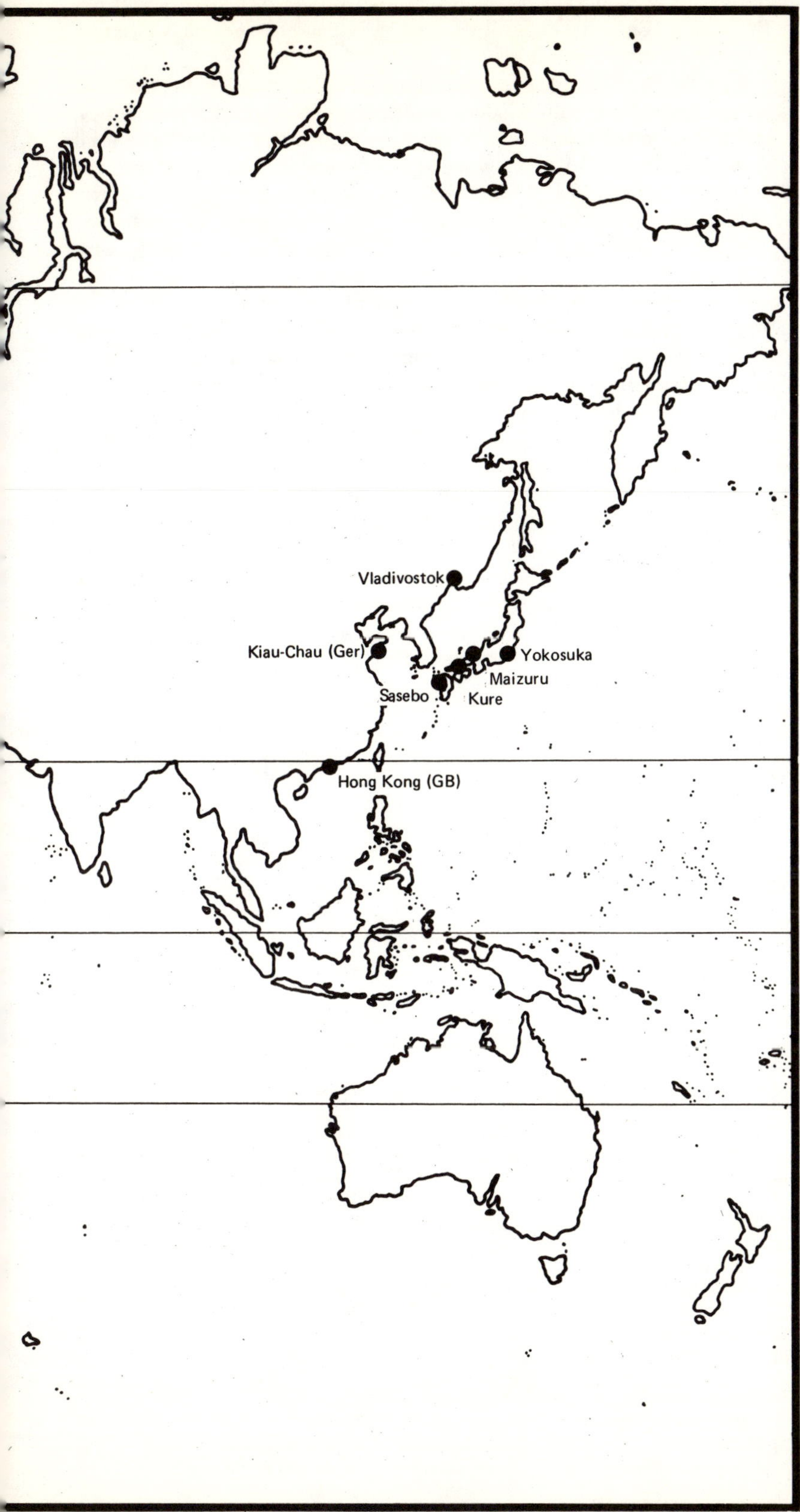

The most important tactical lesson of the Russo-Japanese War was that the existing battle ranges were unrealistic; the Japanese had opened fire at Tsushima at 7000yds, almost twice the range at which any navy was accustomed to fire. The world's major navies studied the Tsushima reports feverishly, and realising that long-range gunnery would be decisive, set about improving their training. In 1899 the British Captain Percy Scott had shown that more scientific methods of training could decrease the human error in gunnery, and as recent improvements in the manufacture of propellants had eliminated some of the irregularity of burning in powder, the scene was set for spectacular progress in gunnery.

The *Dreadnought* evolved because long-range gunnery made certain demands on design. The first attempts to improve long-range gunnery encountered a setback, because the heavy secondary guns in the new ships made a shell-splash almost indistinguishable from that of the 12in main guns. In the days before radar, the only method of ranging naval guns was to spot the shell-splashes, and as late as 1904 it was expected that each gunlayer would correct his own fall of shot. As the distances increased it became more and more difficult for the gunlayers to distinguish their fall of shot, and so salvo firing was adopted, a method whereby groups of guns fired together to give a 'spread' of shells in the area of the target. Provided the guns were accurately calibrated to throw their shells in more or less the same area, the probability was that some shells of the salvo would hit the target.

Once salvo firing was established as the only means of firing at long distances, the next logical step was to build a ship with a large number of 12in guns, so that her salvoes of 12in shells would have the maximum chance of hitting. Thus the *Dreadnought* and the *South Carolina* and *Michigan* came to be built. The way in which the *Dreadnought* came to be built first, and the fact that she had Parsons turbines were due to the organising ability of Admiral Fisher and the technical advantages enjoyed by the British at the time. Both types were inevitable responses to tactical needs, rather than strokes of genius from any individual's fertile brain.

The Americans reintroduced the idea of four centreline turrets, which had been forgotten since the *Prince Albert* of 1864, but apart from a tendency to simplify layout, the ships which followed the *Dreadnought* were mainly improved by increasing their gunpower. Calibres went up from 11in and 12in to 13·5in, 14in and then 15in, while armour protection had to follow suit. Inevitably size increased, and so did cost and complexity. Efficiency of machinery improved steadily, if not as spectacularly as weapons, but by 1914 many dreadnoughts were partially fitted to burn oil fuel, and the British were about to make a momentous switch right away from coal.

Weapons

The chief weapons of the battleship were her big guns. Although ranges varied from calibre to calibre and from mark to mark, the 12in gun which armed the majority of the world's battleships in 1914 could fire at 20,000 yds (approximately 11 land miles). At this range the chances of hitting a moving ship were remote, and the greatest range at which hits were obtained was about 17,000yds. Bigger guns could shoot further, as could old guns specially modified to shoot at high elevation.

Mountings were normally hydraulic, with power-operated hoists and rammers for the shells and cartridges, which had to be brought from the magazines and shell-rooms deep down near the bottom of the ship. Although in theory there were flashtight doors and scuttles through which charges had to be passed, war experience showed that all navies had taken such precautions lightly : in more than one ship these flashtight doors were left open to speed up the rate of fire, and it is probably fair to say that every ordnance expert had underestimated the dangers in 1914.

Twin mountings were normal for heavy guns, but the Russians, Italians and Austrians had already produced triple mountings, and the French had announced that they would be introducing quadruple turrets. Single turrets were also known (and the British introduced a single 18in mounting in 1917) but in general the requirements of long-range gunnery made single mountings an expensive luxury. Secondary guns were usually mounted singly, either in the hull, behind armour, or right out in the open, without protection of any sort. This stemmed from the Russo-Japanese War, when the Japanese had found light protection for smaller guns quite useless. Except in some older Russian ships, 6in guns or under were never mounted in turrets at forecastle or upper deck level.

Torpedo tubes were universally popular, but the above-water tubes found in Victorian battleships had given way to submerged tubes, as it was felt that there was too much risk of torpedoes being detonated on deck by shell hits. In fact, the chances of one battleship torpedoing another were abysmally small, even when looking at nineteenth-century naval actions, but all navies continued to mount tubes in capital ships.

Aircraft

Both the British and the Americans had carried out experiments in launching aircraft from ships in 1911–12, but it was left to the British to develop techniques for flying fighters and reconnaissance aircraft from ships to counter the menace of German airships. These Zeppelins were of great assistance to the High Seas Fleet in reporting the whereabouts of British ships, and the British hoped to use fighter aircraft to destroy the Zeppelins before they could relay information.

The British developed their naval air arm to such a pitch that in 1918 they had 500 aircraft at sea with the Grand Fleet, the battle cruisers and the Harwich Force. Had the war continued into 1919 they were planning for a torpedo-bomber raid on the High Seas Fleet—a project which would have anticipated Pearl Harbour and Taranto by over twenty years.

Both the Americans and the Japanese were also experimenting in 1917–18 with aircraft flying from turret-platforms, but the British were the only ones to make any use of this idea in service.

War Service

The Germans and British inevitably made the North Sea the main arena of the naval struggle, with virtually all their dreadnoughts concentrated there. As the two important actions—Dogger Bank and Jutland ('Skagerrak' to the Germans)—were indecisive, the prewar expectations of a North Sea Trafalgar were not realised. For most of the dreadnoughts the war involved long periods at anchor, punctuated by dreary sweeps in vile weather and the dirty routine of coaling.

The peripheral military campaigns undertaken by the British and French created employment for the older battleships, many of which saw more action than the dreadnoughts. Shore bombardment and patrol duties, as well as the humdrum task of providing a flagship for local naval forces were duties which occupied predreadnought battleships for the whole of the war, and most of the losses were incurred among ships on subsidiary duties. From the list of losses shown in Table 1 it is clear that the mine and the submarine torpedo accounted for most of the battleships sunk in the war. Only 9 out of 36 could be described as being sunk 'in action'—as opposed to being lost by underwater attack or by accident.

The great test of the predreadnought battleships of Great Britain and France came at Gallipoli in 1915, when the combined fleets attempted to silence the Turkish forts on both sides of the Dardanelles. Although the older ships were heavily hit, in general they proved well able to carry out their tasks. Their fire-control was crude, but sufficient to allow them to fire at fixed targets on shore.

By 1917 the Allies had completed enough dreadnoughts to be able to release some of the more modern predreadnoughts for subsidiary duties, and this in turn led to several of the older units being paid off and used as harbour hulks. In 1917, when manning was an acute problem, the British First Sea Lord, Admiral Jellicoe, even offered to put a squadron of the oldest dreadnoughts into reserve, but this was not allowed.

When the war ended, battleship design had progressed so rapidly, with 15in and 16in guns and ships of 40,000tons and more projected, that virtually all the early dreadnoughts were obsolete. The 1919 edition of *Brassey's Naval Annual* stated that ships with 12in guns had no place in naval warfare—which eliminated ships built only seven years before. A long procession of old battleships now went to the ship-breakers, some of them surrendered German and Austrian ships, but most of them belonging to the victorious Allies. In 1921 the British firm of Wards clinched the biggest scrap-metal deal in history, when they bought over 200 warships at a flat rate of £2 10s ($10.00) per ton.

Although the battleship survived to fight in another world war, the 1914–18 war was her heyday; never again would so many battleships and battle cruisers swell the returns of warships, and never again would a nation's strength be gauged by her total of dreadnoughts.

Chronological List of Battleship Losses in World War I		
Ship (Nationality)	Date of Loss	Cause
Audacious (British)	27 October 1914	Mine
Bulwark (British)	26 November 1914	Ammunition explosion
Messudieh (Turkish)	13 December 1914	Submarine torpedo
Formidable (British)	1 January 1915	Submarine torpedo
Bouvet (French)	18 March 1915	Mine
Irresistible (British)	18 March 1915	Mine
Ocean (British)	18 March 1915	Mine
Majestic (British)	27 April 1915	Submarine torpedo
Goliath (British)	18 May 1915	Surface torpedo
Triumph (British)	25 May 1915	Submarine torpedo
Haireddin Barbarossa (Turkish)	8 August 1915	Submarine torpedo
Benedetto Brin (Italian)	28 September 1915	Ammunition explosion
King Edward VII (British)	6 January 1916	Mine
Russell (British)	27 April 1916	Mine
Invincible (British)	31 May 1916	Gunfire
Indefatigable (British)	31 May 1916	Gunfire
Queen Mary (British)	31 May 1916	Gunfire
Pommern (German)	1 June 1916	Surface torpedo
Lützow (German)	1 June 1916	Scuttled after gunfire and torpedo damage
Leonardo da Vinci (Italian)	2 August 1916	Ammunition explosion
Imperatritsa Maria (Russian)	20 October 1916	Ammunition explosion
Suffren (French)	26 November 1916	Submarine torpedo
Regina Margherita (Italian)	11 December 1916	Mine
Gaulois (French)	27 December 1916	Submarine torpedo
Peresviet (Russian)	5 January 1917	Mine
Cornwallis (British)	9 January 1917	Submarine torpedo
Tsukuba (Japanese)	14 January 1917	Ammunition explosion
Danton (French)	19 March 1917	Submarine torpedo
Vanguard (British)	9 July 1917	Ammunition explosion
Slava (Russian)	17 October 1917	Gunfire
Wien (Austrian)	10 December 1917	Surface torpedo
Szent Istvan (Austrian)	10 June 1918	Surface torpedo
Svobodnaya Rossia (Russian)	18 June 1918	Scuttled
Glatton (British)	16 September 1918	Ammunition explosion
Viribus Unitis (Austrian)	10 October 1918	Surface torpedo
Britannia (British)	9 November 1918	Submarine torpedo

Austria-Hungary

Viribus Unitis on gunnery trials in 1913 (Austrian State Archives).

Introduction

The Austro-Hungarian Navy had always been known as a small but efficient force, adequate for defence against Italy, but having no other offensive purpose. The Austrians were in fact most anxious not to afford Italy any excuse for hostile action, and had avoided such gestures as preserving Tegetthoff's old flagship, the *Ferdinand Max*, with too much ostentation, lest she remind the Italians of their defeat at Lissa in 1866. Manning was always a problem, with so many languages and ethnic groups among recruits—officers frequently found it necessary to speak as many as six or seven languages.

The big expansion initiated by Count Montecuccoli had not yet shown many results. Apart from the two dreadnoughts completed, and the second pair completing, only the three *Radetzky* class battleships could be called modern. In addition the geography of the Adriatic was against the Austrians, with the Allies holding the Otranto Straits and thus bottling them in. Nevertheless the Austrians handled their small craft with great daring, and kept the Allied patrols in a constant state of vigilance, and the presence of seven battleships at Pola (now Pula) meant that numerous Allied capital ships were kept at Taranto and Brindisi for three years.

Disposition of the Austro-Hungarian Fleet at the Outbreak of War
1st Division
Tegetthoff (flagship), Viribus Unitis, Prinz Eugen
2nd Division
Erzherzog Franz Ferdinand (flagship), Radetzky, Zrinyi
Reserve
Erzherzog Ferdinand Max, Erzherzog Karl, Erzherzog Friedrich, Habsburg, Babenberg, Arpad, Monarch, Budapest, Wien

---

Some of the older ships were used for shore bombardment early in the war, but once the Italians entered hostilities the number of ships available to the Allies was so great that movement of big ships became more difficult. The only big operation planned was to have been a sweep down the Adriatic, with the four dreadnoughts and supporting vessels, to fall on the Allied ships north of Brindisi and then roll up the Otranto Barrage. Unfortunately an Italian attack on Pola with a motor torpedo boat sank the *Szent Istvan*, and the plan had to be abandoned.

Mutiny began to sap the efficiency of the Fleet from 1917, and the Yugo-Slav movement was very active among the sailors. When the Empire disintegrated in October 1918, the Archduke Charles was prepared to allow the whole fleet to be transferred to the Yugo-Slavs, to keep it out of Italian hands. The dreadnought *Viribus Unitis* was actually handed over at Pola to the Yugo-Slavs on 30 October 1918, and a 21-gun salute fired in honour of the old Austro-Hungarian flag, but on the next day two Italians entered the harbour and placed a limpet mine on her hull which sent her to the bottom.

Dockyards and Shipbuilders
Pola was the principal dockyard, with modern facilities. Cattaro (now Kotor) was used as a base, and because of the nature of the Dalmatian coast, with its deep and narrow channels all the way up the Adriatic, battleships could move between the two main bases with ease. The chain of islands afforded protection, and Austrian forces were able to use them as cover for raids on the blockading Italian ships.

Only three yards were capable of building battleships, the Danubius shipyard and machinery works at Fiume, the Stabilimento Tecnico Triestino at Trieste and Pola Dockyard. The guns came from the Skoda Works at Pilsen, and were of a very high standard.

Weapons
The Skoda Works provided a complete range of weapons of all calibres. The triple mountings of the *Viribus Unitis* class were among the most advanced in the world.

Austro-Hungarian Guns			
Calibre	Length in Cal.	Muzzle Velocity	Shell Weight
9·4in	40cal	2264fps	474lb (A.P.)
12in	45cal	2623fps	992lb (A.P.)
14in	45cal	2526fps	1520lb

The Allies refused to recognise the Austrian negotiations with the Yugo-Slav state, and subsequently the ships were re-allocated. Under the Versailles and St. Germain Treaties Italy received the *Erzherzog Franz Ferdinand*, *Radetzky*, *Tegetthoff* and *Zrinyi*, and these ships were handed over at Venice. *Prinz Eugen* went to France.

Austro-Hungarian Fleet in October 1918
1st Division (at Pola)
Tegetthoff (flagship), Viribus Unitis, Prinz Eugen
2nd Division (at Pola)
Erzherzog Franz Ferdinand (flagship), Radetzky, Zrinyi
3rd Division (at Cattaro)
Erzherzog Ferdinand Max (flagship), Erzherzog Karl, Erzherzog Friedrich
Miscellaneous ships at Pola
Habsburg, Babenberg, Arpad (prison ship), Monarch, Budapest (not in commission)

Obsolete Battleships
The following obsolete ships were used as guardships at Cattaro and Pola respectively during the War:

K. E. Rudolf (1887)
Mars (ex-*Tegetthoff*) (1878)

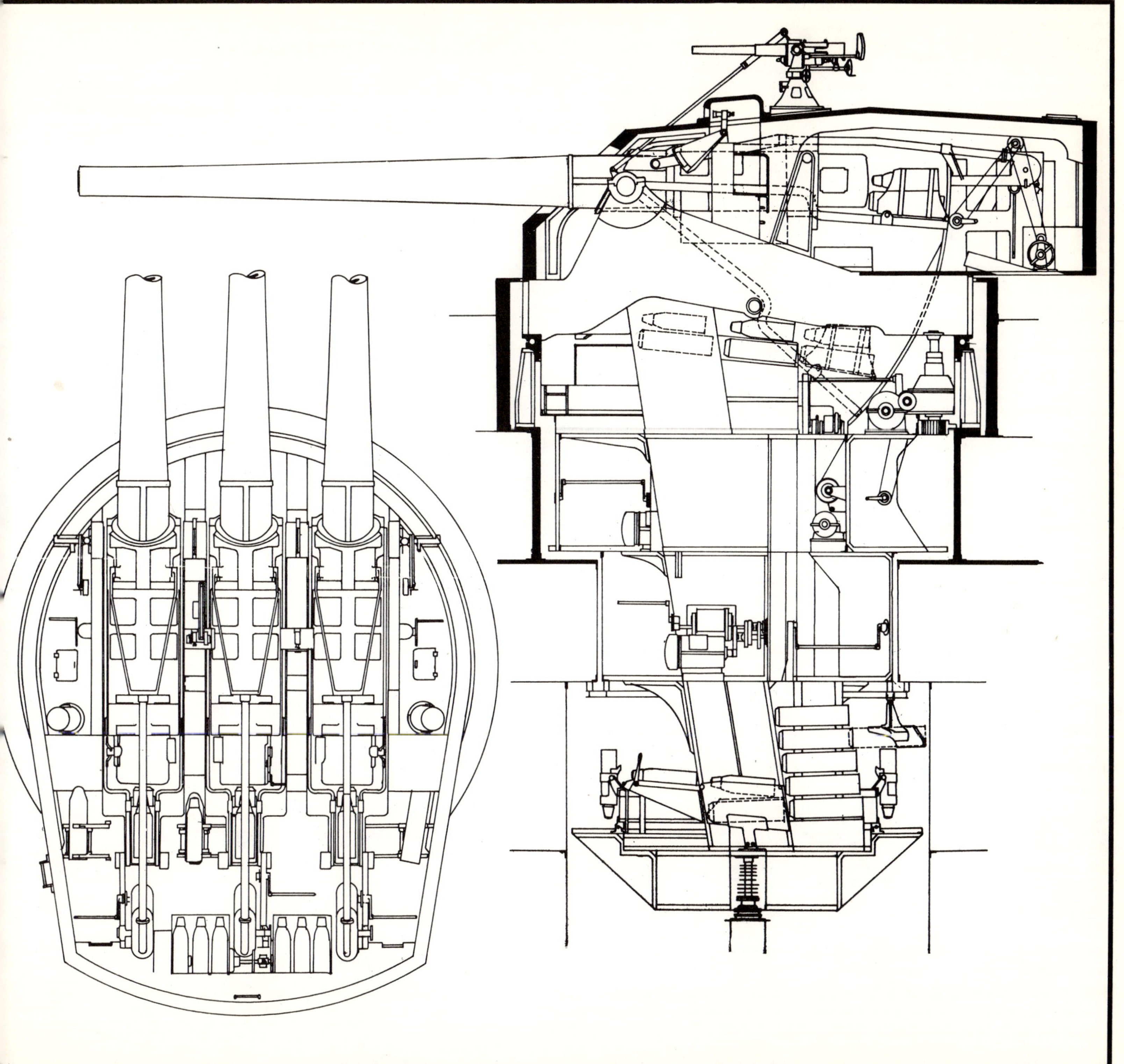

The triple 12in turret of the dreadnoughts of the Viribus Unitis class, manufactured by the famous Skoda-Werke at Pilsen.

Wien class

Displacement: 5600tons normal
Dimensions: 305ft×56ft×21ft (max)
Guns: 4×9·4in Model 1886, 40cal
(2×2)
6×5·9in 40cal (6×1)
2×76mm 18cal
14×3pdrs
Torpedo Tubes: 2×17·7in (above
water, bow and stern)
Armour: 10½–4¾in belt; 2½in deck;
8–5in turrets; 8in CT
Machinery: 2–shaft vertical triple
expansion, 8,500hp = 17knots
(approx. 13×1914); cylindrical
boilers (Belleville in Budapest)
Coal Capacity: 300/500tons
Endurance: Not known
Complement: 400
Cost: Approximately £340,000 each
($1,360,000)

	Laid Down	Launched	Completed	Built/Engined
Wien	1893	July 1895	1896	Stabilimento Technico
Monarch	1893	May 1895	1897	Pola DY
Budapest	1894	Apr 1896	1897	Stabilimento Technico

These ships were due for replacement in 1916 by the dreadnoughts projected to follow the *Viribus Unitis* class, being too old and slow to have any military value. In 1918 *Budapest* was altered to take a 15in howitzer in place of No. 1 turret, but this refit was still incomplete at the end of the war.

Appearance: Their single funnel and large fighting top at base of foremast made them look not unlike the British *Majestic* class on the broadside, but their lack of freeboard was a clear distinction.

Careers

Budapest: Laid up at outbreak of war, and not fully commissioned until 1916, when she and her sisters formed the 5th Division at Cattaro; in 1918 she served as a tender to the Naval Academy at Fiume; refitted 1918 but work still incomplete in October 1918; allocated to Royal Navy and broken up *c.*1920.

Monarch: Service as *Budapest*; accommodation ship 1918.

Wien: Service as *Budapest*, but served during war as tender to the gunnery school at Pola: torpedoed 10 December 1917 at Trieste by an Italian M.T.B.

Above, *two prewar views of the Monarch (IWM and Austrian State Archives).*

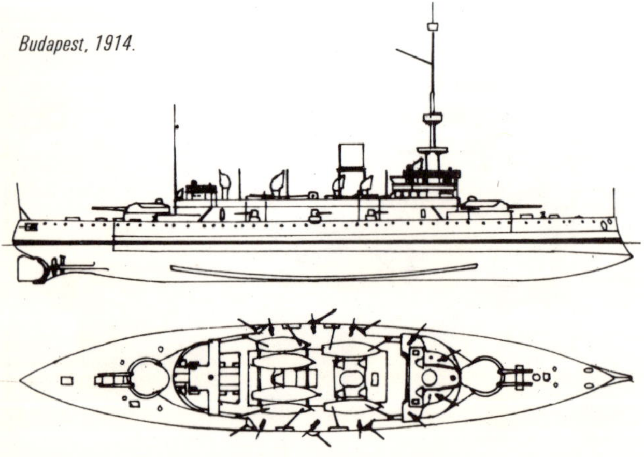

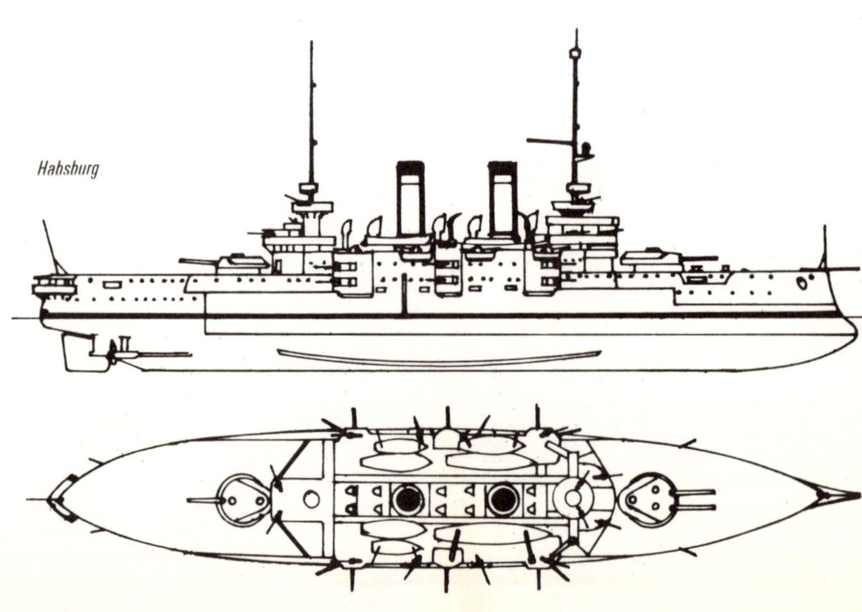

Habsburg class

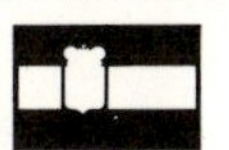

Displacement: 8340tons (normal)
Dimensions: 354ft 4in×65ft 6in× 25ft (max)
Guns: 3×9·4in 40cal (1×2, 1×1)
12×6in 40cal (12×1)
12×76mm (12×1)
Torpedo Tubes: 2×17·7in (beam, submerged)
Armour: $8\frac{3}{4}$–2in belt; $2\frac{1}{2}$in decks; $8\frac{1}{2}$in turrets; 8in C.T.
Machinery: 2-shaft 4-cylinder triple-expansion, 11,900ihp = 18knots; 16 Belleville boilers
Coal Capacity: 500/840tons
Endurance: Not known
Complement: 880

	Laid Down	Launched	Completed	Built/Engined
Habsburg	Feb 1899	Sept 1900	1903	Trieste DY
Arpad	Nov 1899	Sept 1901	1903	Trieste DY
Babenberg	May 1900	Oct 1902	1904	Pola DY

These had been reconstructed just before the outbreak of war, but in spite of this they were fit for little more than coastal defence. During the refit the ventilating cowls were removed, and fire-control was improved, but little else was done to alter their appearance.

Armament: Unusual in having a twin 9·4in turret forward and a single aft. The 76mm guns were arranged above the 6in battery, and in hull-embrasures under the forecastle and quarterdeck.

Appearance: The three double-storied casemates equally spaced amidships gave them a distinctive appearance.

Careers
Arpad: 4th Division 1914–18; training ship 1918; allocated to Royal Navy and broken up *c.*1920.
Babenburg: Service as *Arpad*; accomodation ship 1918; broken up *c.*1920.
Habsburg: Service as *Arpad*; flagship during Ancona raid, 24 May 1915; training ship 1918; broken up *c.*1920.

Top, a pre-1914 view of Arpad, showing the unique arrangement of the secondary battery in three double casemates. Note also the forecastle boom used in handling the anchors (IWM). Above, a view of Babenberg just prior to her refit in 1914 when the ventilating cowls were removed (Austrian State Archives).

Erzherzog Karl class

Displacement: 10,600tons (normal)
Dimensions: 390ft 6in×72ft×24ft 6in (mean)
Guns: 4×9·4in 40cal (2×2)
12×7·6in 42cal (12×1)
14×76mm (12×1)
Torpedo Tubes: 2×17·7in (beam, submerged)
Armour: 8½–2in belt; 2¾–2in deck; 9½in turrets; 8½in C.T.

Machinery: 2-shaft 4-cyl. triple-expansion, 14,000ihp = 19¼knots; 12 Yarrow boilers
Coal Capacity: 550/1315tons

Endurance: Approximately 4000miles at 10knots
Complement: 700
Cost: £912,500 average ($3,650,000)

	Laid Down	Launched	Completed	Built/Engined
Erzherzog Karl	1901	Oct 1903	Feb 1905	Trieste DY
Erzherzog Friedrich	1902	Apr 1904	Oct 1906	Trieste DY
Erzherzog Ferdinand Max	1903	May 1905	Apr 1907	Trieste DY

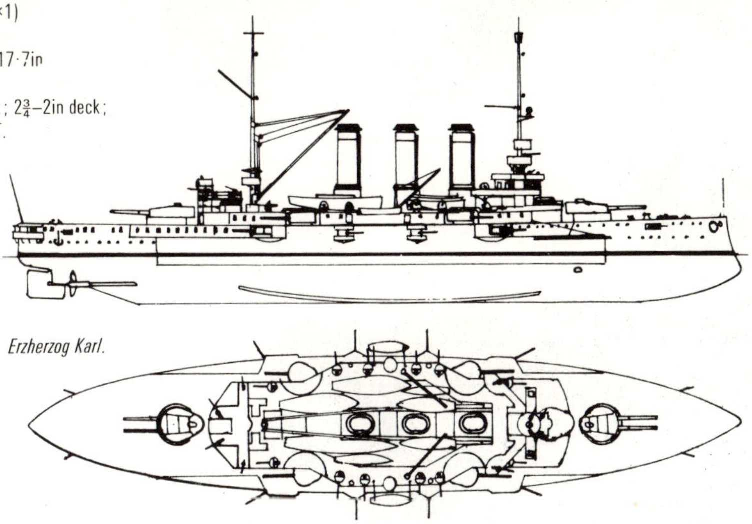

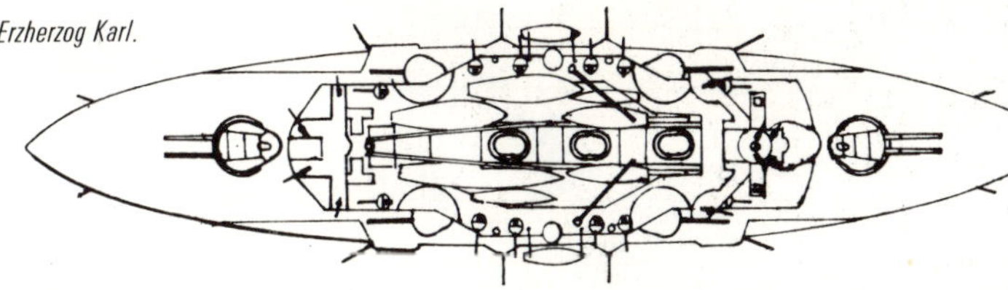

Erzherzog Karl.

These handsome ships suffered, like their contemporaries in the French Fleet from being built too late. Although fine ships for their period, and almost certainly equal to anything the French and the Italians possessed, they could only be used for coastal defence or shore bombardment by 1914.

Armament: The 7·6in guns were arranged in four single turrets at the corners of the superstructure, and in single case-mates at upper deck level. The 76mm guns were, like those in the *Habsburg* class, arranged above the battery. The 9·4in guns had 20° elevation, giving a range of 17,000yds.

Appearance: By 1914 all three had small fire-control platforms on their foremasts.

Careers

Erzherzog Ferdinand Max: Laid up on outbreak of war; Ancona raid 24 May 1915; 3rd Division 1916–18; taken over by Yugo-Slavs in 1919; allocated France and broken up 1920.

Erzherzog Friedrich: Service as *Erzherzog Ferdinand Max.*

Erzherzog Karl: Service as *Erzherzog Ferdinand Max,* but ran aground off Bizerta, while in tow for Toulon; broken up where she lay *c.* 1920.

Top left and below far left, Erzherzog Ferdinand Max (Austrian State Archives). **Below left,** Erzherzog Friedrich shown prewar (IWM).

Right, a pre-1914 view of Erzherzog Karl (Austrian State Archives).

Displacement: 14,500tons (normal); approx. 15,000tons (full load)
Dimensions: 429ft 9in×82ft×26ft 4in (mean)
Guns: 4×12in 45cal (2×2)
8×9·4in 45cal (4×2)
20×4·1in 50cal (20×1)
6×70mm (6×1)
Torpedo Tubes: 3×17·7in (1 bow, 2 beam, all submerged)
Armour: 9–3in belt; 2in deck; 10in turrets; 10in C.T.
Machinery: 2-shaft vertical triple-expansion, 20,000ihp = 20knots; 12 Yarrow boilers
Coal Capacity: 750/1350tons
Endurance: Approximately 4000miles at 10knots
Complement: 880
Cost: Not known

Left, Zrinyi shown before the war. Note her resemblance to the British King Edward VII class (Austrian State Archives).

Left, Radetzky seen running trials in 1910 (Austrian State Archives).

Radetzky class

	Laid Down	Launched	Completed	Built/Engined
Erzherzog Franz Ferdinand	12 Sept 1907	30 Sept 1908	July 1910	Stabilimento Tecnico, Trieste
Zrinyi	15 Nov 1908	12 Apr 1910	July 1911	Stabilimento Tecnico, Trieste
Radetzky	26 Nov 1907	3 July 1909	Oct 1910	Stabilimento Tecnico, Trieste

These ships were laid down after the building of the *Dreadnought* to match the French *Dantons* and the Italian *Vittorio Emmanuele* and *Pisa* classes. They were badly outclassed by the Italian dreadnoughts and were only fit for second-line duties.

Appearance: They strongly resembled the British *King Edward VII* class, with two equal-sized funnels, and turrets at the corners of the superstructure.

Erzherzog Franz Ferdinand: Serving with 2nd Division of Battle Squadron on outbreak of war; bombardment of Ancona 24 May 1915; remained with 2nd Division from 1914–18; interned 1919 at Venice: broken up 1920.

Radetzky: 2nd Division, Battle Squadron 1914–18; bombarded Ancona 24 May 1915; taken over by Yugoslavs in 1918; broken up in Italy 1920.

Zrinyi: Bombarded Ancona 24 May 1915 while serving with 2nd Division; taken over by Yugoslavs in 1918; ceded to U.S.A. as reparations and broken up in Italy in 1920.

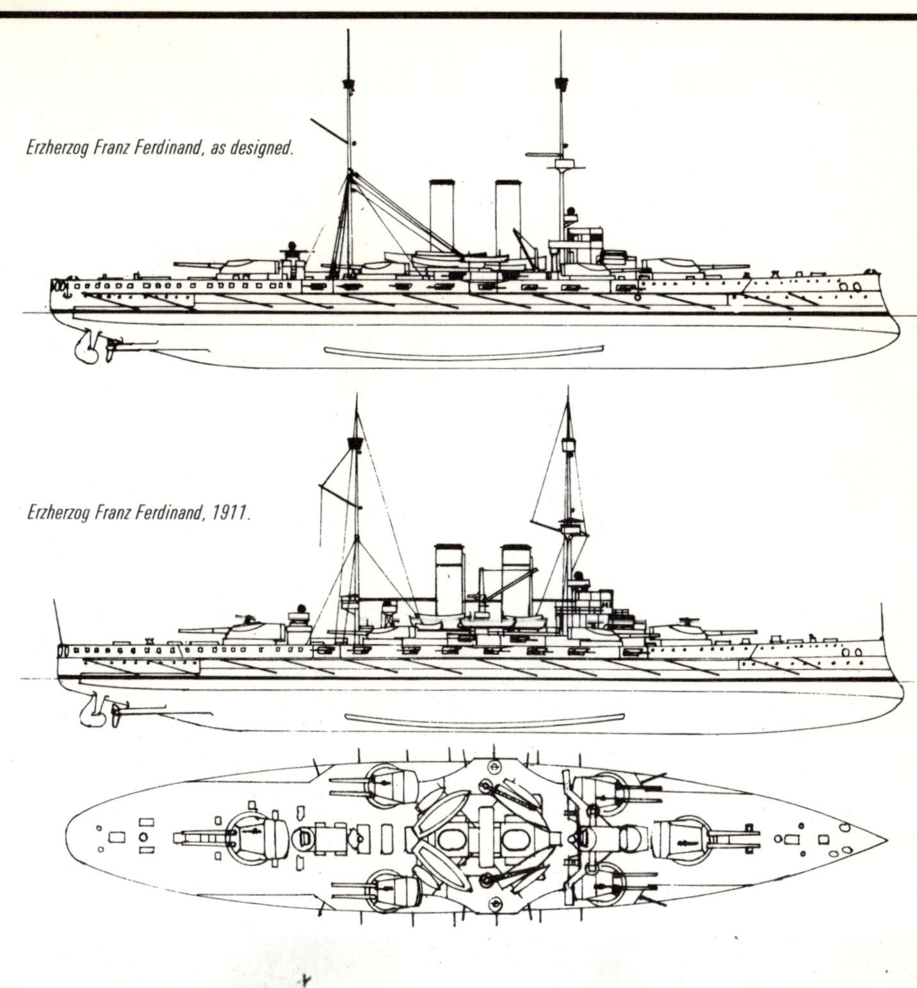

Erzherzog Franz Ferdinand, as designed.

Erzherzog Franz Ferdinand, 1911.

Below, *Erzherzog Franz Ferdinand seen before the war at Pola (IWM).*

Viribus Unitis class

Displacement: 20,000tons normal, 22,000tons full load
Dimensions: 469ft×89ft 6in×27ft (mean)
Guns: 12×12in 45cal (4×3)
12×5·9in cal (12×1)
18×76mm (18×1)
6 smaller
Torpedo Tubes: 4×21in (submerged, beam)
Armour: 11–8in belt; 2½in decks; 11in turrets; 11in C.T.
Machinery: 4-shaft turbines, 25,000hp; 20½knots; ? Yarrow boilers (Babcock in Szent Istvan)
Coal Capacity: 900/2000tons
Endurance: 4200miles at 10knots
Complement: 1000
Cost: £2,500,000 average ($10,000,000)

	Laid Down	Launched	Completed	Built/Engined
Prinz Eugen	16 Jan 1912	30 Nov 1912	July 1914	Trieste DY
*Szent Istvan	29 Jan 1912	17 Jan 1914	Nov 1915	Fiume DY
Tegetthoff	24 May 1910	21 Mar 1912	July 1913	Trieste DY
*Viribus Unitis	24 July 1910	20 June 1911	Oct 1912	Trieste DY

These were handsome, well-proportioned ships. Thanks to the technical ingenuity of the Skoda Works, they enjoyed a heavy broadside without requiring a great length of hull, as in the case of Japanese, American and German ships with twelve guns. However, the lack of experience in building large ships could well have made them less effective in action than their foreign contemporaries.

Appearance: This class bore a superficial resemblance to the British *Queen Elizabeth* class, with two round funnels and four turrets.

Careers

Prinz Eugen: With 1st Division of Battle Squadron 1914–18; bombarded Ancona 24 May 1915; remained at Pola throughout war, and after 1918 surrender ceded to France for use as a target; delivered 25 August 1920 and sunk off Toulon by gunfire from *France* and *Bretagne* 28 June 1922.

Szent Istvan: As *Prinz Eugen* served with 1st Division, Battle Squadron at Pola from 1915–18; torpedoed and sunk off Premuda by Italian M.T.B. *M AS 15* 10 June 1918 (89 lives lost).

Tegetthoff: Flagship of 1st Division of Battle Squadron on outbreak of war, but relieved by *Viribus Unitis* as Fleet Flagship in 1916; remained with 1st Division until Armistice; ceded to Italy and delivered 25 March 1919; broken up at La Spezia 1924–5.

Viribus Unitis: With 1st Division of Battle Squadron 1914–18, and relieved *Tegetthoff* as Fleet Flagship in 1916; with the collapse of the Austro-Hungarian Empire in October 1918 she was handed over to the new Yugoslavian Government on 1 November, but on 10 November she was sunk by an explosive charge placed by Italians, in the harbour at Pola (400 dead).

Above, Prinz Eugen ready for launching in 1915. Note the unusual stern walk and the fact that the armour belt has not yet been fitted (Austrian State Archives).

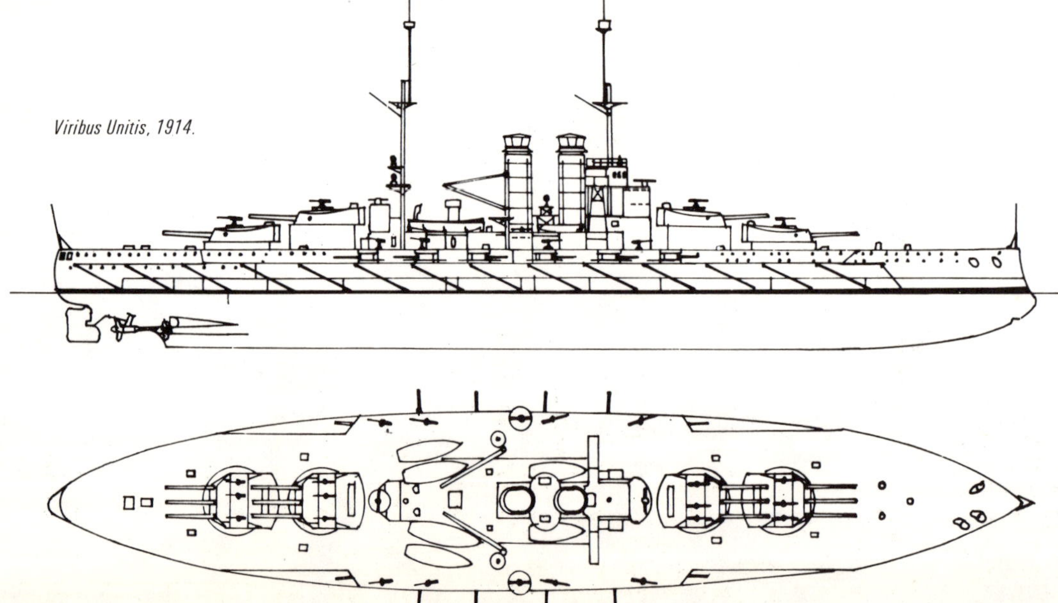

Viribus Unitis, 1914.

Right, Tegetthoff as completed (Austrian State Archives).

Right, Viribus Unitis as she appeared early in the war painted dark grey and still carrying torpedo nets (Austrian State Archives).

Right, a 1920 photograph showing Prinz Eugen in French hands (Musée de la Marine).

Ersatz Monarch class

Displacement: 25,000tons
Dimensions: 574ft (wl)×93ft 6in× 28ft 2in
Guns: 13×14·8in (3×3, 2×2) 45cal 14×5·9in 50cal (14×1) 16×3·4in 50cal
Torpedo Tubes: 4×53cm (submerged, beam)
Armour: 10in belt; 2½in decks; 10in turrets
Machinery: ?-shaft geared turbines, 31,000hp = 21knots; ? boilers
Coal Capacity: 1085/1425tons
Oil Capacity: 855/1425tons
Endurance: approx. 5000miles at 10knots
Cost: not known

	Laid Down	Launched	Completed	Built/Engined
Ersatz Monarch	—	—	—	Trieste DY
Ersatz Budapest	—	—	—	—
Ersatz Wien	—	—	—	—
Ersatz Habsburg	—	—	—	—

These ships were clearly influenced by the Italian *Cavour* class, and mounted a new gun to offset the large numbers of 12in guns mounted by the new Italian ships. The layout of the *Viribus Unitis* was retained, but with twin turrets superimposed over triples, forward and aft. Like the previous class, the superstructure was kept to the minimum, and the secondary battery was concentrated at two levels abreast of the funnels and bridge.

All provided for under the 1914 Programme, but not laid down. Only one builder was announced, and they would probably not have been laid down until 1916 if the war had not broken out in 1914.

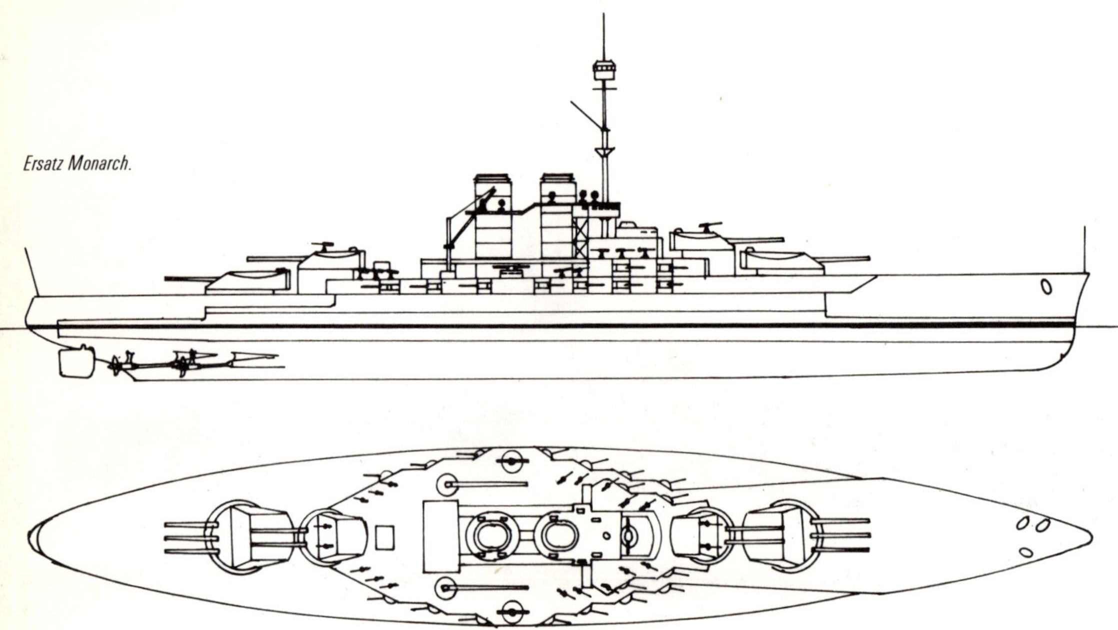

Ersatz Monarch.

Below, Minas Geraes, one of Brazil's two dreadnoughts (Author's collection).

Introduction

The navy of the Republic of Brazil was small by Big Power standards, but it ranked as the largest if not the best of the South American navies. Brazilian resources were almost entirely agricultural, but a short-lived rubber boom had increased prosperity and tempted the government to order two dreadnoughts from Great Britain in 1907. The completion of these two ships in 1910 put Brazil ahead of larger countries such as France and Russia by having dreadnoughts in service.

What followed can only be described as megalomania, for the three major South American nations ordered in turn bigger and costlier battleships. As the rubber boom collapsed it proved impossible to keep up the race, and a further round of battleship-building came to an abrupt stop with the sale of the incomplete *Rio de Janeiro* to Turkey and the cancellation of the gigantic 15in gunned *Riachuelo*.

Like the other South American nations Brazil followed a policy of neutrality, but on 26 October 1917, after assiduous pressure from the United States and some flagrant violations of her neutral status by German U-boats, she joined the Allies. Little was done beyond patrolling the approaches to Rio de Janeiro and other ports, and no losses were incurred.

Marshal Deodoro class

Displacement: 3162tons (normal)
Dimensions: 267ft 6in×47ft 3in× 13ft 9in (max)
Guns: 2×9·4in 45cal (2×1)
4×4·7in 50cal (4×1)
2×6in howitzers
4×6pdrs
2×1pdrs
Torpedo Tubes: 2×14in (above water, beam)
Armour: $13\frac{3}{4}$–4in belt; $1\frac{1}{2}$in deck; 8in turrets; 5in C.T.
Machinery: 2-shaft vertical triple-expansion, 3400ihp = 15knots; 8 Lagrafel d'Allest boilers
Coal Capacity: 246tons
Endurance: 2500miles at 10knots
Complement: 200
Cost: not known

	Laid Down	Launched	Completed	Built/Engined
Marshal Floriano	1897	1899	1899	La Seyne, Toulon
Marshal Deodoro (ex-Ypiranga)	1897	18 June 1898	1899	La Seyne, Toulon

Although too small for offensive operations, these two ships carried out patrol work in the South Atlantic in 1917–18. Their guns were of French design.

Appearance: Their low freeboard and arrangement of superstructure were typical of ships of their vintage. During the war both ships were painted light grey.

Careers

Marshal Deodoro: Served in Central Patrol Area 1917–18; sold to Mexico in 1924 and renamed *Anahuac*.

Marshal Floriano: Served with *M. Deodoro* in Central Patrol Area, based on Rio de Janeiro 1917–18; stricken from effective list in 1936 and sold for breaking up.

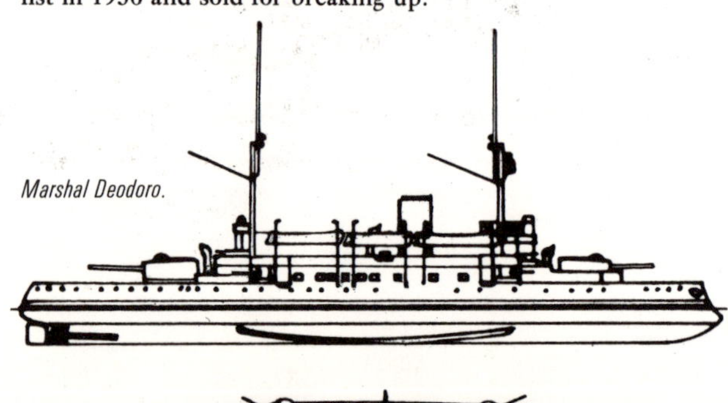

Marshal Deodoro.

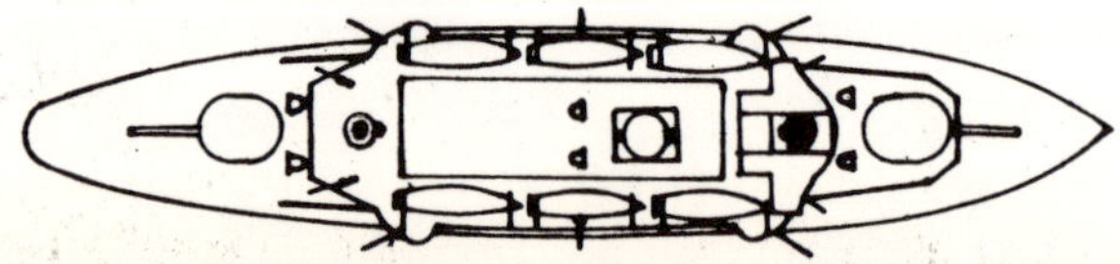

Above, *Marshal Deodoro in the South Atlantic in October 1918 (IWM).*

Minas Geraes class

Displacement: 19,280tons normal, 21,200tons full load
Dimensions: 530ft (wl)×83ft×28ft (max)
Guns: 12×12in 50cal (6×2) 22×4·7in (22×1) 8×3pdrs (8×1)
Torpedo Tubes: Nil
Armour: 9–4in belt; 2¼in deck; 12–8in turrets; 12in CT
Machinery: 2-shaft triple-expansion, 23,500hp = 21knots; ? Babcock boilers
Coal Capacity: 800/2350tons
Endurance: 10,000miles at 10knots (nominal)
Complement: 900
Cost: £616,360 ($2,465,440)

	Laid Down	Launched	Completed	Built/Engined
Minas Geraes	1907	Sept 1908	Jan 1910	Vickers, Barrow
Sao Paulo	1907	Apr 1909	July 1910	Vickers, Barrow

These powerful ships were designed to ensure Brazilian supremacy over her neighbours Chile and Argentina. The British *Dreadnought* was taken as the model, but with greater beam and displacement to allow for a heavier armament. By superimposing No. 2 and No. 5 turrets, it was possible to mount twelve guns, as against ten in the *Dreadnought*, with an extra pair of 12in available to fire on the broadside, and an extra turret firing ahead or astern.

Unfortunately, as we have already seen with the British *Erin* and *Agincourt*, these ships proved rather ambitious for the limited dockyard resources of Brazil, and to keep maintenance costs down they were given two-shaft reciprocating machinery.

When Brazil entered the war in 1917 both ships were refitted at Rio de Janeiro with a view to their serving with the British Grand Fleet. The offer was not taken up, partly on account of the Allies' overwhelming margin of superiority in dreadnoughts, and partly on account of the acute coal shortage, and possibly the difficulty in assimilating the ships into a completely alien organisation.

Appearance: These ships bore a striking resemblance to H.M.S. *Dreadnought*, with a tripod mast between the funnels, but the flush deck and superimposed turrets were distinctive.

Sister ship: The third unit of the class was never laid down, as she was intended to be replaced by a much larger ship to be called *Riachuelo*.

Careers

Minas Geraes: With *Saõ Paulo* formed the Central Area Patrol 1917–18, based on Rio de Raneiro; modernised 1934–7; sold to Italian firm for breaking up in 1953, and towed to Italy 1954.

Saõ Paulo: Central Area Patrol (see *Minas Geraes*) 1917–18; sold 1951 to British firm for breaking up; left Rio in tow for United Kingdom September 1951, but lost without trace north of the Azores, 4 November after the tow had been slipped in bad weather.

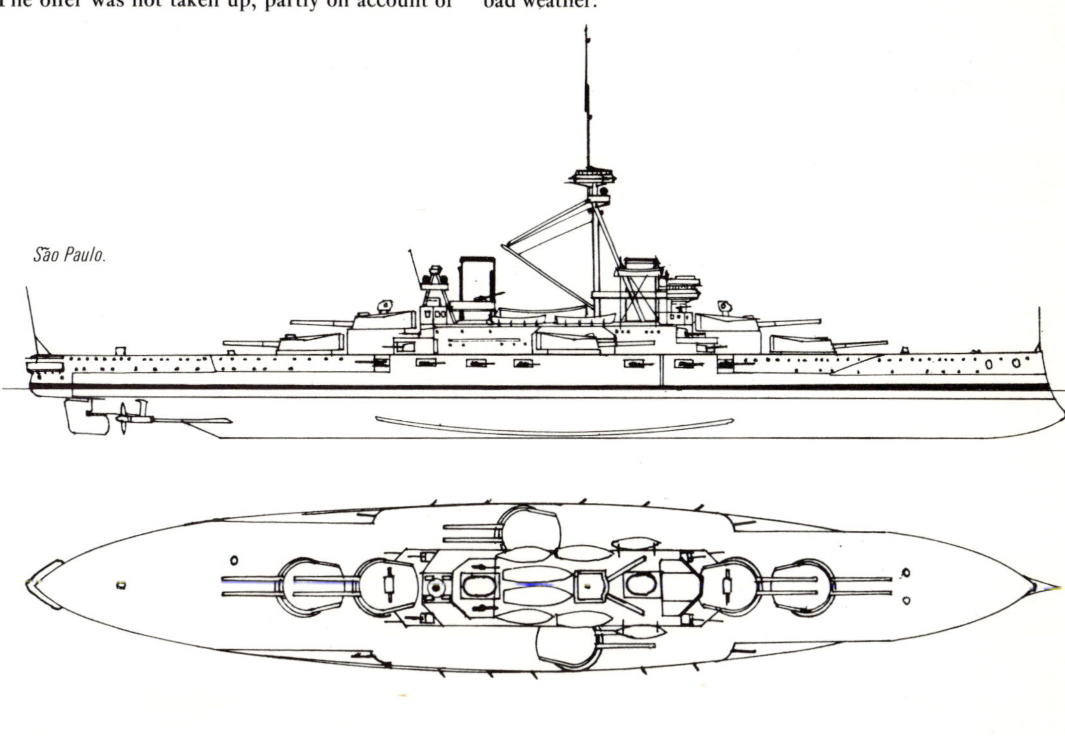
São Paulo.

Two views of the Saõ Paulo, photographed at Rio de Janeiro in 1918 – below, sporting a lurid colour scheme (both IWM).

France

Below, Danton leaving Toulon dockyard on 26 November 1916 (IWM).

Introduction

Although France had maintained a navy of the first rank during the nineteenth century, there had been a dramatic decline in the first decade of the twentieth. The signs had been there earlier, and the French battle fleet had an unenviable reputation as a collection of 'samples', lacking the homogeneity of the British, German and American navies. During the 1880s and 1890s the French tendency to pursue doctrines to absurdly logical conclusions had resulted in an enormous expenditure on torpedo boats and commerce-destroying cruisers at the expense of a balanced fleet.

The conclusion of the Entente between France and Great Britain in 1904 was more than a pious hope: it recognised the common danger of Germany and, by drawing the two former traditional enemies together, it threw out many German calculations. The practical result from the point of view of the French Navy was that it could leave the defence of the Channel to the Royal Navy and concentrate its resources on controlling its vital communications with French North Africa and watching the Italians. There was also an inevitable slackening of effort with the removal of the British Mediterranean Fleet as a potential foe, but more important, in June 1902 the vigorous Minister of Marine, M. Lanessan, was replaced by M. Pelletan. Under Pelletan's erratic guidance the Navy was 'republicanised', which in practice meant that morale was undermined by the promotion of political nominees to high rank.

Pelletan also heralded another period of doctrinaire enthusiasm in French naval circles. After Lanessan's Ministry had raised the Fleet to a peak of efficiency unknown for years, Pelletan announced his preference for the Jeune Ecole (by now sufficiently out of date to be called the Vieille Ecole), which proclaimed the death of the battleship and wanted only a fleet of submarines. He suspended the modernisation of old battleships, cancelled the 1903 manoeuvres, and reduced the vote for coal in order to reduce the time spent at sea.

Pelletan fell from grace because his Anglophobe speeches began to rival the Kaiser's to the point where they embarrassed his Government. After all the diplomatic initiatives which had gone into the Entente it was laughable to find the Minister of Marine saying that Bizerta would be a 'new Carthage' to cut communications between Malta and Gibraltar, and that it was France's duty to prepare for a 'Holy War' against her enemies. He retired in 1905, but the damage he had done was not eradicated for years, and it was clear for all the world to see that France had declined to a second-class naval power.

The most acute problem for the French Navy was the inordinate length of time taken, first to lay down a large ship, and then to get it built. The *Danton* class were all authorised under the 1906 Programme, but despite their lack of sophistication did not join the Fleet until the summer of 1911. The French armament industry did not have the capacity for rapid production of armour plate and heavy guns, these being the components which really determined the length of time taken to build a complete ship.

Dockyards and Bases

Like the British the principal French dockyards had been established for centuries, but with the elimination of Anglo-French competition Brest became far less important than Toulon. From the beginning of the century a lot of money had been spent to create a base at Bizerta, in what is now Tunisia, but it was more of a forward operational base than a dockyard and still lacked the repair facilities of Toulon. Overseas the French had a large number of colonial bases, such as Martinique and Saigon, but during the war their battleships were concentrated in the Mediterranean, so that these had no bearing on dispositions. Like the British, the French had to use Italian facilities, and French ships were based on Taranto; later they used Mudros and Corfu, as well as Alexandria.

French Guns					
Calibre	Length	Model	Wt. of Shell	Range	Notes
10·8in	40cal	1893–6	562lb	unknown	Bouvet, Henri IV etc
12in	40cal	1893–6	750lb	unknown	Jaureguiberry etc
12in	50cal	1906	750lb	19,500yds	Vérité Class etc
13·4in	45cal	1911	1190lb	unknown	Provence Class

Actions

The main French fleet saw no action against enemy heavy units, and it was left to the predreadnoughts to bear the brunt of shore bombardment and convoy duties. The chief commitment in August 1914 was to safeguard the vital troop convoys sailing from Algeria to Marseilles and Toulon against an attack by the *Goeben* and *Breslau*. It must be remembered that on the day the war broke out the French had only one dreadnought, the *Courbet*, ready for service. The *Jean Bart* joined a week later, and the *France* and *Paris* were finished in October, but until these reinforcements were available and the *Goeben* safely blockaded in the Bosphorus the French were unwilling to take any chances.

Britain and France declared war on the Austro-Hungarian Empire at midnight, 12 August, and on 15 August the main French Fleet, including the *Courbet* (flagship), five *Danton* class, the three *Vérités* and two *Républiques* began a sweep against the Austrian forces blockading Montenegro. In a confused action all ships began firing at the light cruiser *Zenta* and the destroyer *Ulan*. Although the range came down from 13,000yds to 4500yds no hits were registered on the destroyer, but the *Zenta* was sunk. One of the more disturbing points about this action was the fact that two 9·4in guns and a 7·6in gun were disabled by premature detonations caused by defective fuses. Otherwise it was a feeble action, in which an overwhelming force had to fire 500 large shells to sink a 2200ton cruiser armed with nothing bigger than 4·7in guns.

The French Fleet continued its blockade of the Adriatic, but on the night of 21 December 1914 the German submarine *U.12* torpedoed the *Jean Bart* off Cattaro. She was not badly damaged, and by good damage control she was able to make Malta for repairs, but the French withdrew their large ships to Navarino in southern Greece, and only brought them back to the Adriatic in January 1915 and again in April, when they heard that the Austrian Fleet had left Pola.

Most of the older French ships went to the Dardanelles in February 1915 for the assault on the Gallipoli Peninsula. Their part in the great

Abbreviated Name	Full Name and Location
Bordeaux	Chantiers de la Gironde, Bordeaux
Brest DY	Arsenale de Brest
La Seyne	Forges et Chantiers de la Mediterranée, Toulon
Lorient DY	Arsenale de Lorient
St. Nazaire (Chau Loire)	Chantiers de la Loire, St. Nazaire
St. Nazaire (Penhoet)	Chantiers de la St. Nazaire
Toulon DY	Arsenale de Toulon

bombardment of 18 March 1915 is described in the British section; not only was the *Bouvet* mined and sunk, but the *Gaulois* and *Suffren* were badly damaged and the others were knocked about. Reinforcements were sent quickly, and the *Gaulois* and *Suffren* eventually rejoined the Fleet.

The little coast-defence ship *Requin* was sent to Egypt early in 1915 to assist in the defence of the Suez Canal. She remained there, and was still actively employed in 1917, when she bombarded Gaza. For the rest of the war, most of the remaining ships spent their time convoying troop-ships and transport from North Africa to France, and from France to Salonika. The main fleet was stationed at Corfu in order to help the Italians in their task of containing the Austrians in the Adriatic, and in 1918 ships were sent to Mudros to prevent a second breakout by the *Yavuz Sultan Selim*.

Disposition of French Fleet at the Outbreak of War
1st Fleet (Toulon)
Flagship of Commander-in-Chief
Courbet (with Jean Bart as relief flagship)
1st Squadron, 1st Division
France (flagship), Paris, Diderot, Mirabeau
2nd Division
Voltaire, Condorcet, Danton, Vergniaud
2nd Squadron, 1st Division
Vérité (flagship), République, Démocratie (refitting)
2nd Division
Justice, Patrie (refitting)
Complementary Division to 2nd Squadron (with reduced complements)
Suffren (flagship), St. Louis, Bouvet, Gaulois
Particular Service Squadron
Jaureguiberry (flagship), Charlemagne
Brest
Carnot, Charles Martel (both laid up but retained on effective list pending completion of the Normandie Class)
Toulon
Massena, Brennus (both laid up but retained on effective list pending completion of the Normandie Class)
Bizerta
Henri IV (flagship), Requin

Disposition of French Fleet in October 1918
Mediterranean Fleet Flagship
Provence
1st Squadron (at Corfu)
Courbet (flagship), Paris, Jean Bart, Condorcet, Lorraine, Bretagne, France
2nd Squadron (at Mudros)
Diderot (flagship), Vergniaud, Mirabeau, Voltaire, Justice, Vérité, Démocratie
Taranto
Henri IV (as depot ship)
Salonika
Patrie
Bizerta
St. Louis

Below, obsolete even before she was laid down, the predreadnought Vergniaud is here shown on trials in 1911 (Musée de la Marine).

Jaureguiberry.

Requin

Displacement: 7214tons normal
Dimensions: 324ft 4in×73ft×23ft (max)
Guns: 2×10·8in (2×1) 8×3·9in (8×1)
Torpedo Tubes: not known
Armour: $19\frac{1}{2}$–$12\frac{1}{2}$in compound belt; 3–4in deck; $9\frac{1}{2}$in turrets

Machinery: 2-shaft compound reciprocating, 11,200hp = $15\frac{1}{2}$knots (in 1908); Niclausse boilers
Coal Capacity: 400/800tons
Endurance: not known
Complement: not known
Cost: not known

	Laid Down	Launched	Completed	Built/Engined
Requin	1875	June 1885	c. 1886	Bordeaux

This vessel was one of the oldest warships to see active service in the war. One of a class of four, she had been retained for training purposes, but after 1908 had not been listed in reference books.
Sister Ships: *Caiman*, *Terrible* and *Indomitable* scrapped by 1908.

Career
Reduced to gunnery school hulk *c*.1908; stationed at Bizerta for coast defence duties August–November 1914; to Egypt December 1914 to assist in defence of Suez Canal; bombardment of Gaza November 1917; broken up *c*.1919–20.

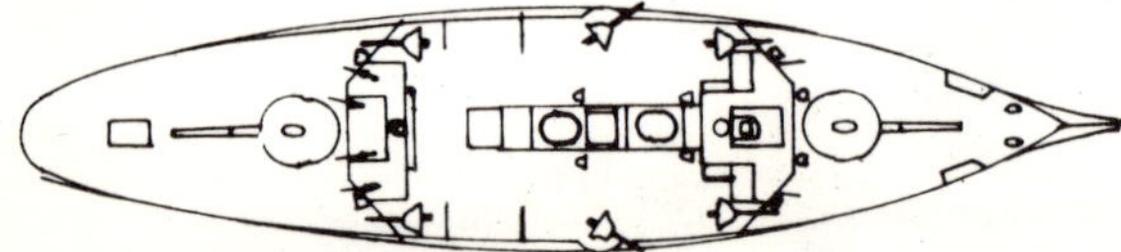

Above right, Requin *seen early in the century, while still painted in traditional colour scheme (Marius Bar).* **Below right,** Requin *seen at Port Said in November 1917 with a French battleship and a Japanese armoured cruiser in the background. Note the peculiar two-tone painting of no. 1 turret which may be a camaflage scheme (IWM).*

Jaureguiberry

Displacement: 11,818tons (normal), 12,229tons (full load)
Dimensions: 109·70m×22·15m× 7·75m
Guns: 2×12in (2×1)
2×10·8in (2×1)
8×5·5in (8×1)
4×2·6in (landing)
14×47mm
Torpedo Tubes: 2×17·7in (beam, submerged)

Armour: 17¾–9¾in belt; 14½ turrets; 9in CT
Machinery: 2-set triple-expansion, 14,300hp = 17·67knots; 24 Lagrafel D'Allest boilers
Coal Capacity: 750/1080tons
Endurance: 3920miles at 10knots
Complement: 597
Cost: Approximately £1,134,000 ($4,536,000)

	Laid Down	Launched	Completed	Built/Engined
Jaureguiberry	8 Apr 1891	27 Oct 1893	Feb 1897	Ch. Mediterranee, La Seyne

The oldest effective battle unit of the French Navy in August 1914, she had always enjoyed a good reputation both as a steamer and as a good seaboat. Like other French ships of the period, the length of time taken for building had made her obsolescent when compared to the British *Canopus* class, whereas she should be regarded as a contemporary of the *Revenge*.

Admiral Guepratte reported after she arrived to replace the *Bouvet* that she was full of inflammable material, magazines not protected by the belt armour, the belt armour itself submerged, and with the stokehold bulkheads rusted through. He also said that the magazine flooding was so defective that the ship might burn, blow up or founder before long.

Appearance: She dated from the period when French warships were given heavy military masts and had high freeboard. In common with other French ships she had exaggerated 'tumble-home' (sloped sides), with the midships turrets in sponsons.

Career

Stationed at Toulon on outbreak of war as Flagship of the Training Squadron of the Armée Navale; escorted troop convoys from Algeria and Egypt; refitted Bizerta December 1914, and became flagship of Syrian Division; sent to Port Said 25 March 1915 to replace the *Bouvet* and *Suffren*; as flagship of Admiral Guepratte she went to the Dardanelles, and provided supporting fire; slightly damaged by gunfire 30 April and 5 May 1915; to Port Said July 1915 and returned to Syrian Division; guardship at Ismailia (Suez Canal) January 1916; transported artillery to Suez 1917; laid up in reserve at Port Said 1918, and left for Toulon 28 February 1919; disarmed as training ship for engineering artificers; condemned and stricken from effective list 20 June 1920 but retained as accommodation hulk until 1932; sold 23 July 1934 for breaking up.

Above, Jaureguiberry in two colour schemes. The top photograph shows her in the early years of the century, the dark colouring of the hull and the light conditions almost concealing the broadside gun position under the boat davits. The second photograph shows her painted grey just prior to 1914. Note the exaggerated tumblehome, which was such a feature in this ship, plus the heavy tubular masts and the apparent great length of the guns in relation to their turrets (top, IWM: bottom, Marius Bar).

# Bouvet

Displacement: 12,205tons (normal);
approx. 14,000tons (full load)
Dimensions: 397ft (wl)×70ft 2in×
28ft 4in
Guns: 2×12in 40cal (2×1)
2×10·8in 40cal (2×1)
8×5·5in 45cal (8×1)
8×3·9in
10×3pdrs
Torpedo Tubes: 4×18in (4 beam,
of which 2 were submerged and 2 above
water)
Armour: 16–10in belt; $3\frac{1}{2}$–$\frac{2}{3}$in
decks; $14\frac{3}{4}$in turrets; 10in C.T.
Machinery: 3-shaft vertical triple-
expansion, 14,000ihp = 17knots
(when new); 24 Belleville boilers
Coal Capacity: 620/800tons
Endurance: 3500miles at 10knots
(approximately)
Complement: 630
Cost: £1,200,000 ($4,800,000)

	Laid Down	Launched	Completed	Built/Engined
*Bouvet	Jan 1893	Apr 1896	1898	Lorient

Similar to the earlier *Massena* which was no longer effective (*qv*), this ship was notable for the number of secondary and tertiary guns in turrets. As in later French ships, little attention was paid to the practical problem of siting guns low down and close together, and one can only speculate on the blast effect of the midships 10·8in guns on the crews in the 5·5in turrets immediately beneath them.

This ship was, according to French sources, in very bad condition when war broke out, but she was suitable for shore bombardment. Her watertight bulkheads were said by Admiral Guepratte to be very rusty.

Armament: The 12in single turrets were disposed forward and aft, while the 10·8in guns were in single turrets a deck lower on the beam, amidships. The 5·5in guns were mounted in single turrets abreast of the forward 12in gun, forward and aft of the 10·8in guns, and just abaft the after 12in gun, below the quarterdeck. The 3·9in guns were disposed on the super-structure.

Career
Sent to Dardanelles January 1915 from Toulon, and joined Admiral de Lapeyrère's force; engaged the outer forts on 19 February 1915, and spotted for the *Suffren*; on 25 February spotted for *Gaulois*; on 18 March she fired at the Narrows forts at 5–6000yds, and even at 12,000yds; she was apparently hit eight times above the waterline, but at about 2.00pm she struck a mine and sank in one-and-a-half minutes; about 660 men were lost.

***Right,** Bouvet shown in 1900 (IWM).*

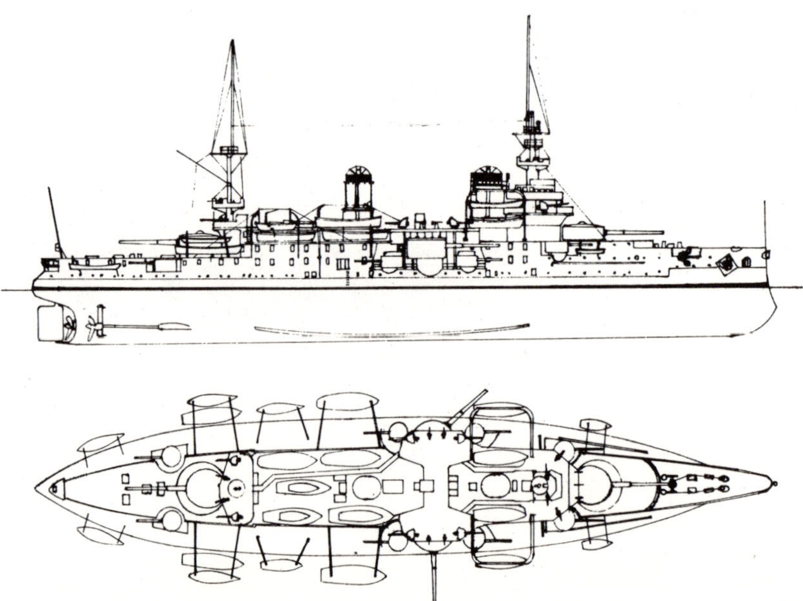

***Right,** Bouvet in 1910, her appearance virtually identical to that at the time of her loss. Note the peculiar arrangement of guns at main deck level amidships and the exaggerated tumblehome (Marius Bar).*

St Louis class

Displacement: 11,108tons normal
Dimensions: 385ft 6in×66ft 6in×27ft 6in
Guns: 4×12in (2×2)
10×5·5in (10×1)
8×3·39in (8×1)
10×3pdrs
4 MGs
Torpedo Tubes: 2×18in (submerged, beam)

Armour: $15\frac{3}{4}$in belt; $3\frac{1}{2}$in decks; $15\frac{3}{4}$in turrets
Machinery: 3-shaft triple-expansion, 15,000hp = 18knots (when new); 20 Belleville boilers
Complement: 730
Coal Capacity: 680/1100tons (max)
Endurance: 4000miles at 10knots
Cost: £1,000,000 average

	Laid Down	Launched	Completed	Builder
Charlemagne	2 Aug 1894	17 Oct 1895	Feb 1898	Brest DY
St. Louis	25 Mar 1895	8 Sept 1896	Feb 1900	Lorient DY
*Gaulois	Jan 1895	Oct 1896	Feb 1899	Brest DY

This class had the reputation of being good seaboats, but lacked protection. They were unique among French ships of the period in belonging to an homogeneous class, since the French tended to build a 'fleet of samples'.

Appearance: These ships had the typical French 'top-hat' funnel caps and heavy military masts. There were several differences in topside detail between the three ships, particularly in the method of handling boats: *St. Louis* had a double-armed swinging davit, whereas *Charlemagne* had a luffing boom.

Careers

Charlemagne: Was gunnery training ship in Mediterranean Training Squadron on outbreak of war; joined special squadron escorting convoys from North Africa to France; to Port Said September 1914 for escort duties; Dardanelles division November 1914–April 1915, during which period she carried out several bombardments; after repairing damage from Turkish gunfire at Bizerta she returned, but was transferred to Salonika in October 1915; refitted May–August 1916 at Bizerta and returned to Salonika division until August 1917; after returning to Bizerta she was recalled to pay off at Toulon; completely disarmed November 1917; condemned 21 June 1920 and sold.

Gaulois: Served in Complementary Division (Reserve Squadron, special complements) to 2nd Squadron of 1st Fleet in Mediterranean August 1914 to February 1915, and escorted convoys from North Africa to France; to Dardanelles March 1915, and sustained heavy damage from Turkish gunfire during the assault on the Narrows 18 March; repaired Toulon April–May, and joined 2nd Division, 2nd Squadron; refitted at Brest late 1916; torpedoed in Mediterranean 27 December 1916.

St. Louis: Escorted Algerian convoys from France from outbreak of war, being one of the Complementary Division (see *Charlemagne*) for the 2nd squadron, 1st Fleet in the Mediterranean; escorted convoys from Port Said October to November; to Dardanelles January 1915, but after refitting at Bizerta joined Syrian Squadron as flagship of Contre-amiral Guepratte; bombardment Gaza 11–13 April and then El Arish 9 May; returned to Dardanelles, where she took part in several bombardments; refitted and repaired at Lorient October 1915–May 1916; to Salonika after refit, where she became Flagship to Division Navale d'Orient in October; recalled to Bizerta March 1917; paid off 5 January 1919; returned to Toulon, where she was disarmed as an overflow ship for the engineers' and stokers' training establishment; condemned 20 June 1920, but retained as accommodation hulk until June 1931; sold 25 April 1933 for Fr 600,230 to Société Metallurgique Méridion for breaking up.

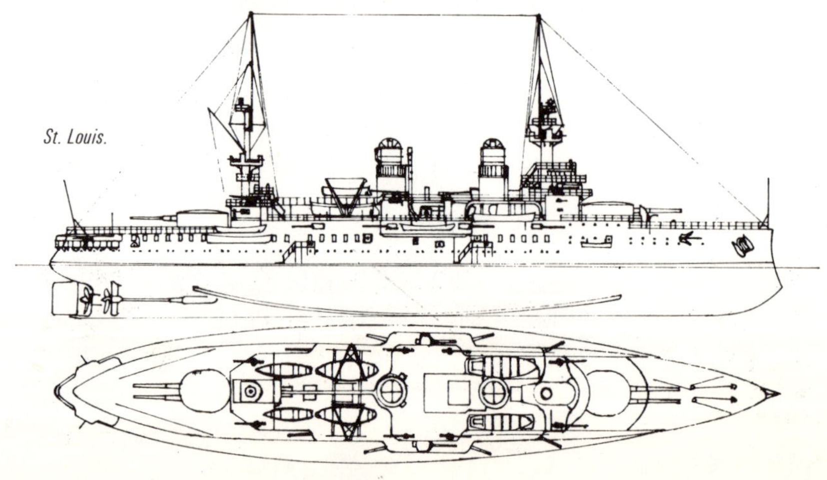

St. Louis.

Left, *Gaulois — an early photograph, showing to good advantage the arrangement of her superstructure (IWM).*

Below left, *St. Louis seen leaving Toulon before the war (Marius Bar).*

Right, *Charlemagne as she appeared during the war (Marius Bar).*

Right, *Gaulois at Mudros in March 1915 before the naval attack in the Narrows (IWM).*

Right, *Gaulois again, after sustaining heavy damage during the attack on the Narrows in April 1915. Note how she is down by the bows, but nevertheless on an even keel (IWM).*

Henri IV

Displacement: 8807tons
Dimensions: 354ft 6in×72ft×23ft
Guns: 2×10·8in (2×1)
7×5·5in (7×1)
12×1·8in
2×MGs
Torpedo Tubes: 2 submerged (beam)
Armour: 11–7in H.S. belt; 3in deck;
11¾in turrets; 5in secondary battery;
4¾in side above main belt
Machinery: 2 sets triple expansion,
11,500ihp = 17·2knots (when new)
but probably not in excess of 13knots
by 1914
Coal Capacity: 735/1100tons
(max)
Complement: 464
Endurance: not known
Cost: £801,248 ($3,204,992)

	Laid Down	Launched	Completed	Builder
Henri IV	July 1897	Aug 1899	1902	Cherbourg DY

This ship had been designed by the great French naval architect Emile Bertin as a seagoing monitor of highly novel design. By combining a low freeboard hull with a built-up superstructure he made her a steady gun-platform without sacrificing weatherliness. But the most interesting point about this small battleship was the fact that she introduced the principle of the superimposed turret: the after 5·5in guns were placed to fire over the 10·8in turret on the quarterdeck. Unfortunately the value of this experiment was quite lost on foreign designers, who harped on the problems of concussion through the sighting hoods—a drawback which could easily be cured by repositioning the sighting hoods.

Although of little use for anything but second-line duties, *Henri IV* rendered useful service throughout the war, and saw as much service as any French capital ship.

Appearance: She was unique, with her high forecastle and low freeboard aft, and square funnels.

Career

At Bizerta on outbreak of war, and remained there until February 1915 as guard ship; to Dardanelles, and in 1916 she joined the Complementary (Reserve) Division of the 3rd Battle Squadron; served for a time with the Eastern Division of the French Mediterranean Fleet, based on Egypt; to Taranto in 1918 to act as a depot ship; returned to Toulon after Armistice and stricken; broken up *c*.1921.

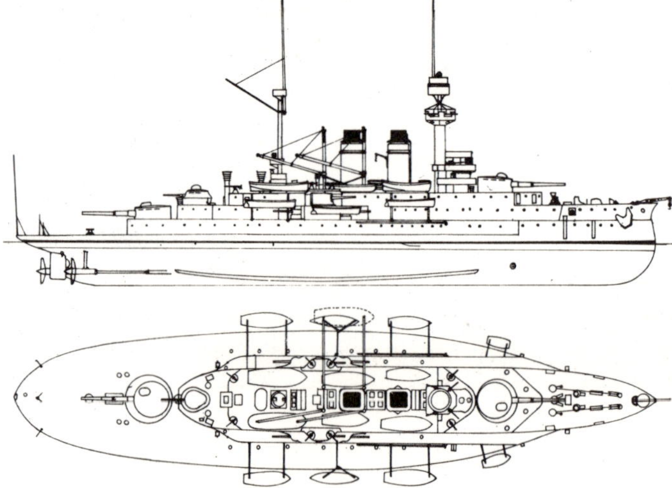

Above and top right, Henri IV seen at Toulon in July 1915 (Marius Bar).

Right, Suffren (see next page) seen running a full-power trial in 1903, at which date she was still painted in the old black and white scheme (Musée de la Marine).

■ Suffren

	Displacement: 12,750tons	Armour: 12–9in belt; 3–1⅔in deck; 13in turrets; 12in CT

Displacement: 12,750tons
Dimensions: 410ft (wl)×70ft×28ft 3in
Guns: 4×12in 45cal (2×2)
10×6·5in 45cal (10×1)
4×3·9in
22×47mm
Torpedo Tubes: 4×18in (4 beam, 2 submerged and 2 above water)

Armour: 12–9in belt; 3–1⅔in deck; 13in turrets; 12in CT
Machinery: 3-shaft vertical triple-expansion, 16,000ihp = 16knots (recent best); 20 Niclausse boilers
Coal Capacity: 820/1150tons
Endurance: not known
Complement: 730
Cost: £1,200,000 ($4,800,000)

	Laid Down	Launched	Completed	Built/Engined
*Suffren	Jan 1899	July 1899	1903	Brest DY

This vessel was closer in fighting qualities to her contemporaries in the Royal Navy, having a more orthodox layout of her main armament than usual. The disposition of the 6·5in guns in turrets is interesting, being some years ahead of other navies.

Appearance: She had the typical heavy foremast and fighting top of French predreadnoughts, but could be distinguished by a less pronounced tumblehome.

Career

She was serving in the Complementary (Reserve) Division of the Mediterranean Fleet; to Dardanelles February 1915; Flagship of Admiral Guepratte, and opened fire on Kum Kale forts 19 February; bombardment of Turkish positions in Gulf of Saros 2 March; hit by Turkish batteries 6 March; bombarded Narrows forts 18 March, and was hit 14 times, and set on fire by a 9·4in shell; in addition the forefunnel was almost destroyed; to Toulon for repairs via Malta 25 March in company with the badly damaged *Gaulois*; returned to Dardanelles in mid-May, with 2nd Division of 3rd Squadron 1916; torpedoed November 1916 in Mediterranean.

Left, Suffren showing details of her after superstructure and sternwalk (Marius Bar).

Above, as she appeared during the war (Marius Bar).

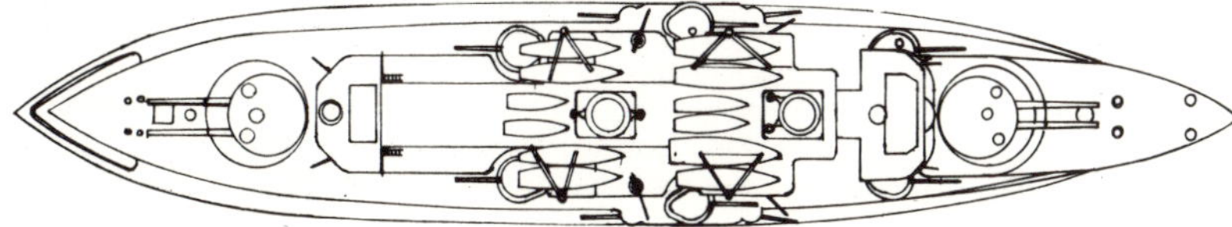

République class

	Laid Down	Launched	Completed	Built/Engined
République	Dec 1901	Sept 1902	1906	Brest DY
Patrie	Dec 1902	Dec 1903	1906	La Seyne, Toulon

Displacement: 14,865tons (normal); approx. 16,000tons (full load)
Dimensions: 439ft (wl)×79ft 6in× 27ft 6in
Guns: 4×12in 45cal (2×2) 18×6·5in 45cal (6×2, 6×1) 25×47mm (25×1)
Torpedo Tubes: 2×18in (2 submerged, beam)
Armour: 11–7in belt; 3in deck; 12½in turrets; 13in C.T.
Machinery: 3-shaft vertical triple-expansion, 17,500ihp = 18knots; 24 Niclausse boilers
Coal Capacity: 900/1850tons
Endurance: 8400miles at 10knots
Complement: 793
Cost: £1,420,000 each ($5,680,000)

These ships were laid down under the 1901 Programme. They continued the practice of mounting some of the secondary armament in turrets, as in the *Suffren*, but for the first time twin turrets were introduced. They were most economical in service, and had the reputation of being good steamers. Although outclassed by later construction they and their half-sisters of the *Vérité* class formed the backbone of the French Battle Fleet for many years.

Armament: The secondary guns were disposed in casemates, two on each side, between the funnels at main deck level and one pair a deck higher abreast of the forward superstructure,

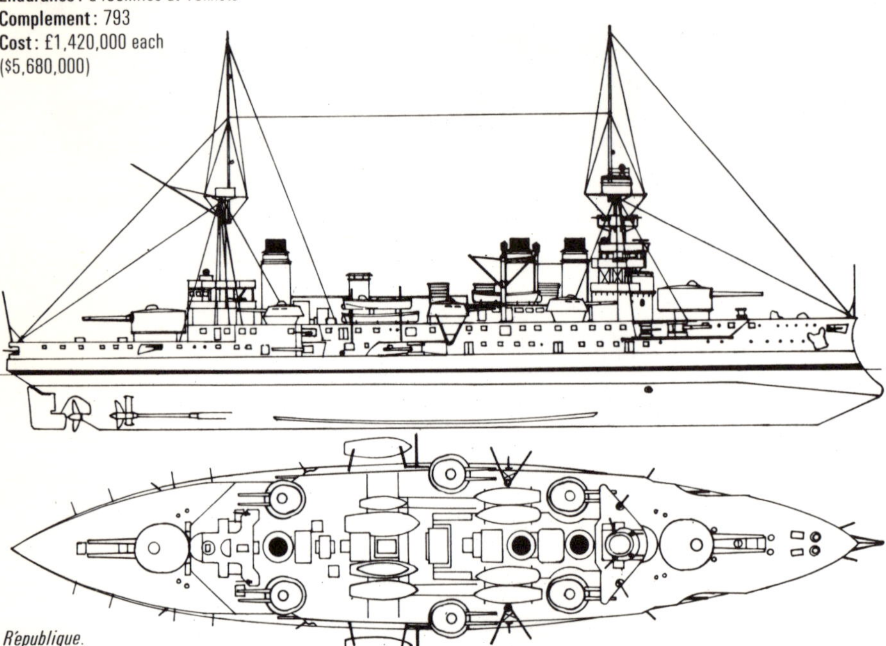

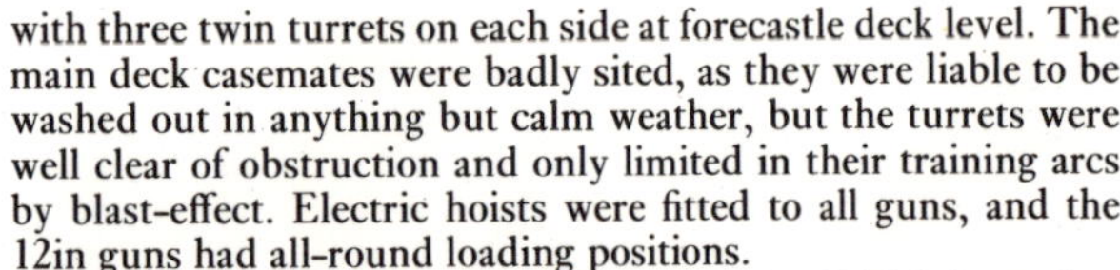

République.

with three twin turrets on each side at forecastle deck level. The main deck casemates were badly sited, as they were liable to be washed out in anything but calm weather, but the turrets were well clear of obstruction and only limited in their training arcs by blast-effect. Electric hoists were fitted to all guns, and the 12in guns had all-round loading positions.

Appearance: Very similar in aspect to the *Vérité* class, they could be distinguished by the twin secondary turrets and the different positions of the main deck battery guns.

Careers

Patrie: With 2nd Squadron (2nd Division) of Mediterranean Fleet August 1914–early 1915; to Dardanelles Squadron as Flagship in mid-1915; Flagship of 3rd Squadron (2nd Division) 1916; at Salamis in March 1917; Eastern Division October 1917–Armistice; stricken 1921 and broken up.

République: With 1st Division of 2nd Squadron of Mediterranean Fleet August 1914–mid-1916; with 3rd Squadron (2nd Division) 1916; at Salamis in March 1917; with Eastern Division from late 1917; stricken 1921 and broken up.

Above, *Patrie at Salonika in November 1915. Note the false bow-wave (IWM).*
Below, *her 1914 appearance (Musée de la Marine).*

Above and below: Répronblique, firstly as she appeared in 1914 (Musée de la Marine) and secondly as she appeared during the war (Marius Bar).

# Vérité class

Displacement: 14,900tons (normal);
15,800tons (full load)
Dimensions: As République class
Guns: 4×12in 50cal (2×2)
10×7·6in 45cal (10×1)
13×65mm (13×1)
6×47mm (6×1)
Torpedo Tubes: 2×18in (submerged, beam)
Armour: As République, but the arrangement differed slightly
Machinery: As Republic, but 18,000ihp, and 22 Belleville boilers in Démocratie and Vérité
Coal Capacity: 905/1825tons
Endurance: 8390miles at 10knots
Complement: 742 (Justice 809 as flagship)
Cost: Approximately £1,425,000 each ($5,700,000)

	Laid Down	Launched	Completed	Built/Engined
Vérité	May 1903	May 1907	Mar 1908	Bordeaux
Justice	May 1902	27 Sept 1904	July 1907	La Seyne, Toulon
Démocratie	May 1903	Apr 1904	July 1907	Brest DY

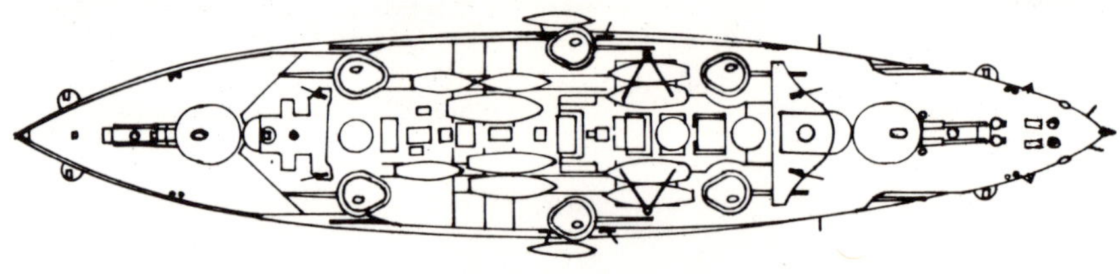

These ships were repeats of the *République* class, but incorporating an improved mark of 12in gun and a heavier secondary battery. Had they been built in less time their deficiencies might not have been so noticeable, but they appeared after the *Dreadnought*, and were quite obviously outclassed. Like the *Républiques* they were always highly regarded for reliability, however, and could on occasion steam at over 17knots for three days.

Sister ship: A fourth ship of this class, the *Liberté*, blew up at Toulon on 25 September 1911.

Armament: The 7·6in guns were arranged much as in the *République* class, but with single turrets at forecastle deck level, and only one gun on each side in casemates at main deck level.

Appearance: They were distinguished from the *Républiques* by the disposition of the main deck battery and the single secondary turrets.

Careers

Démocratie: With 1st Division, 2nd Squadron of Mediterranean Fleet August 1914–February 1915; with 2nd Squadron (2nd Division) 1915–16; 3rd Squadron (1st Division) August 1916; with Complementary (Reserve) Division at Salamis in 1917; at Mudros 1918; stricken 1921 and broken up.

Justice: With 2nd Squadron (2nd Division) August 1914–16, becoming Flagship by August 1915; 3rd Squadron (1st Division) 1916; with Complementary (Reserve) Division at Salamis 1917–19; at Mudros October 1918; stricken 1921 and broken up.

Vérité: Flagship of 2nd Squadron (1st Division) of Mediterranean Fleet August 1914–15; 2nd Squadron (2nd Division) 1915–16; Flagship 3rd Squadron (1st Division) 1916; with Complementary Division at Salamis 1917; at Mudros 1918; stricken 1921 and broken up.

Right, Vérité at Toulon before the war (Marius Bar).

Right, Justice as she appeared in 1914 (Marius Bar).

Right, another 1914 view of Justice (Musée de la Marine).

Right, Démocratie seen leaving Toulon and showing her wartime appearance (Marius Bar).

# Danton class

Displacement: 18,400tons (normal), approx 20,000tons (full load)
Dimensions: 480ft 11in (oa)×84ft 8in ×28ft 8in (mean)
Guns: 4×12in 45cal (2×2)
12×9·4in 50cal (6×2)
16×75mm 65cal (16×1)
8×47mm
Torpedo Tubes: 2×18in (submerged, beam)
Armour: 10–8¾in belt; 2½in deck; 12¾in main turrets, 8·6in secondary turrets; 11½in CT
Machinery: 4-shaft Parsons turbines, 22,500hp = 19¼knots; 26 Belleville boilers (Niclausse in Diderot, Condorcet and Vergniaud)
Coal Capacity: 965/2100tons
Endurance: 3750miles at 10knots
Complement: 852
Cost: £2,190,000 (average) ($8,760,000)

	Laid Down	Launched	Completed	Built/Engined
*Danton	Feb 1908	4 July 1909	Mar 1911	Brest DY
Condorcet	23 Aug 1907	20 Aug 1909	June 1911	St Nazaire (Penhoet)
Vergniaud	July 1908	12 Apr 1910	Sept 1911	Bordeaux
Voltaire	20 July 1907	16 Jan 1909	June 1911	La Seyne
Diderot	20 Oct 1907	19 Apr 1909	June 1911	St Nazaire

These were the last French predreadnoughts, belonging to the 1906 Programme. With their heavy secondary armament they were sometimes equated with the 'intermediate dreadnoughts' of other navies, such as the British *Lord Nelson* class.

It is difficult to see why the French Ministry of Marine authorised these ships, as they were laid down well after the completion of the *Dreadnought*. Had the three later ships been suspended they might have been redesigned as proper dreadnoughts, but as things turned out, all spare dockyard capacity was devoted to producing six battleships of obsolescent design. Although well protected, they proved very slow in service when called on to operate with British and Italian units.

Protection: *Voltaire* appears to have been fitted with 'bulges' in 1917.
Appearance: *Vergniaud* was the only one with single funnel caps, as the others all had double caps. The arrangement of five funnels in two groups was unique.

Careers

Condorcet: Serving in Mediterranean with 1st Squadron, 1st Fleet on outbreak of war to 1916; 2nd Squadron 1916–18; 1931 became the torpedo school at Toulon; scuttled November 1942 and broken up 1947.

Diderot: With 1st Squadron 1914–16; 2nd Squadron 1916–18; discarded 1936 and broken up 1937.

Danton: With 1st Squadron, 1st Fleet on outbreak of war; torpedoed by *U.64* and sunk off Sardinia, 19 March 1917.

Mirabeau: With 1st Squadron, 1st Fleet 1914–16; 2nd Squadron 1916–18; to Black Sea 1919 during Anglo-French intervention in Russian Civil War; ran aground on Crimean coast, near Sevastopol 13 February 1919; refloated April 1919 after the removal of her forward 12in turret and her side armour; condemned 1920 and later expended as a target.

Vergniaud: With 1st Squadron, 1st Fleet (2nd Division) 1914–16, on outbreak of war; left Toulon 3 August 1914 to join search for *Goeben* and escorted troop-convoys from Algeria; in Adriatic operations later in August 1914, which led to destruction of Austrian cruiser *Zenta*; bombardments in Adriatic in September; with 2nd Squadron at Corfu 1917–18, and at Mudros; expended as target for air attack 1921–2.

Voltaire: Flagship of 2nd Division, 1st Squadron, 1st Fleet in Mediterranean 1914–16; 2nd Squadron 1916–18; struck by two torpedoes in 1918, but managed to reach harbour; discarded 1935 and broken up 1939.

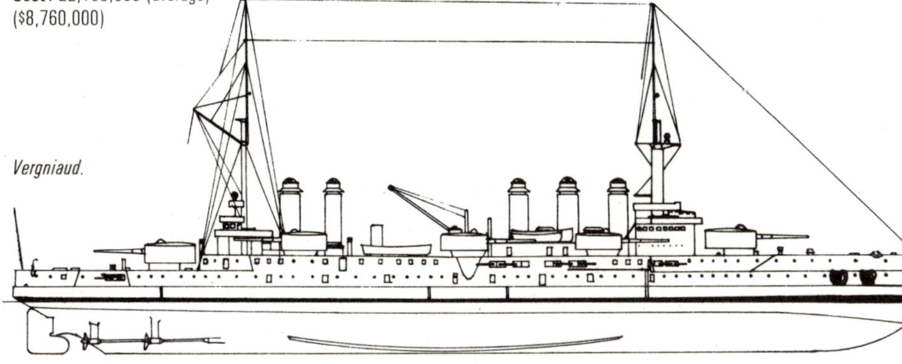

Vergniaud.

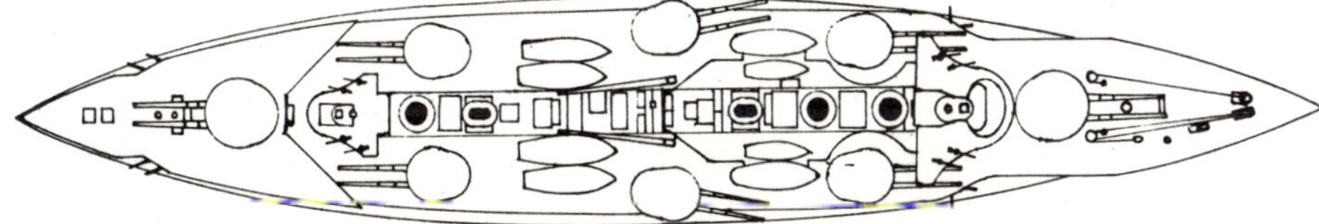

Above left, *Mirabeau seen in 1911 while on full-power trials (Musée de la Marine).*

Below left, *Condorcet shown dressed overall on 30 July 1919, by which time her mainmast had been removed (IWM).*

Right, *Condorcet in Toulon undergoing repairs to her mainmast in mid-October 1916. Note the scaffolding around the mast and the 75mm gun in its embrasure below the quarterdeck (IWM).*

Courbet class

Displacement: 23,100 tons (normal); 26,000 tons (full load)
Dimensions: 541ft 3in (pp) × 88ft 9in ×29ft 9in
Guns: 12×12in 45cal (6×2); 22×5·5in 55cal (22×1) 4×3pdr (4×1)
Torpedo Tubes: 4×18in (submerged, beam)
Armour: 10¾–7¼in belt; 3¾in deck; 12½in turrets
Machinery: 4-shaft Parsons turbines, 28,000shp=20knots; 24 Belleville boilers
Coal Capacity: 900/2706 tons
Oil Capacity: 310 tons
Endurance: 4200 miles at 10 knots
Complement: 998
Cost: £2,475,000 (average) ($9,900,000)

	Laid Down	Launched	Completed	Built/Engined
Courbet	1 Sept 1910	23 Sept 1911	Nov 1913	Brest DY
Jean Bart	15 Nov 1910	22 Sept 1911	June 1913	Lorient
Paris	10 Nov 1911	28 Sept 1912	Aug 1914	La Seyne, Toulon
France	30 Nov 1911	7 Nov 1912	Aug 1914	Ch de Loire

The *Courbet* class were laid down under the 1910 and 1911 Programmes, and were the first French dreadnoughts. The layout was reminiscent of the British *Dreadnought*, but even more of the Brazilian *Minas Geraes* class, with wing turrets (Nos. 3 and 4) abreast of the funnels. However, turrets Nos. 2 and 5 were superimposed, at a time when the British and Germans were only just coming to accept this idea. Unfortunately the *Courbet* class were so long in gestation, and in building (three years) that they were quite outclassed by the later dreadnoughts building abroad.

Armament: A noticeable feature of this design is the lack of attention paid to blast effects. The 12in turrets amidships, Nos. 3 and 4 were no better and no worse placed than wing turrets in British and German ships, but the secondary 5·5in guns were very closely spaced in their casemates, and the mutual interference from blast would probably have made life in the casemates very uncomfortable.

Appearance: They were unmistakable, with a pole mast between the two foremost funnels and the after one. *Jean Bart* differed from the others in having goosenecked boat cranes abreast of the after funnel instead of heavy derricks.

Careers

Courbet: Flagship of C-in-C, Mediterranean Fleet on outbreak of war and continued until 1915; relief Flagship 1916 and then attached to 1st Squadron 1916–18, being stationed at Corfu and Mudros in 1917–18; modernised in 1926–9, but relegated to harbour training in 1939; escaped to United Kingdom after fall of France in 1940, and used as anti-aircraft battery; scuttled to form part of 'Mulberry' harbour breakwater 9 June 1944.

France: Flagship of 1st Squadron, Mediterranean Fleet on outbreak of war; attached to Fleet Flagship 1915, and became Fleet Flagship herself 1916; returned to 1st Squadron 1916–18, and served at Corfu and Mudros; foundered in Quiberon Bay 24 August 1922 after striking an unchartered rock.

Jean Bart: Attached to Fleet Flagship, Mediterreanean as relief flagship in August 1914; torpedoed by *U.12* 21 December 1914 off Antivari; repaired at Malta 1915; 2nd Squadron 1915–16; 2nd Division, 1st Squadron 1916–18, including service at Corfu and Mudros; modernised 1926–9, but paid off in 1936 and relegated to harbour training; renamed *Ocean* to release her name for a new battleship; fell into German hands after the occupation of Toulon in 1942, and was used as a target; sunk by Allied air attack in 1944, and salvaged and scrapped at the end of 1945.

Paris: With 1st Squadron 1914–15; Flagship of 1st Division, 2nd Squadron 1915–16; transferred to 2nd Division of 1st Squadron 1916–18, and served at Corfu and Mudros; modernised 1926–9 and reduced to harbour service in 1939; escaped to United Kingdom after fall of France, and used by Free French Navy as an accommodation ship; returned to France 1945 and broken up 1955.

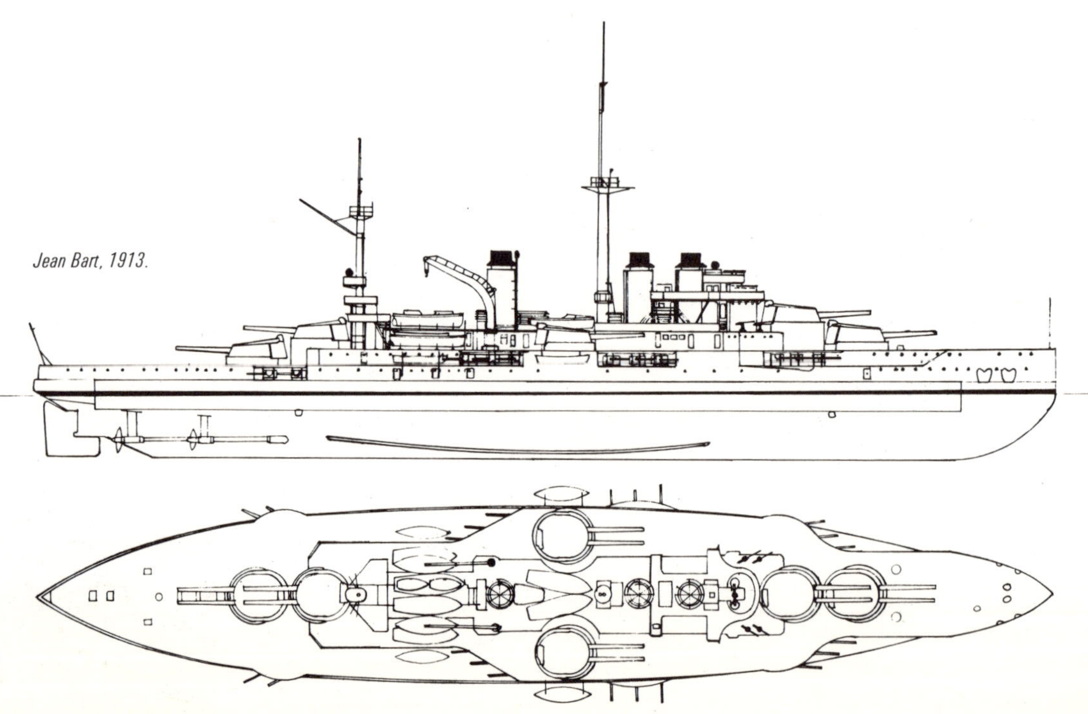
Jean Bart, 1913.

Left, *Paris running her full power trials at the outbreak of the war (Musée de la Marine).*

Left, *France leaving Toulon on 27 December 1916 after repairs (IWM).*

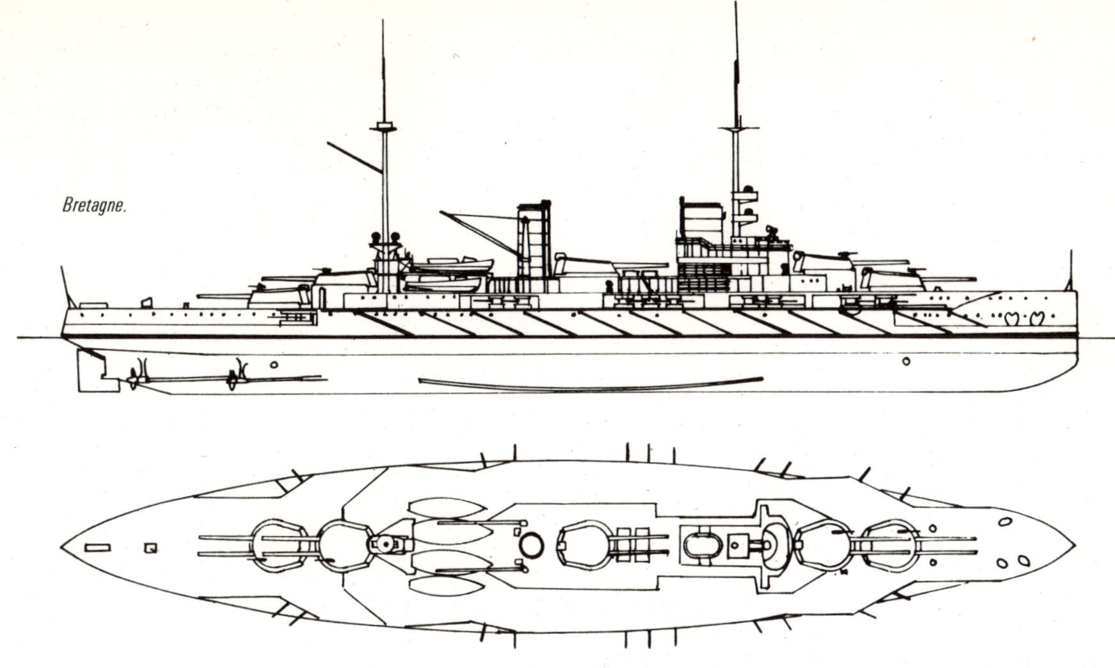

Above left, Bretagne as she appeared on completion in 1915 (Musée de la Marine).

Below left, Provence seen off Dolma Bagche, near Istanbul, on 1 November 1919 (IWM).

Bretagne class

Displacement: 23,230tons (normal); 28,500 (approx. full load)
Dimensions: 541ft 3in×88ft 9in× 29ft 9in
Guns: 10×13·4in 45cal (5×2) 22×5·5in 55cal (22×1) 4×3in
Torpedo Tubes: 4×18in (4 beam, submerged)
Armour: $10\frac{3}{4}$–$7\frac{1}{4}$in belt; $2\frac{3}{4}$–$1\frac{1}{2}$in decks; 13·4in turrets (excepting super-imposed and midships turrets, which had $9\frac{3}{4}$in armour); $11\frac{3}{4}$in CT
Machinery: 4-shaft Parsons turbines, 43,000shp = 21knots; 18 boilers
Coal Capacity: 900/2680tons
Oil Capacity: 300tons'
Endurance: 4700miles at 10knots
Complement: 1124
Cost: not known

	Laid Down	Launched	Completed	Built/Engined
Bretagne	1 July 1912	21 Apr 1913	Sept 1915	Brest DY
Lorraine	1 Aug 1912	30 Sept 1913	July 1916	Penhoet,
Provence	1 May 1912	20 Apr 1913	June 1915	Lorient DY

This trio of handsome vessels were ordered under the 1912 Programme and were the only new construction to join the French battle fleet during the war. After the unfortunate experience with the *Danton* class it was wisely decided to hasten their building time by keeping the hull of the preceding *Jean Bart* class, but allocating the weight to a centreline armament of fewer and heavier guns, to match the increases in gun-calibres in foreign navies. The result was a more handsome and balanced design than the French had produced for a decade.

The secondary armament was unusual in that the casemates were so closely bunched. Apart from the problem of spray interference, no attention seems to have been paid to blast problems. The midships 13·4in turret (No. 3) was carried at an unusual height above water.

Appearance: All four were very similar, with only minor differences (funnels, cranes, etc) to distinguish them. They were typical of French ships of the period, with a straight stem and recessed hawsepipes. They differed from the *Courbet* class by having one broad funnel and one small one between pole masts.

Careers

Bretagne: Joined 1st Division, 1st Squadron of Mediterranean Fleet in 1916; Flagship 1st Squadron 1917–18 and served at Corfu and Mudros; modernised 1919–20 and again in 1932–35; sunk by naval gunfire from British 'Force H' at Oran 3 July 1940.

Lorraine: Ran trials at Toulon in mid-1916 and joined 1st Squadron of Mediterranean Fleet as Flagship; relieved by *Bretagne* 1917 and refitted at Toulon; returned to 1st Squadron and served at Corfu and Mudros; modernised as *Bretagne*; interned at Alexadria in 1940, but rejoined Allies in 1943; broken up 1953.

Provence: Became Fleet Flagship 1916 and continued as such until Armistice; modernised as *Bretagne* and *Provence*; badly damaged by British gunfire at Oran 3 July 1940 but escaped to Toulon, where she was scuttled to avoid capture by the Germans in 1942; raised and scrapped in 1943.

Left, Lorraine in dock at Toulon in December 1916. Note that there are no guns in the after turret, and the ports have been blanked off (IWM).

Below, Bretagne passing through the swing bridge in Toulon dockyard, October 1916 (IWM).

Normandie class

Displacement: 25,230tons
Dimensions: 579ft (wl)×88ft 2in×29ft
Guns: 12×13·4in (3×4), 45cal
24×5·5in (24×1)
4×47mm (4×1)
Torpedo Tubes: 6×18in (submerged, beam)
Armour: 11–7in belt
Machinery: 2-shaft turbines and 2-shaft triple expansion (4 in all), totalling 40,000shp = 21½knots; boilers varied from 21 Guyot du Temple to 28 Bellevilles
Coal Capacity: 900/2700tons
Oil Capacity: 300tons
Endurance: 7000miles at 10knots (approximate)
Complement: 1200
Cost: not known

	Laid Down	Launched	Completed	Builder
Bearn (ex-Vendée)	10 Jan 1914	—	—	La Seyne
Flandre	1 Oct 1913	20 Oct 1914	—	Brest
Gascogne	1 Oct 1913	20 Sept 1914	—	Lorient
Languedoc	18 Apr 1913	1 May 1915	—	Bordeaux
Normandie	18 Apr 1913	19 Oct 1914	—	St. Nazaire

Four new battleships of revolutionary design were ordered under the 1913 Programme. With beam much the same as the *Bretagne* and slightly greater length, the horsepower developed was greater than in the preceeding class. French battleships had come in for some criticism as being slower than their contemporaries, and it was hoped that the new ships would have greater tactical flexibility if they could maintain 21knots.

French experience with turbines had not been a total success, coal consumption tending to be very high at cruising speeds. The *Danton* class had come in for much criticism when they were found to use far more coal than the reciprocating-engined *République* and *Vérité* classes; in an attempt to rectify this the *Normandie* class were to be given turbines on the two inner shafts and triple-expansion machinery on the outer shafts for cruising.

The most advanced feature of the new design was the introduction of quadruple turrets, the first of their kind in the world. As a result, without increasing the dimensions unduly over the preceding maximum, the French produced a design with 20 per cent more gunpower, but without sacrificing the advantage of centreline mountings. Furthermore, with only three large turrets, the economical layout of the superstructure ensured good arcs of fire for all turrets.

The layout of secondary guns was not so good, as all the errors of the previous designs were repeated, with tightly bunched casemate mountings calculated to suffer from maximum blast interference, both from one another and from the main guns.

All five units of this class were suspended in August 1914. It was originally intended to complete them for the postwar fleet, but so much equipment had been appropriated for other ships that it proved uneconomical to do anything with *Flandre*, *Gascogne*, *Languedoc* and *Normandie*. Only *Bearn* was fit for completion, and she was chosen for conversion to an aircraft carrier, the only French vessel of this type to be completed until 1946.

Careers

Bearn: Name changed in 1914 before launching; all work suspended in August 1914, and not restarted until December 1918; redesigned as aircraft-carrier and completed 1923–6; survived World War II and hulked 1947; broken up in Italy in 1967.

Flandre: Work suspended in August 1914; so much of her material, such as boilers, was allocated to patrol vessels during the war that she was not woth completing postwar; the hull was stricken on 18 April 1922 and broken up in October 1924 at Toulon.

Gascogne: Work suspended August 1914; boilers and other material appropriated for torpedo-craft; as with *Flandre*; cancelled 18 April 1922 with *Flandre* and sold for breaking up 13 April 1923; scrapping completed at Lorient 1923–4.

Languedoc: Suspended in August 1914 and cancelled 18 April 1922 with *Flandre* and *Gascogne*; sold for breaking up in 1924, but sunk (?) in May 1925; wreck raised and broken up in May 1929.

Normandie: Suspended August 1914 and cancelled 18 April 1922 with *Flandre*, *Gascogne* and *Languedoc*; as her machinery was 70 per cent complete it was appropriated for the completion of *Bearn*, and her boilers had already been used in torpedo-craft.

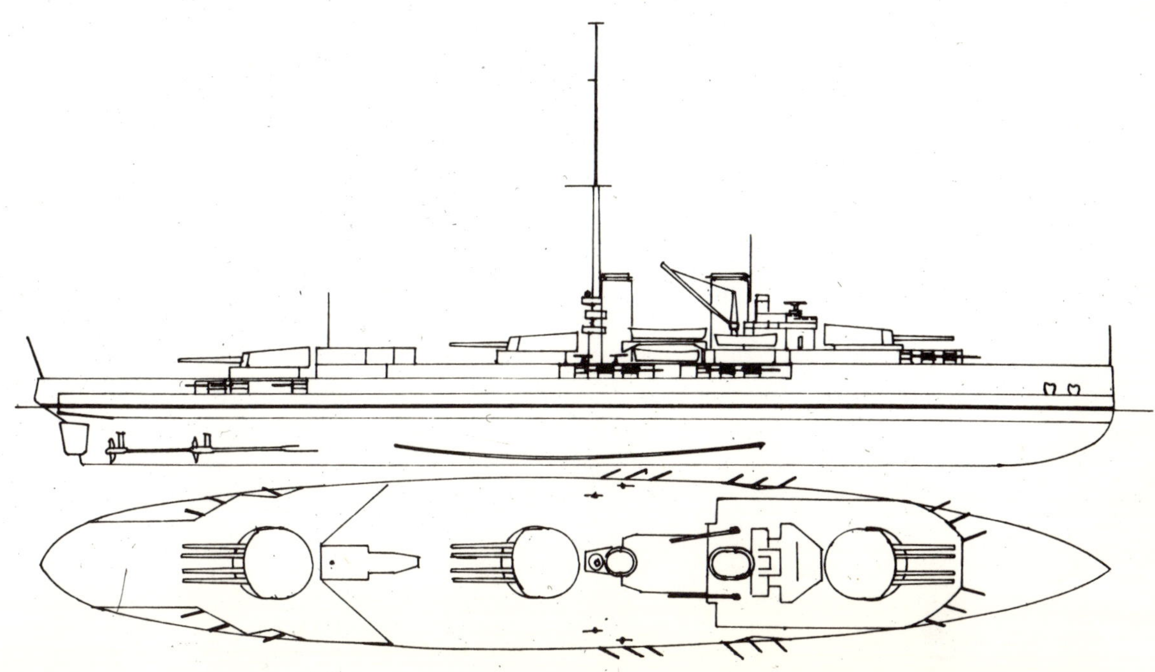

Lyon class

Displacement: 27,500tons (normal) : 29,600tons (full load)
Dimensions: 728ft×110ft×34ft
Guns: 16×13·4in 45cal (4×4)
24×5·5in (24×1)
Torpedo Tubes: 6×18in (submerged, beam)
Armour: Not known
Machinery: 2 sets turbines and 2 sets triple expansion, totalling 44,000shp= 23knots
Fuel: Coal and Oil
Endurance: Not known

	Laid Down	Launched	Completed	Contractors
Lille	—	—	—	La Seyne
Lyon	—	—	—	St. Nazaire
Duquesne	—	—	—	Brest
Tourville	—	—	—	Lorient

These ships were enlarged editions of the *Normandie* class, intended to be laid down under the 1915 Programme. The same quadruple turrets were to be mounted, but with an additional centreline turret between the funnels. In other respects they followed the *Normandie* design closely, but with slightly higher power. They were not laid down by the time war broke out, and construction was cancelled at the same time as work on the *Normandie* class was suspended.

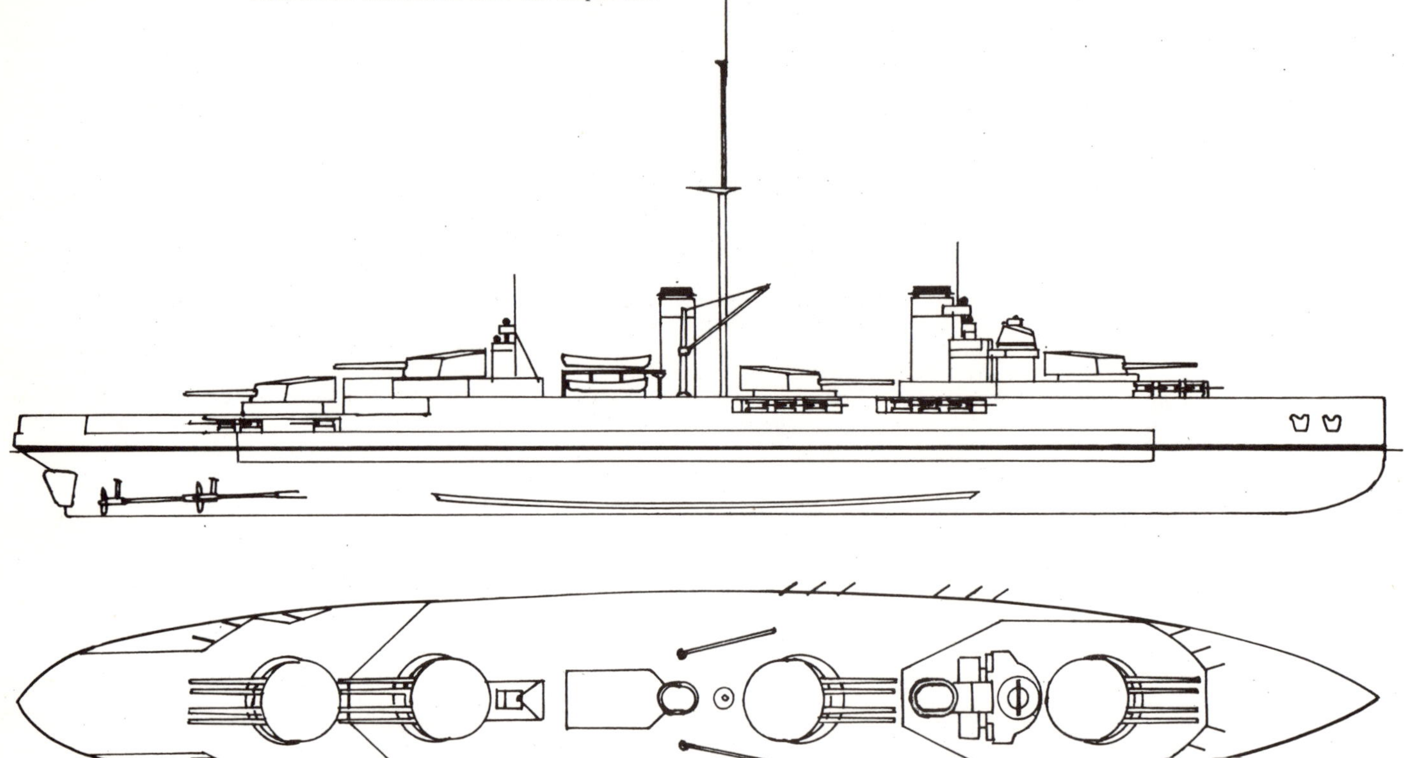

In 1913–14 designs were prepared for a battle cruiser edition of the *Normandie* class. Although never ordered, the following particulars give an idea of their qualities:

Displacement: 27,000tons (approx.)
Guns: 12×13·4in (3×4)
24×5·5in (24×1)
Armour: 11¼in belt (maximum)
Machinery: 4-shaft turbines, 63,000shp=27knots

The design was under review, and other combinations of guns and armour were under consideration.

Germany

Below, Baden returning from Heligoland in 1918 (Bundesarchiv).

Introduction

If Lord Fisher could be described as the presiding genius of the Royal Navy, then Admiral Tirpitz could claim a similar honour for his part in building up the German Navy. From a coast-defence force in 1897 it became the world's second largest navy in less than two decades.

Germany's industrial strength had been growing during the closing years of the nineteenth Century, and with the growth of nationalism, influential Germans began to envy the British their enormous seaborne trade and their colonies. Colonies were regarded as a potent form of economic capital, and it was felt that Germany had fewer than she could have won for herself with a large navy. As Secretary of the German Admiralty, Tirpitz was able to persuade the young and ambitious Kaiser Wilhelm II that a big navy would assist Germany to extend her influence by acting as a threat to Great Britain.

Tirpitz evolved his notorious 'Risk Theory', which was an attempt to avoid the almost impossible challenge of trying to outbuild the Royal Navy. Instead, he argued that, since the British feared above all a combination of two navies (ie: the French and Russian), all the Germans needed was a fleet strong enough to inflict such damage on the Royal Navy as would reduce it below its own 'Two Power Standard'. This 'risk' of damage had an attractive simplicity, which we can now see as naïve: the major flaw in the 'Risk Theory' was that Great Britain might patch up her differences with either France or Russia, and possibly with both, and then be able to crush the German Navy.

There was another unforeseen factor which upset the Germans' calculations—the Kaiser. Egged on by Pan-German propagandists, the Kaiser gave vent to blustering speeches about German ambitions to outbuild the Royal Navy. While the British tradition of isolation from European alliances remained unchanged, whatever threat the German Army might pose, this isolation could not be guaranteed if the British should come to suspect that Germany wanted to be a great naval power. This is exactly what happened, for a combination of inept diplomacy and jingoistic speechmaking by the Emperor alarmed the British, French and Russians to such an extent that they were able to settle their differences and join a Triple Entente by 1907.

The German Navy Laws
Tirpitz persuaded the German Reichstag to pass the First German Navy Law in 1898. This laid down the strength of the Fleet at 19 battleships and 8 coast defence ships:

5 *Wittelsbach* Class	1 *Oldenburg* (old)
5 *Kaiser* Class (old)	6 *Siegfried* Class
4 *Wörth* Class	1 *Odin*
4 *Baden* Class (old)	1 *Aegir*

As the Navy Law laid down effective lives for battleships, and that these vessels had to be replaced within 25 years, considerable new building would have to be undertaken to finish the programme by 1903, as the law required. Not content with this rate of expansion, Tirpitz was able to exploit anti-British feeling during the Boer War and introduced a Second Navy Law in 1900, which replaced the existing establishment with a larger one:

2 fleet flagships	4 battleships (reserve)
32 battleships (4 active squadrons)	plus 8 large cruisers

Naturally the British took this as a direct challenge, and so both nations took their first steps in the fatal arms race which culminated in World War I. The Germans, and Tirpitz in particular, had not wanted a world war, and could not understand why the British were so suspicious of their motives. As time went by the suspicion became mutual, with the Germans insisting that the British would try to 'Copenhagen' them, or in other words, launch a pre-emptive attack on their main bases. The British for their part believed that swarms of German torpedo-craft would swoop out of the mist to destroy their fleet.

The final straw, so far as the British were concerned, was an amendment to the 1900 Navy Law, passed by the Reichstag in 1908. This was a subterfuge to increase the strength of the Fleet, by reducing the 'effective life' of capital ships from 25 to 20 years, and by stipulating that the eight large cruisers provided for should be battle cruisers. In practice the first provision meant that the Reichstag had to allow Tirpitz to lay down four battleships a year for three years, in place of the original three a year; the effect of the second provision was obvious. Taken in total they meant that by 1920 the German Fleet would comprise 58 dreadnoughts, instead of the 38 provided for in 1900.

For Germany the consequences of this chicanery were tragic, for it eliminated any permanent hope of reaching an understanding with Great Britain. Although there was to be much argument and counter-argument between 1908 and 1914, the outcome was that each country built to the limit of its capacity. The irony of it all was that Tirpitz resented bitterly British suggestions that his Navy was an instrument of aggression. He had intended it as a political pawn which could strengthen Germany's power to negotiate in the world, and neither he nor the Emperor he served so loyally ever quite understood the extent (or justification) of the British fears.

The building of the *Dreadnought* wiped out Britain's enormous lead in battleships by making the older ships obsolete, and acted as a tremendous incentive to Germany to try for something approaching parity in numbers. At the same time the Germans began to emerge as the most scientific battleship designers in the world. Although mistakes were made in the early dreadnoughts, their principles of damage control proved to be far in advance of British practice in 1914. Armouring and machinery design were subjected to close scrutiny, and during the war German ships proved that they not only had first-class protection, but also had efficient and economical machinery.

The first battle cruisers offered convincing proof of the excellence of German design, for the *Von der Tann* and the *Moltke* class had all the qualities lacking in their British equivalents, the *Invincible* and *Indefatigable* classes. Yet, the Germans had inflicted certain penalties on their ships which reduced their fighting efficiency. Owing to their belief that the British would implement a close blockade of the German coast, they played down the importance of endurance and seaworthiness. Because ships would only have to put to sea on rare forays, their crews could be accommodated in cramped quarters, and living spaces could therefore be closely subdivided. The training followed suit, and it is significant that the High Seas Fleet had only one large-scale manoeuvre before the war. At Jutland German ship-handling left much to be desired, and more than one ship was lost by collision in the hectic moments of the night action.

Shipbuilders

There were fewer big yards in Germany capable of building battleships than there were in Britain. In general building times were longer, and when the naval arms race entered its final phase the British were able to adopt a policy of 'two keels to one' at a period when German yards were stretched to full capacity. The guns came from the Krupp works, which had been greatly expanded before the war, but after 1914 the Army's needs resulted in a severe shortage, and construction was held up.

Being late in the field German shipbuilders had not been very successful in obtaining foreign orders for battleships, but the Vulkan contract for building the Greek *Salamis* might have been the pointer to future developments.

German Shipbuilders

Abbreviation	Full Name of Builder and Location
Blohm & Voss	Blohm & Voss, Hamburg
Germania	Friedrich Krupp Germaniawerft, Kiel
Howaldt	Howaldtswerfte, Kiel
Kiel DY	Kaiserliche Werft, Kiel
Schichau	Friedrich Schichau, Danzig
Vulkan, Hamburg	A. G. Vulkan, Hamburg
Vulkan, Stettin	A. G. Vulkan, Stettin
Weser	A. G. Weser, Bremen
Wilhelmshaven DY	Kaiserliche Werft, Wilhelmshaven

Dockyards and Bases

The two Imperial Dockyards, Kiel and Wilhelmshaven, had been established in the nineteenth century. Kiel was on the Baltic coast, and its utility had been increased enormously by the building of the Kiel Canal. One of the consequences of the switch to dreadnought building was a considerable increase in dimensions of battleships which made the canal too small. The Kiel Canal was essential for Germany to facilitate deployment of her ships, and so at vast expense the Canal was deepened and widened; the re-opening came in July 1914.

Hamburg, Danzig and Bremerhaven were the other major shipbuilding ports; other centres specialised in smaller craft. There was no shortage of bases on the Baltic coast, but Germany suffered a grave strategic disadvantage in a war with Great Britain, having all her outlets to the North Sea concentrated quite close together. Her only permanent naval base overseas was Kiao-Chau (Tsingtao) which was quickly captured by Anglo-Japanese forces.

Weapons

German naval guns came from the great Krupp factory, and fully earned their fine reputation, both for accuracy and durability. The old 9·4in gun, which dated from the days when the Imperial German Navy was still a coast-defence force, had little to recommend it against the 12in gun which was standard elsewhere but the later 11in and 12in guns were first class. However, the Germans remained wedded to their belief in high muzzle velocity and a light shell, and the disadvantages came to light when the British went to heavier shells and lower muzzle velocities with their 13·5in and 15in.

German chemists were more successful than their British counterparts in producing stable cordite propellants. Although much has been made of the German practice of keeping cartridges in brass cases, the basic stability of German cordite was the most important factor. There were few precautions against flash, and shells and cartridges were stowed together. The danger of flash travelling was underestimated until the disastrous fire in the *Seydlitz* at the Dogger Bank which burnt out the after turrets, but time after time German ships escaped destruction because of the safe nature of their cordite charges. During the war the Germans lost no battleship by an internal ammunition explosion, as against three British losses (excluding Jutland where some were probably due to cordite explosion).

German Guns

Calibre	Length in Calibres	Range	Elevation	Notes
9·4in	40	18,500yds	30°	Old battleships up to Wittelsbach Class
11in	40	20,600yds	30°	Braunschweig and Deutschland classes
11in	45	22,400yds	20°	Westfalen Class and Von der Tann
11in	50	19,700yds	$13\frac{1}{2}$°	Moltke Class and Seydlitz
11in	50	21,000yds	16°	Seydlitz (1916), Moltke later class
11in	50	23,700yds	$22\frac{1}{2}$°	Goeben (1918)
12in	50	21,000yds	$13\frac{1}{2}$°	Helgoland, Kaiser, König and Derfflinger classes
12in	50	22,300yds	16°	Prinzregent Luitpold and Hindenburg (1916) followed by others of class
15in	45	22,200yds	16°	Baden and Bayern

Although the Germans never favoured the idea of a stern torpedo tube, their designs always included a bow tube, housed in the forefoot under the ram. As in other navies, this feature of capital ships proved utterly useless, and there is no record of any battleship hitting anything with a torpedo during the war.

Actions

When War broke out the High Seas Fleet was disposed in three battle squadrons, and the battle cruisers were in a separate squadron. As the pattern of the war emerged more clearly, the oldest coast-defence ships were paid off and converted to humbler but more essential duties, such as distilling ships, accommodation and repair hulks, etc. The manpower saved was diverted to the destroyer and submarine flotillas. The main battle squadrons took part in several sweeps, covering the battle cruisers, but their only action was the Battle of the Skagerrak, known to the British as Jutland.

Disposition of German Fleet August 1914

Fleet Flagship
Friedrich der Grosse (in battle formed part of Squadron I)

Squadron I
Ostfriesland (flagship), Thüringen, Helgoland, Oldenburg, Posen, Rheinland, Nassau, Westfalen

Squadron II
Deutschland (flagship), Braunschweig, Lothringen, Preussen, Hessen, Elsass, Pommern, Hannover, Schleswig-Holstein, Schlesien

Squadron III
König (flagship), Grosser Kurfürst, Kaiser, Prinzregent Luitpold, Kaiserin, König Albert

Scouting Group I
Seydlitz (flagship), Von Der Tann, Moltke

Coast Defence and Local Guardships
Odin, Aegir, Brandenburg, Wörth, Siegfried, Beowulf, Frithjof, Heimdall, Hildebrand, Hagen, Kaiser Friedrich III, Kaiser Wilhelm II, Kaiser Wilhelm der Grosse, Kaiser Barbarossa, Kaiser Karl der Grosse, Mecklenburg, Wettin, Wittelsbach, Schwaben, Zähringen

Mediterranean Squadron
Goeben (flagship)

German policy had for many years been to try whittling down the superiority of the British Fleet to a point where the High Seas Fleet could meet it on equal terms. When in 1914 the British did not institute a close blockade—which would have exposed their battleships to just this sort of attrition—the German strategy was thrown into confusion and new ideas had to be found. The result was a policy of provocative raids, with the battle cruisers crossing the North Sea to bombard towns like Scarborough and the Hartlepools, in the hope of luring a single British squadron into the arms of the full High Seas Fleet. There were a number of narrow escapes on both sides, and then on 24 January 1915 Scouting Group I (*Seydlitz*, *Derfflinger*, *Moltke* and the armoured cruiser *Blücher*) were caught by the British battle cruiser force under Beatty.

The German ships were lucky to escape a severe mauling, and they owed this partly to British signal failures but mainly to Hipper's decision to leave the unfortunate *Blücher* to her fate. As the British ships mistakenly concentrated on the crippled cruiser the 1st Scouting Group disappeared over the horizon; the only serious damage was suffered by the *Seydlitz* ohich lost 159 men in a cordite fire.

The Battle of the Skagerrak, 31 May 1916

With German policy dedicated to avoiding a confrontation between their Fleet and the British, the nature of the Skagerrak battle could be forecast with ease; the British would try to engage, while the Germans would try to disengage, inflicting as much damage as possible.

The battle produced little to reassure the Germans, apart from a justified pride in the excellence of their ships, their gunnery, and their night-fighting organisation. To offset the sinking of three British battle cruisers and three armoured cruisers (of which only the *Queen Mary* had sufficient protection to give her any expectation of survival), the High Seas Fleet lost the old *Pommern* to a torpedo-attack during the night, and the battle cruiser flagship *Lutzow*, which had to be sunk by German forces after battling to stay afloat for hours. The surviving battle cruisers were badly damaged, the *Derfflinger* having two turrets destroyed and the *Seydlitz* being set ablaze.

The High Seas Fleet at the Skagerrak, 31 May 1916
Fleet Flagship
Friedrich der Grosse (Vice-Admiral Scheer) serving with Squadron III
Squadron I
Ostfriesland (Vice-Admiral Schmidt), Thüringen, Helgoland, Oldenburg, Posen (Rear-Admiral Engelhardt), Rheinland, Nassau, Westfalen
Squadron II
Deutschland (Rear-Admiral Mauve), Pommern, Schlesien, Schleswig-Holstein, Hannover (Rear-Admiral Lichtenfels), Hessen
Squadron III*
König (Rear-Admiral Behncke), Grosser Kurfürst, Markgraf, Kronprinz, Kaiser (Rear-Admiral Nordmann), Prinzregent Luitpold, Kaiserin, Friedrich der Grosse (q.v.)
Scouting Group I
Lützow (Rear-Admiral Hipper), Derfflinger, Seydlitz, Moltke, Von der Tann

---

*König Albert refitting

The closing stages of the main fleet action were marked by desperate manoeuvres by Admiral Scheer, who had lost all touch with Jellicoe and was dangerously misinformed about the British position and course. Many years later, Scheer candidly admitted that he had little idea of how to extricate his ships, and had been prepared to sacrifice his Scouting Group I as a last resort. This 'death ride' of the battle cruisers enabled the High Seas Fleet to make a 180° turn away, and the devoted battle cruisers also vanished into the mist and smoke as darkness fell. During the night Scheer's ships managed to force their way through the British screen of light cruisers and destroyers, and it was here that their superior night fighting techniques proved decisive.

Baltic Operations 1915–17

Dreadnoughts were detached from time to time to bolster the forces operating against the Russians. In August 1915 the *Posen* and *Nassau* were in action in the Gulf of Riga, and hit the Russian *Slava* on 17 August. In October 1917 the *Moltke* and Squadrons III and IV of the High Seas Fleet (ten battleships) carried out a big assault on Russian forces in the Gulf once more. On 17 October the *Slava* was set on fire by hits from the *Kronprinz* and *Kaiser*, and was later abandoned by the Russians after being torpedoed by one of their own destroyers.

From 1915 to 1917 British submarines based on Reval were able to affect German operations against the Russians: instead of having total freedom of movement in the Baltic, the Germans were subjected to the constant threat of attack, and in August 1915 the *Moltke* was badly damaged by *E.1*. This threat was only removed when the British submarines were scuttled during the aftermath of the Russian Revolution.

War Modifications and Colour Schemes

In general German ships were not nearly so much modified as British ships. The most important changes effected during the war were the removal of anti-torpedo nets after May 1916 (considerably later than in the Royal Navy) and the provision of anti-aircraft guns. Important modifications to individual ships will be found under the classes, but these were the exception, and not the rule. The colour scheme was light grey overall; funnel bands were discarded on the outbreak of war, but certain battle cruisers had a black cap to the forefunnel. In 1917–18 circles were painted on certain turrets to assist recognition by aircraft. Camouflage schemes were not used.

Decline of the High Seas Fleet

The High Seas Fleet deteriorated after the Battle of Jutland, for its key personnel were drafted to the U-boats and destroyer flotillas in such numbers that efficiency was affected. The result was a lack of contact between officers and ratings which led to the unrest in 1917 and finally open mutiny in 1918. The fact that the High Seas Fleet could boast of not being defeated in battle did not prevent it from surrendering in 1918 without firing a shot, the saddest possible end for a proud navy. Had the Germans showed the same flair for using their capital ships as they had in designing them, the British would have had a far harder job of controlling the North Sea, and this in turn would have jeopardised their entire war strategy.

Another factor in the declining morale of the Fleet was the excessively military flavour of shore training. When ships were in port the crews were inevitably involved in irksome drills and parades. Also, in 1918 the preparations for a sortie were so evident that seditious elements had ample warning to allow them to play on the sailors' fears. Had the ships been more accustomed to cruising, however tedious, the day to day running of the ships might have provided a certain amount of distraction, as it undoubtedly did for the Grand Fleet.

The Armistice signed on 11 November 1918 provided for the surrender of ten battleships and six battle cruisers. Four days later the cruiser *Königsberg* arrived at Rosyth, bringing Rear-Admiral Von Meurer and the plenipotentiaries of the Workmen's and Soldier's Council to negotiate with Admiral Sir David Beatty aboard his flagship, H.M.S. *Queen Elizabeth*. As a result of this the German ships arrived in a melancholy procession at 8.30am on the morning of 21 November.

It must be remembered that the Armistice was not a proclamation of peace, and the British continued to regard themselves as at war with

Germany, pending the signing of a Peace Treaty. Accordingly the surrendered German officers were treated in cavalier fashion, and the British made no secret of their willingness to reopen hostilities if the peace negotiations were not satisfactory. The British and foreign press voiced opinions from time to time about the possible use of the surrendered High Seas Fleet by the Allies against Germany, and although these proposals were never seriously considered, the German internees were well aware of them. Their patriotism and loyalty to their service could never have allowed such a thing to happen, and on 21 June 1919 at Scapa Flow all German ships were scuttled simultaneously. As the British Fleet was away on exercises there were too few British personnel present to do very much, and of the big ships only the *Baden* was successfully beached. The High Seas Fleet, which Tirpitz had created in the space of only twenty years, no longer existed.

German Capital Ships Surrendered 21 November 1918
Battleships (9)[1]
Friedrich Der Grosse, Bayern, Kaiser, Kaiserin, Prinzregent Luitpold, König Albert, Kronprinz Wilhelm, Grosser Kurfürst, Markgraf
Battle Cruisers (5)[2]
Von Der Tann, Moltke, Seydlitz, Derfflinger, Hindenburg

[1] The numbers were short but the König arrived on 4 December.
[2] The Mackensen could not be completed in time, and the Baden arrived in her place on 14 December.

The Fleet Flagship and its crew: SMS Friedrich der Grosse in Norway, 1913, as escort to the Imperial Yacht Hohenzollern (Bundesarchiv).

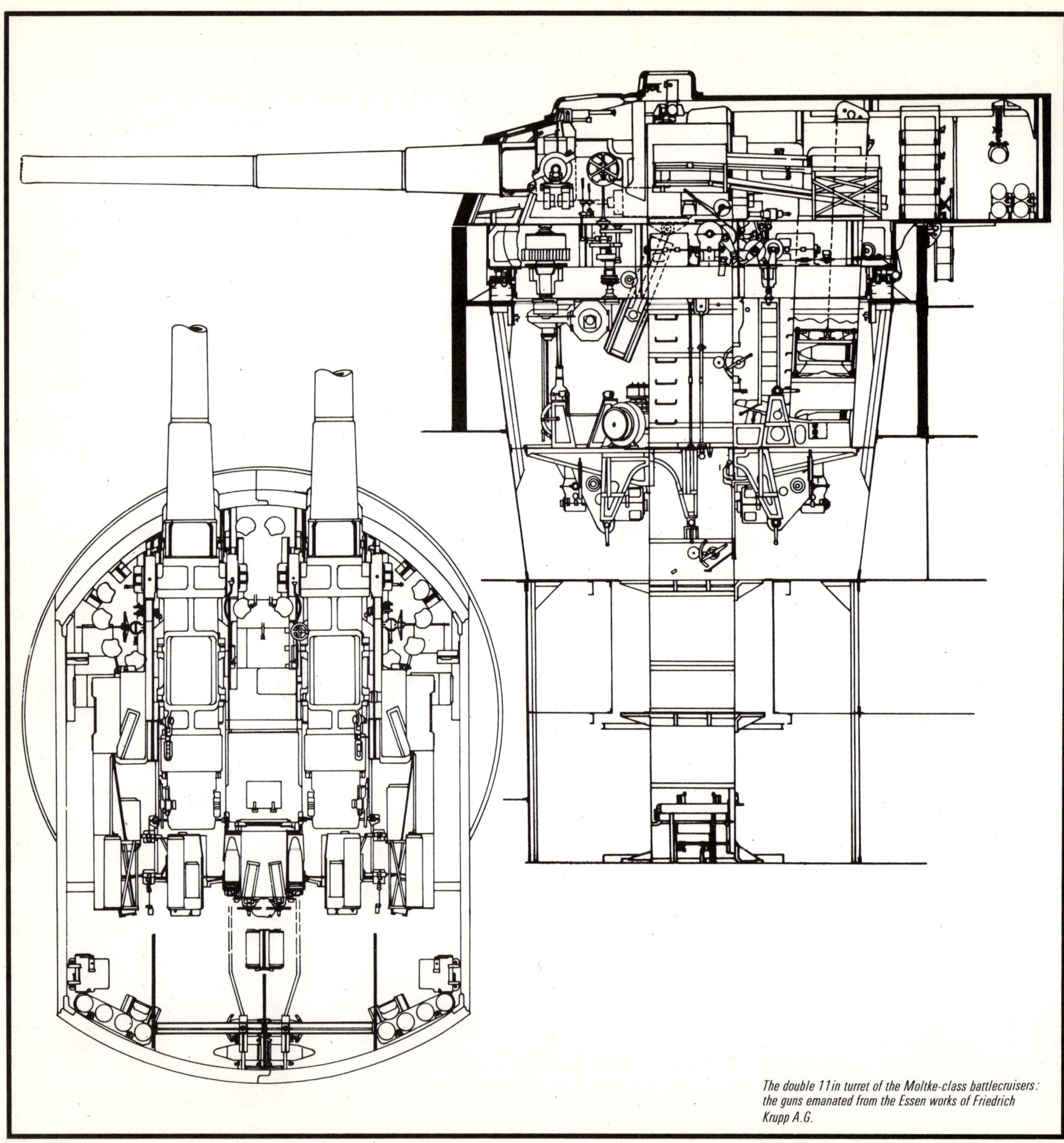

*The double 11in turret of the Moltke-class battlecruisers:
the guns emanated from the Essen works of Friedrich
Krupp A.G.*

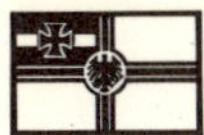

Siegfried class

Displacement: 4058tons (normal), 4225tons (maximum) Aegir and Odin: 4110tons (normal), 4292tons (maximum)

Dimensions: 240ft×49ft 3in×17ft 9in (mean)

Guns: 3×9·4in 35cal (3×1) 10×3·4in 30cal Q.F. (10×1) 6 machine-guns

Torpedo Tubes: 3×17·7in (submerged, 1 stern and 2 beam) 1×13·8in (submerged, bow)

Armour: 9½–7in belt; 1¼in deck (2in in Heimdall and Hagen) 5½in turrets; 7in CT

Machinery: 2-shaft vertical triple expansion, 3-cylinder, 5100hp = 15½knots (in 1904); 8 Schulz-Thornycroft boilers

Coal Capacity: 480/580tons

Endurance: 3980miles at 10knots

Complement: 307 (Hildebrand and Aegir 350 as flagships)

Cost: not known

	Laid Down	Launched	Completed	Built/Engined
Siegfried	1888	10 Aug 1889	Apr 1890	Germania
Beowulf	1890	8 Nov 1890	Apr 1892	Weser
Frithjof	1890	21 July 1891	Feb 1893	Weser
Heimdall	1891	27 July 1892	Apr 1894	Wilhelmshaven DY
Hildebrand	1891	6 Aug 1892	Oct 1893	Kiel DY
Hagen	1891	21 Oct 1893	Oct 1894	Kiel DY
Aegir	1892	3 Apr 1895	Oct 1896	Kiel DY
Odin	1893	3 Nov 1894	July 1896	Schichau

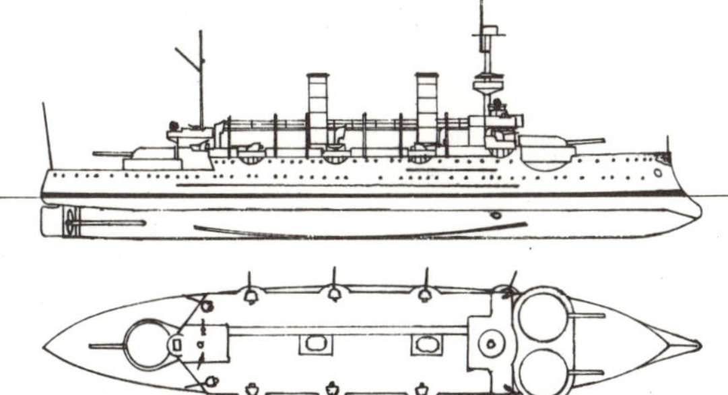

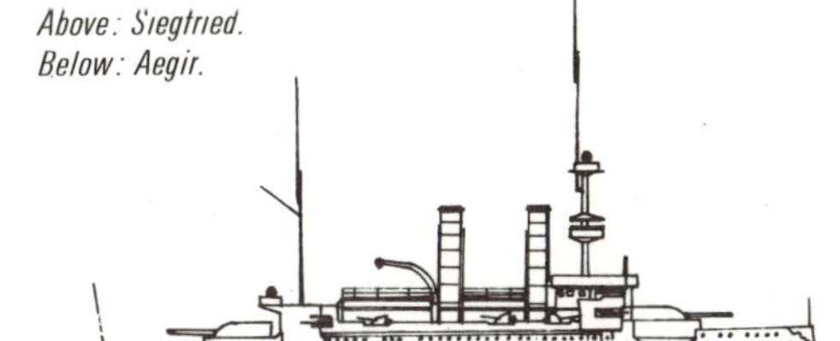

Above: Siegfried.
Below: Aegir.

Right, a pre-1914 photograph of Hagen, which shows the general appearance of this class (IWM).

Originally designed to counter small French coastal battleships, these old ships had little or no military value, and were soon relegated to subsidiary duties.

Careers

Aegir: Served with Squadron VI of the High Seas Fleet in the Baltic August 1914; relegated to coast defence 1915 and disarmed 1916; served as an accommodation ship 1916–18; sold 1922 for conversion to a motor ship for mercantile use; wrecked off Gotland Lighthouse 8 December 1929.

Beowulf: Squadron VI, Baltic 1914–15; coast defence duties 1915–16; disarmed 1916 for service as a U-boat target; used as icebreaker 1918; interned at Stockholm November 1918; sold 1921 and broken up Danzig 1921.

Frithjof: Squadron VI 1914–15; coast defence 1915–16; disarmed and used as accommodation ship at Danzig 1916–18; sold 1923 and converted to motor ship for mercantile use; broken up Danzig 1930.

Hagen: Squadron VI 1914–15; coast defence 1915; disarmed as accommodation ship at Swinemünde 1915; sold and broken up 1919.

Heimdall: Squadron VI 1914–15; coast defence 1915–16; disarmed as accommodation ship at Emden 1916–18; sold 1920 for conversion to salvage vessel, but work abandoned, and broken up at Ronnebeck 1921.

Hildebrand: Squadron VI 1914–15; coast defence 1915–16; disarmed as accommodation ship at Windau 1916–18; sold December 1919 and wrecked off Dutch coast 21 December while in tow to breakers; wreck refloated in 1933 and broken up.

Siegfried: Squadron VI 1914–15; coast defence 1915–16; disarmed as accommodation ship at Wilhelmshaven 1916–18; sold 1920 for conversion to salvage vessel, but work abandoned, and broken up in the same year.

Odin: Coastal defence 1914–16; reduced to tender 1917; sold 1922 and converted to merchant ship; broken up 1935.

Wörth class

Displacement: 10,060tons (normal), 10,727tons (full load)
Dimensions: 340ft 10½in (wl)× 64ft 9in×25ft 4in (mean)
Guns: 6×9·4in (2×2 40cal and 1×2 35cal); disarmed 1916 (see notes)
8×4·1in 35cal (8×1)
8×3·4in (8×1)
12×37mm (12×1)
Torpedo Tubes: 3×17·7in (1 bow, above water and 2 beam, submerged)

Armour: 15¾–11·4/5in belt; 3–2in deck; 9–5in turrets; 11·4/5in CT
Machinery: 2-shaft vertical triple expansion, 3-cylinder, 10,000hp = 17knots in 1905; 12 cylindrical boilers
Coal Capacity: 650/1050tons
Oil Capacity: 110tons
Endurance: 4500miles at 10knots
Complement: 591
Cost: not known

	Laid Down	Launched	Completed	Built/Engined
Wörth	1890	6 Aug 1892	Oct 1893	Germania, Kiel
Brandenburg	1890	21 Sept 1891	Nov 1893	Vulkan, Stettin

These two old ships were suitable only for coast defence in 1914, and had little fighting value.

Sister Ships: Two sister-ships, *Kurfürst Friedrich Wilhelm* and *Weissenburg* were sold to Turkey in 1910, and will be found under the Turkish section.

Careers

Brandenburg: Serving with Squadron V (Baltic) of the High Seas Fleet at outbreak of war; relegated to coast defence in 1915 and disarmed for subsidiary service in 1916; accommodation ship and distilling hulk at Libau 1916–18; conversion to target ship begun in 1918 but not completed; stricken 13 May 1919 and broken up at Danzig in 1920.

Wörth: With Squadron V in August 1914 but relegated to coastal defence in 1915; accommodation ship at Danzig 1916–18; stricken 13 May 1919 and broken up at Danzig.

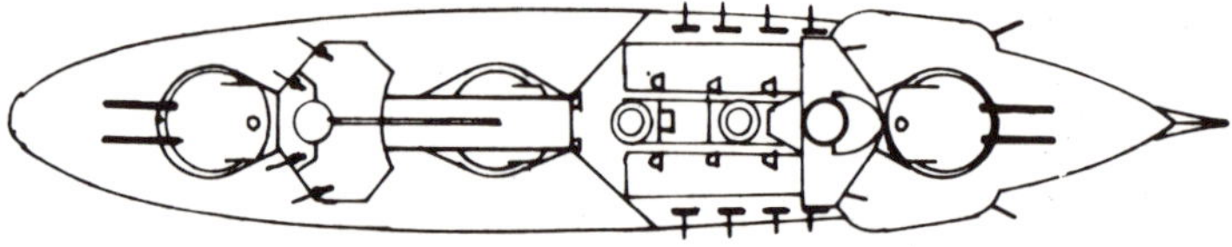

Below, a peacetime view of Brandenburg, showing the distinctive shape of her 9 4in gun turrets (IWM).

Below right, Kaiser Friedrich III in the early years of the century (IWM).

Kaiser Friedrich III class

Displacement: 10,790tons (normal)
Dimensions: 384ft (wl)×65ft 6in× 27ft (max)
Guns: 4×9·4in 40cal (2×2) 14×5·9in 40cal (14×1); Kaiser Karl, 18×5·9in 12×3·4in 12×1pdr
Torpedo Tubes: 6×17·7in (submerged, bow and beam)
Armour: 12–4in belt; 10in turrets; 3in decks; 10in CT
Machinery: 3-shaft 3-cylinder vertical triple expansion, 14,000hp = 18knots (when new); 8 cylindrical and 4 Schultz boilers
Coal Capacity: 650/1050tons
Oil Capacity: 200tons
Endurance: 4500miles at 10knots
Complement: 658
Cost: not known

	Laid Down	Launched	Completed	Built/Engined
Kaiser Friedrich III	1895	1 July 1896	1898	Wilhelmshaven DY
Kaiser Wilhelm der Grosse	1896	1 June 1899	1900	Germania
Kaiser Karl der Grosse	1898	18 Oct 1899	1900	Blohm & Voss
Kaiser Barbarossa	1898	21 Apr 1900	1901	Schichau
Kaiser Wilhelm II	1898	14 Sept 1897	1899	Wilhelmshaven DY

These ships were too slow and weakly armed to be useful even in second-line service, and were quickly relegated to harbour service.

Careers

Kaiser Friedrich III: Accommodation hulk 1914–18; broken up 1920.

Kaiser Wilhelm der Grosse: Torpedo-firing ship at Kiel 1914–18; broken up 1920.

Kaiser Karl der Grosse: Prisoner-of-war accommodation ship at Wilhelmshaven; broken up 1920.

Kaiser Barbarossa: As *Kaiser Karl Der Grosse.*

Kaiser Wilhelm II: H.Q. ship at Wilhelmshaven 1914–18; broken up 1921.

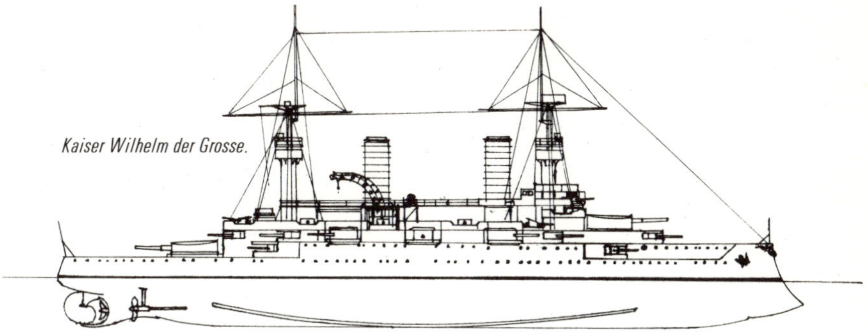

Kaiser Wilhelm der Grosse.

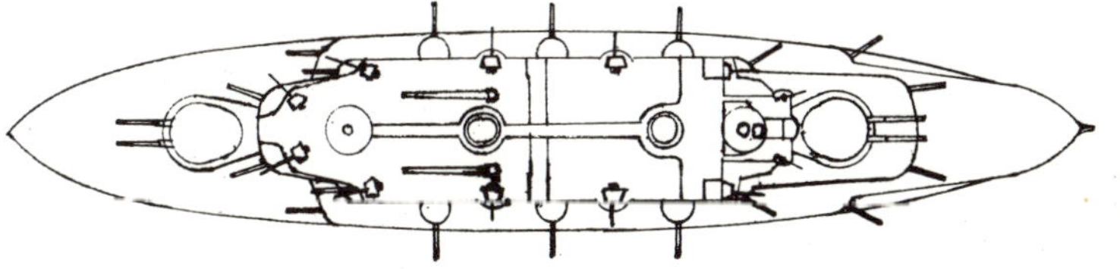

Below, *Kaiser Wilhelm der Grosse just before the war (Musée de la Marine).*

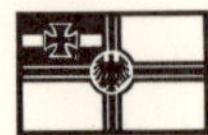

Wittelsbach class

Displacement: 11,800tons normal
Dimensions: 400ft (wl)×67ft×28ft (max)
Guns: 4×9·4in 40cal (2×2)
18×5·9in 40cal
12×3·4in
Torpedo Tubes: 5×17·7in (submerged, bow and beam)
Armour: 9–4in belt; 10in turrets; 3in deck; 10in CT
Machinery: 3-shaft vertical triple expansion, 15,000hp = 18knots; 6 Schulz-Thornycroft and 6 cylindrical boilers
Coal Capacity: 653/1400tons
Oil Capacity: 200tons
Endurance: 5000miles at 10knots
Complement: 650 (715 as flagship)
Cost:

	Laid Down	Launched	Completed	Built/Engined
Wittelsbach	1898	7 Oct 1900	1902	Wilhelmshaven DY
Wettin	1899	6 June 1901	1902	Schichau
Zähringen	1899	12 June 1901	1902	Germania
Mecklenburg	1900	9 Nov 1901	1903	Vulkan, Stettin
Schwaben	1900	19 Aug 1901	1903	Wilhelmshaven DY

Like the earlier German predreadnoughts, this class was too slow and weakly armed for anything but the humblest harbour duty. The 9·4in gun was too weak to give them any value in coast defence, and so they were paid off as soon as possible.

Careers

Wittelsbach: 1914–18 drill ship at Kiel, and subsequently became depot ship for F-boats (minesweepers) at Wilhelmshaven; broken up 1921.

Wettin: 1914–18 drill and depot ship; broken up 1922.

Zähringen: 1914–18 drill ship; converted to radio-controlled target 1927; sunk by aircraft attack in Gotenhafen 18 December 1944.

Mecklenburg: 1914–18 prison ship and accommodation ship for F-boats at Kiel; broken up 1921.

Schwaben: Drill ship and depot ship for F-boats at Wilhelmshaven; broken up 1921.

Mecklenburg.

Right, *a prewar view of Wittelsbach (Druppel).*

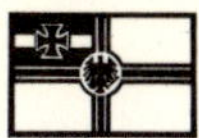

Braunschweig class

Displacement: 13,200tons normal
Dimensions: 398ft 6in×72ft 9in×25ft
Guns: 4×11in 40cal; (2×2)
14×6·7in 40cal (14×1);
14×3·4in (14×1)
2×3·4in A.A. (added during war)
Torpedo Tubes: 6×17·7in (1 bow,
1 stern, 4 beam)
Armour: 8¾–4in belt; 3in deck;
10–6in turrets; 12in CT
Machinery: 3-shaft, 3-cylinder vertical
triple expansion, 16,000hp=18knots;
8 Schulz-Thornycroft and 8 cylindrical
boilers
Coal Capacity: 700/1600tons
Oil Capacity: 200tons
Endurance: 5500miles at 10knots
Complement: 691
Cost: average £1,160,000
($4,640,000)

	Laid Down	Launched	Completed	Built/Engined
Braunschweig	1901	20 Dec 1902	1904	Germania
Elsass	1901	26 Mar 1903	1904	Schichau
Lothringen	1902	27 May 1904	1906	Schichau
Hessen	1902	18 Sept 1903	1905	Germania
Preussen	1902	30 Oct 1903	1905	Vulkan, Stettin

These were the first German battleships to compare favourably for size and armament with British and other foreign battleships. On the enlarged tonnage German constructors were able to produce seagoing battleships which were well armoured, and mounting a heavy secondary battery.

Appearance: The first 3-funnelled German battleships, and very similar in general rig to the following *Deutschland* class, from which they could be distinguished by the secondary turrets amidships, and their uncased funnels.

Careers

Braunschweig: High Seas Fleet August 1914 to 1916, when she was reduced to a drill ship and accommodation ship at Kiel; from 1921 to 1926 served in Reichsmarine as coast defence ship; stricken 31 March 1931.

Elsass: As *Braunschweig*, but recommissioned in Reichsmarine 15 February 1924; stricken 31 March 1931.

Lothringen: August 1914 to 1916 served with High Seas Fleet but became guard ship in Sound that year; the following year she was reduced to drill ship and engineers' training ship for F-boats (minesweepers) at Wilhelmshaven; broken up 1931.

Hessen: At Battle of Jutland with Battle Squadron II; in 1917 became depot ship at Brunsbüttel, during 1923–5 refitted as coast defence ship at Wilhelmshaven for Reichsmarine; stricken from effective list 31 March 1931 but converted at Wilhelmshaven to radio-controlled target ship; handed to the Russians in 1945–6 as *Tsel*; subsequent fate not known.

Preussen: High Seas Fleet August 1914–16, when she became guard ship in the Sound; disarmed 1917 as depot ship for F-boats at Wilhelmshaven; stricken 5 April 1929 and broken up 1931 at Wilhelmshaven, but midships section remained as pontoon for target trials until sunk by Allied bombing in 1945 (named *Vierkant*).

Braunschweig.

Right, *Preussen at speed before the war (IWM).*

Deutschland class

Displacement: 13,200 tons
Dimensions: 398ft 6in×72ft 9in× 25ft 3in (mean)
Guns: 4×11in 40cal (2×2)
14×6·7in 40cal (14×1)
20×3·4in (20×1)
2×3·4in AA added during war
Torpedo Tubes: 6×17·7in (1 bow, 1 stern, 4 beam, all submerged)
Armour: 9–4in belt; 3in decks; 11in turrets; 12in CT
Machinery: 3-shaft 3-cylinder vertical triple expansion, 16,000hp=18knots; 12 Schulz-Thornycroft boilers
Coal Capacity: 800/1800 tons
Oil Capacity: 200 tons
Endurance: 5500 miles at 10 knots
Complement: 729
Cost: not known

	Laid Down	Launched	Completed	Built/Engined
Deutschland	29 June 1903	19 Nov 1904	Aug 1906	Germania
Hannover	Nov 1904	29 Sept 1905	Oct 1907	Wilhelmshaven
*Pommern	Apr 1904	2 Dec 1905	Aug 1907	Vulkan, Stettin
Schleswig-Holstein	Aug 1905	7 Dec 1906	July 1908	Germania/ Schichau
Schlesien	1905	28 May 1906	May 1908	Germania/ Schichau

These vessels were improved editions of the *Braunschweig* class. The 6·7in gun was continued, but all mounted in casemates, not turrets. Although slow they remained with the High Seas Fleet until after the Battle of Jutland in 1916.

Armament: The 6·7in gun was criticised on the grounds that it was too heavy for hand-loading. The 6·7in ammunition stowage arrangements, with the shells stowed nose-outwards in wing magazines almost certainly caused the loss of the *Pommern*; she was the only battleship to be *blown up* by a single torpedo-hit throughout the war.

Appearance: They could be distinguished from the *Braunschweig* class by the absence of the turrets amidships. In *Deutschland* and *Hannover* the forward searchlight was carried on a small platform above the fighting top on the foremast; the others carried it on the top. Unlike the *Braunschweig* class, the funnels were half-cased, with the casing rising higher on the foremost funnel.

Careers

Deutschland: Flagship of Squadron II; High Seas Fleet; Jutland 31 May 1916; 1917 reduced to accommodation ship at Wilhelmshaven; broken up 1920.

Hannover: Squadron II, High Seas Fleet; Jutland 31 May 1916; 1917 guardship in Sound; broken up 1920.

Pommern: Squadron II, High Seas Fleet; torpedoed during night action following Jutland, 1 June 1916 by British destroyers *Marvel* or *Obedient*, and was lost with all hands.

Schleswig-Holstein: Squadron II, High Seas Fleet; Jutland 31 May 1916; accommodation and depot ship 1917; modernised postwar and served in World War II.

Schlesien: Squadron II, High Seas Fleet; Jutland 31 May 1916; drill and training ship from 1917; modernised postwar and served in World War II.

Above right, *Schleswig-Holstein (Musée de la Marine).*

Below right, *Schlesien (Druppel). Both are prewar photographs.*

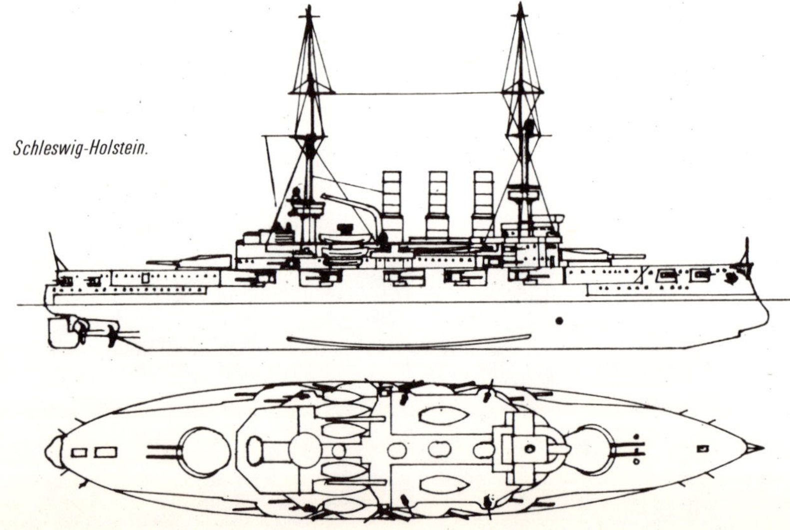

Schleswig-Holstein.

Right, two prewar photographs of Nassau. The lower photograph shows her prominent wireless gaffs; these were later reduced (IWM and Musée de la Marine).

66

Westfalen class

Displacement: 18,900tons (normal);
20,210tons (full load)
Dimensions: 478ft×89ft×27ft 6in
Guns: 12×11in 45cal (6×2)
12×5·9in 45cal (12×1)
16×3·4in (16×1); reduced to 14 in
1915 and replaced altogether in
1916/17 by 4×3·4in A.A.
Torpedo Tubes: 6×17·7in (45cm),
(1 bow, 1 stern, 4 beam, all submerged)
Armour: 11½–4in belt; 4in decks,
11in turrets; 12in CT
Machinery: 3-shaft vertical triple
expansion, 22,000ihp = 19½knots;
12 Marine boilers
Coal Capacity: 935/2952tons
Oil Capacity: 157tons (as altered in
1915)
Endurance: 9400miles at 10knots
Complement: 963–1008

	Laid Down	Launched	Completed	Built/Engined
Rheinland	1 June 1907	26 Sept 1908	Apr 1910	Vulkan, Stettin
Posen	11 June 1907	12 Dec 1908	May 1910	Germania
Nassau	22 July 1907	7 Mar 1908	Oct 1909	Wilhelmshaven DY
Westfalen	12 Aug 1907	1 July 1908	Nov 1909	Weser

The *Rheinland* was the first German 'dreadnought', built at top speed to counter the British lead in the new type. Despite the great haste with which German designers tackled the problem of keeping up with the Royal Navy, it was six months after the completion of the *Dreadnought* before the first keel was laid in Germany; even then, they took 2 or 3 years to complete as against the year for building the British ship.

To reduce the delay in designing the *Westfalen* class no attempt was made to provide turbines, and the well-tried three-shaft arrangement of triple-expansion machinery of the *Deutschland* class was duplicated, but slightly higher horsepower to offset the greater displacement. The designed horsepower was exceeded on trials, the *Posen* making 20knots with 28,117ihp; in 1915 all four were modified to burn oil fuel, sprayed on the coal as in British ships.

The *Westfalens* set new standards of protection, achieved by means of greater beam and colse subdivision of the hull below water. Protection was in no way sacrificed to improve gunpower, and the penalties of a broadside of only eight 11in guns (6080lb) were accepted.

Armament: Owing to the hasty preparation of designs for this class the layout of magazines, particularly those serving the wing turrets, was very cramped. The layout of the 5·9in battery was good, but the 3·4in guns were badly placed forward and aft. The pair of guns bearing right aft had to be removed in 1915, as they proved utterly useless; the other guns were removed from their bow and stern sponsons, and from the superstructure in 1916–17, when anti-aircraft guns replaced them.

Appearance: Generally similar in layout and appearance to the big armoured cruiser *Blücher*, with the foremost funnel very close to the bridgework and mast. The light gun positions forward, aft and in the superstructure were plated over after Jutland.

Careers

Nassau: Served with Battle Squadron I of the High Seas Fleet from 1914; Jutland 31 May 1916, and collided with the British destroyer *Spitfire* during the night action, losing some plating and ground tackle; hit by two medium calibre shells, and completed repairs by mid-July; stricken 5 November 1919; ceded to Japan under Treaty of Versailles, but sold for breaking up to British firm, who in turn sold her to Dutch shipbreakers; broken up at Dordrecht, Holland in June 1920.

Posen: Served as divisional flagship of Squadron I, High Seas Fleet from 1914; at Jutland 31 May 1916, but sustained no damage; Baltic operations 1917; stricken 5 November 1919 and ceded to Great Britain under Treaty of Versailles; handed over 14 May 1920; broken up at Dordrecht 1921.

Rheinland: Served with Squadron I, High Seas Fleet; Battle of Jutland 31 May 1916, when she was struck by a single medium-calibre shell; repaired in two weeks, and transferred to Baltic for operations against Russians; badly damaged by grounding off Finnish coast 11 April 1918; towed to Kiel and laid up as an accommodation ship; stricken 5 November 1919 and handed over to Allied control 28 June 1920; broken up at Dordrecht 1921.

Westfalen: Served with Squadron I of High Seas Fleet; Jutland 31 May 1916, and hit by a medium-calibre shell; repairs completed mid-June, but on 19 August she was hit by a torpedo from the British submarine *E.23*; repairs completed late in October 1916; Baltic operations 1917–18; became gunnery training ship in September 1918; stricken 5 November 1919 and ceded to Great Britain under the Treaty of Versailles; handed over 5 August 1920 and broken up at Birkenhead in 1924.

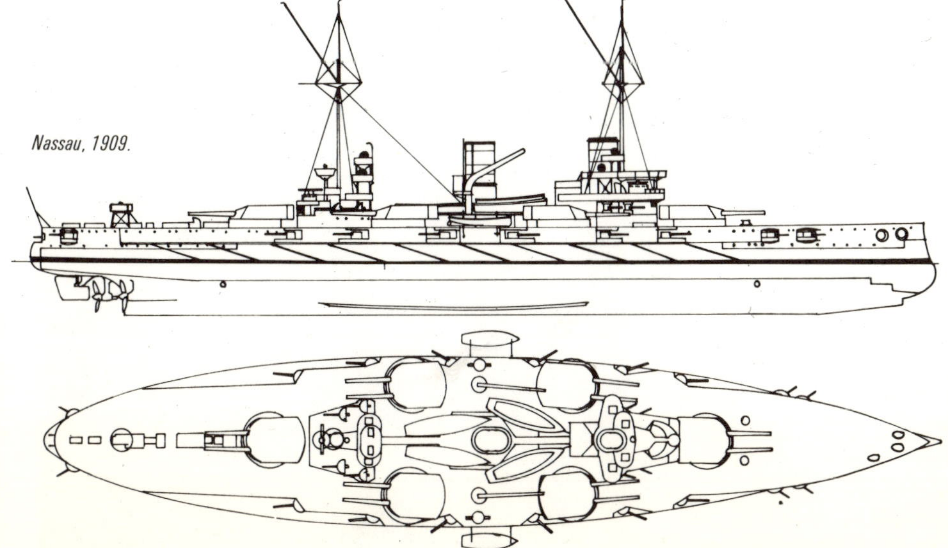

Nassau, 1909.

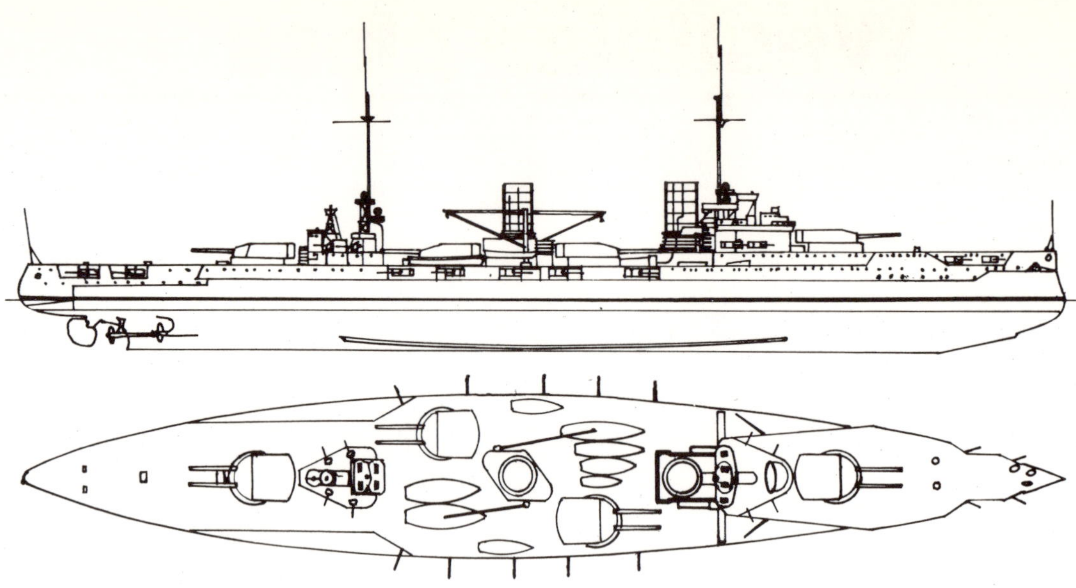

Von der Tann

Displacement: 19,400tons (normal);
21,000tons (full load)
Dimensions: 562ft 9in×87ft×27ft 6in
Guns: 8×11in 45cal (4×2)
10×5·9in 45cal (10×1)
16×3·4in (16×1); reduced to 12 in
1916 and replaced by 2×3·4in A.A.
(2×1); all removed by 1918
Torpedo Tubes: 4×17·7in (45cm),
(1 bow, 1 stern, 2 beam, all submerged)
Armour: 9½–4in belt; 2½in decks;
9in turrets; 9½in CT
Machinery: 4-shaft Parsons turbines,
42,000shp = 24·8knots;
18 Schulz-Thornycroft boilers
Coal Capacity: 984/2756tons
Endurance: Approximately 6500miles
at 10knots
Complement: 998 (wartime)
Cost: £1,833,000 ($7,332,000)

	Laid Down	Launched	Completed	Built/Engined
Von der Tann	25 Mar 1908	20 Mar 1909	Sept 1910	Blohm & Voss

This was the first German battle cruiser, laid down as a reply to the British *Invincible*. A glance at the silhouettes will show how similar the layout of guns is, but thereafter the similarities end. The *Von der Tann* was a great improvement over the original British battle cruiser concept, both on account of her good protection and also for her layout of machinery, which enabled the superstructure to be placed well clear of the turrets.

The *Von der Tann* was a battle cruiser, and many sacrifices of fighting power had to be made in favour of speed, but although she had thinner armour than the contemporary *Westfalen*, it was well arranged, and with eight and a half feet more beam than the *Invincible* her underwater protection was extremely good. On the other hand, the *Von der Tann* lacked the freeboard of the British battle cruiser, which in combination with the heavier British guns, could have left her at a disadvantage in rough weather.

Appearance: In 1916 the four 3·4in guns on the after superstructure were removed and two anti-aircraft guns were substituted. Apart from the removal of other light guns from the positions under the forecastle and quarterdeck, there were no major alterations of her appearance during the war.

Machinery: She was the first German ship engined with Parsons turbines and the first with quadruple screws. On trials *Von der Tann* developed 79,000 horsepower and touched 27·4knots.

Career

Served with the Scouting Group (Admiral Hipper) attached to the High Seas Fleet, from 1914 to 1918; bombarded Yarmouth during raid on British coast, 3 November 1914; bombarded Scarborough during raid, 6 December 1914; refitting at the time of the Battle of the Dogger Bank, January 1915; Jutland 31 May 1916, when she was hit four times; under repair until early August; interned at Scapa Flow after surrender in November 1918, and scuttled June 1919; raised and broken up 1930–4.

Left, *Von der Tann as she appeared after June 1916 and the removal of her torpedo nets (Druppel).*

Left, *Von der Tann as guard ship in the Jade river, 1918 (Bundesarchiv).*

Above right, an aerial view of Oldenburg in 1917 or 1918. Note the recognition circles painted on No. 1 and No. 6 turrets (Druppel).

Below right, prewar view of Thüringen (Druppel).

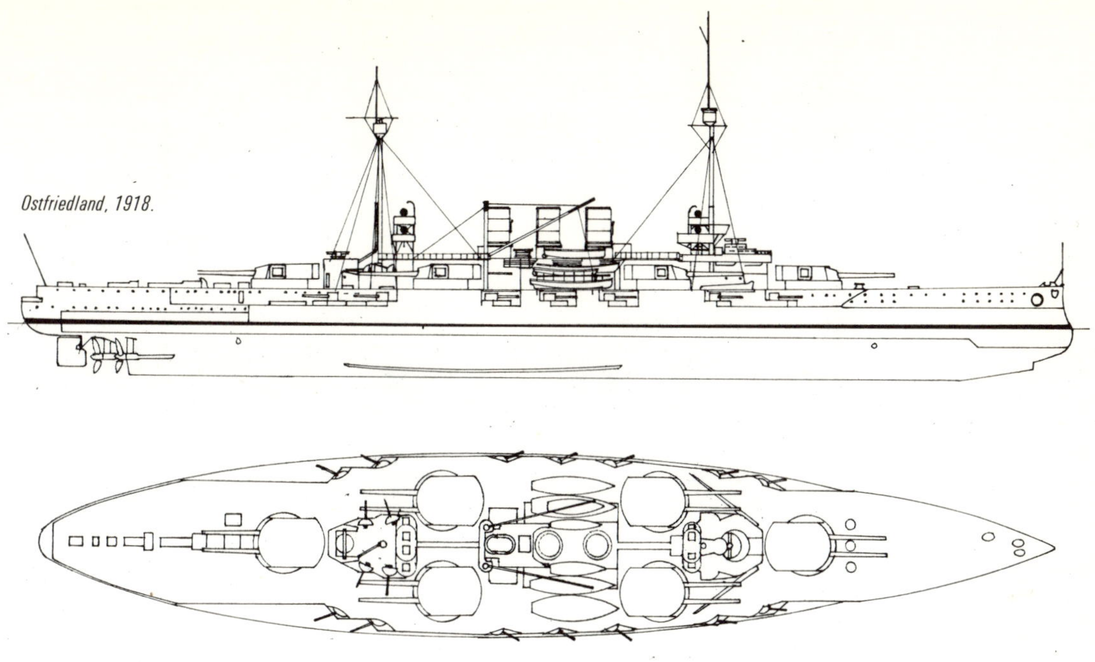

Ostfriedland, 1918.

Helgoland class

Displacement: 22,800tons (normal), 24,312tons (full load)

Dimensions: 546ft×93ft 6in×27ft 6in

Guns: 12×12in 50cal (6×2)
14×5·9in 45cal (14×1)
14×3·4in (14×1); reduced to 12 in 1913, and all replaced 1916–17 by 4×3·4in A.A.

Torpedo Tubes: 6×19·7in (50cm), (1 bow, 1 stern, 4 beam, all submerged)

Armour: 11¾–4in belt; 3in decks; 11in turrets; 12in CT

Machinery: 3-shaft vertical triple expansion, 28,000ihp = 20knots; 15 Marine boilers

Coal Capacity: 984/2756tons

Oil Capacity: 197tons (as altered in 1915)

Endurance: 9400miles at 10knots

Complement: 1113

Cost: not known

	Laid Down	Launched	Completed	Built/Engined
Ostfriesland	19 Oct 1908	30 Sept 1909	Aug 1911	Wilhelmshaven DY
Thüringen	2 Nov 1908	27 Nov 1909	July 1911	Weser
Helgoland	24 Nov 1908	25 Sept 1909	Aug 1911	Howaldt
Oldenburg	1 Mar 1909	30 June 1910	May 1912	Schichau

To match the British battleships' advantage in weight of broadside the *Helgoland* class were given 12in guns; this was a powerful weapon which proved superior in practice to the contemporary British Mark XII gun, although the range (21,000yds) remained the same.

The layout of armament of the *Westfalen* class was repeated, but with even greater beam and extra length to allow for higher speed. The internal layout was altered, however, to allow all the boilers to be grouped together. This resulted in a better arrangement of the wing magazines, and left the funnels clear of the foremast and bridgework. With four more feet on the beam they were less cramped than their predecessors and better protected against underwater damage.

German yards were hard put to match British yards in speed of building. In view of the need to accelerate their programme the Germans were forced once more to retain reciprocating machinery, as turbines could not be supplied in time. Despite this the average building time was nearly three years.

Armament: The 3·4in guns proved to be mounted in unworkable positions, and the aftermost pair (under the quarterdeck, as in the *Westfalens*) had to be removed in 1913. The remainder were removed in 1916–17, when four 3·4in anti-aircraft guns were mounted on the after superstructure. The ports under the forecastle were plated over.

Appearance: Their three short funnels set close together amidships made them distinctive. They were also easily recognisable by their lack of any prominent bridgework.

Careers

Helgoland: Served with High Seas Fleet 1914–18; at Battle of Jutland 31 May 1916, with Battle Squadron I; received one hit, and repaired at Wilhelmshaven by mid-June; stricken 5 November 1919, disarmed and delivered to Great Britain on 5 August 1920 as reparation for the ships scuttled; broken up at Morecambe in 1924.

Oldenburg: With Battle Squadron I, High Seas Fleet; Jutland 31 May 1916, when she was hit by a medium-calibre shell; repaired at Wilhelmshaven by mid-June; stricken 5 November 1919 and disarmed, but handed over to Japan as reparations, and sold to a British firm to break up, who sold her to a Dutch firm; broken up at Dordrecht.

Ostfriesland: With Battle Squadron I, High Seas Fleet 1914–18; Jutland 31 May 1916 and sustained no hits, but hit a mine while returning to base; repaired at Wilhelmshaven and did not return to Fleet until 26 July; stricken 5 November 1919, but ceded to United States as reparations, and transferred 7 April 1919; used as target for aerial bombing and gunfire, and in the course of tests became known as the 'unsinkable' ship after hits from 80 bombs of various sizes and 24 shells; finally hit by six 1000kilo bombs in special demonstration off Cape Henry by Colonel Mitchell, 21 July 1921, and sank in ten minutes.

Thüringen: With Battle Squadron I, High Seas Fleet 1914–18; Jutland 31 May 1916 but not damaged; stricken 5 November 1919 and disarmed, but on 29 April 1920 she was ceded to France and used as a target; broken up at Lorient in 1923, but remnants of the hull are believed to have survived until 1933.

Above right, Moltke in 1913/14 with crew manning ship (Bundesarchiv).

Below right, Moltke arriving to surrender at Scapa Flow in November 1918 (IWM).

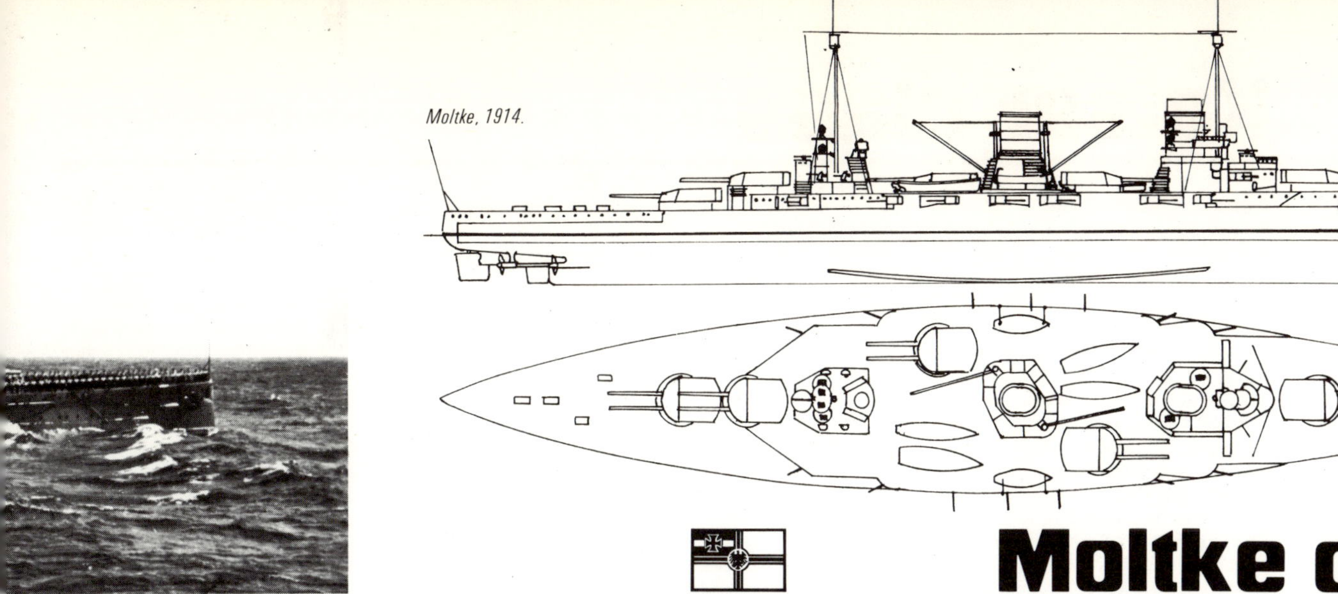

Moltke, 1914.

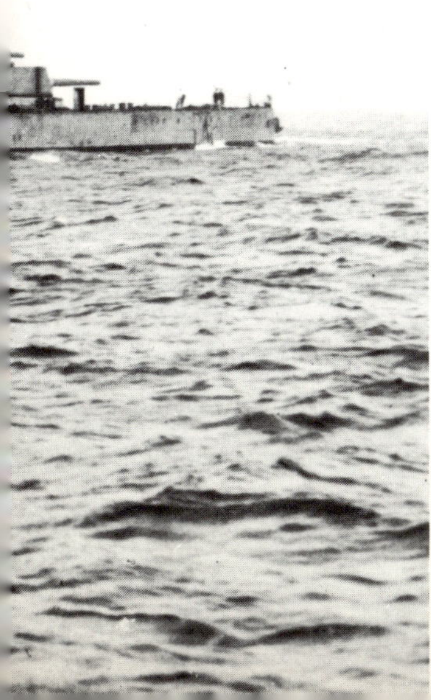

Moltke class

Displacement: 22,616tons (normal); 24,999tons (full load)
Dimensions: 610ft×96ft 9in×27ft
Guns: 10×11in 50cal (5×2)
12×5·9in 45cal (12×1)
12×3·4in (12×1); reduced to 8 in 1916 and replaced by 4×3·4in A.A.
Torpedo Tubes: 4×19·7in (50cm), (1 bow, 1 stern, 2 beam, all submerged)
Armour: 11–4in belt; 2½in deck; 10in turrets; 10in CT
Machinery: 4-shaft Parsons turbines, 52,000shp = 25½knots; 24 Schulz-Thornycroft boilers
Coal Capacity: 984/2952tons
Endurance: 6500miles at 10knots (approximate)
Complement: 1053
Cost: Approx. £2,200,000 each ($8,800,000)

	Laid Down	Launched	Completed	Built/Engined
Moltke	7 Dec 1908	7 Apr 1910	Sept 1911	Blohm & Voss
Goeben	7 Dec 1909	28 Mar 1911	July 1912	Blohm & Voss

These ships were enlarged versions of the *Von der Tann*, built under the 1908 and 1909 Programmes. The layout of the *Kaiser* class battleships was copied, but with 11in guns in place of 12in; the scale of protection was almost on a par with battleships, and they were a step towards the concept of the fast battleship.

The principal weakness lay in the relatively low freeboard forward, which meant that the forecastle was awash in anything but calm weather. The beam turrets were not ideal, for their nominal arcs of fire could not be used to the maximum owing to blast-effect and the strain of cross-deck firing.

Armament: The positions of the 3·4in (88mm) guns under the forecastle proved so wet as to be unusable, so they were suppressed completely by 1918; the four on the after superstructure gave way to anti-aircraft guns in 1916.

Appearance: Very similar to the *Von der Tann*, but distinguished by extra turret aft, and the prominent cap to the forward funnel. In addition they had a heavier look, which was due partly to the bigger funnels.

Careers

Goeben: Had been serving in Mediterranean since 1912, the only German capital ship to serve outside the High Seas Fleet throughout the war; eluded British squadron August 1914 and escaped to Turkish waters (see under Turkish section); interned at Constantinople 10 August 1914 and purchased by Turkey as *Yavuz Sultan Selim*.

Moltke: With High Seas Fleet Scouting Group 1914–18; bombarded Yarmouth 3 November 1914, and Hartlepool 16 December; in action with British battle cruisers at Battle of Dogger Bank 24 January 1915, but not damaged; Baltic operations 1915, and torpedoed off Riga by British submarine *E.1*; repaired at Hamburg after limping home with 450tons of water on board; Lowestoft Raid April 1916; hit by four shells at Jutland 31 May 1916, and repaired by her builders June–July; Baltic operations 1917; during the High Seas Fleet's last major sortie in April 1918 she stripped one of her turbines, and was limping back under escort when, on 23 April, she was torpedoed aft by the British submarine *E.42*; as a result of damage to the engine room and the torpedo–hit she had 2100tons of water on board, but managed to get home; surrendered November 1918 and scuttled at Scapa Flow June 1919; raised and broken up 1927–9.

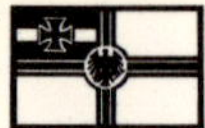

Kaiser class

Displacement: 24,380tons (normal), 26,573tons (full load)

Dimensions: 564ft×95ft 3in×27ft 3in

Guns: 10×12in 50cal (5×2)
14×5·9in 45cal (14×1)
12×3·4in (12×1); reduced to 10 by 1915, and all replaced by 4×3·4in A.A. in 1916–17

Torpedo Tubes: 5×19·7in (50cm) (1 bow, 4 beam, all submerged)

Armour: 13¾–7¾in belt; 3in decks, 11¾in turrets; 13¾in CT

Machinery: All except Prinzregent Luitpold: 3-shaft Parsons turbines, 31,000shp = 21knots; 16 Schulz-Thornycroft boilers Prinzregent Luitpold: 2-shaft Parsons turbines, 26,000shp+single-shaft 6-cylinder Diesel, 12,000bhp= 20knots; 14 Schulz-Thornycroft boilers

Coal Capacity: 984/2952tons (Prinzregent Luitpold 492/3,051tons)

Oil Capacity: 197tons (Prinzregent Luitpold 98·4/394tons)

Endurance: 9500miles at 10knots (Prinzregent Luitpold could steam 2000miles at 12knots under Diesel power only)

Complement: 1084

Cost: not known

	Laid Down	Launched	Completed	Built/Engined
Friedrich der Grosse	26 Jan 1910	10 June 1911	Oct 1912	Vulkan, Hamburg
Kaiserin	July 1910	11 Nov 1911	May 1913	Howaldt
König Albert	July 1910	27 Apr 1912	July 1913	Schichau
Prinzregent Luitpold	Oct 1910	23 Mar 1911	Aug 1912	Germania
Kaiser	Oct 1910	22 Mar 1911	Aug 1912	Kiel DY

In this class German designers incorporated all the lessons learned from the British and other foreign navies. Having solved their problems with turbine machinery, the *Kaiser* class became the first German dreadnoughts powered by the Parsons tubine, although *Prinzregent Luitpold* went further in being the first warship designed for a combination of diesel and steampower. In this ship the centre shaft was to be coupled to a 6-cylinder Germania–designed Diesel engine, while the turbines were to be coupled to the outer shafts. However, the engine was never installed, and it is not known if it was even built. The *Prinzregent Luitpold* was completed with only two shafts, and remained the slowest of her class as a result.

The armament layout was obviously influenced by the British *Neptune* and *Colossus* group, but without the cumbersome flying decks found in that class. With their great beam the protection of the *Kaiser* class was far superior to that of the *Neptune*, and they were much closer to the *Orion* class in fighting power, despite the disparity in weight of broadside (9800lb against 12,500lb).

Armament: Like the British *Neptune* the advantages of the layout of beam turrets amidships were more apparent than real, for blast effects ruled out ahead and astern fire, and cross-deck firing on the broadside tended to strain the hull. The 3·4in guns right aft were removed early in the war, and after Jutland the remaining positions under the forecastle and in the superstructure were suppressed. Four 3·4in anti-aircraft guns were sited on the after structure at this time.

Appearance: The funnels were widely spaced, at either end of the citadel with turrets No. 2 and No. 3 between *en echelon*.

The 3·4in guns were gradually reduced, the positions right aft under the quarterdeck going in 1914–15 and the others in 1916–17. *Friedrich der Grosse* was refitted in 1914 as the Fleet Flagship and given a heavy tubular foremast and enlarged spotting top, which distinguished her from the rest of the class.

Machinery: The adoption of small–tube boilers made the *Kaiser* class good steamers, and they all developed much more than their designed power. The *Kaiser* was the best, and on her trials made 23·4knots with over 55,000hp.

Careers

Friedrich der Grosse: Flagship of Commander-in-Chief, High Seas Fleet 1914–16; at Jutland 31 May 1916, but not hit; at the end of 1916 she joined Battle Squadron IV when relieved as Fleet Flagship by *Baden*; surrendered 1918 under terms of Armistice and interned at Scapa Flow; scuttled 21 June 1919; salvaged 1936–7 and broken up.

Kaiser: With Battle Squadron III, High Seas Fleet 1914–18; at Jutland 31 May 1916 and hit twice; rejoined Fleet in August; with *Kaiserin*, she engaged British light forces in the Heligoland Bight on 17 November 1917; surrendered November 1918 and interned at Scapa Flow; scuttled 21 June 1919; raised 1929 and broken up at Rosyth in 1930.

Kaiserin: With Battle Squadron III, High Seas Fleet 1914–18; at Jutland 31 May 1916 but did not sustain any damage; with *Kaiser* in action against British forces in November 1917; surrendered 1918 and interned at Scapa Flow, where she was scuttled 21 June 1919; raised 1936 and broken up.

König Albert: With Battle Squadron III of High Seas Fleet 1914–18; only one of her class to miss Jutland as she had trouble with her condensers; surrendered 1918 and scuttled at Scapa Flow 21 June 1919; raised and broken up 1935–6.

Prinzregent Luitpold: Served along with her sisters in Battle Squadron III of High Seas Fleet; at Jutland 31 May 1916 but not damaged; surrendered to Grand Fleet November 1918 and scuttled at Scapa Flow on 21 June 1919; raised and broken up 1931–3.

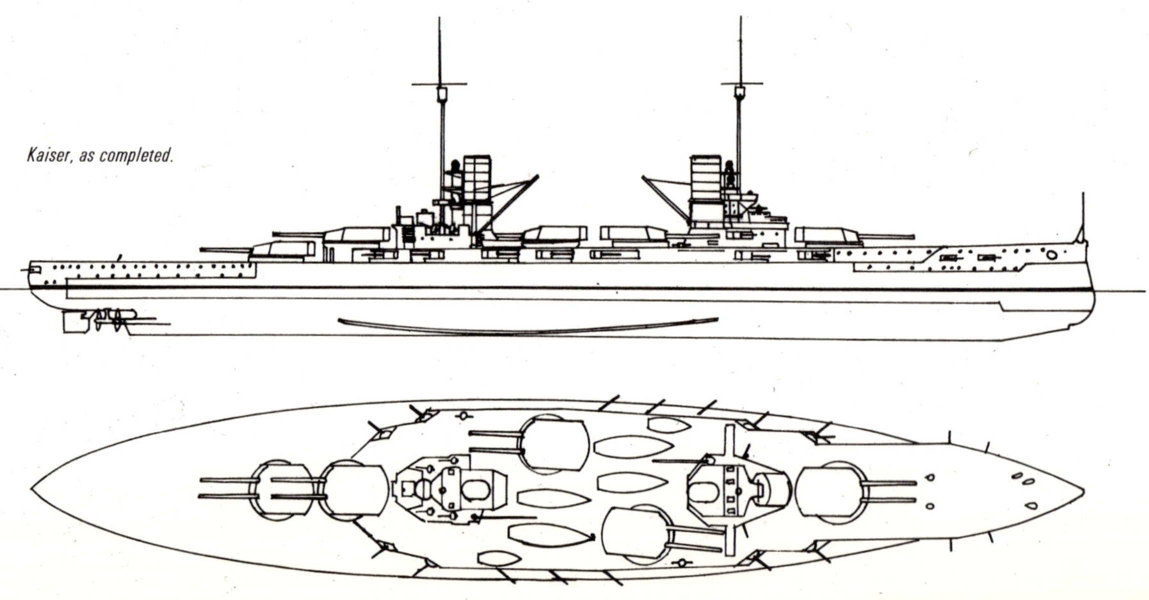

Kaiser, as completed.

Above left, Kaiserin shown late in the war with torpedo nets removed and a heavy spotting top added to the foremast. Note also the square life-rafts lashed to the turrets' side (IWM).
Above right, König Albert as completed. Note the holes for the rammers on the rear face of No. 4 turret (IWM).

Left, Kaiser as completed. Note the inconspicuous bridgework (IWM).

Below left and right, Prinzregent Luitpold and Friedrich der Grosse seen arriving at Scapa Flow in November 1919. Note the heavy foremast on Friedrich der Grosse (both IWM).

Seydlitz

Displacement: 24,610tons (normal);
28,550tons (full load)
Dimensions: 656ft×93ft 6in×27ft
Guns: 10×11in 50cal (5×2)
12×5·9in 45cal (12×1)
14×3·4in (14×1); reduced to 12 in
1916 and replaced by 2×3·4in A.A.
in 1916; remainder removed by 1918
Torpedo Tubes: 4×19·7in (50cm),
(1 bow, 1 stern, 2 beam, all submerged)
Armour: 11–4in belt; 2½in deck;
10in turrets; 10in CT
Machinery: 4-shaft Marine turbines,
67,000shp = 26½knots;
27 Schulz-Thornycroft boilers
Coal Capacity: 984/3543tons
Endurance: Approximately 6500miles
at 10knots
Complement: 1068
Cost: not known

	Laid Down	Launched	Completed	Built/Engined
Seydlitz	4 Feb 1911	30 Mar 1912	May 1913	Blohm & Voss

Seydlitz, 1913.

Above left, Seydlitz entering the Firth of Forth at the surrender of the German fleet in November 1918 (IWM).

This ship was laid down under the 1910 Programme as an improved *Moltke*. The main improvement was to raise the forecastle, thus remedying the poor seakeeping of the earlier ships.

To increase speed a different hull form was chosen, with beam reduced by 3ft 3in and length increased by 46ft. Despite this unusual reduction of beam (so far as German ships were concerned) she proved no less capable of absorbing punishment than any other German ship, and was hit more times than any other ship to survive Jutland. Despite 21 heavy hits (12in, 13·5in and 15in), two medium calibre hits and a 21in torpedo-hit, she managed to reach Jade River.

Armament: As a result of two large calibre hits from British battle cruisers at the Battle of the Dogger Bank the two after turrets (Nos. 4 and 5) were burnt out when the cordite caught fire. As a result German ammunition-handling arrangements were overhauled. From 1916 the 3·4in guns were reduced, until in 1918 only the two anti-aircraft guns remained. After Jutland the control top on the foremast was enlarged.

Career

Served with Scouting Group attached to High Seas Fleet 1914–18; bombardments of Yarmouth November 1914 and Hartlepool December 1914; hit by two shells at Battle of Dogger Bank 24 January 1915 and suffered heavy casualties from fire; mined on return from Lowestoft Raid, 25 April 1916 and returned to port with 1400tons of water on board; heavily damaged at Battle of Jutland 31 May 1916, and had to be beached in Jade River the following day as she drew too much water to enter the harbour; under repair until mid-September at Wilhelmshaven; surrendered November 1918 and scuttled at Scapa Flow June 1919; raised and broken up 1928–30.

Below left, Seydlitz under repair at Wilhelmshaven after the battle of Jutland. Note that the guns have been removed from No. 1 turret, and the ship is in a sinking condition. The ship in the next dock is one of the König class, with the battle cruiser Derfflinger and older battleships in the background (IWM).

Right, a famous picture of Seydlitz limping home after Jutland with dense clouds of smoke pouring from her and with 5,000 tons of water aboard (IWM).

König class

Displacement: 25,390tons (normal), 28,148tons (full load)
Dimensions: 580ft ×97ft×28ft 6in
Guns: 10×12in 50cal (5×2)
14×5·9in 45cal (14×1)
6×3·4in (6×1)
2×3·4in A.A. (2×1); increased to 4 in 1916–17
Torpedo Tubes: 5×19·7in (50cm), (1 bow, 4 beam, all submerged)
Armour: 14–10in belt; 4½in decks; 14in turrets; 14in CT
Machinery: 3-shaft Parsons turbines, 31,000shp=21knots; 12 Schulz-Thornycroft boilers
Coal Capacity: 984tons
Oil Capacity: 689/3543tons
Endurance: 10,000miles at 10knots
Complement: 1150–1218
Cost: not known

	Laid Down	Launched	Completed	Built/Engined
König	Oct 1911	1 Mar 1913	Aug 1914	Wilhelmshaven DY
Grosser Kurfürst	Oct 1911	5 May 1913	July 1914	Vulkan, Hamburg
Markgraf	Nov 1911	4 June 1913	Oct 1914	Weser
Kronprinz	Nov 1911	21 Feb 1914	Nov 1914	Germania

These ships were authorised under the 1909–10 Programme, and were the newest German ships in service on the outbreak of war. Although retaining the 12in gun, the *König* class compared favourably with the British *Iron Duke* class in protection, both above and below water. With 7ft 6in more beam, the German ship could be better subdivided, and as the midships turret (No. 3) was carried a deck higher it was less likely to be washed out in a seaway. However, the Germans are open to criticism for clinging to the 12in gun when foreign navies had turned to the 13·5in and 14in. The retention of a lighter shell meant a higher muzzle velocity in order to keep up the range and penetration, but in ballistic terms this proved self-defeating, as the lower muzzle velocity of the bigger foreign guns improved their shooting and reduced barrel wear.

The internal layout of the *Kaiser* class was retained, two boiler rooms forward and one aft, grouped with the machinery. This resulted in the same general appearance as the previous class, with a funnel at either end of the superstructure in similar manner to the Italian dreadnoughts. By modern standards this seems a clumsy alternative to grouping all boilers together or staggering the engine rooms, but it must be remembered that German designers (like their opposite numbers abroad) could not allow a battleship to have fewer than ten guns, at a time when number of guns was taken as a simple yardstick of a warship's strength. Only when battle cruisers and 15in gunned ships were on the drawing board could eight guns be considered, and then it was seen as a compromise.

Armament: The clumsy layout of the midships turrets seen in the *Kaiser* class was dropped in favour of superimposed turrets forward and aft (Nos. 2 and 4) and a centreline turret (No. 3) between the funnels. As in the Vickers-built *Erin* the No. 3 turret was carried at the level of the forecastle deck, which ensured a good command and freedom from spray interference in bad weather. The light armament was much reduced and concentrated in the forward superstructure; for the first time the useless hull-embrasures forward and aft were omitted, and reliance was placed on a few guns well sited. For the first time anti-aircraft guns were fitted, a 3·4in weapon in either side of the mainmast.

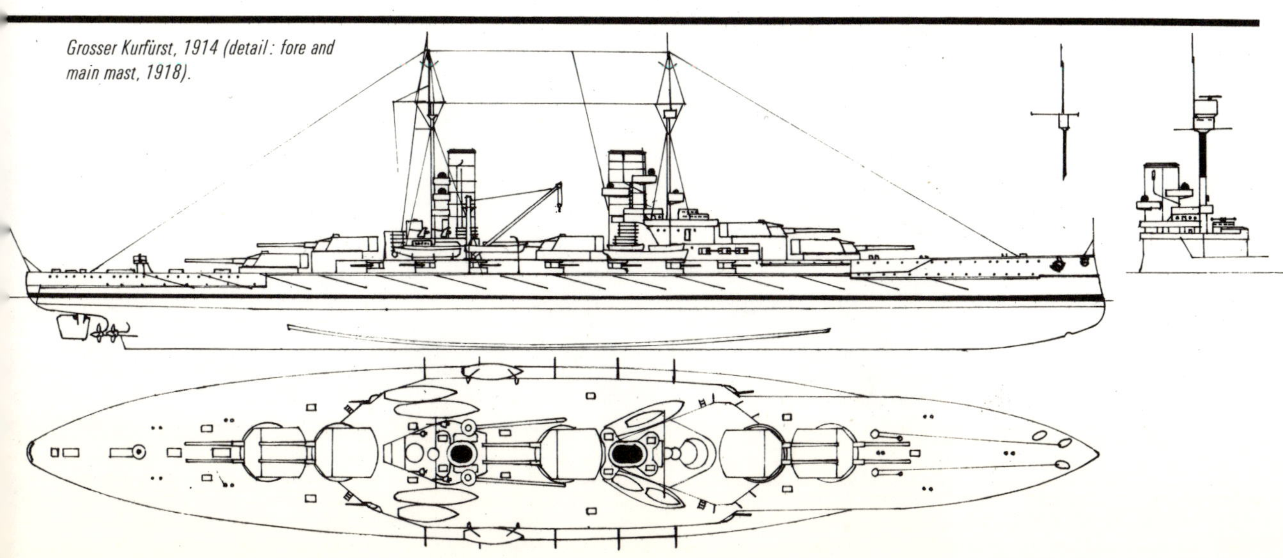

Above left, *König as she appeared before 1916 with torpedo nets still fitted (Bundesarchiv).* **Above right,** *Kronprinz Wilhelm at Scapa Flow after the surrender. Note the heavy spotting top and the absence of torpedo nets (IWM).*

Grosser Kurfürst, 1914 (detail: fore and main mast, 1918).

Appearance: For the first time a heavy tubular foremast control top was adopted in place of the light mast and spotting top of earlier ships. *Grosser Kurfürst* and *König* at first had a lighter version, but by 1916 all had the heavy type.

Nomenclature: On 27 January 1918 the *Kronprinz* was renamed *Kronprinz Wilhelm* by the Kaiser to commemorate the victories won by his son, the Crown Prince.

Machinery: It was originally hoped to adopt the combined steam-diesel installation tried out in the *Prinzregent Luitpold*, but that fiasco forced the designers to revert to conventional three-shaft steam machinery.

Careers

Grosser Kurfürst: Joined Battle Squadron III, High Seas Fleet on outbreak of war; hit eight times at Battle of Jutland, 31 May 1916; repairs completed by original builders at Hamburg by mid-July; torpedoed by British submarine *J.1* off Horns Reef 5 November 1916, but without serious damage; collided with *Kronprinz* in Heligoland Bight 5 March 1917; Baltic operations October 1917, during the course of which she was damaged by a mine; surrendered to Grand Fleet in November 1918 and scuttled at Scapa Flow 21 June 1919; raised and broken up 1936.

König: Joined Battle Squadron III of the High Seas Fleet on outbreak of war; Jutland 31 May 1916, when she was hit ten times; repairs completed at Kiel on 21 July; in action in Baltic against Russian *Slava* in October 1917; surrendered November 1918 and scuttled at Scapa Flow; salvage and clearance work on the wreck has been going on since 1962.

Kronprinz: Still completing when war broke out, but joined Battle Squadron III at the end of 1914; served with High Seas Fleet throughout the war; undamaged at Jutland, 31 May 1916; torpedoed by British submarine *J.1* off Horns Reef 5 November 1916 (see also *Grosser Kurfürst*); repaired by early December but was damaged in collision with *Grosser Kurfürst* on 5 March 1917, and was under repair until May; renamed *Kronprinz Wilhelm* 27 January 1918 (see above); surrendered November 1918 and scuttled at Scapa Flow June 1919; wreck has been under salvage since 1962.

Markgraf: Joined Battle Squadron III of the High Seas Fleet after outbreak of war; hit five times at Battle of Jutland, 31 May 1916, and repaired by her original builders in June–July; surrendered to Grand Fleet November 1918, and scuttled at Scapa Flow June 1919; since 1962 the wreck has been under salvage.

Derfflinger class

Displacement: 26,180tons (D), 26,318tons (L), 26,513tons (H) (normal); 30,707–31,002tons (full load)

Dimensions: 689ft×95ft×27ft 6in

Guns: 8×12in 50cal (4×2) 14×5·9in 45cal (14×1); Derfflinger 12×5·9in 4×3·4in (4×1), Derfflinger only; removed 1916 8×3·4in A.A.; added in Derfflinger but others completed thus

Torpedo Tubes: 4×19·7in (50cm), (1 bow, 1 stern, 2 beam, all submerged)

Armour: 12–5in belt; 2½in deck; 11in turrets; 11in CT

Machinery: Derfflinger & Lützow: 4-shaft Marine turbines, 63,000shp = 26½knots; 14 coal-fired boilers and 4 double-ended oil-firing boilers Hindenburg: as others, but 72,000shp = 27knots

Coal Capacity: 738/3642tons

Oil Capacity: 246/984tons

Endurance: 9,000miles at 10knots (approximate)

Complement: 1112–1182

Cost: Nearly £3,000,000 per ship ($12,000,000)

Above left, Derfflinger and Hindenburg seen on arrival at Scapa Flow in 1918. Note the heavy tripod and funnel tops of Hindenburg compared to those on Derfflinger (IWM).

Below left, Derfflinger shown sinking after her scuttling in 1919 (IWM).

	Laid Down	Launched	Completed	Built/Engined
Derfflinger	1 Jan 1912	12 July 1913	Sept 1914	Blohm & Voss
Lützow	July 1912	29 Nov 1913	Aug 1915	Schichau
Hindenburg	30 June 1913	1 Aug 1915	May 1917	Wilhelmshaven DY

These ships were a great advance on previous German battle cruisers. Intended as the battle cruiser equivalent of the new *König* class battleships, they foreshadowed the 8-gun layout of the *Bayern* class, but were unique among German capital ships in having a flush deck. Without doubt probably the best ships for their displacement in World War I.

With greater beam than the *Seydlitz* their subdivision was very good. The *Lützow* sank after hours of battering from 24 heavy shell-hits and a 21in torpedo-hit, and had she not been driven too hard she might well have stayed afloat. The *Derfflinger* also displayed an enormous capacity to withstand punishment, with 17 large calibre shell-hits and still able to steam.

The flush deck layout with lower freeboard was adopted to offset the increase in topweight caused by having two super-imposed turrets (Nos. 2 and 3). This reduction in freeboard was the worst feature of the design, as it put the class at a disadvantage in any gun-duel with British capital ships. However, in practice the combination of poor shell and bad cordite in British ships wiped out any advantage they had in gunpower and seaworthiness.

Appearance: The *Derfflinger* class were the only German battle cruisers to be fitted with tripod foremasts and superimposed turrets. All three still had pole foremasts at Jutland, but the two survivors received a heavy tripod in 1916 (in *Hindenburg*'s case, during fitting out). *Lützow* and *Hindenburg* differed from *Derfflinger* in having an extra 5·9in gun amidships in the battery. All three had different funnels: *Derfflinger* had deep caps showing above the casings, with the forefunnel slightly raised, *Lützow* had a fully cased forefunnel and a half-cased after funnel of equal height, while *Hindenburg* had shallow caps showing above the casings (see illustrations).

Careers

Derfflinger: Joined Scouting Group of High Seas Fleet just after outbreak of war; bombardment of Scarborough December 1915; hit once at Battle of Dogger Bank 24 January 1915; Lowestoft Raid April 1916; heavily damaged at Battle of Jutland 31 May 1916; under repair at Wilhelmshaven until mid-October; surrendered November 1918 and scuttled at Scapa Flow June 1919; raised and broken up 1934–6, but the last traces of her did not disappear until 1948.

Hindenburg: Took part in action with British light forces in Heligoland Bight 17 November 1917; surrendered November 1918 and scuttled at Scapa Flow in June 1919; raised 1930 and broken up 1931–2 at Rosyth.

Lützow: Served with Scouting Group attached to High Seas Fleet; as a result of considerable turbine trouble she was not fully effective until March 1916; Lowestoft Raid April 1916; heavily damaged in action with British battleships and battle cruisers at Jutland, 31 May 1916; with 7500tons of water aboard and 116 dead, Admiral Hipper gave the order to sink her in the early hours of 1 June; after taking off the crew she was sunk with two torpedoes by the destroyer *G.38*.

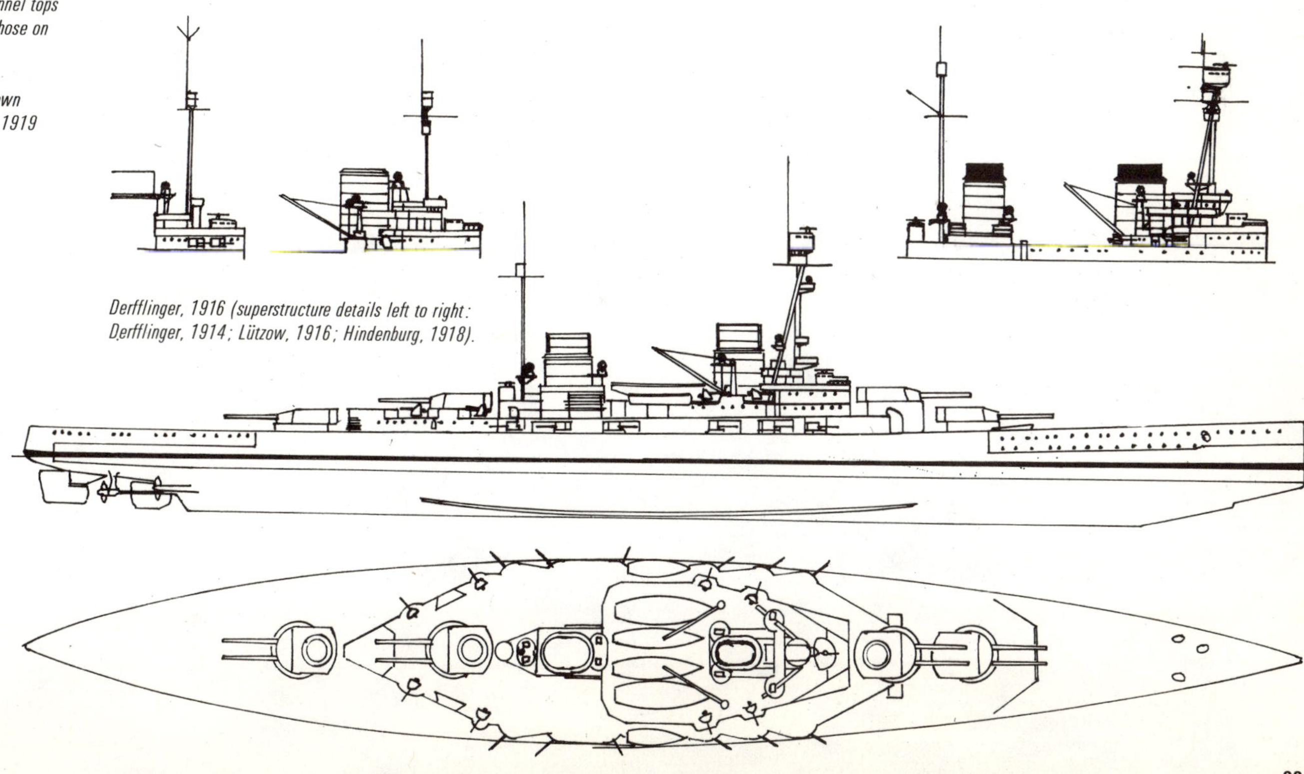

Derfflinger, 1916 (superstructure details left to right: Derfflinger, 1914; Lützow, 1916; Hindenburg, 1918).

Left, Lützow as she appeared in 1916 just before Jutland, still carrying torpedo nets (Bundesarchiv).

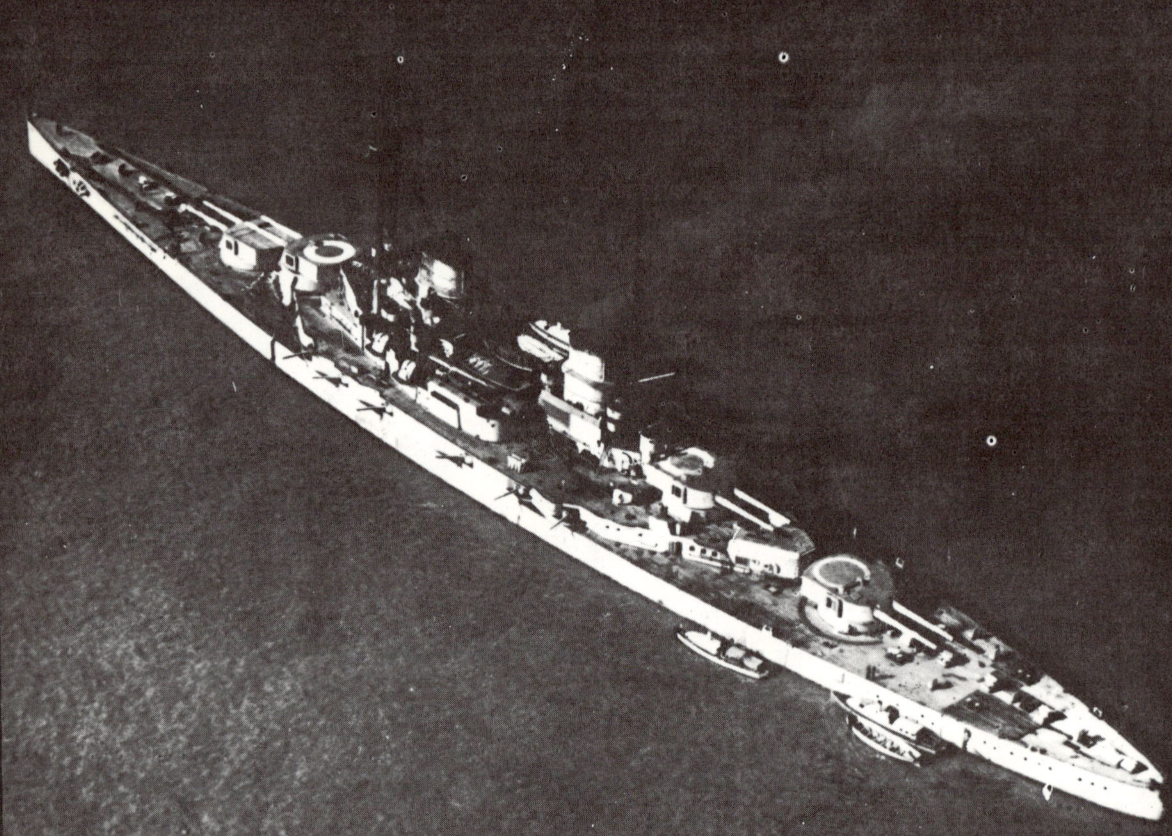

Left, Derfflinger in the Jade river in 1917 (Bundesarchiv).

Left, an aerial view of Hindenburg taken from a Zeppelin in 1918 (Bundesarchiv).

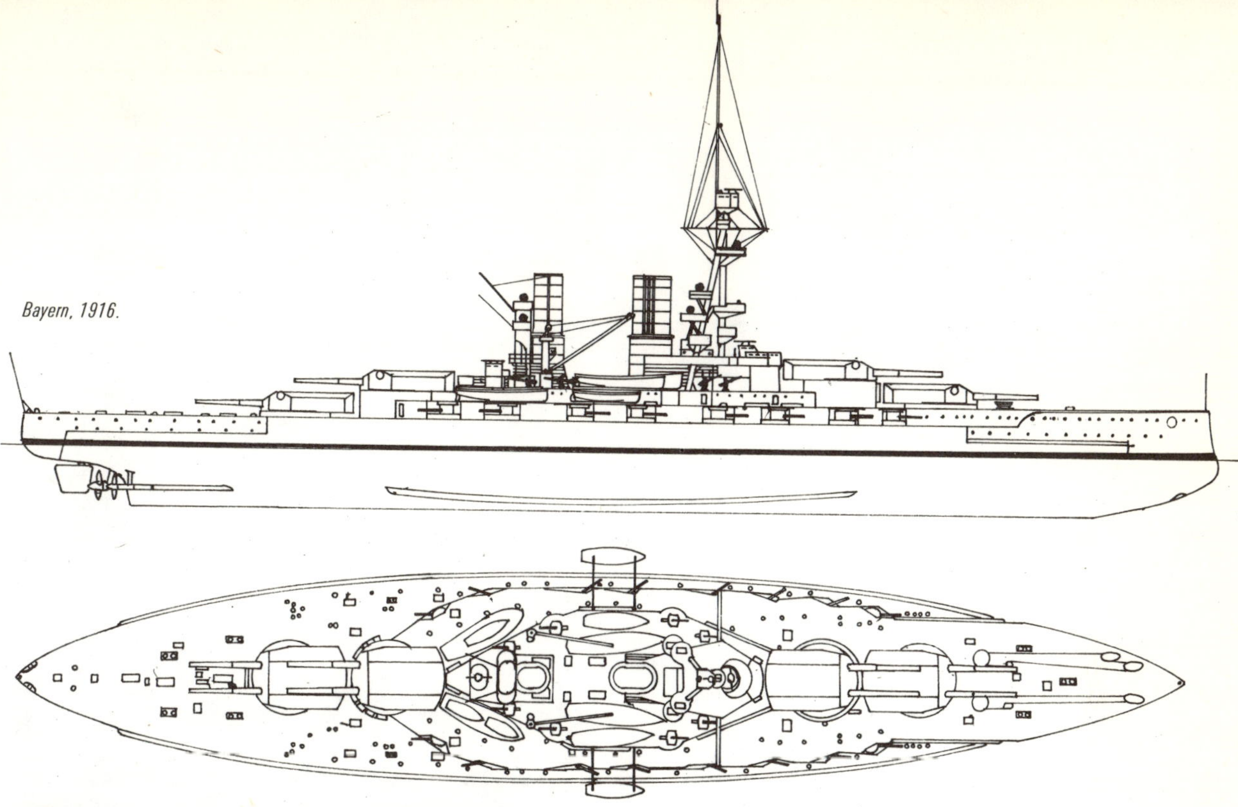

Bayern, 1916.

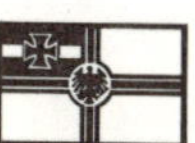

Bayern class

Displacement: 28,000tons (normal)
Dimensions: 560ft 6in×99ft×27ft 9in
Guns: 8×15in 45cal (4×2)
16×5·9in 45cal (16×1)
8×3·4in A.A. (4×2)
Torpedo Tubes: 5×23·6in (1 bow, 4 beam, all submerged)
Armour: 13¾–6in belt; 4¾in decks; 13¾in turrets; 13¾in CT
Machinery: 3-shaft turbines, 52,000shp = 22¼knots; 11 coal-fired 3 oil-fired boilers (Württemberg 12 coal-fired boilers)
Coal Capacity: 886/3346tons
Oil Capacity: 197/610tons
Endurance: 9000miles at 10knots
Complement: 1171–1271
Cost: not known

	Laid Down	Launched	Completed	Builder
Baden	29 Sept 1913	30 Oct 1915	Oct 1916	Schichau
Bayern	20 Sept 1913	18 Feb 1915	Mar 1916	Howaldt
Württemberg	4 Jan 1915	20 June 1917	—	Vulcan, Hamburg
Sachsen	1914	21 Nov 1916	—	Germania

When the Germans learned of British plans for the *Queen Elizabeth* they laid down four ships of equal gunpower under the 1912 and 1913 Programmes. As the German battle cruisers were so battleworthy they did not feel the need to create a 'fast division' of 25knot battleships in the way that the British did, and so the *Bayern* class emerged more as equivalents of the *Revenge* class. As such they are an interesting example of how separate threads of development in different countries can eventually run together. Comparison of the *Revenge* and *Bayern* reveals a remarkable similarity: the same layout of guns, the same calibre and even the same standard of protection.

Like other German ships the *Bayern* class had only moderate freeboard when compared to British ships; this was quite adequate for normal North Sea conditions, but they would have been at a disadvantage if forced to fight further afield. Their metacentric height was 8·3ft (greater than any existing capital ship), which would have made them very stiff, and able to stay upright even after heavy flooding of side compartments. This would have produced a very lively gun-platform in the Atlantic.
Armament: With only 16° elevation for the 15in guns, their range was only 22,200yds (just over 12·5miles). The shell weighed 1653lb (ie: about 300lb less than the British 15in) and the maximum rate of fire under ideal conditions was one round every 26 seconds—7 shells every 3 minutes for each gun.
Sister Ships: The *Sachsen* and *Württemberg* proceeded very slowly after 1915 as steel was in short supply and the Army had requisitioned 15in guns for the Western Front and the

Belgian coast. When the need for more U-boats was apparent *Württemberg* was suspended but work on *Sachsen* continued up to the Armistice.
Appearance: *Baden* and *Bayern* were the first German capital ships to be built with tripod masts. As built *Bayern* had no mainmast, but by 1918 both she and *Baden* had a pole mast stepped against the second funnel. *Baden* differed from *Bayern* in having slightly more extensive bridgework. *Sachsen* would have differed considerably from the first two.
Machinery: The forward boilers were oil-fired, and the after ones coal-fired. The machinery of *Württemberg* would have differed slightly in having 12 boilers, while *Sachsen* had 2-shaft Parsons turbines, and a single shaft M.A.N. diesel engine on the centre shaft.
Careers
Baden: Replaced *Friedrich der Grosse* as Fleet Flagship on completion; not originally among ships to be surrendered under terms of Armistice, but had to be substituted for *Mackensen* and arrived 14 December 1918; scuttling at Scapa Flow 21 June 1919 was unsuccessful, and British boarding parties managed to beach her; repaired and towed to Portsmouth, where she was put through exhaustive comparative trials with H.M.S. *Revenge*, involving armour, guns and construction; sunk as target for battleships on 21 August 1921.
Bayern: Running trials at time of Battle of Jutland in May 1916; Baltic operations 1917, and mined 12 October; surrendered November 1918 and scuttled at Scapa Flow June 1919; raised and broken up 1934–5.
Sachsen: She was approximately nine months away from completion at the Armistice; stricken 3 November 1919 and broken up 1029–1 at Kiel.
Württemberg: Stricken 3 November 1919 and broken up 1920–21 at Hamburg.

Above, Baden at speed – a photograph taken from a Zeppelin in 1918 (Bundesarchiv).

Above left, Bayern shown down by the head after striking a mine in October 1917 (IWM).

Centre left, Bayern at sea with other units of the High Seas Fleet (Bundesarchiv).

Below left, Bayern seen towards the war's end (IWM).

Below centre, a British salvage craft lies alongside the Baden after her unsuccessful attempt to scuttle herself at Scapa Flow, 1919. A light cruiser can be seen in the background (IWM).

Below right, A view from the quarterdeck of Baden's after 15in guns and turrets; this photograph was taken after the 1919 salvage, when the ship was stripped for examination by the British designers (IWM).

Mackensen class

Displacement: 30,510 tons (normal); 34,742 tons (full load)
Dimensions: 731ft 7in (wl)× 99ft 6in×30ft 6in
Guns: 8×14in 50cal (4×2) 14×5·9in 45cal (14×1)
8×3·4in A.A. (8×1)
Torpedo Tubes: 5×23·6in (1 bow, 4 beam, all submerged)
Armour: not known
Machinery: 4-shaft turbines, 90,000shp = 27knots; 24 single-ended coal-firing boilers, 8 double-ended oil-firing
Coal Capacity: 788/3937 tons
Oil Capacity: 295/1968 tons
Endurance: Approximately 10,000 miles at 10 knots

	Laid Down	Launched	Completed	Built/Engined
Mackensen	30 Jan 1915	21 Apr 1917	—	Blohm & Voss
Graf Spee	30 Nov 1915	15 Sept 1917	—	Schichau
Ersatz Freya	1 May 1915	13 Mar 19102	—	Blohm & Voss
Ersatz Friedrich Carl	3 Nov 1915	—	—	Wilhelmshaven DY

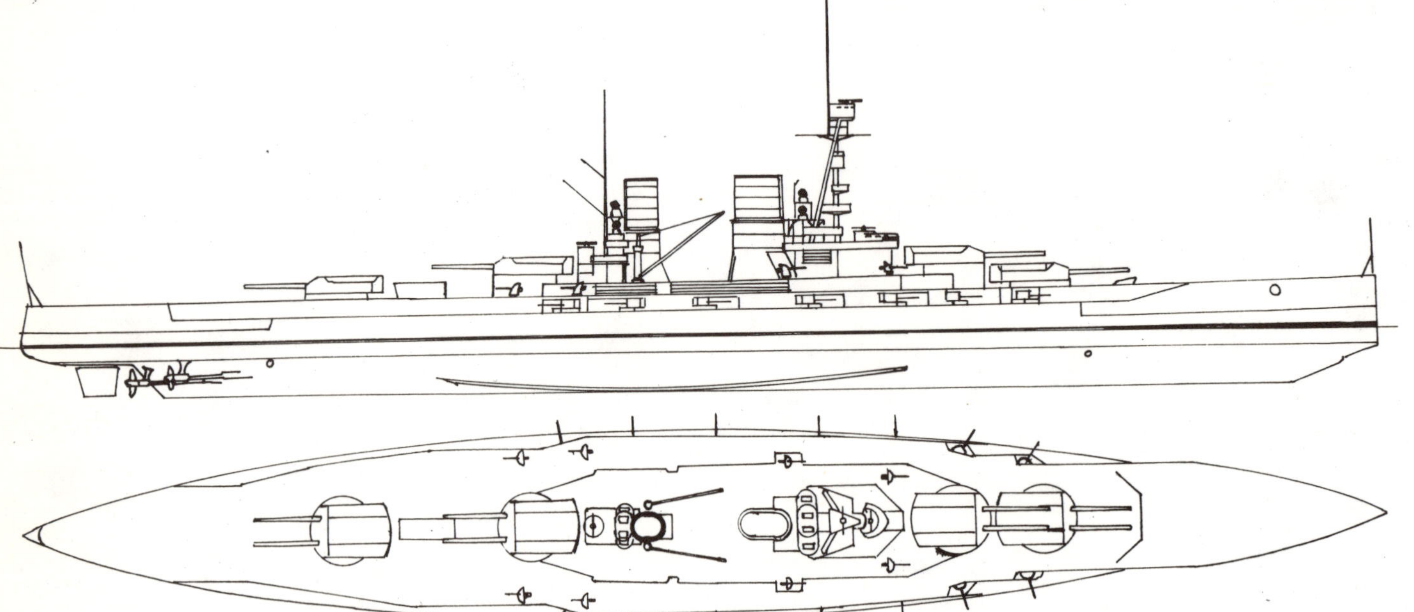

These magnificent ships were laid down under the war programme, but with steel in short supply and difficulties in production of heavy gun-mountings there was never much likelihood of them coming into service. They were basically an expansion of the *Derfflinger*, with the same flush deck and layout of turrets, but with the funnels closer together, and mounting a new 14in gun. This gun had initially been designed to match the British 13·5in and Japanese and American 14in, and although superseded by the 15in/38cm gun, it had been retained for the new battle cruisers.

Nomenclature: In accordance with German practice, names for new construction were not announced in advance, merely the ship to be replaced under the Navy Law concerned; ie if a Ship 'A' was to replace the *König*, she would be known as 'Ersatz König' or '*König* Replacement'. Thus the names *Prinz Eitel Friedrich* and *Fürst Bismarck* were allocated for *Ersatz Freya* and *Ersatz Friedrich Carl*, but never actually given.

Work was suspended on all four in 1917. *Mackensen* was to be surrendered under the Armistice terms, but she was so far from completion that the *Baden* had to be substituted. *Ersatz Freya* was launched in 1920 to clear the slipway and broken up 1920–2 at Hamburg, as was the hull of *Graf Spee* at Kiel in 1921–3. Ship 'A' or *Ersatz Friedrich Carl* was broken up on the slipway, between 1919 and 1922.

Ersatz Yorck

Displacement: 33,000 tons (normal); 37,500 tons (full load)
Dimensions: 747ft 4½in (wl)× 99ft 6in×30ft 6in
Guns: 8×15in 50cal (4×2) 12×5·9in 45cal (12×1) 8×3·4in A.A. (8×1)
Torpedo Tubes: 3×23·6in (60cm), (1 bow, 2 beam, all submerged)
Armour: 11¾–9¾in belt; 3½in deck; 10in turrets; 13¾in CT
Machinery: 4-shaft turbines, 90,000shp = 27·3 knots; 8 coal-fired boilers, 8 oil-fired

	Laid Down	Launched	Completed	Built
Ersatz Yorck	1916	—	—	Vulkan, Hamburg
Ersatz Gneisenau	1916	—	—	Germania
Ersatz Scharnhorst	1916	—	—	Blohm & Voss

This class was an improved version of the *Mackensen* class, with similar layout, but having all boiler uptakes trunked into one funnel. Like the *Mackensens* they made so many demands upon the supply of strategic materials that they had to be suspended in 1917. The basic aim to provide a 15in gunned reply to the British *Repulse* and *Renown*, although those ships, with their 6in armour, would have been no match for the *Seydlitz* or the *Derfflinger* in battle.

Below, stern view of Revenge taken shortly after the war (Admiralty).

Introduction

The Royal Navy was by far the largest navy in the world when war broke out in August 1914. Allied to a glittering tradition of victories going back to Queen Elizabeth I was a numerical superiority over its rivals which had been maintained since the end of the Napoleonic Wars. For many years this supremacy had been kept at a level which made the Royal Navy numerically equal to any two foreign navies—the famous 'Two Power Standard'. The introduction of the dreadnought had made this level of superiority harder to maintain by forcing the Royal Navy to start almost level with Germany, but nonetheless Great Britain had completed 29 dreadnoughts against 18 German and 10 American by the start of the war. Furthermore, she could still fall back on 40 pre-dreadnoughts to match 22 German and 25 American ships.

There were grave weaknesses in the Royal Navy, in the realms of ship design, training and organisation, as might be expected in a fighting force which had enjoyed virtually effortless supremacy for a century. Many reforms had been effected by the titanic energy of Lord Fisher, who as First Sea Lord from 1904 to 1910 reorganised the dockyards, introduced radically new warships and overhauled the manning of the Fleet. Fisher's reforms were far-reaching, and affected the whole organisation of the Navy, but in the field of warship design he is famous for introducing the *Dreadnought* as the prototype for all future battleships, as well as the battle cruiser. He saw the clash of British and German interests as inevitable, and built up the strength of the Royal Navy in time for the outbreak of war, at the same time organising a new system of manning reserve ships to ensure maximum efficiency in peacetime.

Dynamic personalities like Fisher nearly always have flaws in their character to balance their virtues. Fisher was a man of slogans, and he coined the dangerously facile maxim 'speed is protection'. This found its expression in the battle cruiser, a type of ship designed to replace the armoured cruiser by combining an armament on the scale of the *Dreadnought* with cruiser-scale protection to allow for very high speed. Had the battle cruiser remained nothing more than a superior breed of cruiser (which it could not, as it was too expensive and too heavily armed) all would have been well, but it soon came to be used as a fast battleship. Here was the problem, for a British battle cruiser in the battle-line would be fighting the one type of ship she had been designed to avoid.

The great enthusiasm for higher speeds shown by Fisher proved contagious, for Fisher could be vindictive to anyone who opposed his dogmas. One cannot escape the conclusion that some designers and senior officers must have been either very myopic or simply sycophantic during the Fisher era, for some capital ship designs should have struck them as inefficient, if not unsound. British designers grew accustomed to sacrificing protection in favour of speed and gunpower, and as the dreadnought race went on British battleships in some cases had *less* armour than their predecessors, despite constant improvements in gun-performance.

Fisher and his disciples had absolute faith in the destructive power of the naval gun, and all their assumptions were based on the theory of single devastating hits. Hence Fisher's insistence on bigger and bigger guns, forcing gun calibres upwards from 12in to 13·5in, to 15in and finally to 18in. Gunnery became the key to high rank in the Royal Navy, and battleships and tactics came by a strange process of logic to conform to the requirements of gunnery officers. Thus errors like the layout of the turrets in the *Lion* class were perpetrated: because the gunnery branch thought in terms of broadside firing, nobody thought of the problems inherent in siting the No. 3 turret between the funnels. Similarly gunnery and fire-control requirements were sufficient to inhibit any progress away from the excessively formal and rigid line-of-battle tactics laid down for the Battle Fleet.

One should not fall into the common trap of viewing British problems too narrowly, however, for the German Navy had its rigidity of doctrine too, and all the major navies believed in the formal line-of-battle. But the Royal Navy preached gunnery and weight of gunpower, and the haphazard approach to detailed organisation that characterised Fisher's regime was echoed by the gunnery branch's failure to perceive that its armour-piercing shells were too sensitive and that they tended to break up on striking armour obliquely. Tests showed this in 1911, but at the Battle of Jutland, five years later, it became obvious that nothing had been done to rectify matters.

The second point of weakness also affected gunnery, if only indirectly. British cordite propellant charges proved to be unstable in action, and no fewer than four major warships—including battleships—were lost by detonation of their magazines. The loss of the *Queen Mary* and the near loss of her sistership *Lion* proved how unsafe cordite could be, particularly when carelessly handled, but the major portion of the blame for both shell and propellant failure can be laid at the door of the manufacturers. The advantages of TNT as a filler for shells were well known, but to avoid expense the old lyddite filling was retained as long as possible.

However, British designers did not remain completely sunk in sloth, and there is ample evidence that the spur of German competition had been felt before 1914. The introduction of the 15in gun and the adoption of oil fuel showed that radical departures could be made without hesitation. The fact that both the Parsons turbine and the 15in gun, to name only two major innovations, could be introduced with no failure whatsoever showed what British designers could do—both projects were fraught with political and technical hazards, and failure would have endangered the military effectiveness of the Navy, but both were completely successful.

Composition of the Battle Fleet

The Royal Navy had a large fleet of predreadnoughts, which had been built between 1893 and 1908, numbering some forty ships in all. The pace of construction and technical development after the building of the *Dreadnought* (1905–6) made even the best of these obsolescent, but it was obvious that the more modern predreadnoughts would still have a role in wartime.

The small coast-defence battleship had not been popular since mid-Victorian days, and the Royal Navy regarded this function as suitable for its most elderly battleships. Those ships completed between 1901 and 1904 were intended to act as a reserve force in case of any losses in the main fleet.

The main strength of the Royal Navy was concentrated in its eighteen dreadnought battleships, of which two were still completing. Ten more were under construction, the most powerful battleships the world had yet seen, and there were also nine dreadnought battle cruisers, with a tenth about to finish her trials. One of the battle cruisers, H.M.A.S. *Australia*, was the property of the Commonwealth of Australia, but in the decade leading up to the war Imperial solidarity had been so well fostered that the Royal Navy could count on this ship. Also, in the uncertain days after the Sarajevo Incident the British Government refused to allow Turkish crews to take over their new dreadnoughts *Reshadieh* and *Sultan Osman I*: when war broke out they were seized and added to the Royal Navy.

During the war five *Queen Elizabeth* class and five *Revenge* class were completed, the *Canada* was taken over from Chile, and the *Repulse*, *Renown*, *Glorious* and *Courageous* were built. An additional unit, the *Furious*, was so much altered that she cannot be classed as a capital ship, whatever she was in her original condition. Two small coast-defence battleships building for Norway were also taken over for shore bombardment; the only other capital ships begun during the war (*Hood* class) were still incomplete at the Armistice in 1918.

Builders

The builders of British capital ships were all traditionally specialist firms, who had made their name in the nineteenth century when iron shipbuilding was a new industry. They were concentrated mainly on the great rivers, the Tees, Tyne, Clyde and Thames, etc., but ships were also built in the Royal Dockyards as a matter of naval policy, to ensure that the private yeards did not have monopoly of expertise. The following are the builders mentioned in this book; shown as abbreviated and in full:

British Shipbuilders

Abbreviation	Full Name	Location
Armstrong, Elswick	Sir W. G. Armstrong, Whitworth & Co.	Elswick, Tyne
Beardmore	Wm. Beardmore & Co.	Dalmuir, Clyde
Clydebank	John Brown & Co.	Clydebank, Glasgow
Chatham DY	H.M. Dockyard, Chatham	Kent
Cammell Laird	Cammell Laird & Co.	Birkenhead, Merseyside
Devonport DY	H.M. Dockyard, Devonport	Plymouth, Devon
Fairfield	Fairfield Shipbuilding & Engineering Co.	Govan, Clyde
Harland & Wolff	Harland & Wolff Ltd.	Belfast, Northern Ireland
Hawthorn Leslie	R. & W. Hawthorn, Leslie & Co.	Hebburn, Tyne
Palmer	Palmer's Shipbuilding & Engineering Co.	Jarrow, Tyne
Portsmouth DY	H.M. Dockyard, Portsmouth	Hampshire
Pembroke DY	H.M. Dockyard, Pembroke	South Wales
Scotts	Scott's Shipbuilding & Engineering Co.	Greenock, Clyde
Thames I.W.	Thames Iron Works Ltd.	Blackwall, Thames
Vickers, Barrow	Vickers Ltd.	Barrow-in-Furness, Lancashire

Battleship Weapons

British hydraulic turret-machinery had developed along very sound lines since the 1880s, and all the mountings in service had been developed from the highly successful model in the *Albion* and *Glory* (1896). Electric machinery had been tried in the *Invincible* in 1907, but hydraulic machinery continued to be standard and in the 15in twin turret, designed in 1913, probably reached its peak of perfection. No gun mounting since has been able to match its combination of ruggedness and simplicity.

Twin mountings were the rule for British capital ships, although the 18in turret was single, simply because of its weight. Multiple mountings (ie: triple and quadruple) had been proposed by the big gun-manufacturing firms, but the gunnery branch was firmly against them on the grounds that salvo firing was easier to control with twin turrets. Although this may sound odd to modern ears, British experience with triple and quadruple mountings in later years confirmed that the roominess and simplicity of the twin mounting were very important advantages.

Elevation of guns increased as greater ranges became possible. Thus 13·5° was enough for the old *Majestic* class in 1896, but the *Queen Elizabeth* had 20° in 1915. Muzzle velocities of the various marks of 12in rose higher and higher as improvements were made to propellants and shells, but the quality of shooting fell off until it was realised that a light shell and high velocity combine to produce inaccuracy at long range. When the 13·5in and 15in guns were introduced muzzle velocity dropped, and as the shell weight went up considerably these guns proved far more accurate than the 12in. As a bonus, it was found that barrel wear was also drastically reduced. It should also be remembered that an improvement in accuracy at extreme ranges was far more important than any slight increase in range, as the percentage of possible hits at extreme distances was extremely low.

Principal British Guns

Calibre	Mark	Length	Elevation	Range	Notes
12in	not known	40cal	20°(?)	c.16,000yds	Relined 13·5in 35cal old Revenge
12in	Mk.VIII	35cal	13½°	13,750yds	Majestic and Canopus Cl
12in	Mk.IX	40cal	13½°	15,000yds	Formidable Cl etc
10in	Mk.VI Mk.VII	45cal	13½°	14,700yds	Triumph Cl
12in	Mk.IX	40cal	13½°	15,600yds	King Edward VII Cl (with heavier charge)
12in	Mk.X Mk.XIII	45cal	13½°	16,350yds	(with 2cal radius head) Lord Nelson Cl Dreadnought and Invincible Cl (see below)
12in	Mk.XIII	45cal	13½°	19,000yds	(with 4cal radius head) Bellerophon, Indefatigable Cl Agincourt; also Dreadnought and Invincible in 1916
12in	Mk.XI Mk.XII	50cal	15°	c.21,500yds	St. Vincent and Colossus Cl
13·5in	Mk.V	45cal	20°	c.24,000yds	(1250lb shell) Lion and Orion Cl
13·5in	Mk.V	45cal	20°	23,800yds	(1400lb shell) King George V, I. Duke Cl, Q. Mary and Tiger
13·5in	Mk.VI	45cal	20°	23,000yds	Erin
14in	Mk.I	45cal	20°	c.24,200yds	Canada
15in	Mk.I	42cal	20°	24,300yds	Q. Elizabeth, Revenge Cl etc
18in	Mk.I	40cal	30°	29,000yds	Furious
9·2in	Mk.XII	51cal	40°	39,000yds	Glatton Cl (with 8crh shell and super-charge)

Torpedo tubes were fitted below water in all British capital ships, and proved utterly useless. In particular stern tubes proved unworkable, and were all removed or made inoperable during the war. The battle cruisers *Repulse*, *Renown*, *Courageous* and *Glorious* were given above-water torpedo tubes, but these also proved to be of little value.

Machinery

The *Dreadnought* introduced the Parsons turbine, which became the standard method of propulsion for British battleships. The four-shaft installation was the only one used once the turbine was adopted, whereas the older ships all had two shafts. The standard 3-cylinder and 4-cylinder inverted triple-expansion engines remained almost unaltered in general layout, from the *Majestic* to the *Lord Nelson*, but there were many permutations and combinations of boilers. The 'battle of the boilers' had raged in the 1890s, but eventually the water-tube boiler had won the day.

Battleship machinery was subjected to stresses and wear far beyond anything imagined by designers. The British in particular kept their ships at sea so much that any inherent flaws were bound to appear. Yet, despite the thousands of miles steamed by British battleships, their machinery proved reasonably reliable. The dreadnoughts tended to suffer from condenser trouble, and the age of the machinery in older ships caused a lot of worry, but at no time were any great number of ships badly incapacitated. The worst case was the *Indomitable*, which was long overdue for a refit in August 1914, and had difficulty in maintaining 22knots while chasing the *Goeben*.

Fleet Bases

The Royal Navy had built up its chain of bases to fight the French and Dutch in the seventeenth and eighteenth centuries; consequently they were situated in the Channel and in the Thames Estuary (Devonport, Portsmouth, Chatham and Sheerness), and in South Wales (Pembroke and Milford Haven), to enable ships to maintain a close blockade of Dutch and French ports. When it became clear that Germany would be the next enemy it was realised that these traditional bases would be too far from the northern exits to the North Sea, so in 1906 work started on Rosyth, on the Fifeshire side of the Firth of Forth. This was to be a huge new yard capable of docking any capital ship in the Navy, but by 1914 the Fleet had expanded at such a rate that Rosyth could not handle it, and a second northerly base was needed.

Some years before 1914 the Admiralty had prepared contingency plans to use Scapa Flow in the Orkney Islands as a Fleet anchorage. It had two perfect qualities—first, enough space to anchor not only battleships, but all the cruisers, destroyers and support ships necessary: second, it was close to the Germans' only feasible route to the Atlantic. The distance between Orkney and Norway is less than the distance from Orkney to London, and it was relatively easy to patrol the exit routes. Of course Scapa Flow had serious drawbacks, principally because no money had been spent on equipping it as a Fleet base. Having no defences and nothing but a fuel depot, it was impossible to maintain the Fleet there until guns had been mounted, net-booms laid, and repair facilities set up.

After a submarine scare in 1914 the Grand Fleet went from anchorage to anchorage, while Scapa Flow was made secure. Then came the German battle cruiser raids on the East Coast, and public outcry forced the Admiralty to station some ships at Rosyth. The Grand Fleet came to use the Firth of Forth regularly for repairs and recreation, since Scapa was too remote and bleak to be totally self-sufficient.

Overseas bases existed in great numbers in 1914, the legacy of a century of imperial expansion, and this made it possible to disperse ships all over the world without much trouble. Nevertheless, temporary bases had to be set up, such as the advanced base at Mudros for the Dardanelles expedition. Base facilities were also granted by the Italians, and a force of British battleships was based at Taranto from 1915–18.

The Fleet on the Outbreak of War

The Home Fleet became the Grand Fleet on 7 August 1914, thus reviving a term which went back centuries. The battle squadron organisation of the old Home Fleet was then reconstructed to form a new Channel Fleet, which incorporated the old battleships which had come forward from the Reserve and were making up their full complements. At this point the battle fleets were distributed as follows:

Strength of the Grand Fleet and Battle Cruisers on the Outbreak of War

Grand Fleet
Fleet Flagship
Iron Duke
1st Battle Squadron
Marlborough (Vice-Admiral), St. Vincent (Rear-Admiral), Colossus, Hercules, Neptune, Vanguard, Collingwood, Superb
2nd Battle Squadron
King George V (Vice-Admiral), Orion (Rear-Admiral), Ajax, Audacious, Centurion, Conqueror, Monarch, Thunderer
3rd Battle Squadron
King Edward VII (Vice-Admiral), Hibernia (Rear-Admiral), Commonwealth, Africa, Zealandia, Dominion, Britannia, Hindustan
4th Battle Squadron
Dreadnought (Vice-Admiral), Temeraire, Bellerophon
6th Battle Squadron
Russell (Flagship), Cornwallis, Albemarle, Duncan, Exmouth
1st Battle Cruiser Squadron
Lion (Vice-Admiral), Princess Royal, Queen Mary, New Zealand
plus 8 armoured cruisers
Channel Fleet
Fleet Flagship
Lord Nelson
5th Battle Squadron
Prince of Wales (Vice-Admiral), Queen (Rear-Admiral), Agamemnon, Venerable, Irresistible, Bulwark, Formidable, Implacable, London
7th Battle Squadron
Prince George (Flagship), Caesar, Jupiter, Majestic
8th Battle Squadron
Albion (Flagship), Canopus, Glory, Ocean, Vengeance
9th Battle Squadron
Hannibal (Flagship), Victorious, Mars, Magnificent, Illustrious (paid off to provide crew for Erin)
Mediterranean Fleet
2nd Battle Cruiser Squadron
Inflexible (Flagship), Indefatigable, Indomitable
plus 4 armoured cruisers
East Indies
Station Flagship
Swiftsure
Australasia
Australia, New Zealand
China
Station Flagship
Swiftsure
plus 1 armoured cruiser

The predreadnought battle squadrons were thinned out early in 1915, when bombarding ships were needed for the Dardanelles Expedition. The *Lord Nelsons*, *Duncans*, and most of the older ships went, including two of the *Majestic* class. The remaining *Majestics* were either disarmed to provide guns for monitors or dispersed as guardships for subsidiary duties. The new *Queen Elizabeths* were earmarked for the now defunct 5th Battle Squadron, which was transferred to the Grand Fleet; in addition the arrival of the last two units of the *Iron Duke* class and the ex-Turkish *Erin* and *Agincourt* made a slight reorganisation of the squadrons necessary.

The old concept of close blockade was impossible to operate, for it would have involved the British battle squadrons patrolling off German bases, and would certainly have led to a high rate of attrition from submarines and mines. In 1912 the new War Staff had rejected any such ideas, and in the summer of 1914 the happy compromise of a 'distant blockade' was finally accepted; this involved patrolling a line from Scapa Flow to

Norway, and from Dover to Cap Gris Nez. At a stroke German hopes of wearing down the British strength by using their submarines, torpedo-boats and destroyers were dashed. Instead, the Germans had to adopt a policy of trying to trap a weak portion of the Grand Fleet so that it could be annihilated by their own fleet.

As a result of this unexpected reversal of war plans, the war at sea so far as the Grand Fleet and the High Seas Fleet were concerned became a long drawn-out business of patrolling and waiting. The British had to try to tempt the Germans out, and thus had to use their battle cruisers as the bait, while the Germans resorted to pinprick bombardments of the British East Coast. This was an exhausting business, and the British fleet always ran the risk of having a squadron cut off and destroyed, but the game was far more lethal for the Germans, who generally got the worst of it.

Detailed descriptions of the naval battles of the First World War are not part of this book, but the following summary shows what actions involved the Grand Fleet:

Heligoland Bight, 1914

On 28 August 1914 British light forces began a sweep into the Bight to roll up the German outposts. Thanks to the state of the tide no German heavy units came out, but their light cruisers joined in and began to punish the British for their temerity. In response to a plea from Commodores Tyrwhitt and Keyes for support, the Admiralty allowed Sir David Beatty to take his battle cruisers in, but as a result of appalling staffwork, nobody in the British forces already engaged had any inkling of this. However, the gamble paid off, and the *Lion*, *Princess Royal*, *Queen Mary*, *New Zealand* and *Invincible* thundered into the Bight and, without suffering any damage, sank the cruisers *Mainz*, *Köln* and *Ariadne*. The event bolstered British morale at an uncertain stage of the war, but it was hardly more than an extremely lucky raid, which could have ended disastrously if the German battle cruisers had been able to arrive earlier.

Dogger Bank 1915

The German raids on the East Coast in 1914 caused Beatty's battle cruisers to be shifted from Scapa Flow to Rosyth, and this redeployment led to the next action. On 24 January 1915 Beatty's force, including the *Lion*, *Tiger*, *Princess Royal*, *New Zealand* and *Indomitable*,[1] as a result of a decoded German signal, intercepted the German Scouting Group I off the Dogger Bank. The action developed into a stern chase, with only the bigger British battle cruisers able to fire at ranges which started at 22,000yds. The Germans, handicapped by the presence of the slow (25knots) armoured cruiser *Blücher*, concentrated on the *Lion* and disabled her with twelve hits. A misunderstood signal caused the remaining British ships to abandon the pursuit and they fell on the hapless *Blücher*. After an heroic fight she sank, but the only chance the British would get to destroy a portion of the High Seas Fleet was gone for ever.

Jutland, 1916

On 31 May 1916, again as a result of cryptographic analysis, the British were able to get Vice-Admiral Sir David Beatty and his Battle Cruiser Force to sea in time to intercept Rear-Admiral Hipper's Scouting Group I. What neither admiral knew was that his opponent was supported by the full battle fleet. The months of missed chances were over, and the scene was set for the greatest sea battle the world had ever seen.

[1] Missing ships: Queen Mary en route to Portsmouth for docking; Invincible at Gibraltar; Inflexible in Mediterranean.

Strength of the Grand Fleet and Battle Cruisers, 31 May 1916

Grand Fleet
Fleet Flagship
Iron Duke (with 4th B.S.)
1st Battle Squadron, 5th Division
Colossus, Collingwood, Neptune, St. Vincent
1st Battle Squadron, 6th Division
Marlborough, Revenge, Hercules, Agincourt
2nd Battle Squadron, 1st Division
King George V, Ajax, Centurion, Erin
2nd Battle Squadron, 2nd Division
Orion, Monarch, Conqueror, Thunderer
4th Battle Squadron, 3rd Division
Iron Duke (q.v.), Royal Oak, Superb, Canada
4th Battle Squadron, 4th Division
Benbow, Bellerophon, Temeraire, Vanguard
3rd Battle Cruiser Squadron[1].
Invincible, Indomitable, Inflexible
Battle Cruiser Force
1st Battle Cruiser Squadron
Lion, Princess Royal, Queen Mary, Tiger
2nd Battle Cruiser Squadron
New Zealand, Indefatigable
5th Battle Squadron[2].
Barham, Valiant, Warspite, Malaya

[1] Detached from B.C.F. for gunnery practice. In addition the Australia was in dock.
[2] Detached from Grand Fleet to replace 3rd B.C.S. Queen Elizabeth refitting.

The opening phase was a hard fight between the opposing battle cruisers, and Beatty's six ships were badly hammered by Hipper's five—a bad moment at which to discover the inherent weakness of British battle cruisers. The *Von der Tann* scored a fatal hit on the *Indefatigable's* fore turret, causing her to blow up with the loss of practically all her company. Just over twenty minutes later the *Queen Mary*, which had been firing (to quote a German onlooker) with 'fabulous rapidity' blew up after a fire in No. 3 turret. *Lion* had already been hit in the same spot, but after a near-disaster a gallant Royal Marine officer—Major Harvey—flooded the magazines and saved the flagship.

At this point the tide began to turn in favour of the British, for their four massive *Queen Elizabeth* class battleships, which had been stationed astern of the battle cruisers, caught up and began to fire accurately at the Germans at the enormous range of 18,500yds. The German fire began to slacken, and Beatty ordered his destroyers to attack in order to gain time. The Germans broke away, and for the first time the British saw the full strength of the High Seas Fleet—22 battleships in all. Beatty, bearing in mind that his principal duty was to deliver the German fleet to the Grand Fleet, began his 'run to the north'. As he drew near, with the German Scouting Group I in pursuit, Jellicoe ordered Hood's 3rd Battle Cruiser Squadron forward in support, and for a time they rendered very timely assistance. But suddenly, in the fluctuating visibility which made Jutland so confusing, the *Invincible* was silhouetted against the setting sun; the *Derfflinger* and possibly the *König* registered on her, scored hits amidships, and the British ship blew up with the loss of 1026 men.

The last stage of the battle, as far as British capital ships were concerned, was a series of intermittent actions between the main fleets, with the British ships hidden in mist and smoke, and firing at German ships as they appeared and reappeared out of the mist patches. The German Commander-in-Chief, Vice-Admiral Scheer, tried to extricate himself from the trap, but twice blundered into the centre of the British line and withdrew to avoid annihilation. Only nightfall enabled him to escape, and after a confused night action his battered ships drove through the British destroyers and reached the safety of the Horns Reef Channel.

The British had good reason to be discontented with the Battle of Jutland: the long-sought battle had been fought, but 37 capital ships had failed to destroy 27; one German battlecruiser, the *Lützow*, had been scuttled after heavy damage, and the old predreadnought *Pommern* had been torpedoed, but the Battle Cruiser Force had lost three battle cruisers, of which so much had been expected. The war had not been decided at a stroke, and everyone in the Grand Fleet knew that the heartbreaking futility of patrolling the North Sea had to go on. But in another sense Jutland had sealed the fate of Germany: the Kaiser was so appalled at the risks run by Scheer that he forbade any future attempt to entice the British into action; despite German claims to a victory on the grounds that they had suffered fewer losses, they knew that 'the Grand Fleet's prisoner had only assaulted its jailer, but was now safely back in prison'.

The Grand Fleet underwent a radical reorganisation after Jutland. New methods of co-ordinated fire control were introduced, new methods of night fighting, and above all, new armour-piercing shell. Reports from neutral Sweden confirmed what people had suspected, that British shell had not been as destructive as German shell. This turned out to be due to over-hardening of the nosecaps, which affected only A.P. shells; by comparison the Common shell was very well designed, and was highly thought of by the Germans.

The significant point about Jutland was the presence of the bulk of the Grand Fleet off Jutland Bank on the morning of 1 June 1916, searching for the High Seas Fleet. But there was no enemy to contest the return of crippled destroyers, and Jellicoe was able to round up his stragglers without hindrance. All capital ships immediately began a programme of refits to improve protection to magazines and to provide better flashtight shutters to ammunition hoists. Both this and the provision of improved shell took time and the Grand Fleet could not be said to have been completely re-equipped until 1917. The results of all this were not to be seen for the rest of the war, and indeed the real benefits were not evident until 1939.

Heligoland Bight, 1917

On 17 November 1917 British capital ships had their last sight of German heavy units. 'Light' forces, including the battle cruisers *Courageous* and *Glorious* and eight light cruisers, were ordered to destroy German minesweepers in the Bight. A confused action followed, hampered by smoke screens and the large areas sown with mines, and as was to be expected, the two battle cruisers made little impression with their 15in guns. The *Repulse* came up in support, and fired at the German battleships *Kaiser* and *Kaiserin* at extreme range, while covering the retreat of the light cruisers.

Battleships in Other Theatres

With the most modern capital ships concentrated in the North Sea to contain the German Fleet, it was inevitable that the older ships would be dispersed on lesser duties. As the British immediately launched military campaigns overseas, battleships and supporting warships were needed to provide convoy escorts and shore bombardment. The German Navy was unable to interfere with the passage of ships to the various theatres of war, such as the Cameroons, Gallipoli and Mesopotamia, as their commerce-raiding cruisers were soon either destroyed or immobilised.

The Battle of the Falklands

The old battleship *Canopus* was sent to South America to support Admiral Cradock's cruisers, but she was too late for the Battle of Coronel (1 November 1914). Her 12in guns might have turned the scale, but Cradock had not wanted to be held back by her lack of speed. However, the old ship played her part in the prelude to the Battle of the Falklands, when she was beached at Port Stanley to strengthen the local defences, in expectation of an attack by the squadron of Graf Spee.

As soon as the news of the disaster at Coronel reached London the First Sea Lord, Lord Fisher (who had been recalled from retirement) despatched the battle cruisers *Invincible* and *Inflexible* to the Falklands. The chase after Spee could have lasted months in the Pacific, but the German commander chose to attack the British colony at the Falklands, and arrived on 8 December 1914 just as the two battle cruisers were coaling. At this point the *Canopus* opened fire with her forward 12in guns, and Spee's scouting cruisers withdrew. The two dreadnoughts soon worked up to full speed, and after a stern chase of some hours Spee's armoured cruisers were sunk without causing more than superficial damage to the British ships. It was the only time that battle cruisers were to be used in their designed role of hunting down armoured cruisers, and in this they proved highly successful.

The Belgian Coast Operations

Late in 1914 the Royal Navy was able to intervene in the land fighting by bombarding the German Army's right flank on the Belgian Coast at Nieuport. A scratch force of old gunboats, requisitioned monitors and modern warships was assembled under Rear-Admiral Hood to shell the German positions. The old battleship *Revenge* was hurriedly fitted out, and the *Venerable* was used for a time, until the specially-built 12in-, 14in- and 15in-gunned monitors were ready.

The Dardenelles Expedition and Overseas Operations

After Turkey's declaration of war on 1 November 1914 the British and French took offensive action quickly and on 3 November the *Indefatigable* and *Indomitable* with the French *Vérité* and *Suffren* fired on the outer Dardenelles forts. Thus warned, the Germans and Turks strengthened the defences with the result that when the Allies decided to force the Dardanelles to give support to Russia they found the Gallipoli Peninsula heavily fortified.

Despite the poor showing that ships have made against shore fortifications throughout history, the Admiralty cheerfully sanctioned a purely naval assault on the Dardanelles. Hopelessly optimistic forecasts were made as to the number of shells needed to knock out shore guns, and the new 15in-gunned battleship *Queen Elizabeth* was sent out to calibrate her guns against the forts. After some preliminary preparations the outer forts were once more bombarded by the *Cornwallis*, *Triumph*, *Albion* and *Inflexible*, with the French *Bouvet* and *Suffren* on 19 February. After another month of desultory bombarding, the big attack was launched on 18 March 1915.

The order of battle on that fateful day was as follows:

Line 'A': *Prince George*, *Queen Elizabeth*, *Agamemnon*, *Lord Nelson*, *Inflexible*.

Line 'B': *Vengeance*, *Irresistible*, *Albion* and *Ocean*.

In support: *Majestic*, *Gaulois*, *Charlemagne*, *Bouvet*, *Suffren*, *Swiftsure* and *Triumph*.

The Allied ships had no experience of spotting against mobile howitzers, and the battleships made little impression on the Turkish defences.

A cleverly-laid minefield accounted for the loss of the *Bouvet*, *Irresistible* and *Ocean*, and damaged the *Inflexible* severely. In addition, many of the ships had been badly knocked about by gunfire and so the whole scheme was abandoned on 23 March. It had been a badly planned operation, and despite the fact that the old predreadnoughts had specifically been sent out as expendable, the loss of two obsolete British ships was held to be disastrous.

After troops had been landed on the Gallipoli Peninsula the old battleships were retained to provide supporting fire. However, the *Goliath* was torpedoed by a Turkish torpedo-boat on 13 May, and then a U-Boat (*U.21*) sank the *Triumph* and *Majestic* off the beaches. Henceforward fire support for the troops had to be provided by destroyers, 'bulged' cruisers and monitors, and the battleships had to be withdrawn to Mudros and Salonika.

Under an Anglo-Italian agreement four predreadnoughts then had to be sent to Taranto to stiffen the Italian Navy. In May 1915 the *Queen*, *Prince of Wales*, *Venerable* and *London* were transferred from the Dardanelles, and all except the *London* remained there until 1918.

Other predreadnoughts served in East Africa, the East Indies and the White Sea, to name only a few stations, usually as Flagships. The older battleships in many ways saw more activity, if not action, than the dreadnoughts patrolling the North Sea. The *Jupiter* astounded the Russians when she was sent to Murmansk as an icebreaker in February 1915, for no ship had ever reached there so early in the year.

The Surrender of the German Fleet

After the ceaseless patrolling and frustration of four years, the sudden collapse of the German war effort in November 1918 was almost an anticlimax. The naval conditions of the Armistice included the surrender of six battle cruisers and ten battleships for internment until the Peace Conference. As a result, on 21 November 1918 the British and American battleships of the Grand Fleet mustered to witness a strangely distasteful sight—the surrender of the cream of a once-proud High Seas Fleet. The German ships, led by the small cruiser H.M.S. *Cardiff* were led between two lines of capital ships comprising 33 battleships and 10 battle cruisers.

War Modifications and Colour Schemes

British capital ships were in general far more liable to changes of appearance than those of any other navy. Early in the war wireless topmasts were struck, and gradually torpedo-nets were removed. From 1916 funnel-caps began to appear, but only in dreadnoughts, while control tops were constantly being extended and enlarged to cope with improvements in fire control.

Many predreadnoughts had their main deck guns resited in open batteries higher up, and stockless anchors began to replace the old pattern. Anti-aircraft guns appeared in all ships, usually high-angle 12pdrs (3in) but often converted 3pdrs (47mm) and 6pdrs (57mm). Although anti-torpedo 'bulges' were fitted to the old *Revenge* and to a pair of the later *Revenge* class, this did not come in as a war modification in any ships, with the exception of the *Commonwealth*, which was modified for shore bombardment in 1918.

All battleships retained the 'Home Fleet grey' of prewar days for some time into 1915, although ships in the Mediterranean were given some partial camouflage schemes at this time. In 1916 a lighter grey came into vogue for the Grand Fleet, and this remained standard until 1918. From 1917 as part of the post-Jutland improvements in fire control dread-

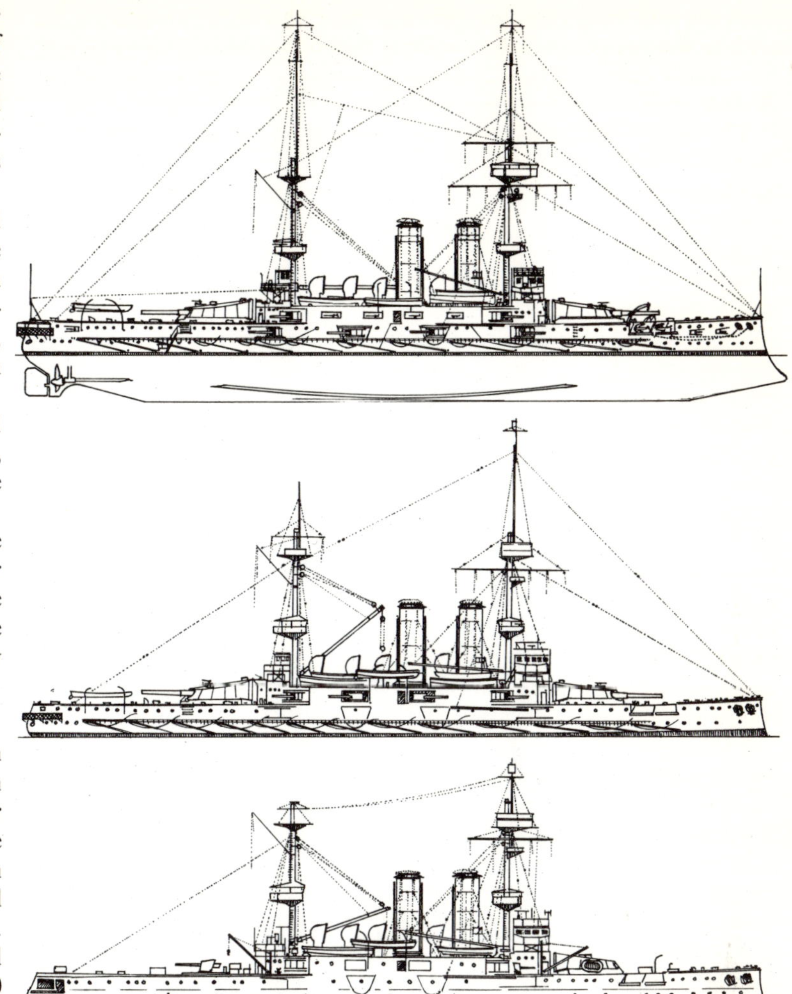

Above, three drawings showing how drastically some of the predreadnought battleships were modified during the course of the war; top, *Irresistible* in 1912, centre, *Implacable* in 1917, bottom, *London* in 1918.

noughts had deflection scales painted on turrets and turret-crowns, and carried rangeclocks on their masts.

The rangeclock and deflection scales were both devices to improve gunnery, particularly in confused conditions likely to be encountered in the North Sea. It should be remembered that wireless telegraphy was still relatively undeveloped, and ship-to-ship communication still relied solely on the flashing lamp or flag hoists. At Jutland, with ships pouring out dense clouds of coal-smoke, it was frequently impossible to read any information about the bearing and range of an enemy squadron; by the time the information was available the mist might have closed in, and the opportunity to open fire had gone.

The rangeclock simply expressed the range of the target in thousands of yards, and the figures on its face could be read by a ship astern or ahead in the line. The bearing of that target would be read off from the deflection scales on the turrets, and with these two items of information, the ship coming up astern would have her guns aimed in the right direction should there be any sudden improvement in visibility.

Apart from early camouflage schemes, several ships in home waters were painted in dazzle schemes in 1917–18. With few exceptions the Grand Fleet dreadnoughts did not receive dazzle schemes, but a number of predreadnoughts were painted in a weird assortment of stripes.

The most radically altered British battleship (apart from the old *Revenge*) was the *London*, which became a minelayer in 1918. All ships surrendered a varying number of light guns in 1915–16 to provide defensive guns for merchant ships. The most noticeable change in armament for war-built ships was the disappearance of the broadside casemate gun; instead guns were mounted in shields at forecastle deck level, to keep them clear of spray and blast.

Conclusions

The problems of the Royal Navy in 1914–18 were unique, for it had worldwide commitments. Its losses in capital ships were heavy—three by internal explosion, five by mine, three in action, and six torpedoed.

But, the total strength was little affected and, as the French had found in the Napoleonic Wars, the numerical strength of the Royal Navy enabled it to sustain disasters which would have crippled a smaller force.

The British ships were not individually superior to those of their opponents in many cases, but with a combination of far-sighted strategy and offensive tactics they achieved a very real victory. The Grand Fleet could have 'lost the war in an afternoon' had it been beaten at Jutland, and the real proof that it had not been beaten came in 1917, when the High Seas Fleet was unable to prevent the Allies from bringing hundreds of thousands of American soldiers to Europe. Indeed, during the whole war, the British ferried nine million soldiers across the Channel without the loss of a single man. Many other ships were sunk to achieve this, but in the final analysis the price was not too high, for the Allies always retained the use of the sea, while their enemies could only dispute that possession from time to time.

Name	Aug. 1914	Sep. 1915	Jan. 1918	Apr. 1918
	Pendant Numbers worn by British Battleships 1914–18			
Revenge	P.55	N.12	N.84	N.84
Majestic	D.04	—	—	—
Caesar	D.27	P.02	P.10	P.10
Hannibal	D.36	P.45	N.54	N.54
Illustrious	D.40	P.40	P.97	P.97
Jupiter	D.50	P.50	N.64	N.64
Magnificent	D.13	P.83	P.3A	P.3A
Mars	D.42	P.01	P.6A	P.6A
Prince George	D.46	P.86	P.9A	P.9A
Victorious	D.48	P.65	P.3C	P.3C
Canopus	N.29	N.29	N.17	N.17
Albion	N.48	N.48	N.00	N.00
Glory	P.08	P.08	P.92	P.92
Goliath	N.54	—	—	—
Ocean	N.56	—	—	—
Vengeance	N.57	N.57	N.1A	N.1A
Formidable	50	—	—	—
Bulwark	95	—	—	—
Implacable	63	63	72	N.48
Irresistible	64	—	—	—
London	70	70	81	N.41
Prince of Wales	81	81	94	N.46
Queen	82	82	96	96
Venerable	96	96	A.8	N.36
Duncan	43	43	59	N.53
Albemarle	07	07	06	N.39
Cornwallis	33	33	—	—
Exmouth	12	12	63	N.44
Russell	23	23	—	—
Swiftsure	not known	not known	P.05	P.05
Triumph	not known	—	—	—
King Edward VII	66	66	—	—
Africa	25	25	02	N.07
Britannia	27	27	21	N.40
Commonwealth	31	31	44	31 (then N.88 in June 1918)
Dominion	41	41	54	41 (then N.90 in June 1918)
Hibernia	60	60	70	N.66
Hindustan	62	62	71	N.67
Zealandia	73	73	2C	19 (then N.89 in June 1918)
Lord Nelson	04	04	82	cancelled
Agamemnon	01	01	03	cancelled
Dreadnought	00	00	56	73
Bellerophon	72	72	11	63
Superb	49	49	A0	49
Temeraire	48	48	A2	92
Collingwood	26	26	42	03
St. Vincent	16	16	7A	85
Vanguard	39	39	—	—
Colossus	93	93	43	24
Hercules	47	47	69	54
Neptune	02	02	89	79
Orion	52	52	91	86
Conqueror	06	06	47	95
Monarch	55	55	88	60
Thunderer	32	32	A3	36
King George V	61	61	77	70
Ajax	40	40	05	46
Audacious	54	—	—	—
Centurion	21	21	35	83
Iron Duke	94	94	76	14
Benbow	75	75	14	51
Emperor of India	11	11	60	16
Marlborough	79	79	85	66
Agincourt	53	53	04	09
Erin	56	56	61	76
Canada	28	28	26	01
Queen Elizabeth	10	10	97	00
Barham	97	97	10	34
Malaya	3.A	3.A	84	06
Valiant	34	34	A6	43
Warspite	57	57	A9	12
Royal Sovereign	59	59	5A	89
Ramillies	74	74	98	·21
Resolution	8A	8A	1A	57
Revenge	98	98	2A	29
Royal Oak	67	67	4A	38
Invincible	85	85	—	—
Indomitable	77	77	74	05
Inflexible	83	83	75	47
Indefatigable	13	13	—	—
Australia	C6	C6	09	81
New Zealand	08	08	90	53
Lion	22	22	79	67
Princess Royal	29	29	95	68
Queen Mary	14	14	—	—
Tiger	42	42	A4	91
Renown		64 (Jan. 1916)	99	23
Repulse		54 (Jan. 1916)	0A	26
Courageous			51	94
Glorious			67	56
Furious			65	40
Glatton		N.03	N.50	N.50
Gorgon		P.59	N.51	N.51

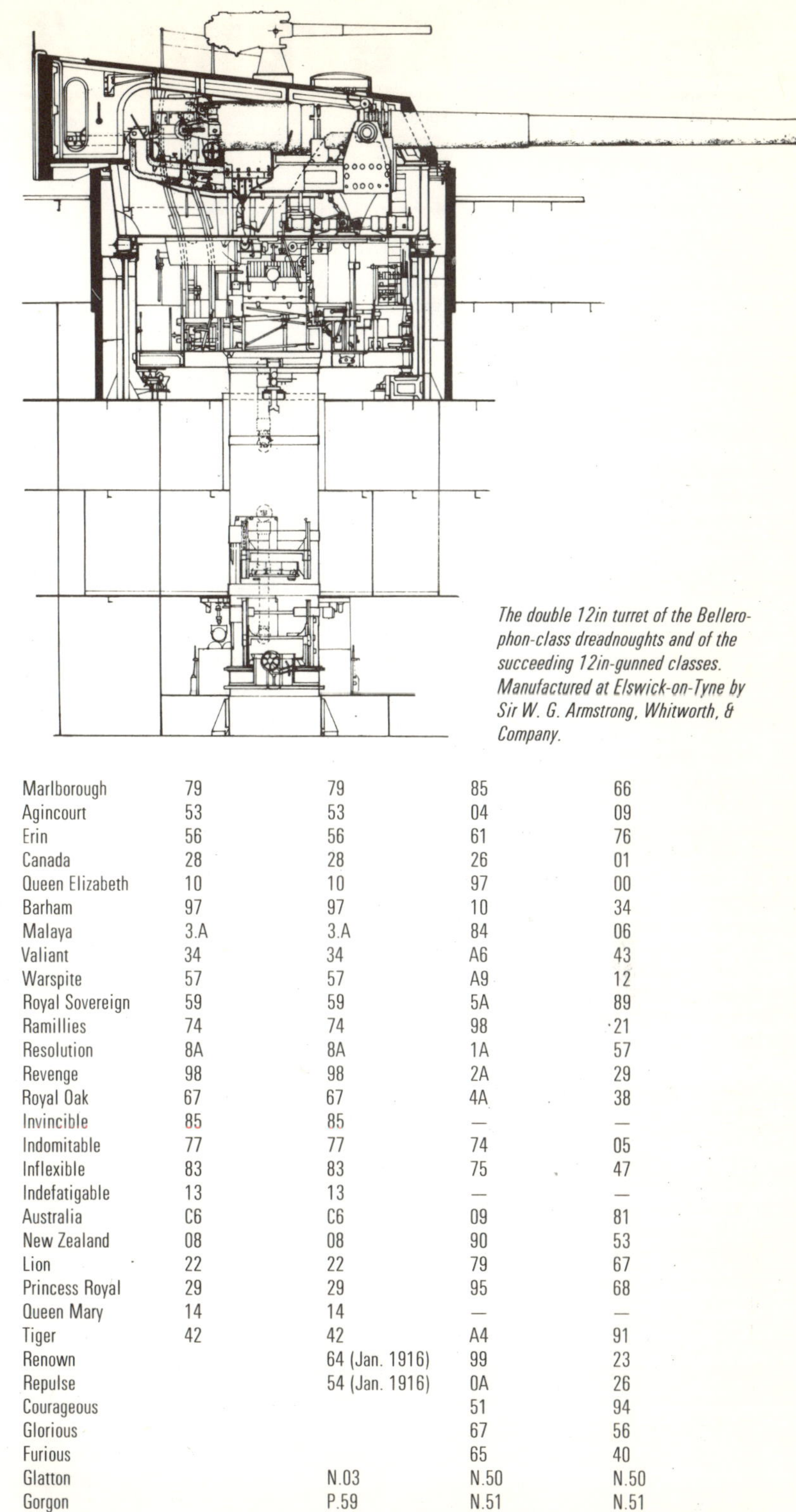

The double 12in turret of the Bellerophon-class dreadnoughts and of the succeeding 12in-gunned classes. Manufactured at Elswick-on-Tyne by Sir W. G. Armstrong, Whitworth, & Company.

Note: When the period point (.) is omitted between a numeral and a letter, this means that there is no flag superior; in its place the 'answering pendant' is used. Thus A2 means 'Answering pendant No. 2', whereas A.2 means' Flag superior A, followed by numeral pendant 2'.

Revenge/Redoubtable class

Displacement: 14,635tons (at load draught, 1914)

Dimensions: 380ft (pp)×75ft× 28–29ft

Guns: 4×13·5in (2×2), later 4×12in (see notes) 10×6in QF (10×1), later 6×6in (see notes) about 12×3pdrs carried in fighting tops on superstructure and elsewhere

Torpedo Tubes: 2 submerged (forward) 4 above water (beam) and 1 above water (stern)

Armour: 18–14in belt, 3–2½in decks, 17–11in barbettes etc

Machinery: 2 sets vertical 3-cylinder triple expansion, 9000hp=13knots (by 1914); 8 cylindrical boilers

Coal Capacity: 1000tons

Endurance: 4700miles at 10knots

Complement: 661 (1913)

Cost: £950,000 ($3,800,000)

	Laid Down	Launched	Completed	Built
Revenge	12 Feb 1891	3 Nov 1892	Mar 1894	Palmer, Jarrow

This elderly unit (the oldest British battleship to see active service) was laid up in reserve awaiting sale in August 1914. She and her sisters had been the pride of the Channel and Mediterranean Fleets in the 1890s, but all had been struck off the effective list from 1911 onwards. *Revenge* had in fact been towed to the Motherbank (Isle of Wight anchorage for ships awaiting sale) in April 1913, and had not found a buyer when war broke out in 1914.

Having been used as a gunnery training ship since 1906 the old battleship had been fitted with modern fire control and was suitable for shore bombardment. In October 1914 she was towed to Portsmouth Dockyard for refit. The German positions on the Belgian coast were vulnerable to British naval bombardment, and the *Revenge* was the biggest unit available. Her main drawback was her great draught, and of course if she had been sunk her prestige value as a battleship, however old, would have been great. As bulges were fitted for protection against torpedoes, H.M.S. *Revenge* made history as the first warship to use this device in service. She was also fitted with an early form of minesweeping gear invented by Sir Arthur Wilson, and similar in principle to the better-known paravane gear.

After carrying out a number of successful shoots against the German right flank the *Revenge* was renamed *Redoubtable* on 2 August 1915 to release the name for the new *Royal Sovereign* class battleship. When the 12in gunned monitors came into service later that year the old ship was redundant, but she took part in long-range gunnery trials in the Thames before paying off in October 1915. She recommissioned as a tender to H.M.S. *Victory* from 1918 to February 1919, and was sold 6 November 1919 to Wards and broken up at Briton Ferry.

Gunnery: At first her original short-barrelled 13·5in guns were retained to use up stocks of obsolete shell; the lack of elevation of the mounting (only 16°) made it necessary to list the ship to give greater range. When stocks of old pattern 13·5in shell were exhausted her guns were relined to take 12in ammunition, increasing their effective range to 16,000yds. Photographs indicate that her four main deck 6in guns were suppressed, but it is not certain if this was a wartime or prewar alteration.

Sister ships: *Royal Sovereign, Royal Oak, Ramillies, Resolution, Repulse* and *Empress of India* all broken up 1911–14; near-sister *Hood* sunk as blockship at Portland in August 1914.

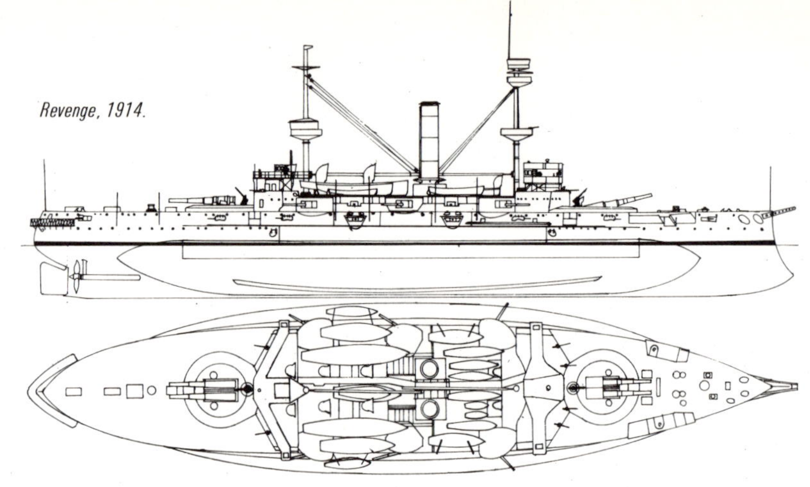

Revenge, 1914.

Above right, Revenge shown heeling to increase the range of her guns during a shoot off the Belgium coast in 1914–15. Note the false bow wave and the horns of the mine-sweeping gear over the bows (IWM).

Below right, sporting an early form of camouflage (IWM).

Majestic class

Displacement: 14,560–14,890tons (at load draught)
Dimensions: 390ft×75ft×26ft 6in–27ft 6in
Guns: 4×12in 35cal (2×2); later removed from some ships (see notes) 12×6in (12×1); 8 later removed from some ships (see notes) 16×12pdrs, 12×3pdrs; many of these removed during the war
Torpedo Tubes: 4 submerged 18in (beam), 1 above water 18in (stern)
Armour: 9in belt (Harvey steel), 14–7in barbettes, 4–2½in decks
Machinery: 2 sets triple expansion, 10,000hp = 13–14knots (by 1914); 8 cylindrical boilers
Coal Capacity: 900/1900tons
Oil Capacity: 400tons in all but Jupiter and Illustrious
Endurance: 4700miles at 10knots
Complement: 673
Cost: £950,000 average ($3,800,000)

	Laid Down	Launched	Completed	Built/Engined
*Majestic	Feb 1894	31 Jan 1895	Dec 1895	Porsmouth DY
Caesar	25 Mar 1895	2 Sept 1896	Jan 1898	Portsmouth DY
Hannibal	1 May 1894	28 Apr 1896	Apr 1898	Portsmouth DY
Illustrious	11 Mar 1895	17 Sept 1896	Apr 1898	Chatham DY
Jupiter	26 Apr 1894	18 Nov 1895	May 1897	John Brown
Magnificent	18 Dec 1893	19 Dec 1894	Dec 1895	Chatham DY
Mars	2 June 1894	30 Mar 1896	June 1897	Lairds, Birkenhead
Prince George	10 Sept 1894	22 Aug 1895	Nov 1896	Portsmouth DY
Victorious	28 May 1894	19 Oct 1895	Nov 1896	Chatham DY

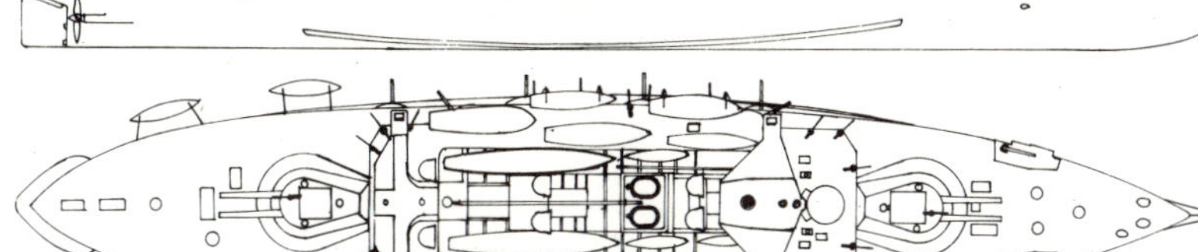

Majestic, 1914.

Left, *Majestic (Author's collection).*

This was the oldest class on the effective list in the Royal Navy in August 1914. Built 1893–8, they were the model for battleships all over the world, and they served as the pattern for development until the *Dreadnought*. Had war not broken out, they would soon have gone to the breakers, and in any event they were earmarked for subsidiary duties. *Majestic, Caesar, Jupiter* and *Prince George* commissioned from the Reserve (nucleus crews) to form the 7th Battle Squadron in August 1914 and *Hannibal, Victorious, Mars* and *Magnificent* formed the 9th B.S., but as soon as it became clear that there was no immediate prospect of a fleet action they were dispered as guardships. Early in 1915 the 12in guns and turrets were removed from *Magnificent, Mars, Hannibal* and *Victorious* to provide the armament for the eight *General Wolfe* class monitors; the ships themselves were then converted to troop transports, retaining only their forecastle deck casemate guns.

Careers

Caesar: 7th B.S. 1914, including covering crossing of B.E.F.; North America and West Indies Station and Atlantic escort duties 1915–18; Mediterranean and Black Sea 1918–19; sold 8 November 1921 to Slough Trading Co. and then towed for breaking up in Germany July 1922.

Hannibal: 9th B.S. 1914; sent to Humber as guard ship late 1914 until disarmed early 1915; to Mediterranean as troopship 1915–16 and subsequently in East Indies and Egyptian waters; sold 28 January 1920 to Montagu Yates and broken up in Italy.

Illustrious: August 1914 sent to Loch Ewe as guard ship, and to Lough Swilly etc subsequently; Channel 1915; used as ammunition store ship in Tyne and at Portsmouth 1916–19 (it is not clear from records whether or not she was disarmed between 1915 and 1918, but her turrets may well have been used as spares for the monitors); paid off March 1920 and sold 18 June 1920 to Wards, Barrow.

Jupiter: 7th B.S. 1914, and later guard ship for Tyne and Humber; at end of that year sent to Archangel to break through ice, and became the first vessel ever to dock in the month of February; Channel May 1915, followed by service in East Indies and Egypt 1915–16; Special Service 1917–18 and paid off 1919; sold 15 January 1920 to Hughes Bolckow.

Magnificent: 9th B.S. 1914; disarmed 1915 and became troopship in Mediterranean 1915–17; in January 1918 became an ammunition store at Rosyth until paid off 1919; sold 9 May 1921 to Ward, Inverkeithing.

Majestic: 7th B.S. 1914; escorted Canadian convoy to U.K. October 1914; Channel early 1915 and bombarded Belgian coast; March 1915 to Dardanelles for naval assault; torpedoed by *U.21* 27 May 1915, while carrying out bombardment off Gaba Tepe, the day after she became flagship.

Mars: 9th B.S. 1914; disarmed 1915 and served as troopship in Mediterranean 1915–16; 1916 became depot ship at Invergordon; sold 9 May 1921 to Ward and broken up at Briton Ferry.

Prince George: Commissioned as Flagship 7th B.S. August 1914 for service in Channel covering passage of B.E.F. transports; transferred to Dardanelles March 1915 and suffered slight damage during bombardment on 2 May from Turkish artillery; took part in Sulva Bay landing and evacuation of Cape Helles,

during which she was hit by a defective torpedo; paid off late
1916 at Chatham and used as auxiliary sick bay; later converted
to destroyer depot ship, and renamed *Victorious II* in 1918; sold
29 January 1921 to Cohen, but resold and stranded off Kamper-
duin while in tow to Germany.

Victorious: Commissioned in 9th B.S. 1914; disarmed 1915 and
sent to Longhope in the Orkneys in March 1916 to act as a base
ship for repair workers; remained at Scapa Flow until 1919;
renamed *Indus II* 1920; sold 19 December 1922 to A. J. Purves
and resold 1923 to Stanlee for breaking up at Dover.

Below, *a prewar view of Jupiter, showing details of her boats and upperworks (Author's collection).*

Canopus class

Displacement: approximately 13,150tons (at load draught)
Dimensions: 390ft×74ft×25ft 10in–26ft 6in
Guns: 4×12in 35cal (2×2) 12×6in (12×1); 4 later removed from some ships
10×12pdrs (10×1), 6×3pdrs (6×1); many of these removed during the war
Torpedo Tubes: 4 submerged 18in (beam)

Armour: 6–2in belt (Krupp Cemented), 12–6in barbettes, 2–1in decks
Machinery: 2 sets 3-cylinder triple expansion, 13,500hp=13–15knots (by 1914); 20 Belleville boilers
Coal Capacity: 800/1800tons
Endurance: 4500miles at 10knots
Complement: 683
Cost: £900,000 average ($3,600,000)

	Laid Down	Launched	Completed	Built
Canopus	4 Jan 1897	12 Oct 1897	Dec 1899	Portsmouth DY
Albion	3 Dec 1896	21 June 1898	June 1901	Thames I.W.
Glory	1 Dec 1896	11 Mar 1896 (floated out)	Oct 1900	Lairds, Birkenhead
*Goliath	4 Jan 1897	23 Mar 1898	Mar 1900	Chatham DY
*Ocean	15 Feb 1897	5 July 1898	Feb 1900	Devonport DY
Vengeance	23 Aug 1898	25 July 1899	Apr 1902	Vickers, Barrow

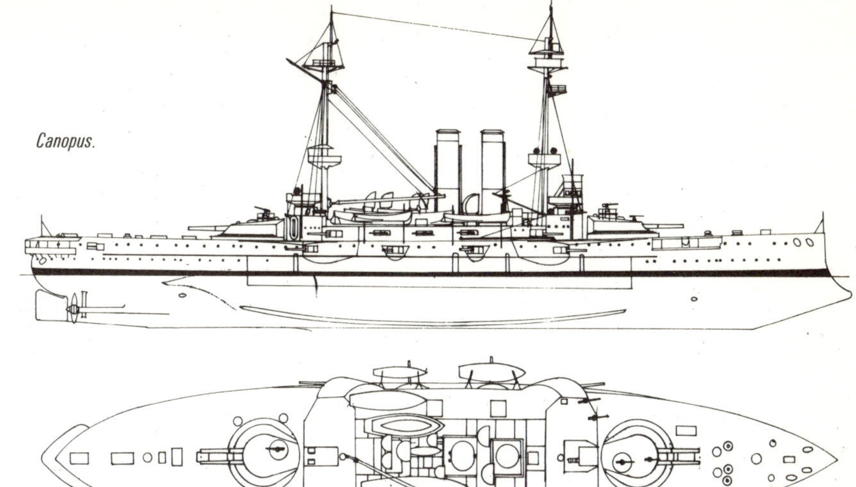

Canopus.

These were smaller editions of the *Majestic* class, and were the oldest British capital ships to see much action. After commissioning to form the 8th Battle Squadron on the outbreak of war they were dispersed on a variety of secondary duties, and served all over the world.

Appearance: Distinguished from *Majestics* by discarding side-by-side funnels in favour of the fore-and-aft arrangement. The shortage of light weapons for smaller ships led to the eventual stripping of 12pdr and 3pdr guns from their battery decks and upper works, and in 1917 *Canopus*, *Glory* and *Vengeance* had their main deck 6in casemate guns suppressed (the forward and after positions remained in *Vengeance*); in *Canopus* and *Glory* two of the guns were resited in the former 12pdr battery, thus improving their command and general utility. Small anti-aircraft guns were mounted on turrets in most of the class, and stockless anchors replaced the old pattern.

Below, one of the two views of *Vengeance* in 1917 on her return to home waters following service in East Africa. She is flying the flag of a Rear-Admiral (NMM).

Careers

Albion: August 1914 8th B.S. (Flagship); transferred to Cape of Good Hope November 1914–February 1915 and then to Dardanelles; carried troops to Salonika October 1915; stationed on east coast of England as guardship 1916–18 and became accommodation ship at Devonport late 1918; sold 11 December 1919 to Ward and broken up at Morecambe.

Canopus: August 1914 B.S., and transferred October to South America Station; although ordered to join Sir Christopher Cradock's cruiser squadron before the Battle of Coronel, she was too far away to be of assistance; following destruction of Cradock's force she was berthed on mud at Port Stanley, Falklands, to act as guard ship; fired 12in salvoes at Von Spee's cruisers during opening stages of Falklands Battle, and provided 12pdr guns for coast-defence; to Mediterranean for Dardanelles, March 1915; returned to Chatham to pay off in 1916; accommodation ship 1916–18; sold 18 February 1920 to Stanlee, and broken up at Dover.

Glory: August 1914 B.S.; October 1914 Flagship, North America and West Indies Station; Mediterranean June 1915–16 and then to Murmansk for duty as guard ship and depot ship; returned to Rosyth as depot ship and renamed *Crescent* 1 May 1920; sold 19 December 1922 to Granton Shipbreaking Co.

Goliath: August 1914 8th B.S., but sent to Loch Ewe as guard ship; bombardment duties off Belgian coast; September 1914 to East Indies Station (East Africa); Rufiji River operations against *Königsberg*; to Dardanelles April 1915 and sunk by Turkish torpedo-boat *Muavenet*, 13 May 1915.

Ocean: 8th B.S. August 1914, and transferred with *Goliath* to East Indies Station in September; Persian Gulf October 1914; defence of Suez Canal February 1915 and then to Dardanelles; on 18 March during bombardment of Narrows she was hit by shell-fire and then fouled a mine in Erenkui Bay (laid by Turkish *Nusret*); abandoned at 7.30pm and sank about three hours later.

Vengeance: 8th B.S. August 1914; to Cameroons in November and then to Egypt and Cape Verde; Flagship of Sir John de Robeck, January 1915, for Dardenelles expedition; returned to Egypt November 1915 as guard ship, and subsequently served in East Indies, Egypt again, East Africa and the Cape; ordnance depot at Devonport 1918–19 and sold 1 December 1921 to Stanlee; arrived at Dover for breaking up 9 January 1923.

Displacement: 15,000tons (Navy List tonnage) but varied from 14,100 to 14,500tons at load draught
Dimensions: 400ft×75ft×25ft–26ft 6in
Guns: 4×12in 40cal (2×2); see Notes for removal from London and Queen
12×6in 45cal (12×1); reduced to 8 in some, and to 3 in London (see Notes)
16×12pdrs (16×1); reduced in most ships
6×3pdrs (6×1); reduced in most ships
A.A. guns added in some ships, e.g. 1×4in in London
Torpedo Tubes: 4 submerged 18in (beam)
Armour: 9–3in belt (Krupp Cemented in Londons and Queens, Harvey steel in earlier trio), 3–1in decks, 12–6in barbettes
Machinery: 2 sets triple expansion, 15,000hp=18knots; 20 Belleville boilers
Coal Capacity: 900/2000tons
Endurance: 3000miles at 10knots
Complement: 780–810
Cost: £1,000,000 average ($4,000,000)

Below, Vengeance in 1917 again. Note that two of the main deck 6in guns on each side have been removed and small anti-aircraft guns have been added on the turret crowns, while stockless anchors have also been fitted (NMM).

Formidable/London/Queen classes

	Laid Down	Launched	Completed	Built
*Formidable	21 Mar 1898	17 Nov 1898	Sept 1901	Portsmouth DY
*Irresistible	11 Apr 1898	15 Dec 1898	Feb 1902	Chatham Dy
Implacable		11 Mar 1899	Sept 1901	Devonport DY
London	8 Dec 1898	21 Sept 1899	June 1902	Portsmouth DY
*Bulwark	20 Mar 1899	18 Oct 1899	Mar 1902	Devonport DY
Venerable	2 Jan 1899	2 Nov 1899	Nov 1902	Chatham DY
Queen	12 Mar 1901	8 Mar 1902	Mar 1904	Devonport DY
Prince of Wales	20 Mar 1901	25 Mar 1902	Mar 1904	Chatham DY

Improved *Canopus* class, with heavier armour and a longer pattern of 12in gun. Although often regarded as forming one homogeneous group, the three classes were distinguished in several ways. As Krupp armour could not be shaped as easily as earlier steel, the turrets in the *Londons* and *Queens* had angled sides. Owing to the passage of time between laying down the first and second classes, a number of internal modifications authorised for the later *Duncan* class were included in the *Londons*.

Their service was varied and arduous, and unlike earlier British predreadnoughts, those which survived were mostly still in full active commission in 1918. *London* was the most drastically altered of all, as she spent most of 1917 converting to a minelayer. This involved the complete removal of the after 12in turret and barbette to allow the conversion of the after part of the main deck to a mine-deck, with rails discharging over the stern. The guns were removed from the forward turret, but for some reason the turret itself remained in place. Most of the 6in guns were removed, excepting the upper casemate guns abreast of the bridge, and an additional 6in gun was added on the quarterdeck.

Appearance: Distinguished from *Canopus* class by heavier look, and funnels further apart. The 12pdr positions abaft the hawsepipes differed between groups, but these had nearly all been plated in by 1914. The two *Queens* had an open 12pdr battery between the 6in guns. By the end of 1916 *Implacable*, *London* and *Venerable* had two 6in guns mounted in place of 12pdrs in the upper battery, and had the lower casemates plated over making a total of four guns a side. By 1918 *Queen* was partially disarmed, having had the 12in guns removed from her turrets.

Careers

Bulwark: In commission with 5th B.S. on outbreak of war; blew up at Sheerness 26 November 1914 while taking on ammunition (only 12 saved out of 750).

Formidable: In commission with 5th B.S. on outbreak of war; Channel patrol duties from August 1914, covering passage of B.E.F.; torpedoed by *U.24* about 20 miles from Start Point 1 January 1915 with heavy loss of life.

Implacable: In commission, 5th B.S. August 1914; Dardanelles March 1915, and endeared herself to the Lancashire Fusiliers by coming in very close to the shore and destroying Turkish gun positions with her 12in guns; Cape Helles landing 24 April 1915 and other operations; May 1915 ordered to Adriatic to support Italian Fleet with her sisters; Egypt and East Indies 1915–16, then returned to Mediterranean 1916–17; Northern Patrol 1918–19; sold 8 November 1921 to Slough Trading Co. for breaking up.

Irresistible: In 5th B.S. in August 1914; to Dardanelles February 1915; took part in attack on Narrows 18 March, and struck mine in Erenkui Bay at 4.15pm; drifted under the Turkish guns and was eventually sunk by gunfire around 7.30pm.

London: In commission, 5th B.S. in August 1914; Dardanelles March 1915; with *Implacable*, *Venerable* and *Prince of Wales* sent to Taranto in May 1915 to reinforce Italian Fleet; withdrawn 1917 to return home for conversion to minelayer; January 1918 joined 1st Minelaying Squadron; in reserve acting as depot ship 1919 and sold 4 June 1920.

Prince of Wales: In commission, 5th B.S. in August 1914; Dardanelles March 1915; Taranto May 1915; returned to home waters 1918; sold 12 April 1920.

Queen: In commission, 5th B.S., on outbreak of war; to Dardanelles March 1915; Taranto May 1915, and remained there until 1918, by which time she had been partially disarmed as a depot ship; recalled to home waters and sold 4 September 1920.

Venerable: in commission with 5th B.S. August 1914 but allocated to Vice-Admiral, Dover, for bombardment duties off Belgian coast in October 1914; bombarded Westende batteries March 1915; sent to Dardanelles May 1915 to replace *Queen Elizabeth*; bombardment and other duties, Suvla Bay August 1915, and then transferred to Taranto to support Italian Fleet; recalled 1918 and still in service as depot ship 1919; sold 4 June 1920.

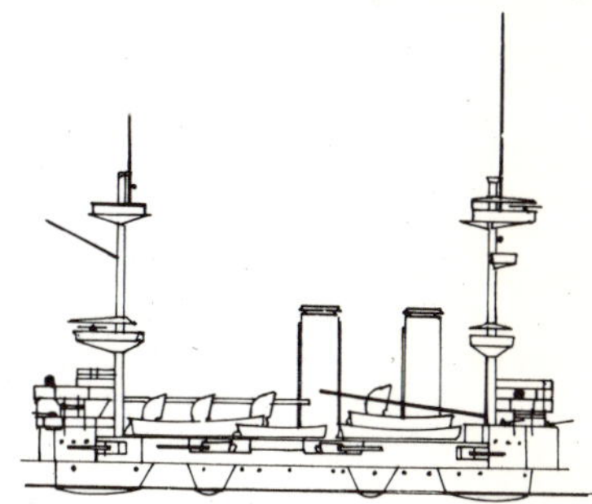

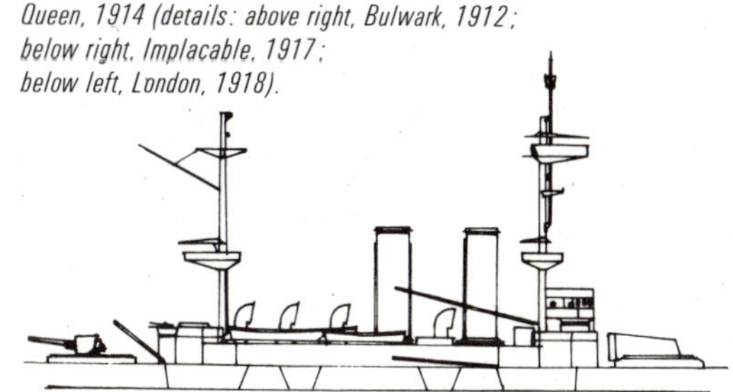

Queen, 1914 (details: above right, Bulwark, 1912; below right, Implacable, 1917; below left, London, 1918).

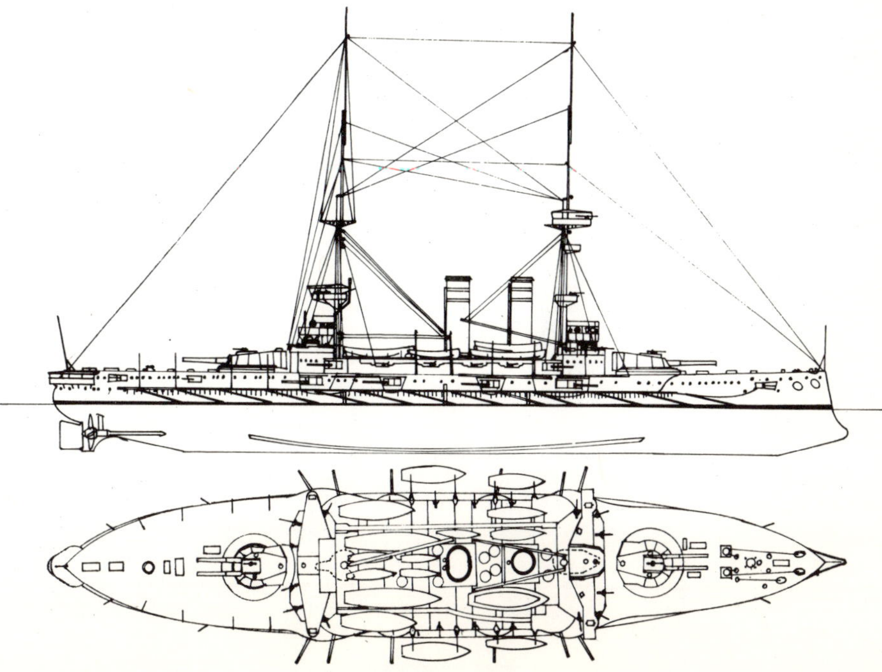

Above left, Prince of Wales in 1912, with tall wireless masts typical of prewar British ships. Note that she has funnel bands and torpedo nets, but stockless anchors (NMM).

Above, Queen in 1914, still with funnel bands but without torpedo nets (NMM).

Left, Irresistable just before the outbreak of war. The fighting tops have been converted to fire control positions (NMM).

Below left, Bulwark in 1914, virtually as she was at the time she was lost. Note that her torpedo nets have been removed and that the original fighting tops have been fitted with screens and converted to fire control positions (NMM).

Below centre, London painted in dazzle scheme (IWM).

Above right, a prewar view of Prince of Wales taken at Portsmouth, showing details of the boat stowage and the upperworks. Note HMS Victory afloat in the background (Author's collection).

Below right, London shown in 1919 after her conversion to a minelayer. Note that No. 1 turret was retained minus its 12in guns whereas No. 2 turret aft was entirely removed. The 6in guns were all removed and the 12pdrs were plated in. Note also that stockless anchors were fitted in place of the original stocked pattern – this had been carried out on many surviving predreadnoughts by 1917 (NMM).

Duncan class

Displacement: 13,500tons at load draught

Dimensions: 405ft×75ft 6in×25ft 2in–26ft 3in

Guns: 4×12in 40cal (2×2) 12×6in 45cal (12×1); Albemarle had only 8 in 1917 10×12pdrs (10×1); reduced in all 6×3pdrs (6×1); reduced in all

Torpedo Tubes: 4 submerged 18in (beam)

Armour: 7–3in belt, 2–1in decks, 11–4in barbettes

Machinery: 2 sets triple expansion, 18,000hp = 19knots; 24 Belleville boilers

Coal Capacity: 900/2240tons

Endurance: 3000miles at 10knots

Complement: 720

Cost: £1,093,800 average ($4,372,000)

	Laid Down	Launched	Completed	Built
Duncan	10 July 1899	21 Mar 1901	Oct 1903	Thames Ironworks
*Cornwallis	19 July 1899	13 July 1901	Feb 1904	Thames Ironworks
Exmouth	10 Aug 1899	31 Aug 1901	May 1903	Lairds, Birkenhead
*Russell	11 Mar 1899	19 Feb 1901	Feb 1903	Palmers, Jarrow
Albemarle	23 Nov 1899	5 Mar 1901	Nov 1903	Chatham DY

Slightly smaller and faster editions of the *Formidable* group, originally built to counter the Russian ships *Oslyabia* and *Peresviet*. As such they were the last of the straightforward developments of Sir William White's original *Majestic* type, with four 12in guns and twelve 6in. Henceforward new pressures influenced the Board of Admiralty in its choice of armament, and the passing of Sir William White from the scene marked the end of a remarkably stable decade in British ship design. Although generally similar to the previous classes, the *Duncans* had equal-sized round funnels, and continued the practice initiated in the *Queens* of carrying their 12pdrs in an open battery.

Appearance: *Albemarle* was the only one of the class to have stockless anchors in 1914, but this refinement was extended to the others during wartime refits. *Exmouth* was refitted in 1915 for bombardment at Gallipoli, and had extra-heavy torpedo nets. In 1917 *Albemarle* had her main deck casemate 6in guns removed, and mounted two per side in the former 12pdr battery. In common with other old battleships, the ships surrendered a number of light weapons from 1915 onwards in order to provide defensive armament for merchant ships, and as a simple way of compensating for increases in topweight.

Sister ship: A sixth ship of this class, *Montagu*, was wrecked off Lundy 30 May 1906.

Careers

Albemarle: Serving with 6th B.S. at outbreak of war, but acting as gunnery tender at Portsmouth; transferred to Grand Fleet August 1914 for Northern Patrol duties; 6th B.S., Channel February 1915 (later 3rd B.S.); in November 1915 had her bridge washed away in heavy weather in Pentland Firth; after repairs rejoined 3rd B.S. at Scapa December 1915, and was transferred to Archangel the following January as ice-breaker and guard ship; recalled September for a refit; May 1917 to November 1918 in reserve as overflow ship at Naval Barracks, Devonport; sold 19 November 1919 and broken up.

Cornwallis: Serving with 4th B.S., Home Fleet prior to war, but transferred to 6th B.S. in August 1914 for service in Channel; to Mediterranean January 1915 and made history as the first ship to open fire against the Turkish defences at Gallipoli, 18 February; saw service throughout Dardanelles Campaign, firing 500 rounds of 12in and 6000 rounds of 6in; torpedoed and sunk by *U.32* near Malta, 9 January 1917.

Duncan: Gunnery tender at Portsmouth (2nd Fleet) prewar, but commissioned in 6th B.S. in August 1914; after Northern Patrol duties she joined the *King Edward* class in the 3rd B.S. in November, and subsequently served in Channel area; to Mediterranean early in 1915, but not sent to Dardanelles; paid off 1917 and not recommissioned; sold 18 February 1920.

Exmouth: Gunnery training ship at Devonport prewar, but joined 6th B.S. in Grand Fleet; later served on Northern Patrol on 3rd B.S.; joined Channel Fleet November 1914, and bombarded Zeebrugge; sent to Dardanelles May 1915 with *Venerable* to replace *Queen Elizabeth* (refitted with heavier nets as a result of loss of *Majestic* and *Triumph*); became flagship of Admiral Nicholson at Cephalo, the only battleship allowed to lie off the beaches; returned to home waters 1917 and paid off; sold 15 January 1920.

Russell: Serving with 2nd Fleet at Nore prewar, but commissioned as Flagship 6th B.S., Grand Fleet in August 1914; November 1914 transferred to Channel, and took part in bombardments off Belgian coast; to Mediterranean early in 1915, and became stand-by battleship at Mudros with *Hibernia*; evacuation of Cape Helles January 1916; mined off Malta 27 April 1916.

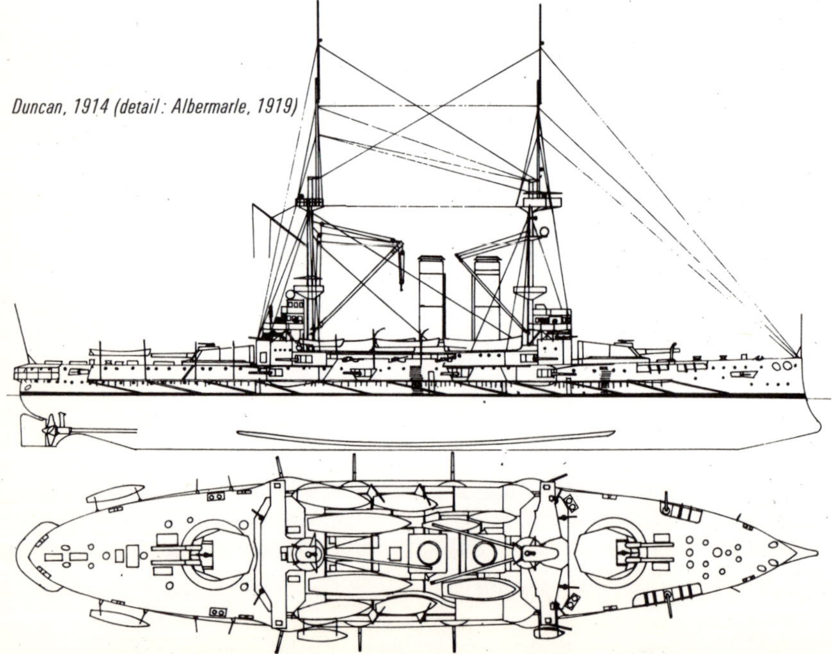

Duncan, 1914 (detail: Albermarle, 1919)

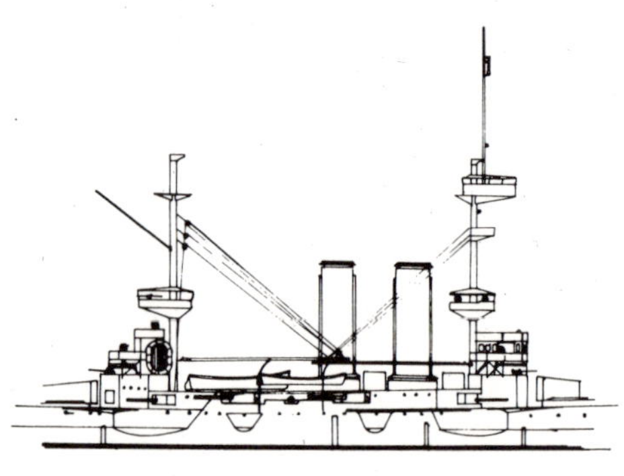

Above right, Russell in April 1905 at Devonport (Admiralty).
Below right, Albemarle shown in 1914 with torpedo nets removed (NMM).

Triumph class

Displacement: 12,175tons (at load draught)

Dimensions: 436ft×71ft×25ft 4in

Guns: 4×10in (2×2)
14×7·5in (14×1); some or all removed from Swiftsure in 1917
14×14pdrs (14×1); main deck guns removed from Swiftsure in 1916 (others may have been removed later)

Torpedo Tubes: 2 submerged 18in (beam)

Machinery: 2 sets triple expansion, 12,500hp = 19knots; 12 Yarrow boilers

Coal Capacity: 800/2000tons

Endurance: 6250miles at 10knots

Complement: 802

Cost: £847,000 average ($3,388,000)

	Laid Down	Launched	Completed	Built
*Triumph (ex-Constitucion)	26 Feb 1902	12 Jan 1903	June 1904	Armstrong, Elswick
Swiftsure (ex Libertad)	26 Feb 1902	15 Jan 1903	June 1904	Vickers, Barrow

These two battleships were taken over from Chile while completing in British yards, in order to prevent their purchase by the Russians, which would have upset the balance of naval power in the Far East on the outbreak of the Russo-Japanese War. They were smaller and lighter armed than their Royal Navy contemporaries, and as they were not homogeneous they were used as flagships on distant stations up to 1914.

Appearance: Distinctive on account of their large goosenecked cranes amidships, but could be distinguished from one another by their bridge-wings. *Triumph* had conspicuous shelters on each wing, whereas *Swiftsure* had none.

Careers

Swiftsure: Flagship of East Indies Squadron on outbreak of war, and carried out patrol and escort duties in Red Sea; defended Suez Canal November 1914, and transferred to Dardanelles March 1915; returned to Chatham late in 1916 to pay and disarm; was under consideration for use as block ship for projected Zeebrugge operation in 1917, but became overflow ship; stripped in 1919 and used as a target; sold 18 June 1920 to Stanlee Shipbreaking Co.

Triumph: In reserve at Hong Kong on outbreak of war, but hurriedly recommissioned with crews of laid-up Yangtze gunboats; assisted Japanese forces in capture of Tsingtau; transferred to Dardanelles early in 1915, and after taking part in various support duties, torpedoed by *U.21* while firing off Gaba Tepe 25 May 1915. This loss, coupled with that of *Majestic* two days later, caused the withdrawal of all battleships from the Gallipoli beach-heads.

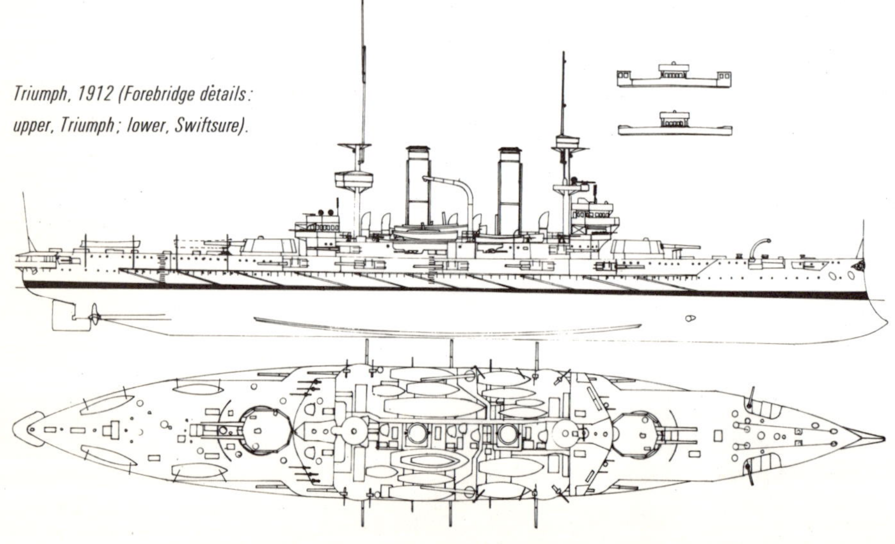

Triumph, 1912 (Forebridge details: upper, Triumph; lower, Swiftsure).

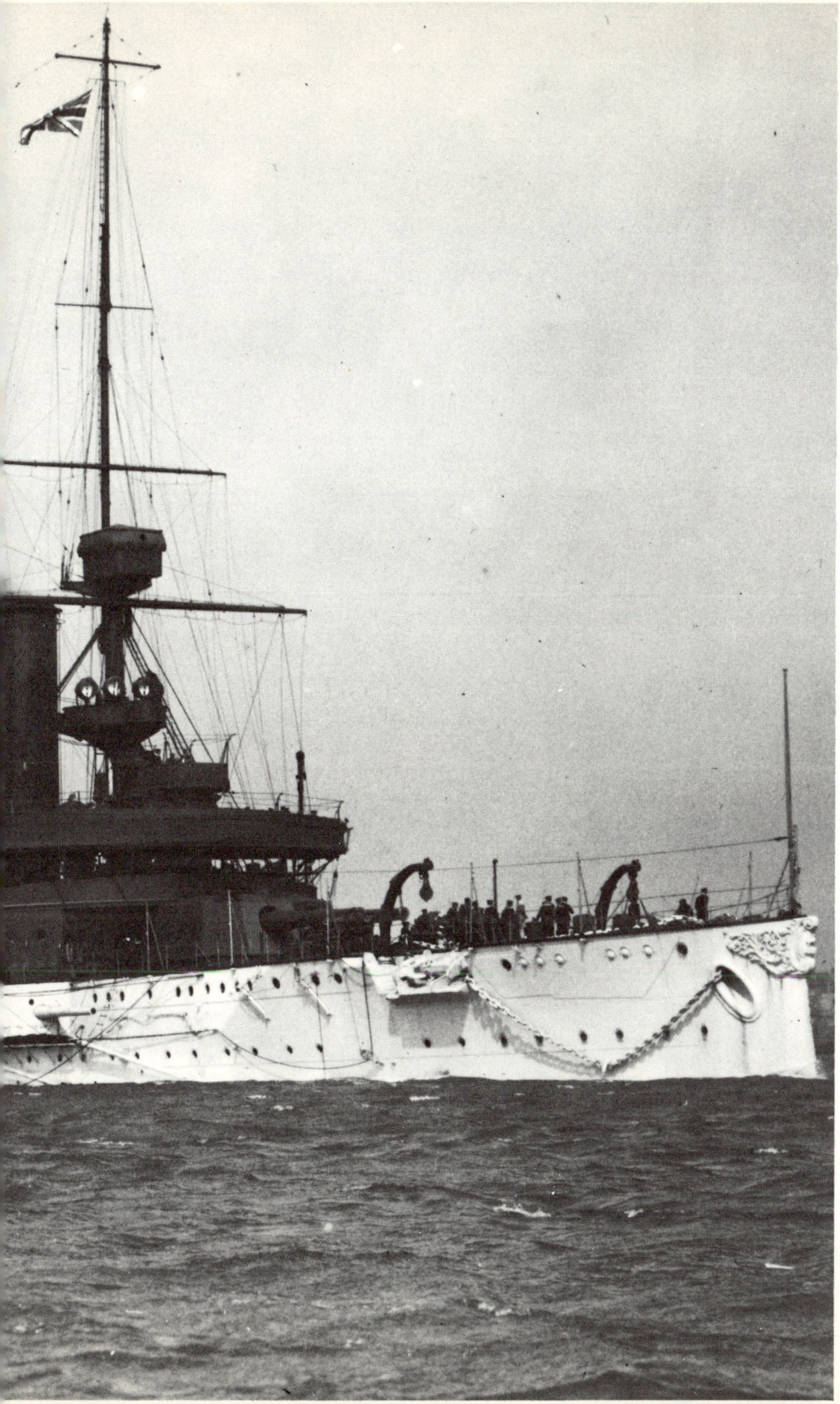

Above, *Triumph at Gallipoli exercising her torpedo nets (IWM).*

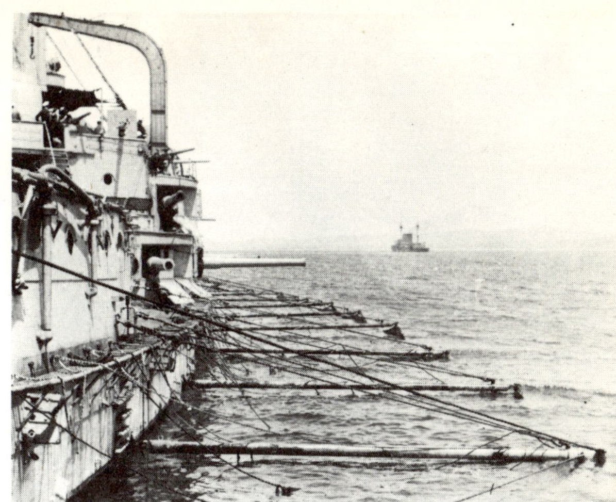

Left, *Swiftsure in 1913–14 in Far East paint scheme. Note the large gooseneck cranes amidships typical of this ship and her sister, and the searchlight platform above the bridge. This was the former fighting top. Note also the torpedo nets carried below the 7·5in gun battery (NMM).*

Above left, Britannia in 1913–14 showing the main features of the King Edward class – large equal-size funnels, masts without fighting tops, and 9·2in turrets at the corners of the superstructure. Note that the 6in guns amidships have been run in and housed; this was done to avoid fouling boats lying alongside – in time of war these guns would normally be visible (NMM).

Above right, King Edward VII sinking after striking a mine off Cape Wrath, 6 January 1916 (IWM).

Left, Britannia sinking after having been torpedoed on 8 November 1918 by German submarine U.50 (Authors collection).

Below left, Africa in 1916 (IWM).

Below right, Commonwealth in 1920 with considerable wartime modifications for shore bombardment. The pole foremast has been replaced by a tripod and the three midships 6in guns in the main deck battery have been replaced by two 6in guns between the 9·2in turrets. Also note the enlarged searchlight positions on the after superstructure and on the fire control platform on the mainmast (NMM).

King Edward VII class

Displacement: 15,700tons (at load draught)
Dimensions: 425ft×78ft×24ft 6in–26ft 9in
Guns: 4×12in 40 cal (2×2)
4×9·2in 45cal (4×1)
10×6in 50cal (10×1)
14×12pdrs (14×1); most removed
14×3pdrs (14×1); most removed
Torpedo Tubes: 4 submerged 18in (beam)
Armour: 9–4in belt, 2½–1in decks, 12–6in barbettes
Machinery: 2 sets 4-cylinder vertical triple expansion, 18,000hp = 18½knots; 10–16 boilers of various makes (see Notes)
Coal Capacity: 950/2200tons+380tons (all excepting Zealandia)
Endurance: 7000miles at 10knots
Complement: 777
Cost: £1,300,000 average ($5,200,000)

	Laid Down	Launched	Completed	Built
*King Edward VII	8 Mar 1902	23 July 1903	Feb 1905	Devonport DY
Hibernia	6 Jan 1904	17 June 1905	Jan 1907	Devonport DY
Dominion	23 May 1902	25 Aug 1903	July 1905	Vickers, Barrow
Commonwealth	17 June 1902	13 May 1903	Mar 1905	Fairfield
Hindustan	25 Oct 1902	19 Dec 1903	July 1905	John Brown
Zealandia (ex-New Zealand)	9 Feb 1903	4 Feb 1904	June 1905	Portsmouth DY
*Britannia	4 Feb 1904	10 Dec 1904	Sept 1906	Portsmouth DY
Africa	27 Jan 1904	20 May 1905	Nov 1906	Chatham DY

These handsome ships were the last in a line of continuous development back to the 1880s. Although the final design work was completed by Sir Philip Watts, in appearance they reflect the ideas of their initiator, Sir William White. Designed at a time when the need for heavier gunpower was evident, they were in their day the most powerful battleships afloat. After the introduction of the term 'dreadnought' they were often described as 'intermediate dreadnoughts' as a tribute to their powerful secondary armament.

The 9·2in gun had been chosen for the secondary armament since with capped shell it was equal to the heaviest battleship armour at the modest battle-ranges in vogue in 1901–2. However, later experience showed that the similarity in size between 12in and 9·2in shell-splashes made long-range gunnery difficult. As a result, further impetus was given to the development of the 'all-big-gun' type both in England and abroad.

Machinery: As the class were laid down while the last arguments of the fatuous 'Battle of the boilers' raged, their boiler arrangements were oddly assorted. *King Edward VII* had 10 Babcock & Wilcox and 6 cylindrical boilers; *Dominion* and *Commonwealth* had 16 Babcock & Wilcox; *Zealandia* had 12 Niclausse and 3 cylindrical boilers; the remaining four had 12 Babcock & Wilcox and 3 cylindrical boilers.

Appearance: Their big round funnels made the class the most handsome of the British predreadnoughts, and they were also distinguished as the first to have fire-control positions on both masts in place of the fighting tops found in older ships. From 1915 onwards they underwent the usual modifications, and in 1916–17 *Commonwealth*, *Zealandia*, *Britannia*, *Africa* and *Hibernia* lost all ten 6in guns from the battery in return for four single guns in shields on the upper deck.

Commonwealth was altered for coastal bombardment in 1918, with tripod foremast, director control top, and anti-torpedo bulges fitted. *Zealandia* was similarly altered but did not receive bulges.

Careers

Africa: With 3rd B.S. Home Fleet prewar, but with the rest of that squadron transferred to Grand Fleet in August 1914; April 1917–November 1918 attached to 9th Cruiser Squadron; accommodation ship from April 1919; sold 30 June 1920 for breaking up.

Britannia: 3rd B.S. as *Africa*; badly damaged by two-day stranding off Inchkeith in January 1915; with 3rd B.S. transferred to Nore early 1916 to guard Thames Estuary; torpedoed 9 November 1918 by *U.50* while on passage from Freetown to Gibraltar (although hit by 2 torpedoes, she floated upright for three-and-a-half hours).

Commonwealth: With 3rd B.S. as *Africa*; refitted December 1914–February 1915 before returning to Grand Fleet; refitted 1918 for shore bombardment (see above); seagoing gunnery training ship at Invergordon 1919–21; sold 18 November 1921 and broken up in Germany.

Dominion: 3rd B.S. as *Africa*; temporarily Flagship 3rd B.S. Grand Fleet August – September 1915; with 3rd B.S. to Nore 1916; April 1918 accommodation ship at Chatham; sold 9 May 1921 for breaking up.

Hibernia: 3rd B.S. as *Africa*; November 1915 transferred from Grand Fleet to Dardanelles as Flagship of Admiral Fremantle; accommodation ship at Nore 1919; sold 8 November 1921.

Hindustan: 3rd B.S. as *Africa*; with 3rd B.S. transferred from Grand Fleet to Nore early May 1916; 1917–18 based in Swin as depot ship for personnel and ships training for Zeebrugge operations; sold 9 May 1921.

King Edward VII: Flagship 3rd B.S. Grand Fleet from August 1914; flag shifted to *Dominion* August – September 1915 during repairs to guns; while a private ship mined 6 January 1916 off Cape Wrath (minefield laid by raider *Möwe*); both engine rooms flooded, and with a rising sea she had to be abandoned after 13 hours' struggle to save her.

Zealandia: Was *New Zealand* until December 1911, when the name was transferred to the new battle cruiser purchased by the Dominion of New Zealand; pre 1914 with 3rd B.S. as *Africa*; transferred from Grand Fleet to Dardanelles November 1915; refitted for shore bombardment in 1918 (see above); accommodation ship at Portsmouth 1919; sold 8 November 1921.

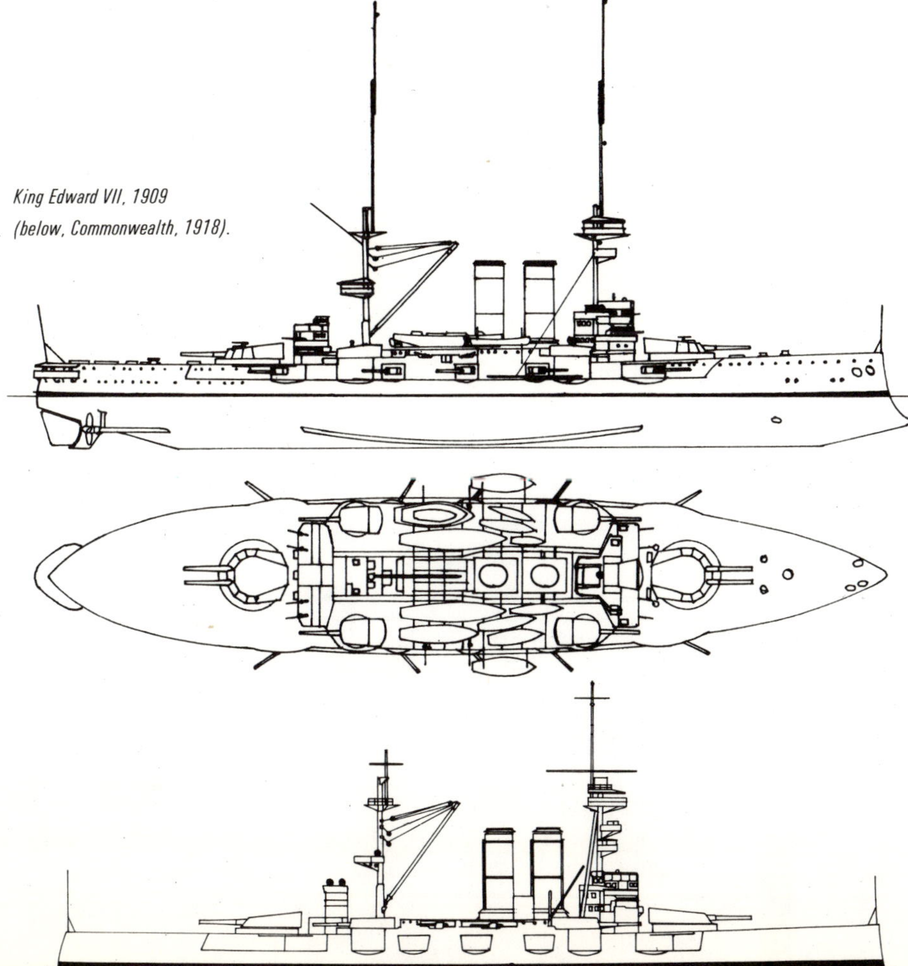

King Edward VII, 1909 (below, Commonwealth, 1918).

Britannia at Portsmouth in October 1906 (Admiralty).

Dreadnought

Displacement: 17,110tons (at load draught)
Dimensions: 490ft×82ft×26ft 6in
Guns: 10×12in 45cal (5×2) 24×12pdrs 18cwt (24×1); reduced to 10 by 1916
Torpedo Tubes: 5 submerged 18in (4 beam, 1 stern)
Armour: 11–4in belt, 11in barbettes, 3–1½in decks
Machinery: 4-shaft Parsons turbines, 23,000hp = 21knots; 18 Babcock & Wilcox boilers
Coal Capacity: 900/2900tons
Oil Capacity: 1120tons
Endurance: 6620miles at 10knots
Complement: 695–773
Cost: £1,783,883 ($7,135,532)

Below, Dreadnought as she appeared at the outbreak of war, still painted in Home Fleet dark grey, with torpedo nets and 12pdr guns on the turrets (IWM).

	Laid Down	Launched	Completed	Built
Dreadnought	2 Oct 1905	10 Feb 1906	Oct 1906	Portsmouth DY

The *Dreadnought*'s effect on history is too well known to be recapitulated here, but it is necessary to point out the important features which she introduced: steam turbines with quadruple shafting, multiple heavy gun positions, and tripod masting, etc. The Parsons turbines not only delivered greater power, raising battleship speeds to 21 knots, but lowered the centre of gravity, and so enabled a much heavier armament to be carried at a good height above the waterline. The greater reliability and smooth running of the turbine reduced maintenance costs, and enabled the Fleet to spend more time at sea.

The rapid pace of naval expansion which followed the building of the *Dreadnought* meant inevitably that she was soon outclassed by newer ships. Even before Jutland she was released from the Grand Fleet with the *King Edwards* to be stationed in the Thames. There were a number of weak points in her design, particularly in layout, but these were far outweighed by her overwhelming supremacy in gunpower, speed and protection. Her period of construction, 366 days from keel-laying to trials, remains unsurpassed even in these days of prefabrication, and nothing better demonstrates the great advantage held by the British before 1914; even if they did not always produce the very best ships, they were able to outbuild any nation.

Appearance: During refit in 1915 the topmasts were reduced in height, and the control top was enlarged to take a director position. By 1916 12pdrs had been removed from No. 1 turret, both beam turrets, and from all positions in the superstructure with the exception of those port and starboard of the bridge.

In common with later dreadnoughts her bridge was enlarged and extended during 1916–17 to accommodate the growing numbers of bridge personnel. Anti-aircraft guns were added, two 12pdrs on the after quarterdeck, and two 12pdrs were also added on disappearing mountings, but their position cannot be verified (probably one on each beam turret). In 1917 the after control position on the dwarf tripod mainmast was suppressed, having always been useless, and it became a searchlight platform.

Career
Flagship 4th B.S. on outbreak of war (Home Fleet); joined Grand Fleet August 1914 with remainder of 4th B.S.; while carrying out a sweep in the North Sea on 18 March 1915, she rammed and sank *U.29* (Otto Weddigen); major refit in Spring 1916; in May of that year transferred to 3rd B.S. as flagship, based on Sheerness to guard against German raid on Thames Estuary; rejoined Grand Fleet March 1918 (4th B.S.) until paid off July 1918; joined Reserve at Rosyth February 1919; on Sale List 31 March 1920, and sold 9 May 1921 to T. W. Ward for £44,000 ($176,000), less than 2½ per cent of her original cost; arrived at Inverkeithing 2 January 1923 for breaking up.

Dreadnought (detail: 1910).

Lord Nelson class

	Laid Down	Launched	Completed	Built
Lord Nelson	18 May 1905	4 Sept 1906	Oct 1908	Palmer
Agamemnon	15 May 1905	23 June 1906	June 1908	Beardmore

Displacement: 16,000tons approx
(at load draught): 16,500 Navy List
Dimensions: 410ft×79ft 6in×25ft 3in
–27ft
Guns: 4×12in (2×2)
10×9·2in (4×2, 2×1)
24×12pdrs (24×1); some removed
c.1916–17
10×3pdrs (10×1); some removed
c.1916–17
Torpedo Tubes: 5 submerged 18in
(4 beam, 1 stern)
Machinery: 2 sets triple expansion,
16,750hp = 18knots; 15 Yarrow
boilers
Coal Capacity: 900/2171tons
Oil Capacity: 1090tons
Endurance: 9180miles at 10knots
Complement: 800/817
Cost: £1,540,000 ($6,160,000)

With the *King Edward VII* class, these were the most battle-worthy of the older British ships—and they were actually newer than the *Dreadnought*, having been completed a year later. They were an alternative to the *Dreadnought* design, and would have been the prototype for future development if the Admiralty had not sanctioned the change to oil fuel, turbines and a uniform armament. As with the *King Edwards*, the 9·2in gun caused trouble when long-range gunnery came into vogue, as its shell-splash was too similar to the 12in. Note the increase of radius brought about by better bunker-capacity; the oil capacity was also greatly increased as compared with the *King Edwards*.

Appearance: Quite unlike other British ships, having a distinctly French look. Both refitted at Malta Dockyard in 1917 with taller funnels. The first British battleships since the *Captain* (1870) with a tripod mast, which became standard in later ships.

Agamemnon: In August 1914 serving with 5th B.S., and took part in Channel patrols; to Dardanelles February 1915, taking part in the early bombardments; in May 1916 shot down Zeppelin *L.85* at Salonika; with *Lord Nelson* alternated between Mudros and Salonika in readiness for a sortie by the *Goeben*; unfortunately, when the *Goeben* and *Breslau* made their sortie in January 1918 both ships were off station, leaving the German ships free to sink two monitors without trouble; armistice with Turks signed on board November 1918; returned to Chatham to pay off February 1919; recommissioned April 1923 as disarmed target for gunnery and aircraft (wireless-controlled); paid off for disposal 31 December 1926 and broken up.

Lord Nelson: Flagship of 2nd B.S. August 1914 and covered B.E.F. transports; Dardanelles February 1915 with *Agamemnon*; spent the remainder of the war in the Mediterranean, including Aegean and Black Sea operations; returned to home waters in May 1919 and paid off into reserve at Sheerness; sold 4 June 1920 to Stanlee Co., Dover, who resold her 8 November 1921 to Slough Trading Co. for breaking up in Germany.

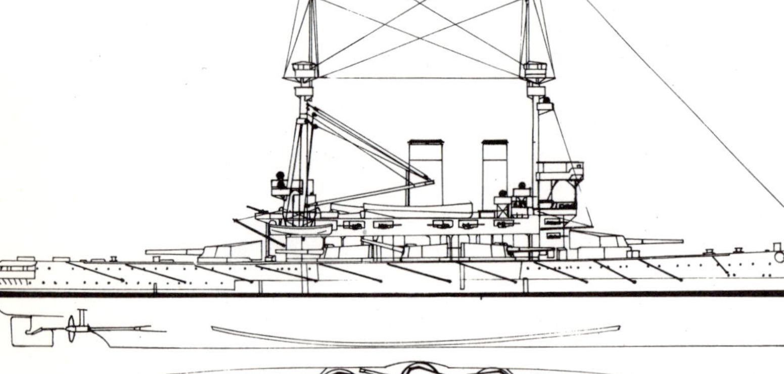

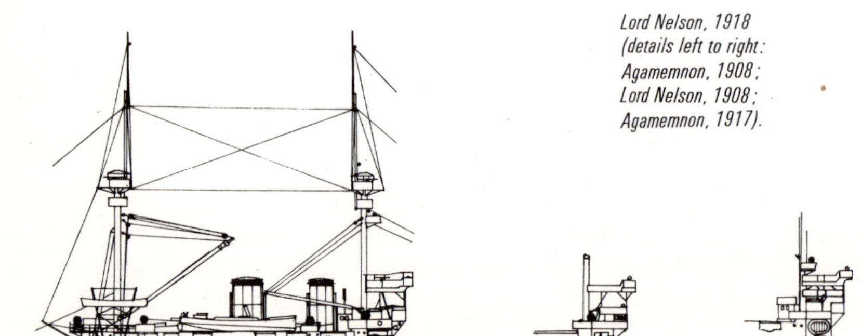

*Lord Nelson, 1918
(details left to right:
Agamemnon, 1908;
Lord Nelson, 1908;
Agamemnon, 1917).*

Above right, *Lord Nelson in 1914, with torpedo nets and additional searchlight platforms on the tripod mainmast. Note the radically different appearance of this ship and her sister, with an unbroken flush deck and three 9·2in turrets on each side between the 12in turrets (NMM).*

Below right, *Agamemnon at Mudros in 1915 with her torpedo nets out. Note the false bow-wave and the mottled camouflage scheme on the turrets and upperworks (IWM).*

Left, *Lord Nelson at Mudros in 1916 still with torpedo nets and short funnels (IWM).*

Left, *Agamemnon after returning home from the Mediterranean 1918–19 (IWM).*

Left, *Lord Nelson laid up at Sheerness in June 1919 with Queen alongside (IWM).*

Invincible class

Displacement: 17,250tons (Navy List), 17,370 at load draught
Dimensions: 530ft×78ft 6in×26ft 3in
Guns: 8×12in 45cal (4×2) 16×4in Q.F. (16×1): 12 by 1917, and 3×4in AA (3×1) 1×3in 7 MG
Torpedo Tubes: 5×18in submerged (4 beam, 1 stern)
Armour: 6in belt; 7in turrets; 10in conning tower; 2½–1in decks
Machinery: 4-screw Parsons turbines, 41,000hp = 25knots; 31 Yarrow boilers (Babcock in Indomitable)
Coal Capacity: 1000/3084tons
Oil Capacity: 710–725tons
Endurance: 3090miles at 10knots
Complement: 784
Cost: £1,600,000 ($6,400,000)

	Laid Down	Launched	Completed	Built/Engined
Indomitable	1 Mar 1906	16 Mar 1907	June 1908	Fairfield, Govan
Inflexible	5 Feb 1906	26 June 1907	Oct 1908	John Brown
*Invincible	2 Apr 1906	13 Apr 1907	Mar 1908	Armstrong

These ships remain the most controversial ships of their period. Lord Fisher had been the driving force behind the design, which was meant to provide a 'dreadnought' equivalent to the old armoured cruiser, with sufficient armour to allow her to reconnoitre without fear of being driven off by hostile battleships, but enough speed to avoid action. Unfortunately, Fisher insisted that his design must have 12in guns, which inevitably led to them being thought of as capital units. Had they been armed with the 9·2in already in service they would never have been mistaken for ships fit to lie in the line of battle, and it is possible that they might not have suffered so badly at Jutland. But as things turned out, it was asking too much of any flag officer to have 17,000ton ships armed with 12in guns and not to use them in the battle line.

The main features of the *Dreadnought* were adopted: a heavy outfit of 12in guns, Parsons turbines driving four shafts, tripod masting, and a light secondary armament, but the enormous increase in boiler power meant that one turret had to be dropped, and armour was five inches thinner. To achieve a margin of four knots over the *Dreadnought*, horsepower was almost doubled and a finer hull form was adopted. As length was so much increased it proved possible to adopt an echelon arrangement for the 12in turrets, which meant that the new ships could fire all eight guns on the broadside. However, blast effect made this advantage largely theoretical, and cross-deck firing caused a considerable degree of strain on the hull.

Whatever criticism can be levelled against Fisher and the Board of Admiralty which he persuaded to pass the design of the *Invincibles*, one should be wary of criticising the design itself. As Sir Philip Watts pointed out, he had been asked to produce a ship capable of mounting eight 12in guns and steaming at 25 knots, but armoured against 11in and 12in shells fired at a range of 9000yds. The mistake lay in assuming that a ship designed to fight efficiently at a given range would have any choice in actual battle; the *Indefatigable* engaged German battle cruisers at Jutland at a range of 15,500yds. Even so, the scanty evidence available on the Jutland losses leads modern historians to look very closely at the possibility of all three battle cruisers, *Invincible*, *Indefatigable* and *Queen Mary* having been sunk by a failure of their cordite handling, rather than armour penetration.

First, there is the fact that all three were hit on turrets— No. 2 or No. 3 in the *Invincible*, No. 1 and No. 4 in the *Indefatigable*, and No. 3 in the *Queen Mary*. Apart from their heavy armour, turrets were designed to prevent flash from shell bursts travelling down to the magazines and shellrooms. From the explosion which nearly sank the *Lion* we know that British cordite did flash off when it should merely have burned, whereas German cordite under the same conditions tended to be stable. From lack of battle experience all navies had tended to assume that their magazine arrangements were adequate, and some time saving had been achieved during gunnery practices by leaving flashtight scuttles open, or by stowing too many shells and charges in the turrets and working chambers. The Germans learned their lesson with the *Seydlitz* at the Dogger Bank in 1915 (and naturally the British had no chance to profit from their experience).

On the solitary occasion when the *Invincibles* were used in one of their designed roles, ie: to run down enemy armoured cruisers on the trade routes, their speed and gunpower proved decisive, but what was overlooked was the fact that any of the more modern British armoured cruisers could have sunk the *Scharnhorst* and *Gneisenau* without any great difficulty, and at far less cost. For their other roles, pursuing stragglers in a fleet action or carrying out enveloping movements, they proved too lightly built and would have had to be 60 per cent larger (like the *Queen Elizabeth* class) to combine the necessary protection and speed.

Appearance: *Indomitable* and *Inflexible* had their fore funnels raised 1910–11 on account of the bridges being smoked out, but

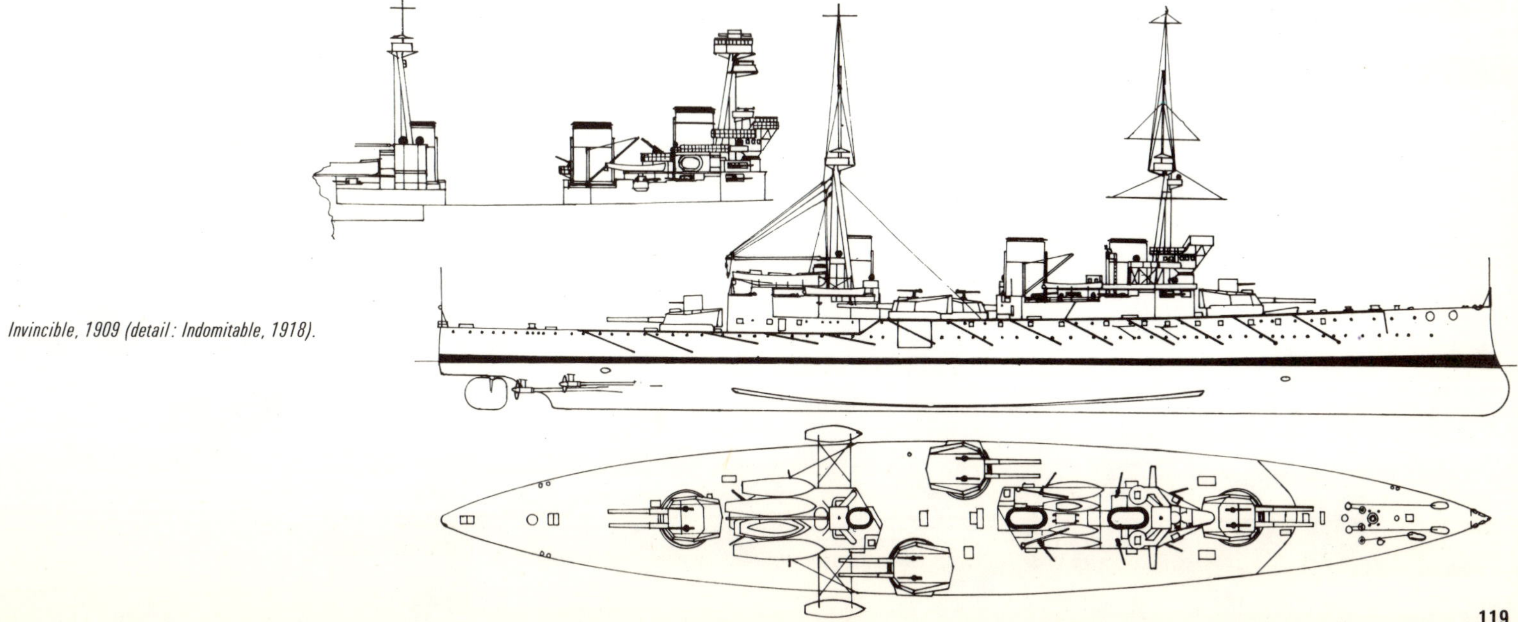

Invincible, 1909 (detail: Indomitable, 1918).

Above, Invincible in 1907 (Author's collection). *Below,* Inflexible in 1918 with torpedo nets removed, large control tops, and aircraft on turrets 2 and 3. Note also the anti-aircraft gun between the first and second funnels (NMM). *Bottom of page,* Indomitable in 1913 after her forefunnel had been raised. Note the original bridgework, 4in guns on turret roofs, torpedo nets and so on. The double row of scuttles shows that there is only a thin strake of armour along the waterline (NMM). *Right,* a prewar view of Inflexible showing clearly the arrangement of the boat stowage (NMM).

Invincible's was not raised until after the Battle of the Falklands in December 1914. In 1917 the two survivors had their search-lights resited in towers around the third funnel, shields fitted to the 4in guns, and the bridgework and control top extended.

Armament and Protection: After Jutland it was realised that the battle cruisers were very vulnerable, and steps were taken to remedy the most glaring deficiencies. Additional armour was added to the roofs of all turrets and to the magazine crowns, the ammunition supply was overhauled, and better flashtight shutters provided. In 1917 improved fire-control was installed, and range clocks were added on the masts, with corresponding deflection scales on the turrets. All 4in guns were removed from the turret tops in 1916–17, and in 1917 four 4in guns were resited in new positions on either side of the forward super-structure, and three 4in anti-aircraft guns were added. Aircraft platforms were provided on No. 2 and No. 3 turrets.

Careers

Indomitable: In Mediterranean on outbreak of war, having been with 2nd Battle Cruiser Squadron since August 1913; took part in search for *Goeben* and *Breslau* 4–10 August 1914; to Dardanel-les for blockade August–November, and took part in long-range bombardment of Sedd-el-Bahr on 3 November; returned home to refit before joining the Grand Fleet (3rd Battle Cruiser Squadron); in action at Dogger Bank 26 January 1915, and towed the damaged *Lion* home at 7knots; in action at Jutland, 31 May 1916, but suffered no damage; June 1916 transferred to 2nd Battle Cruiser Squadron, until January 1919, when she paid off; Flagship of Nore Reserve from February to July 1919 and finally paid off for disposal 31 March 1920; on Sale List 7 April 1920 and sold December 1922.

Inflexible: On outbreak of war Flagship, 2nd Battle Cruiser Squadron and Commander-in-Chief, Mediterranean Fleet; took part in search for *Goeben* and *Breslau* 4–10 August 1914; ordered home 19 August and sent to Humber; Shetland Patrol 1–10 October, covering the passage of the big Canadian troop convoy; ordered to South America 4 November following the news of the disastrous Battle of Coronel, and repairs completed by Devonport Dockyard by 11 November; arrived at Fort William, Falkland Islands on 7 December; coaling began im-mediately, but she and *Invincible* had to raise steam when the enemy was sighted next morning; suffered no damage in ensuing action against *Scharnhorst* and *Gneisenau*; took part in subsequent search for cruiser *Dresden* but ordered to Mediterranean 19 December and called at Gibraltar to refit; 24 January 1915 relieved *Indefatigable* as Flagship of Dardanelles squadron; took part in naval attack on the Narrows 18 March; hit in bridge and forward control top by Turkish shellfire (9 casualties) and mined later that day; withdrew with heavy underwater damage in way of fore torpedo flat, and flooded with 2000tons of water on board (29 killed); repaired at Gibraltar and rejoined Grand Fleet 19 June 1915 (3rd Battle Cruiser Squadron); at Jutland 31 May 1916, but suffered no casualties; paid off into Nore Reserve January 1919 and laid up for disposal 31 March 1920; sold December 1922.

Invincible: Flagship 1st Battle Cruiser Squadron on outbreak of war; in action at Battle of Heligoland Bight 28 August 1914, and then joined 2nd Battle Cruiser Squadron; hoisted flag of Admiral Sturdee 4 November and left Cromarty for Devonport; sailed for South America with *Inflexible* 11 November; Battle of Falklands 8 December, and hit twice below waterline and had foreleg of tripod shot away (1 casualty); rejoined Grand Fleet and 2nd Battle Cruiser Squadron as Flagship March 1915; May 1915 became Flagship of 3rd Battle Cruiser Squadron, which was attached to Grand Fleet to replace 5th Battle Squadron just before Jutland; at Jutland 31 May 1916, and blew up at 6.34pm under heavy fire from *Derfflinger* and *König* (Admiral Hood and over 1000 men killed, with only 5 survivors).

Bellerophon class

Displacement: 18,800tons (at load draught)
Dimensions: 490ft×82ft 6in×27ft
Guns: 10×12in 45cal (5×2) 16×4in Q.F. (16×1)
Torpedo Tubes: 3 submerged 18in (2 beam, 1 stern)
Armour: 10–5in belt ; 9–5in barbettes, 3–1½in decks, 2–1in torpedo bulkhead
Machinery: As Dreadnought, Parsons turbines, 23,000hp = 20¾knots; 18 Babcock boilers (Yarrow in Temeraire)
Coal Capacity: 900/2468tons
Oil Capacity: 842tons
Endurance: 5720miles at 10knots
Complement: 780
Cost: £1,723,000 average ($6,892,000)

	Laid Down	Launched	Completed	Built
Bellerophon	3 Dec 1906	27 July 1907	Feb 1909	Portsmouth DY
Superb	6 Feb 1907	7 Nov 1907	May 1909	Armstrong, Elswick
Temeraire	1 Jan 1907	24 Aug 1907	May 1909	Devonport DY

Virtually repeat *Dreadnoughts*, with slightly increased beam, thinner armour and so on to compensate for an additional tripod mast and heavier secondary armament. The most glaring fault in the *Dreadnought*, the siting of the control top abaft the forward funnel, was rectified by stepping the funnel abaft the mast, but the designers virtually committed the same error by siting the second tripod and control top where it would be smoked out by the forward funnel.

The other weak point of the *Dreadnought* was her puny armament of 12pdr guns, which were the smallest guns capable of disabling a destroyer or torpedo-boat. The *Bellerophons* adopted a smaller number of 4in weapons, but similarly disposed on turret-tops and in the superstructure. An important innovation was the anti-torpedo bulkhead, the first fitted in a British capital ship. This was an inner longitudinal bulkhead to localise the effect of torpedo hits.

Appearance: After the outbreak of war topmasts were reduced in height. In 1916 all 4in were removed from the turrets, where they were constantly exposed to blast and spray; new double-decked positions were provided in the superstructure, thus keeping the number to sixteen. However, in the following year a 4in and a 3in anti-aircraft gun were added aft (one on the quarterdeck and one on the after superstructure). Many minor variations were carried out between 1917 and 1918, including the fitting of a clinker screen or funnel cap to the forward funnel in *Bellerophon*.

Careers
Bellerophon: 1st B.S. Home Fleet on outbreak of war, but transferred to 4th B.S. Grand Fleet August 1914; Jutland 31 May 1916; reduced to reserve 1919 at Sheerness; served as turret drill ship there 1919–20; sold 8 November 1921 to Slough Trading Co. and left in tow for Germany 14 September 1922.
Superb: Service as *Bellerophon*, but Flagship; to Mediterranean in 1918, and as Flagship of Vice-Admiral Gough-Calthorpe led Allied Fleet through Dardanelles after Turkish surrender; 1919 in reserve as turret drill ship, and used subsequently as target; sold 12 December 1922 for breaking up by Stanlee Shipbreaking Co. at Dover.
Temeraire: Service as *Bellerophon* and *Superb*; to Mediterranean 1918; served as seagoing training ship for cadets in 1919; sold 1 December 1921 to Stanlee Shipbreaking Co., Dover.

Below, *Bellerophon in 1909 (Admiralty).*

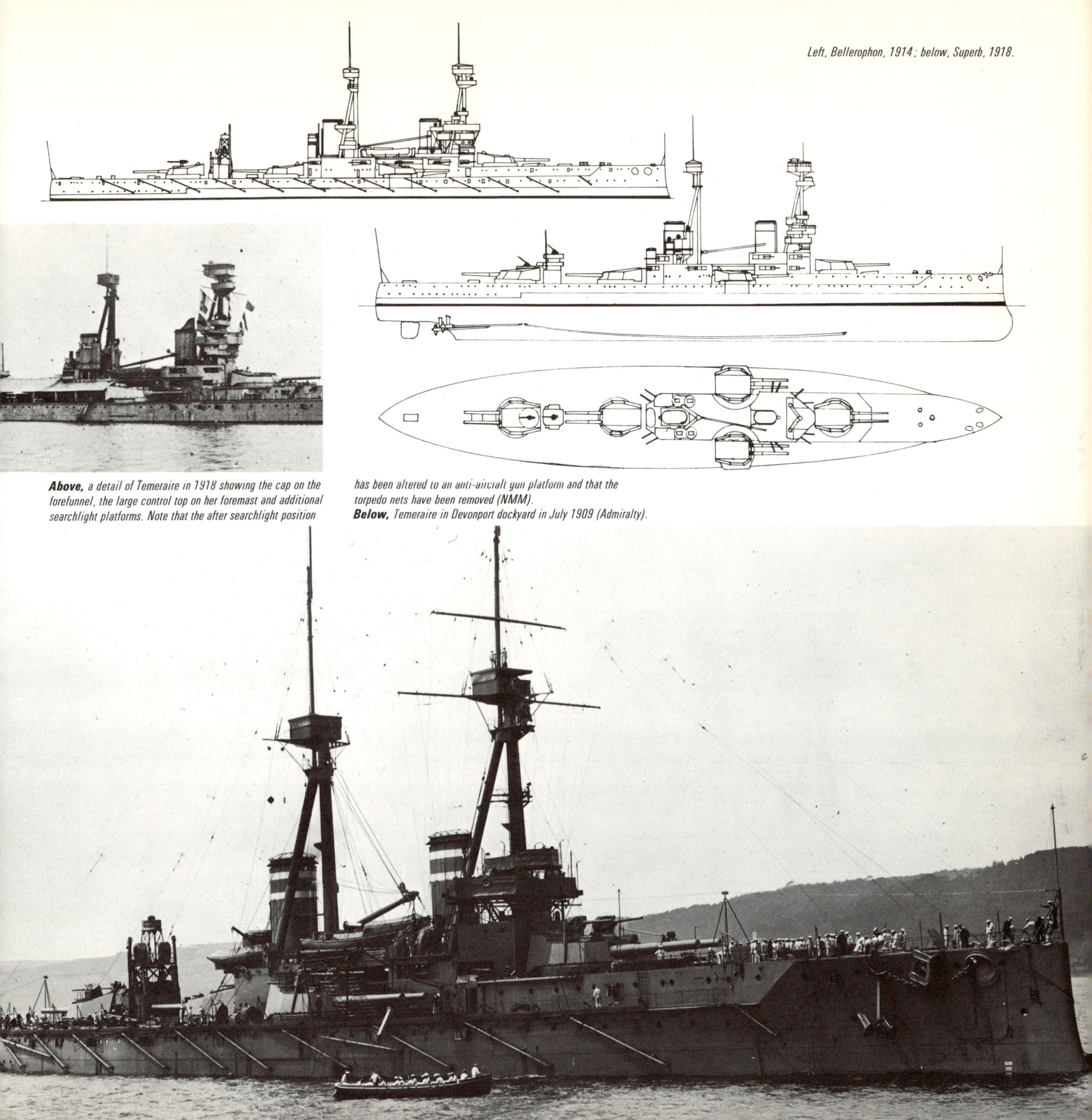

Above, a detail of Temeraire in 1918 showing the cap on the forefunnel, the large control top on her foremast and additional searchlight platforms. Note that the after searchlight position has been altered to an anti-aircraft gun platform and that the torpedo nets have been removed (NMM).

Below, Temeraire in Devonport dockyard in July 1909 (Admiralty).

Vanguard, 1911 (detail, Collingwood, 1918).

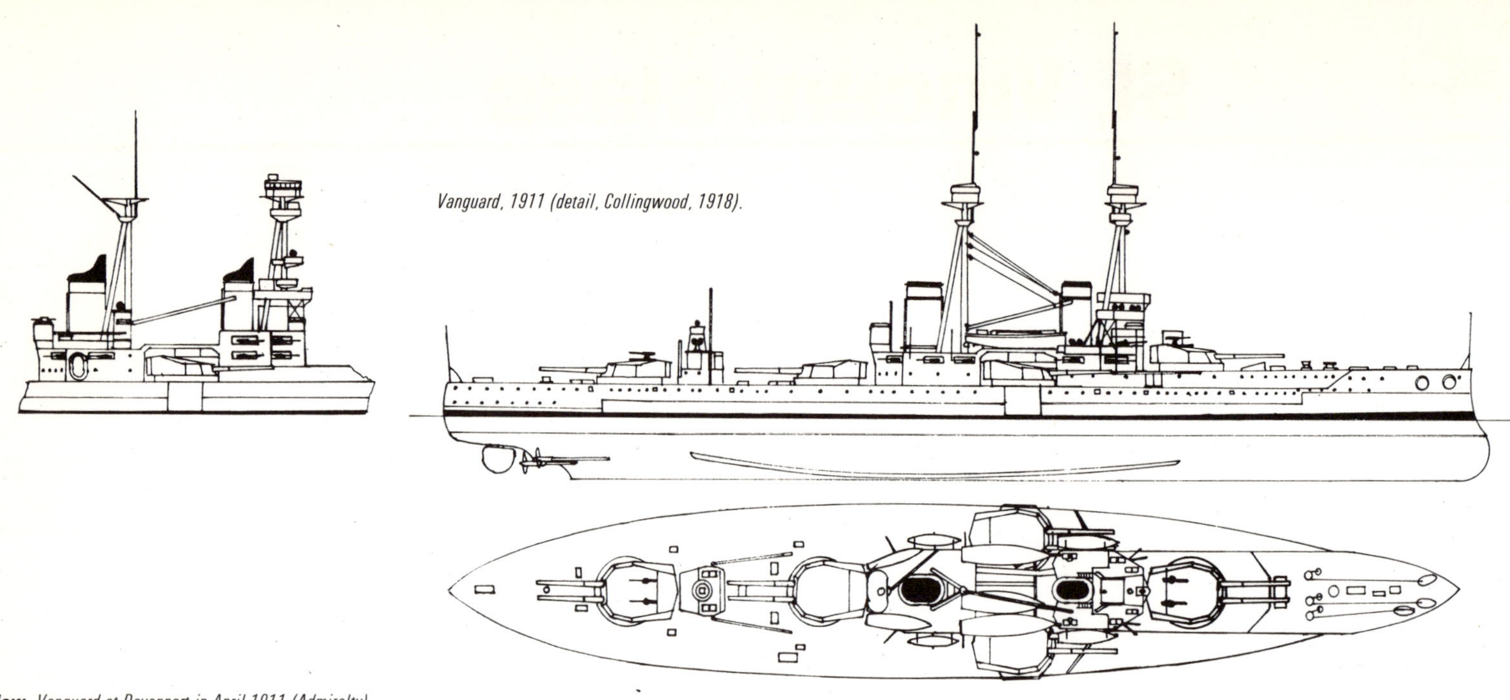

Below, *Vanguard at Devonport in April 1911 (Admiralty).*

St. Vincent class

Displacement: 19,560tons (normal load condition), 21,060tons normal load after 1916–17 alterations

Dimensions: 500ft×84ft×28ft 7in

Guns: 10×12in 50cal (5×2) 18×4in Q.F. (18×1); by 1918 only 13×4in, including 1×4in AA 4×3pdrs

Torpedo Tubes: 3×18in (2 beam, 1 stern, but stern TT removed 1916)

Armour: As Bellerophon, but thinner plating at bow and stern

Machinery: 4-screw Parsons turbines, 24,500hp = 21 knots; 18 Babcock boilers (Yarrow in Collingwood)

Coal Capacity: 900/2800tons

Oil Capacity: 940tons+190tons patent fuel

Endurance: 6900tons at 10knots

Complement: 758

Cost: £1,700,000 average ($6,800,000)

	Laid Down	Launched	Completed	Built/Engined
Collingwood	3 Feb 1907	7 Nov 1908	Apr 1910	Devonport DY/ H. Leslie
St. Vincent	30 Dec 1907	10 Sept 1908	May 1909	Portsmouth DY/ Scotts
*Vanguard (ex-Rodney)	2 Apr 1908	22 Feb 1909	Feb 1910	Vickers, Barrow

Slightly improved versions of the *Bellerophons*, with a more powerful 12in gun, and slightly more horsepower to offset the rise in displacement. The reduction in beam and draught, coupled with the slightly increased length resulted in greater efficiency, and the *St. Vincents* achieved their design speed easily.

Appearance: By August 1914 all had short topmasts. They differed from the *Bellerophons* in having a thicker after funnel, and the 12in gun turrets were differently shaped. Two 4in on No. 1 turret had been removed before the war, and by 1917 another five had been removed from the superstructure. One of two 3in anti-aircraft guns mounted in 1915–16 was replaced by a 4in anti-aircraft gun on the quarterdeck by 1918.

Torpedo nets were removed in 1916 (before Jutland), and in 1916–17 all three had clinker screens added to the fore funnel (plus after funnel in *Collingwood*); the after control top on the mainmast was suppressed at the same time, having been rendered useless by smoke interference. *Collingwood* was fitted with aircraft platforms on two turrets.

Careers

Collingwood: August 1914 1st Battle Squadron (having been Flagship up to that time) and joined Grand Fleet; notable as the ship in which the late King George VI, then H.R.H. The Duke of York, served as a lieutenant; Jutland 31 May 1916, and suffered no damage; post-Jutland joined 4th Battle Squadron, until paid off in 1919; from 1919 to 1922 in Reserve at Devonport serving as gunnery training ship; sold 12 December 1922 to Cashmore, Newport for breaking up.

St. Vincent: August 1914 she was already serving as Flagship 1st Battle Squadron, and as such joined the Grand Fleet; Jutland 31 May 1916, and suffered no casualties; relieved as Flagship 1917 and transferred to 4th Battle Squadron; paid off 1919 into Portsmouth Reserve for service as turret drill ship; sold 1 December 1921 to Stanlee for breaking up at Dover.

Vanguard: Serving in 1st Battle Squadron and joined Grand Fleet in August 1914; Jutland 31 May 1916, suffering no damage; destroyed by a magazine explosion at Scapa Flow on the night of 9 July 1917, with the loss of 804 men (believed to have been caused by unstable cordite); one of only two British dreadnought battleships lost during the war.

Right, *1914 views of St. Vincent (top) and Vanguard (bottom) showing funnel bands and torpedo nets still in place. Note that the bridges have been enlarged (NMM).*

Displacement: 19,680tons (load condition)
Dimensions: 510ft×85ft×28ft 6in
Guns: 10×12in 50cal (5×2)
16×4in Q.F. (16×1)
4×3pdrs
Torpedo Tubes: 3×18in (2 beam, 1stern); stern tube suppressed 1916
Armour: 10–2½in belt; 9–5in barbettes; 11in turrets and CT; 3–¾in decks
Machinery: 4-shaft Parsons turbines, 25,000hp = 21 knots; 18 Yarrow boilers
Coal Capacity: 900/2710tons
Oil Capacity: 790tons
Endurance: 6330miles at 10knots
Complement: 759
Cost: £1,527,916 ($6,111,664)

Hercules and Colossus

Displacement: 20,225tons (load condition)
Dimensions: As Neptune, but maximum draught 28ft 9 in
Guns: As Neptune; 13×4in guns in 1917 (including 1×4in A.A.) and 1×3in A.A.
Torpedo Tubes: 3×21in (2 beam, 1 stern); stern tube later removed
Armour: 11–7in belt; 11–4in barbettes; 11in turrets and CT; 4–1½in decks
Machinery: As Neptune, but 18 Babcock boilers in Colossus
Coal Capacity: 900/2900tons
Oil Capacity: 800tons
Endurance: 6680miles at 10knots
Complement: 755
Cost: £1,535,000 average ($6,140,000)

	Laid Down	Launched	Completed	Built/Engined
Neptune (ex-Foudroyant)	19 Jan 1909	30 Sept 1909	Jan 1911	Portsmouth DY/ Harland & Wolff
Colossus	8 July 1909	9 Apr 1910	July 1911	Scotts
Hercules	30 July 1909	·10 May 1910	Aug 1911	Palmers

Neptune

The *Neptune* was the first breakaway from the original *Dreadnought* layout, in an attempt to overcome the disadvantage of losing the fire of one or other beam turret when firing on the broadside. The U.S. Navy had shown the way with the centreline turrets in the *Michigan* and subsequent classes, and the original proposals for the *Dreadnought* had included suggestions for superimposed turrets. The British were hampered by the design of their turrets, as the sighting hoods at the front end of the turret made it impossible for No. 2 turret to fire over No. 1 turret without concussing the occupants of the sighting hoods.

As a compromise the *Neptune* was given echeloned guns amidships, as in the *Invincible*, but as ten guns were considered essential for a battleship, No. 4 turret had to be superimposed in order to avoid a great increase of length which would in turn increase the cost. The design of the turrets meant that No. 4 turret could never fire dead astern, but as strength of broadside was the main criterion this was not considered any severe handicap. As with the *Invincibles* the strain of crossdeck firing caused trouble; she reflects the muddled state of British theories of battleship design during this period.

Appearance: *Neptune* retained the long 12in guns (50cal) of the *St. Vincent* class in their distinctive turrets. Although completed with level funnels she had her fore funnel heightened in 1912 to reduce smoke interference. To keep the decks clear the boats were all carried on a 'flying bridge' between the funnels, but this was so obviously in danger of being wrecked by shellfire and becoming a hazard that the forward one was removed just after the outbreak of war.

In 1916 the twin searchlights were replaced by singles, and the

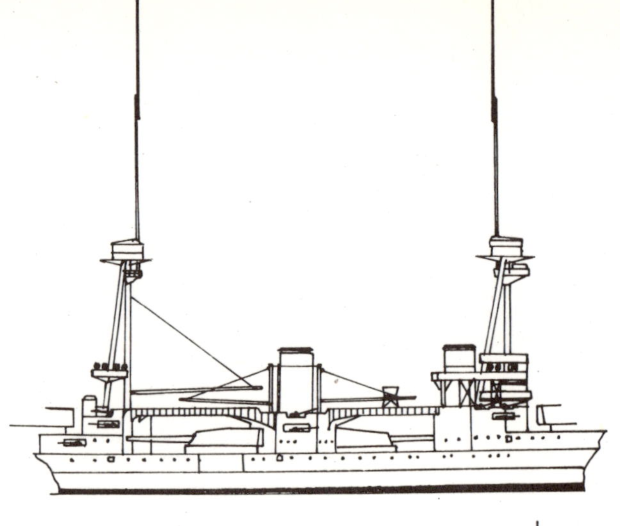

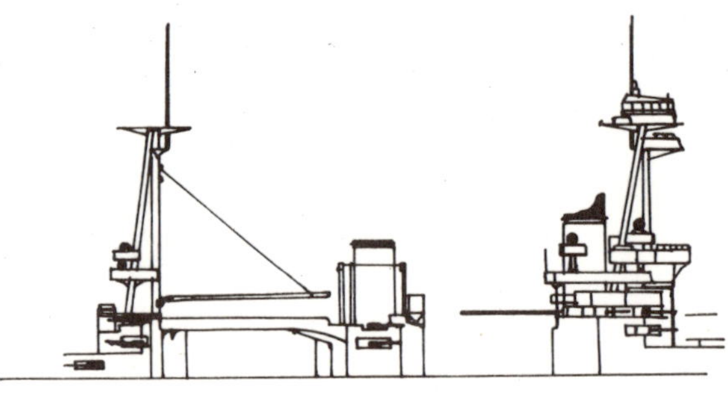

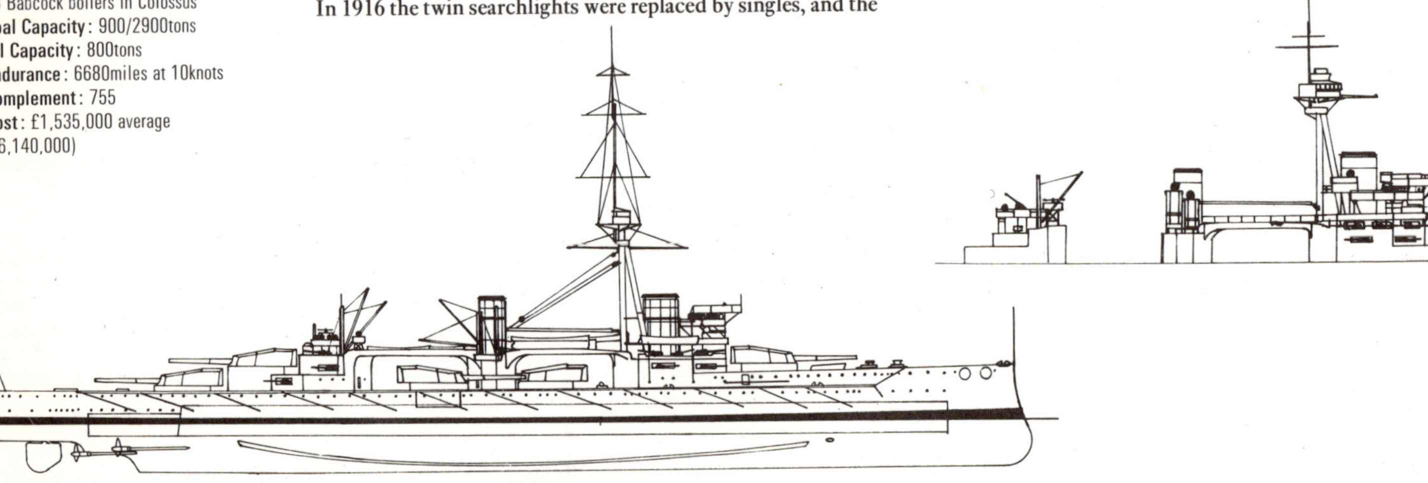

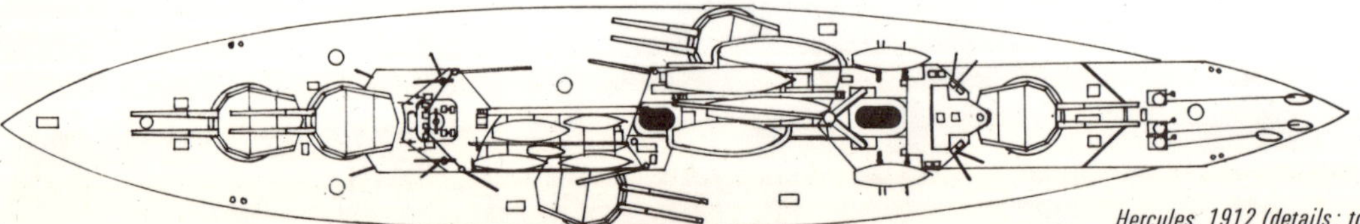

Hercules, 1912 (details: top, Neptune, 1911; middle, Neptune, 1918; bottom, Colossus, 1918).

fore funnel was given a clinker screen, as it was still smoking out the bridge. In common with other dreadnoughts her bridge structure was enlarged, a director top was added to the fore tripod, and the after tripod control position was suppressed.

Hercules and Colossus

Built one year later (1909 Programme) as sisters of the *Neptune*, but incorporating several improvements. First, the 21in torpedo was much more effective than the 18in in range and speed, and although now seen as totally useless in this role, the torpedo was assumed to be essential in battleship *versus* battleship tactics. Second, the effect of smoke on the after control position was at last admitted, and as weight-saving was very important in this design, the after tripod was dropped, and did not reappear in any subsequent design for the Royal Navy.

The other important difference between the *Hercules* and *Neptune* was in protection. The *Dreadnought*'s 11in barbette armour had been reduced in the *Bellerophon*, and then further reduced until it was only 9in thick in the *Neptune*, and other armour reflected the same tendency to be whittled down in order to save weight and restrict dimensions. The *Hercules*, however, was given an 11in belt; but to compensate for this extra protection the anti-torpedo bulkhead was omitted. Thus in the four years between the laying down of the *Dreadnought* and the laying down of the *Hercules*, protection of British battleships had not been improved in contrast to foreign navies.

Appearance: Once again funnels proved one of the most troublesome features of the design, which seems yet more evidence of the muddled state of British design at this time. The fore funnel had to be raised to stop smoke interference with the bridge, but as the single tripod and its control position had been sited just behind the funnel, the control top now became virtually unusable. This arrangement had been severely criticised when the *Dreadnought* appeared, and it had been dropped; now it re-appeared, at a time when good gunnery and fire-control were more important than they had ever been.

Hercules had shields to her 4in guns, whereas *Colossus* had open ports with dropping lids. As with *Neptune* one of the flying decks was removed soon after the outbreak of war, but in this case it was the after one. Alterations to bridges, control tops and so on, conformed to those for *Neptune* during the war, but no funnel cap was fitted. After the Armistice *Colossus* was used as a training ship, and appeared in Victorian black and white livery, which looked utterly incongrous. Unlike *Neptune*, the 4in were nearly all mounted in the forward superstructure.

Careers

Colossus: Serving with 1st Battle Squadron in August 1914 and joined Grand Fleet; Flagship 1st B.S. at Jutland 31 May 1916, and was hit during main fleet action, the only one of Jellicoe's battleships to be damaged (2 shells hit in forward superstructure, causing 5 casualties); transferred to 4th Battle Squadron subsequently to 1919; recommissioned 1919 as cadets' training ship at Devonport, and sold in July 1928 to the Alloa Shipbreaking Co.

Hercules: Serving with 1st Battle Squadron on outbreak of war, and transferred to 8th Battle Squadron, Grand Fleet; Jutland 31 May 1916, and later Flagship 4th Battle Squadron; on 3 December 1918 carried International Armistice Commission to Wilhelmshaven; sold 8 November 1921 to Slough Trading Co. and arrived at Kiel to be broken up October 1922.

Neptune: With 1st Battle Squadron prewar, and joined Grand Fleet August 1914; collided with neutral steamer in fog 23 April 1916; 4th Battle Squadron 1917–18 and in Reserve 1919–22; sold 1 September 1922 to Hughes Bolckow and broken up at Blyth.

Top, Neptune in 1913 and as she appeared at the outbreak of war. Note the torpedo nets, high topmast and funnel bands (NMM). Centre, Colossus in 1918 after the flying bridge between the second funnel and the after superstructure had been removed. Note also that the bridgework had by this time been extended (NMM). Bottom, Hercules in 1918; she has had the after flying bridge removed, searchlight towers have been added and the bridgework has been extended (NMM)

Indefatigable class

Displacement: 18,500tons (load condition); 22,080tons (full load)
Dimensions: 555ft×80ft×27ft
Guns: 8×12in 50cal (4×2)
16×4in Q.F. (16×1)
4×3pdrs
Torpedo Tubes: 2×18in (beam, submerged)
Armour: As Invincible class
Machinery: 4-shaft Parsons turbines, 44,000hp = 25knots; 31 Babcock & Wilcox boilers
Coal Capacity: 1000/3170tons
Oil Capacity: 840tons
Endurance: 6330miles at 10knots
Complement: 800
Cost: £1,600,000 average ($6,400,000)

	Laid Down	Launched	Completed	Built/Engined
*Indefatigable	23 Feb 1909	28 Oct 1909	Feb 1911	Devonport DY/ John Brown
New Zealand	20 June 1910	1 July 1911	Nov 1912	Fairfield
Australia	23 June 1910	25 Oct 1911	June 1913	John Brown

As the tempo of construction speeded up after the appearance of the *Dreadnought* and then the *Invincible*, the British were tempted to save time by producing a second trio of battle cruisers only slightly better than the *Invincibles*. This expedient undoubtedly worked well, as a reluctant Parliament was persuaded to sanction the building of one under the 1908 Estimates, while the Dominions of Australia and New Zealand paid for two more. As the cost worked out at £82 10s ($329) per ton, the *Indefatigable* was the cheapest capital ship built in this century, and in that respect the British and Dominion Parliaments could feel satisfied that their taxpayers' money had been well spent. However, the economy of cost was achieved by repeating the *Invincible* hull, but 'stretching' it to allow the midships turrets to fire more effectively on either beam. The design of the original battle cruisers could be justified in the light of the speed with which it was prepared, but to repeat all the errors in a later class was inexcusable.

The misjudgement of Lord Fisher's regime in sanctioning

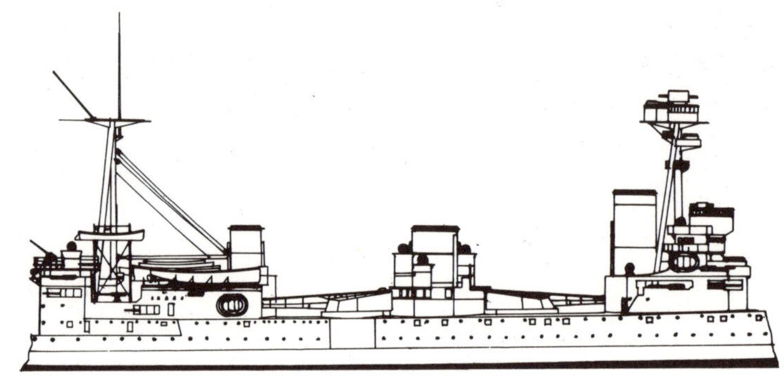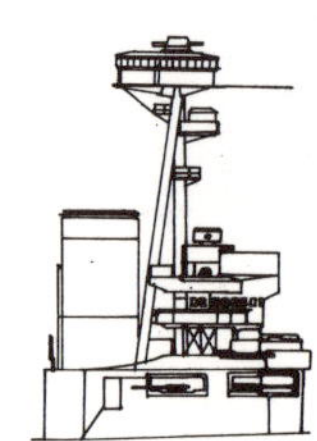

New Zealand, 1913 (details: above left, New Zealand, 1918; above, Australia, 1918).

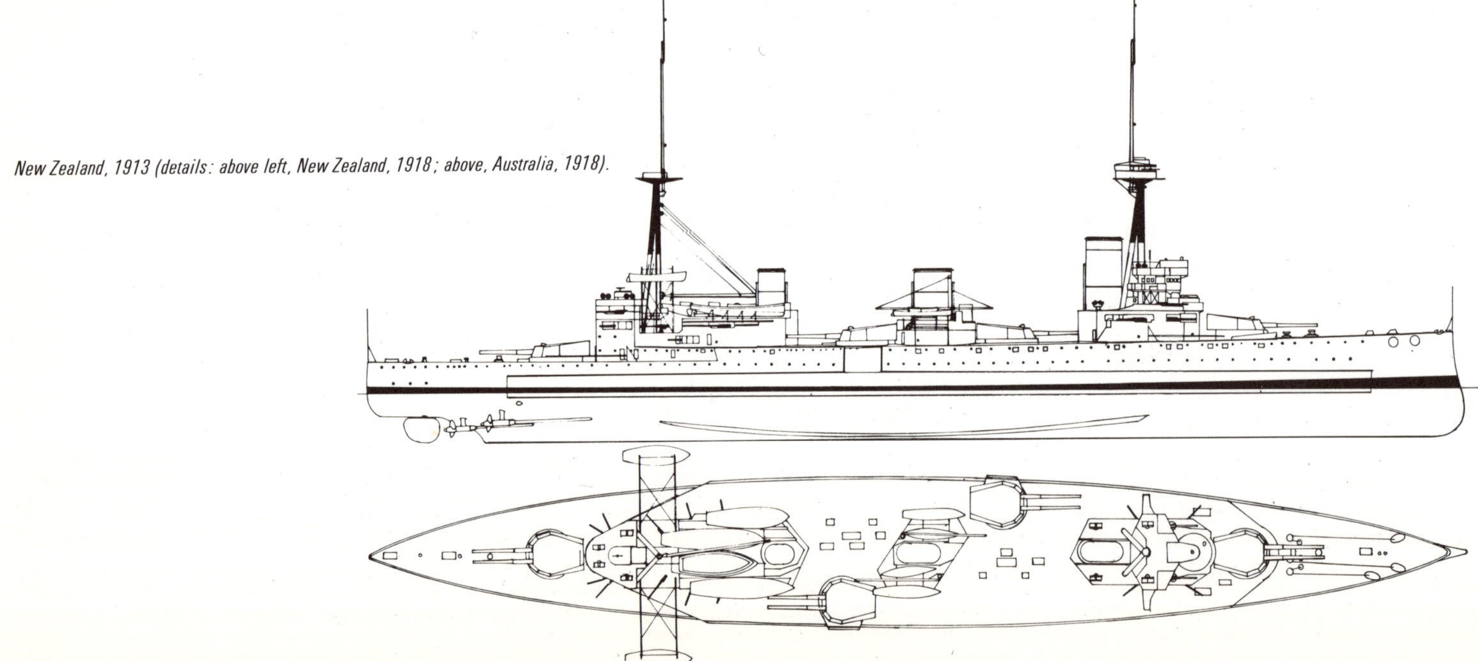

the building of the *Indefatigables* was apparent as early as 1908, when it was known that the Germans would be building their own battle cruisers. It was no longer a question of the *Invincible* type destroying enemy cruisers by sheer weight of gunpower, but of standing up to 11in or 12in gunfire, which should have been out of the question. Unfortunately the zeal with which Fisher lobbied the British Press trapped him, for the published protection of the *Indefatigable* (like the *Invincible* before her) was overstated by one or two inches. Thus Press and Parliament were told that these handsome ships were on a par with the German *Von der Tann*, when the German battle cruiser prototype had nearly four inches more armour on the belt, and nearly two inches more deck armour.

The tragedy of the *Indefatigable* design is that it could have been a lot better, even allowing for the inherent dangers of poor magazine protection. The enormous freeboard absorbed far too much tonnage, and her allowance of fuel was too generous for North Sea operations. Another 1000tons, coupled with some attempt at reduction of freeboard and superstructure would have produced a capital ship worthy of the name.

Appearance: With the same tall tripods and flat-sided funnels, they resembled the *Invincibles*, but they were distinguished by the wide spacing of the funnels. In all three the forward funnel was raised during building to avoid smoke interference. During World War I, *c*.1916–17, the after control top was suppressed as a result of smoke interference in both *New Zealand* and *Australia*. Throughout her service with the Grand Fleet *New Zealand* was distinguished by having a white ensign painted on either side of her control top; both ships had the usual additions to bridgework in 1917–18, and aircraft platforms etc.

Career

Indefatigable: Transferred to Mediterranean in December 1913 and still serving there in August 1914 to cover the German battle cruiser *Goeben* (2nd Battle Cruiser Squadron); took part in search for *Goeben* and in early Dardanelles operations; bombarded Cape Helles 3 November 1914 and temporary Flagship of Admiral Carden until relieved January 1915 by *Inflexible* and sent to refit at Malta; rejoined 2nd Battle Cruiser Squadron in Grand Fleet in February; took part in first phase of battle cruiser action at Jutland 31 May 1916 but blew up under fire 1605 hours and sank with the loss of nearly all her company.

New Zealand: Completed for New Zealand Government, but on account of manpower and maintenance difficulties she was thereupon presented to the Royal Navy. With 1st Battle Cruiser Squadron of Grand Fleet from August 1914; became Flagship, 2nd Battle Cruiser Squadron during January and February 1915, and fought at Battle of Dogger Bank 24 January 1915; fired at *Blücher*, and Rear-Admiral Moore succeeded to command when *Lion* was temporarily out of action; damaged in collision with *Australia* 22 April 1916 but repairs completed in time for Jutland, 31 May 1916; hit once on No. 4 turret but suffered no casualties; transferred to 1st Battle Cruiser Squadron June 1916 but reverted to 2nd B.C.S. when relieved by *Renown* September 1916; in 1919 conducted Admiral Jellicoe on his tour of the Dominions and listed for disposal under Washington Treaty; sold December 1922.

Australia (H.M.A.S.): In Australian waters on outbreak of war as Flagship of Royal Australian Navy; to North American and West Indies Station as Flagship November–December 1914 and hunted German armed merchantmen after Battle of Falklands; January 1915 joined Grand Fleet as Flagship of Rear-Admiral Pakenham (2nd Battle Cruiser Squadron); in collision with *New Zealand* (q.v.) April 1916 and missed Jutland; rejoined 2nd Battle Cruiser Squadron June 1916 as Flagship to November 1918; returned to Australia 1919 to become Flagship, R.A.N. once more; listed for disposal under Washington Treaty 1922, and ceremonially scuttled off Sydney Heads.

Above, *Indefatigable at Devonport on 14 June 1911 (Admiralty).*

Above, *Australia as she appeared on completion in 1912, with the original simple bridgework. Note that the after fire control platform (on the mainmast) has still to be fitted (NMM).*

Above, *New Zealand in 1918, showing a complete range of wartime modifications. Note the enlarged forward control top, and the removal of the control top on the mainmast. Note also the aircraft and platform on No. 2 turret, the deflection scales on No. 4 turret, and the removal of torpedo nets (NMM).*

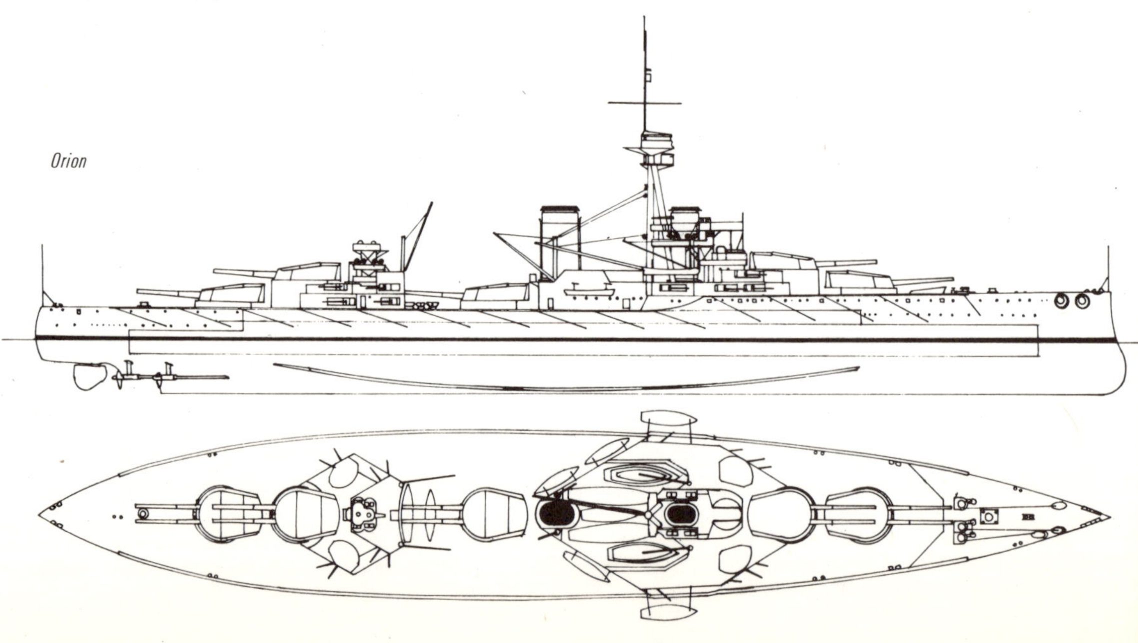

Orion

Right, two views of Monarch. Above, as she was in 1913–14 with torpedo nets, high wireless mast and funnel band. Note that she has a director control position added below the main fire control top on the tripod mast. This class was the first to receive the director firing system which later extended to all dreadnoughts, and also to some earlier ships (NMM).

Orion class

Displacement: 22,200tons (load draught); 25,870tons (deep load)
Dimensions: 545ft×88ft 6in×28ft 9in
Guns: 10×13·5in 45cal (5×2) 16×4in Q.F. (16×1); reduced to 13 1916–17 including one 4in A.A. 4×3pdrs
Torpedo Tubes: 3×18in (2 beam, 1 stern, submerged); stern tube removed 1916
Armour: 12–8in belt; 10–2in barbettes; 11in turrets and CT; 4–1in decks
Machinery: 4-shaft Parsons turbines, 27,000hp = 21knots; 18 Babcock boilers (Yarrow in Monarch)
Coal Capacity: 900/3300tons
Oil Capacity: 800tons
Endurance: 6730miles at 10knots
Complement: 752
Cost: £1,900,000 ($7,600,000)

	Laid Down	Launched	Completed	Built/Engined
Conqueror	5 Apr 1910	1 May 1911	Nov 1912	Beardmore
Monarch (ex-King George V)	1 Apr 1910	30 Mar 1911	Mar 1912	Armstrong, Elswick/H. Leslie
Orion	29 Nov 1909	20 Aug 1910	Jan 1912	Portsmouth DY/ Wallsend Slipway
Thunderer	13 Apr 1910	1 Feb 1911	June 1912	Thames I.W.

This class represented such a great increase in size and power that the Press immediately dubbed them 'superdreadnoughts'. They introduced many new features to British design—centreline superimposed turrets, the 13·5in guns, armour to upper deck level and so on, but they represent above all the end of that muddled period in British capital ship design typified by the *Indefatigable* and *Colossus*. The essence of the *Orion* class layout is simplicity, combined with a healthy balance between offence and defence. Unfortunately the old design of sighting hood was retained for the 13·5in turrets, which meant that the benefits of superimposed turrets were lost when firing on certain bearings, as the observers in the lower turrets would be concussed by blast.

The great innovation was the reversion to a calibre of 13·5in for the main armament for the first time since the *Revenge*. It had become obvious that there was a limit to improvements which could be made to the 12in gun: the length had been increased from 35 calibres to 50 calibres between 1893 and 1909, but whatever theoretical advantages might be gained in terms of muzzle velocity, range or penetration from a lighter shell and a longer gun, the fact remained that the latest mark of 12in gun did not fire accurately at the longer ranges. By dropping the muzzle velocity and increasing the bore it was found that shooting improved dramatically and that in addition there was less wear and tear on the barrel.

Despite their increase in gunpower and protection the *Orion* class suffered in one important respect when compared with their German contemporaries, the *Helgolands*. For the first time it was laid down that an increase in beam to provide better protection against underwater damage was not permissible, owing to the lack of large docks. The *Helgoland* class, with no such limits placed, had a beam five feet greater for roughly similar overall size, which allowed greater subdivision, a wing passage and torpedo bulkhead. In another respect the *Orions* were unfortunate, as the pernicious mast/funnel arrangement of the

Dreadnought and *Colossus* was revived, in spite of ample evidence against it.

Appearance: These were the last British dreadnoughts to have the tripod abaft the forward funnel. As built, the bridgework was very restricted and had to be extended during the war. *Thunderer* was the first ship fitted with director-firing gear, and had the distinctive director control top below the main top on the tripod; this was extended to the others by the outbreak of war. During 1917–18 all were given range clocks, deflection scales on turrets, and turret-platforms for aircraft.

Armament: The earlier mark of 13·5in gun (Mark V) was mounted, firing a 1250lb shell.

Careers

Conqueror: Serving in 2nd Battle Squadron at outbreak of war, and joined Grand Fleet; collided with *Monarch* and damaged her bows badly, 27 December 1914; with 2nd B.S. at Jutland 31 May 1916, but suffered no damage or casualties; served in postwar Fleet until discarded to conform with Washington Treaty; sold 19 December 1922 to Upnor Shipbreaking Co.

Monarch: Service as *Conqueror*; served in postwar Fleet until 1922, when she was discarded under Washington Treaty; used as a fleet target 20 January 1925, and attacked off Scilly Islands by aircraft, cruisers and battleships in turn; as she was still afloat at dusk she had to be sunk by deliberate fire from the *Revenge*.

Orion: Serving with 2nd Battle Squadron of Home Fleet on outbreak of war, and became Flagship, 2nd B.S. with the Grand Fleet; wore flag of Rear-Admiral A. C. Leveson at Jutland, 31 May 1916, suffering no damage; served in postwar Fleet until discarded in 1922; sold 19 December 1922 to Cox & Danks and broken up at Upnor.

Thunderer: Service as *Orion* and others, with 2nd Battle Squadron, Grand Fleet; although surplus to requirements under the Washington Treaty she was retained as a seagoing training ship for cadets until 1926 (replacing *Colossus*); sold to Hughes Bolckow 10 December 1926 but ran aground on her way to Blyth 24 December and did not arrive for breaking up until 14 April 1927.

Below, *Thunderer in Devonport dockyard, February 1913. Note that the torpedo nets are being rolled up and stowed on their shelf (NMM).*

Lion class

Displacement: 26,270tons (normal load); 29,680tons (full load)
Dimensions: 660ft×88ft 6in× 28ft 10in
Guns: 8×13·5in 45cal (4×2) 16×4in Q.F. (16×1): 15×4in (1917) and 1×3in A.A., 1×4in A.A. (Lion and Princess Royal) 4×3pdrs
Torpedo Tubes: 2×21in (beam, submerged)
Armour: 9–4in belt and turrets 10in CT 2½–1in decks
Machinery: 4-shaft Parsons turbines, 70,000hp = 27knots; 42 Yarrow boilers
Coal Capacity: 1000/3500tons (Queen Mary, 3700tons maximum)
Oil Capacity: 1135tons (Queen Mary 1130tons)
Endurance: 5610miles at 10knots
Complement: 997
Cost: £2,080,000 ($8,320,000)

	Laid Down	Launched	Completed	Built/Engined
Lion	29 Nov 1909	6 Aug 1910	May 1912	Devonport DY/ Vickers, Barrow
Princess Royal	2 May 1910	29 Apr 1911	Nov 1912	Vickers, Barrow
*Queen Mary	6 Mar 1911	20 Mar 1912	Sept 1915	Palmer/John Brown

To match the gunpower of the *Orions* a new class of battle cruisers was ordered in 1909. As the new ships were to make 27knots all restrictions on tonnage were lifted, and for the first time the term 'capital ship' was used to describe both battleships and battle cruisers. The *Lion* class displaced 4000tons more than the *Orions*, and nearly three times the horsepower, so it is not surprising that they made a tremendous impression on all who saw them. However, they were not the splendid ships that they seemed, for their armour only accounted for 23 per cent of displacement (as compared to the *Seydlitz*, 31 per cent).

Taking into account all the trouble with tripods and with unorthodox arrangements of turrets in earlier dreadnoughts, the layout of the *Lion* class can only be ascribed to a serious lapse on the part of the Admiralty Board or the Director of Naval Construction. First, the midships or No. 3 turret was restricted to arcs of 120° fire on either beam, when logic dictated that it should be superimposed aft, with normal arcs of fire. Second, the tripod foremast was put over a *raised* forefunnel, with the result that the control top became unusable from the heat as well as smoke. Last of all, the antiquated custom of placing the

bridge on top of the conning tower, where it was a dangerous encumbrance, was reintroduced for no apparent reason.

The layout of the turrets could not be changed, but the mast/ funnel combination could be. Despite opposition from the Board the new First Lord of the Admiralty, Winston Churchill, voted sufficient funds (£120,000) to take the two completed ships in hand for drastic modifications. As a result they became very handsome ships, with three tall funnels and a light pole foremast, the first seen in H.M. ships since the *Lord Nelson* and *Agamemnon*.
Protection: After the loss of the *Queen Mary* and the two earlier battle cruisers at Jutland it was immediately assumed that the *Lion* class suffered from too thin a belt. However, later research casts some doubt on this: true, the *Lions* were underarmoured for ships of their size, but there is no proof from analysis of the hits on *Princess Royal*, *Lion* or *Tiger* that 9in armour was easily penetrated by German heavy shell. Furthermore, *Queen Mary* was hit on No. 3 turret, as was *Lion*, which makes a cordite fire more likely as the cause of her loss. Whereas the *Invincible* and *Indefatigable* could have been destroyed by a penetration of their belt armour, this was not obviously so with the *Queen Mary*.
Appearance: *Queen Mary* differed slightly from the earlier two, in having round funnels instead of oval, and a single-storyed 4in gun battery forward. During 1917 the customary towers for searchlights were added on the third funnel in *Lion* and *Princess Royal*, and in 1918 *Lion* was given a clinker screen on her forefunnel. Both ships also received aircraft platforms on No. 3 and

Queen Mary, 1914 (details left to right: inset, Princess Royal; Lion, 1918; Queen Mary 1916; Lion, 1918).

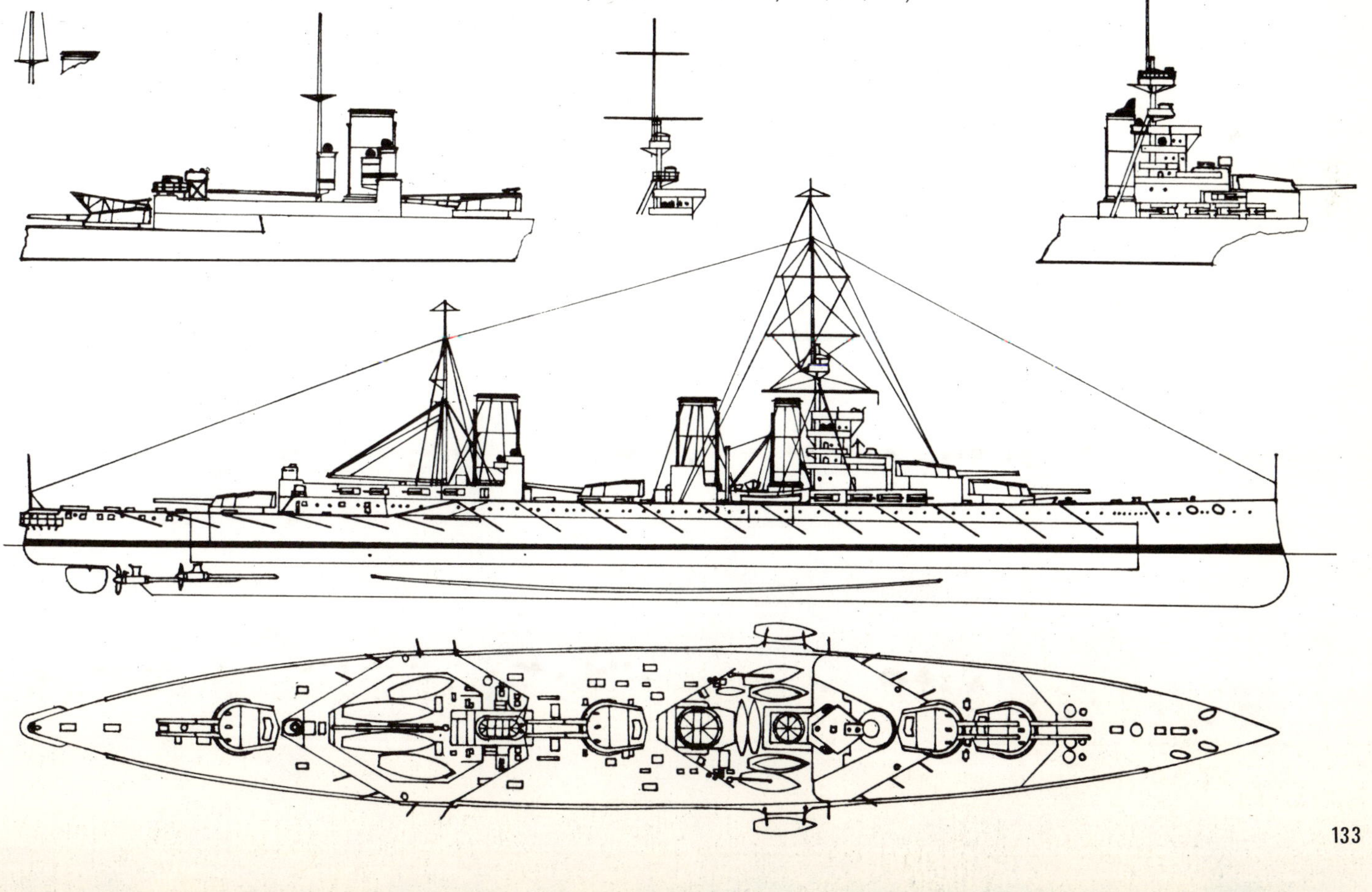

No. 4 turrets. After Jutland *Lion* had No. 3 turret removed for repairs, and went to sea with only three turrets for some weeks.

Careers

Lion: Flagship of 1st Battle Cruiser Squadron at outbreak of war, and joined Grand Fleet; Flagship Battle Cruiser Force 1915 to 1918 (Beatty relieved by Vice-Admiral Pakenham November 1916); Battle of Dogger Bank 24 January 1915, when she was hit by several German shells, including two which punched in plates and caused flooding; owing to contaminated feedwater she lost speed, and eventually had to be towed home by *Indomitable*; at Jutland 31 May 1916, and lost 100 men killed and 50 injured, mostly from hit on No. 3 turret which burned out the turret and nearly sank the ship.

Princess Royal: 1st Battle Cruiser Squadron August 1914, and took part with *Lion* and *Queen Mary* in Battle of Heligoland Bight 28 August 1914; Dogger Bank action 24 January 1915; became Flagship 1st Battle Cruiser Squadron after *Lion* became Flagship, Battle Cruiser Force; Jutland 31 May 1916, and extensively damaged, with hits on main fire control, 4in gun position, No. 4 turret, and after engine-room casings; fires only put out with difficulty as a result of damage to lighting systems and fire main; served postwar (1919–23) with 1st Battle Cruiser Squadron, but discarded to conform with Washington Treaty; sold December 1926.

Queen Mary: With 1st Battle Cruiser Squadron on outbreak of war, and joined Grand Fleet; Heligoland Bight action 28 August 1914; Dogger Bank action 24 January 1915; sunk by gunfire at Jutland, from *Derfflinger* and *Seydlitz*; she blew up in a tremendous explosion, with the loss of 1276 men (7 survivors).

Above left, *Princess Royal in 1914. Note that the forward net booms are in position, whereas the after booms are stowed (NMM).*

Above right, *Lion in 1918 with wartime modifications. She has lost her torpedo nets and has aircraft platforms on No. 3 and No. 4 turrets. A clinker screen was later added to her forefunnel (NMM).*

Below left, *a portrait view of Queen Mary taken on 30 August 1913 (Admiralty).*

King George V class

	Laid Down	Launched	Completed	Built/Engined
Ajax	27 Feb 1911	21 Mar 1912	Mar 1913	Scotts
*Audacious	23 Mar 1911	14 Sept 1912	Oct 1913	Cammell Laird
Centurion	16 Jan 1911	18 Nov 1911	May 1913	Devonport DY/ H. Leslie
King George V (ex-Royal George)	16 Jan 1911	9 Oct 1911	Nov 1912	Portsmouth DY/ Parsons

Displacement: 23,000tons (load draught), 25,700tons (full load)
Dimensions: 555ft×89ft×28ft 8in
Guns: 10×13·5in (5×2) 16×4in (16×1); reduced to 12 1915–17 and 2×4in A.A. added 1916–17 4×3pdrs
Torpedo Tubes: 3×21in (2 beam, 1 stern, all submerged); stern tube removed
Armour: 12–8in belt; 11in turrets and CT; 4–1in decks
Machinery: 4-shaft Parsons turbines, 27,000hp = 21knots; 18 Babcock boilers (Yarrow in Audacious and Centurion)
Coal Capacity: 900/3150tons (King George V maximum only 2870 tons)
Oil Capacity: 800tons
Endurance: 6730miles at 10knots
Complement: 782
Cost: £1,960,000 average ($7,840,000)

Slightly improved *Orions*, with redistributed secondary guns. Although designed to have the tripod between the funnels, the *Lion* fiasco caused them to have the mast before the funnels, and this became standard. When they appeared they were strongly criticised for having nothing bigger than a 4in armament to deal with torpedo-boats and destroyers—at a time when American ships had 5in, Japanese and French 5·5in, and the Germans and Austrians 5·9in guns. This was partly due to financial restrictions, as the Liberal Government which had just come to power in England was not prepared to sanction an increase in displacement to allow a 6in gun armament—and with Lord Fisher still at the Admiralty when the design was prepared there was no possibility of his 'all-big-gun' theories being abandoned.

Armament: A slightly improved 13·5in gun was carried, firing a 1400lb shell. For the first time rangefinders were incorporated in the turret roofs, which made it possible for turrets to go into local control at much greater ranges if necessary. For the first time since the beginning of the century secondary guns were mounted below the forecastle firing through open ports; this arrangement proved useless in rough weather, and the four guns were removed from all ships during the war.

Appearance: For the first time appeared that combination of heavy foremast and two large funnels which was to become typical of British capital ships up to the *Hood*. As completed all had a light pole mast, as in the *Lions*, since it was felt that the director did not require a heavy tripod. However, the pole was not rigid enough to support the weight, and gradually struts and flanges were tried and discarded in turn, until by 1917 all three survivors had a normal tripod similar to later ships.

The 4in guns in their ports abreast of No. 1 and No. 2 turrets were often hard to distinguish, as the ports were kept closed. By 1917 they had been plated in and the normal wartime alterations to appearance had been affected, including searchlight towers on the second funnel, aircraft platforms and so on.

Careers

Ajax: Serving with Home Fleet at outbreak of war; joined 2nd Battle Squadron of Grand Fleet in August 1914; Jutland 31 May 1916; to Mediterranean 1919 to take part in operations in Black Sea, covering withdrawal of White Russians; returned home to pay off 1924 and remained in Reserve at Nore until August 1926; sold November 1926 to Alloa Shipbreaking Co. for breaking up.

Audacious: With Home Fleet at outbreak of war; joined 2nd Battle Squadron, Grand Fleet; while based on Lough Swilly, she put to sea on 27 October 1914 for target practice; at 9am while under helm off Tory Island she struck a mine abreast of the port engine room; flooding in the port and centreline engine

Right, prewar view of King George V, showing her after 13·5in guns trained to port (Author's collection—the vertical line running down the mast is a crack on the negative).

KING GEORGE V.

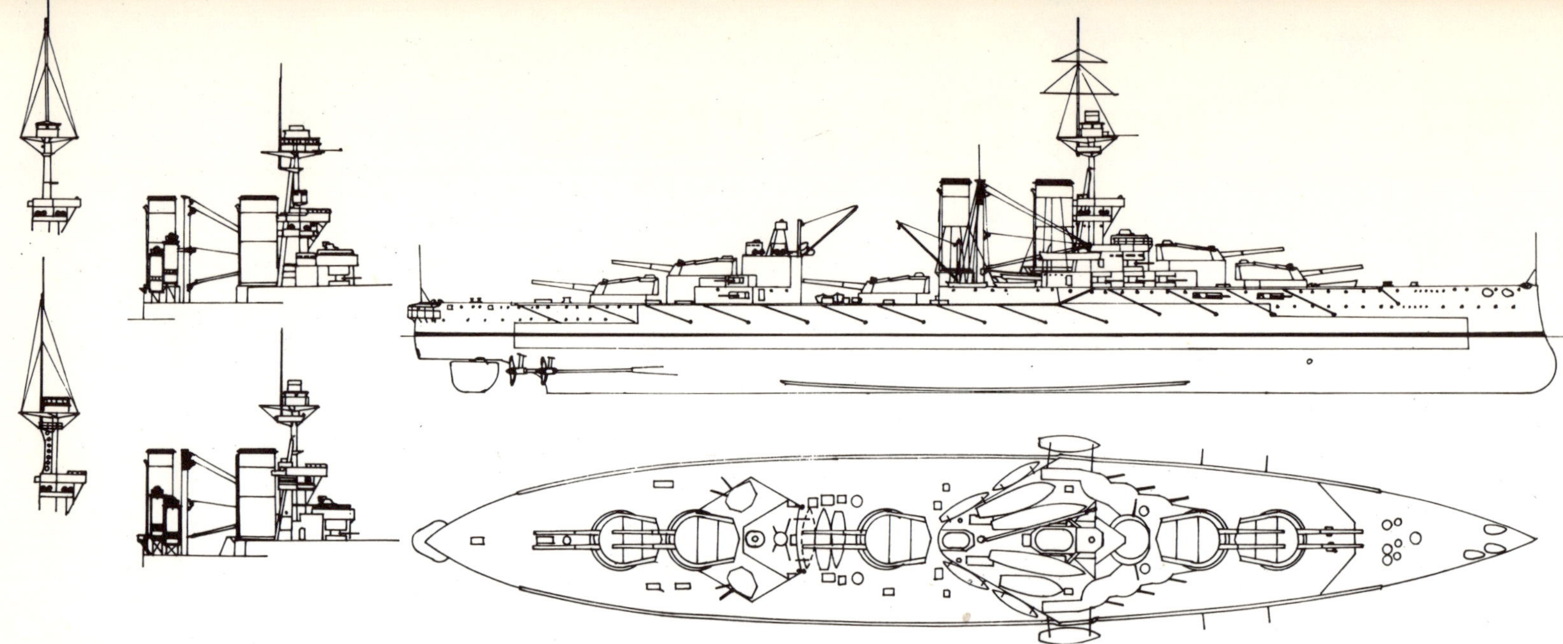

Audacious, 1913 (details:
top left, King George V, 1912;
bottom left, King George V, 1914;
top right, Centurion, 1917;
bottom right, King George V, 1918).

Right, Centurion in 1918, with torpedo nets removed, searchlight towers added and bridgework enlarged (NMM).

Below right, King George V seen late in the war, with her kite ballon aloft (IWM).

rooms caused a list, and it was necessary to flood certain starboard compartments to bring her on to an even keel; unfortunately, many compartments thought to be watertight proved not to be, and the rate of flooding proved too great; despite tremendous efforts to tow the *Audacious* to Lough Swilly by ships which included the White Star liner *Olympic*, the heavy seas running made salvage impossible; at 9.00pm, after all her complement had been rescued, she blew up and sank; strenuous efforts were made to keep the loss of the *Audacious* secret, despite the knowledge that a number of Americans had taken photographs from the *Olympic*, and her loss can be attributed to the crude state of damage control in the Royal Navy at the time rather than any abnormal weakness of design, although the problem of leaks through so-called watertight bulkheads was common to all navies at the time, and was not eradicated until war experience had brought it to light.

King George V: Flagship of Home Fleet (Vice-Admiral Sir George Warrender) to outbreak of war; became Flagship 2nd Battle Squadron of Grand Fleet (Vice-Admiral Sir Thomas Jerram) in August 1914 and remained so until 1919 (in action at Jutland, with no casualties); to Mediterranean 1919, and paid off in 1923 in Reserve at Devonport; served as gunnery training ship until 1926; sold 2 December 1926 to Alloa Shipbreaking Co. for breaking up.

Centurion: With Home Fleet to August 1914, when she and the rest of the class joined the 2nd Battle Squadron, Grand Fleet; Jutland 31 May 1916, but no damage; Mediterranean 1919–24, including operations in support of White Russians; paid off in Reserve at Portsmouth 1924–6, but in 1927 she completed conversion to a radio-controlled target ship; served in World War II as dummy battleship for convoy escort, and scuttled to form part of Mulberry Harbour 9 June 1944.

Iron Duke class

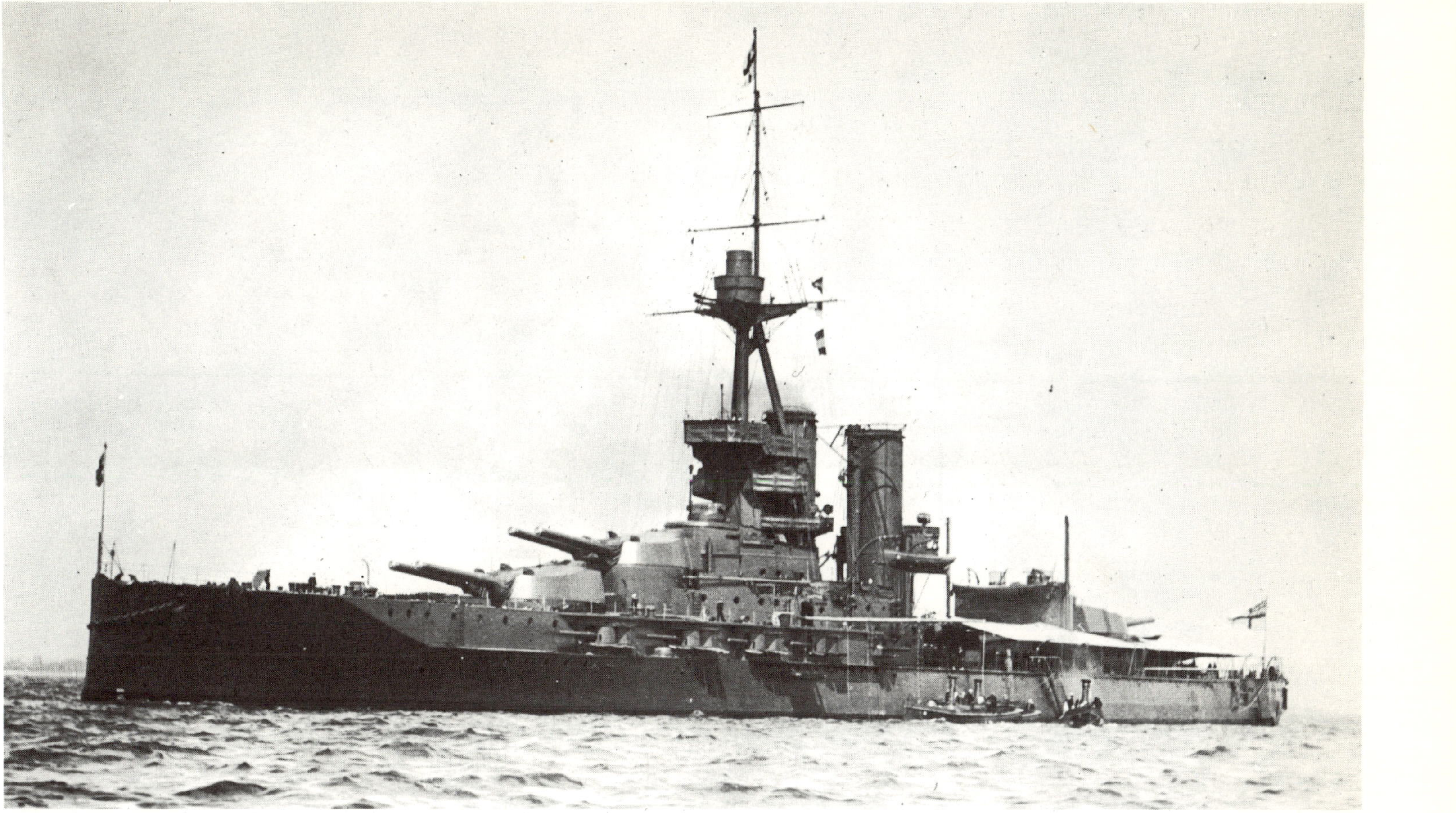

Displacement: 25,820tons (normal load); 30,380tons (full load)
Dimensions: 580ft×90ft×29ft 6in
Guns: 10×13·5in 45cal (5×2)
12×6in Q.F. (12×1)
2×3in A.A. (2×1)
4×3pdrs
Torpedo Tubes: 4×21in (submerged, beam)
Armour: 12–4in belt; 6–2in battery; 2½–1in decks; 11in CT and turrets
Machinery: 4-shaft Parsons turbines, 29,000hp = 21knots; 18 Babcock boilers (Yarrow in Marlborough and Emperor of India)
Coal Capacity: 900/3250tons
Oil Capacity: 1050tons (+550tons in emergency tanks)
Endurance: 7780miles at 10knots
Complement: 925–942 (wartime up to 1022)
Cost: £2,042,800 average $8,171,200)

	Laid Down	Launched	Completed	Built/Engined
Benbow	30 May 1912	12 Nov 1913	Oct 1914	Beardmore
Emperor of India (ex-Delhi)	31 May 1912	27 Nov 1913	Nov 1914	Vickers, Barrow
Iron Duke	12 Jan 1912	12 Oct 1912	Mar 1914	Portsmouth DY/ Cammell Laird
Marlborough	25 Jan 1912	24 Oct 1912	June 1914	Devonport DY/ Hawthorn Leslie

This class consituted an improved *King George V* and *Orion* type, but with one important addition, a heavy secondary armament of 6in guns. The previous classes had been subjected to growing criticism in and out of the Service for their puny 4in guns at a time when foreign destroyers were growing in size and when all foreign designs had gone over to the idea of a properly arranged secondary armament. As Fisher had left the Admiralty early in 1910, designs of battleships no longer had to conform to his prejudices about the effect of 13·5in shell against torpedo-craft, and as the quickening tempo of rivalry between Great Britain and Germany meant that more money was available, the additional cost of a 6in battery was not questioned.

The *Iron Dukes* rectified many of the faults found in earlier British dreadnoughts; their greater beam gave them more protection against underwater damage, in addition to providing stability for the 6in guns. However, they were more lightly armoured than their German contemporaries, the *Königs*, to offset the great preponderance of gunpower.

Gunnery: No. 3 turret tended to suffer from wetness in rough weather, as a result of the low freeboard aft. The 6in guns proved particularly troublesome, as the battery was low, and too far forward to escape constant interference from spray. Although the gun embrasures could be closed by segmented ports in rough weather, it was found that these were washed away constantly. Before the end of 1914 it was found necessary to unship the ports altogether, and to provide watertight india-rubber joints between the revolving shield and the ship's side. This improvement was incorporated into the *Tiger* and the *Queen Elizabeth* class.

The solitary 6in guns positioned right aft at main deck level to port and starboard of No. 5 turret was designed to be used against torpedo-craft silhouetted against the setting sun. As the freeboard was about three feet, the mounting was constantly flooded, and spray would have made shooting impossible in all but a flat calm. When the alterations to the battery described above were carried out late in 1914, the two 6in guns were moved to the forecastle deck level, and put in unarmoured

casemates on either side of the bridge. The old positions were plated in, and the new arrangement proved most satisfactory.

Iron Duke was the first battleship of the Royal Navy fitted with anti-aircraft guns, as she went to sea for trials in 1914 with two 12pdr high-angle guns (some authorities say these were 3pdrs, but this seems to be a misreading of 3in, the alternative description of the 12pdr). They were mounted on the after superstructure.

Appearance: Differed from the *King George V* class in having thin round funnels of equal size, and a prominent derrick-post between the funnels. The heavy tripod was reintroduced, and as the war progressed the tops were enlarged. Other improvements were made to fire-control during the war, including the provision of range clocks on masts and deflection scales on turrets. In 1918 aircraft platforms were also introduced.

The *Iron Duke* herself ran trials early in 1914 with torpedo nets but they were removed before commissioning, and the rest of the class did not receive them. No further battleships were to be fitted with them in the Royal Navy.

Careers

Benbow: Joined 4th Battle Squadron, Grand Fleet on 10 December 1914 (Flagship of Sir Douglas Gamble until February 1915, when he was relieved by Sir Doveton Sturdee); Jutland 31 May 1916; Mediterranean 1919–24, including Black Sea operations supporting White Russians; transferred to Atlantic Fleet 1926–9, and sold 14 March 1931 to Alloa Shipbreaking Co.

Emperor of India: Joined Grand Fleet (4th Battle Squadron) in December 1914, with which she served until 1919; during this time she was at Jutland, and also served as Flagship of 1st Battle Squadron (Rear-Admiral A. L. Duff); to Mediterranean 1919 and served in Black Sea in support of White Russians; refitted 1922, and returned to Home waters in 1926; Atlantic Fleet 1926–9; sunk by gunfire as target off Owers Bank 1 July 1931; wreck raised and sold to Alloa Shipbreaking Co. arriving at Rosyth 16 February 1932.

Iron Duke: Flagship of Home Fleet (Admiral Sir George Callaghan) at outbreak of war, and became Flagship of the Grand Fleet (Sir John Jellicoe) in August 1914; Jutland 31 May 1916; relieved as Fleet Flagship by *Queen Elizabeth* late in 1916 and joined 2nd Battle Squadron until 1919; Mediterranean 1919–26, including Black Sea operations in support of White Russians; Atlantic Fleet 1926–9; converted to 'demilitarised' status to conform with conditions of London Naval Treaty and became gunnery training ship; served as depot ship at Scapa Flow 1939–45 (damaged by aircraft attack October 1939) and sold February 1946 to British Iron and Steel Corporation and broken up at Faslane.

Marlborough: Served as Second Flagship of Home Fleet to outbreak of war, and then become Flagship of 1st Battle Squadron, Grand Fleet (Sir Lewis Bayly, until relieved December 1914 by Sir Cecil Burney); torpedoed at Jutland 31 May 1916, probably by the cruiser *Wiesbaden* and spent three months under repair; hit amidships, and had a hole 70ft × 20ft, but kept station at 17knots and fired fourteen salvoes in six minutes; twenty-four hours later, after she had been detached, she was drawing 39ft and making 10knots as she made for the Humber; to Mediterranean 1919, where she took part in Black Sea operations with the remainder of the class; refitted 1920–2, and transferred to Atlantic Fleet 1926–9; sold May 1932 to Alloa Shipbreaking Co. and arrived at Rosyth 25 June 1932.

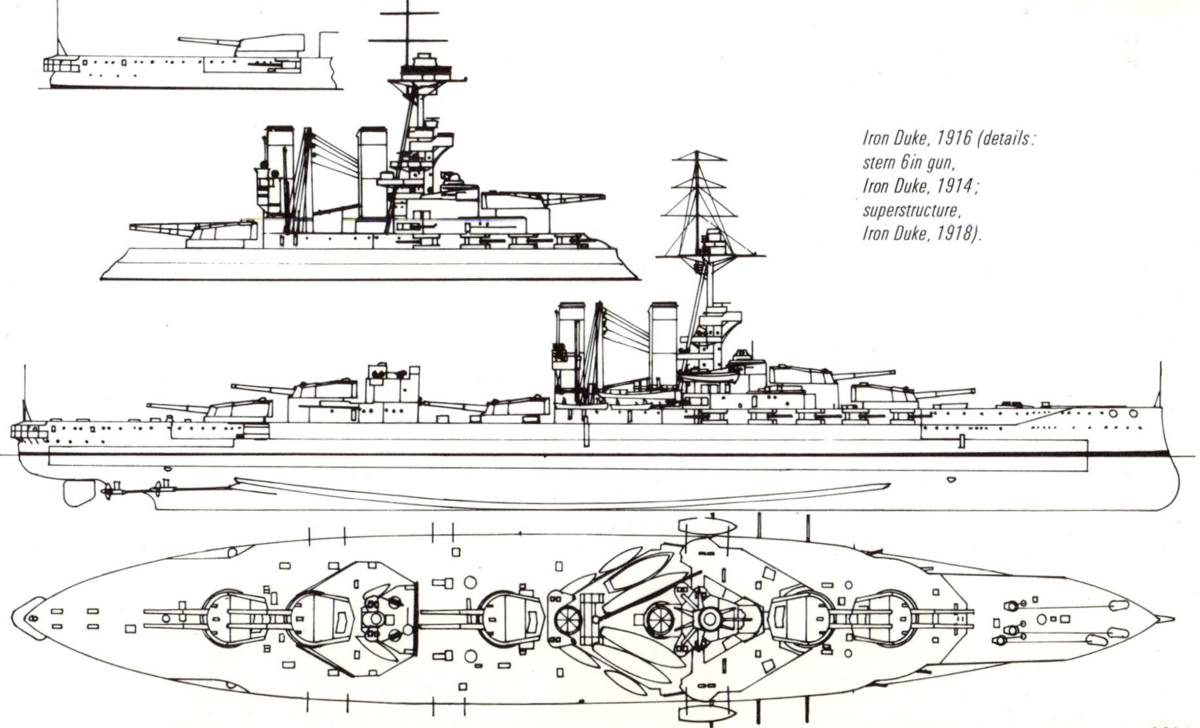

Above, *Emperor of India – a 1919 view showing the clinker screen (funnel cap) added to her forward funnel. Note also the aircraft platforms on No. 2 turret and No. 3 turret (NMM).*

Iron Duke, 1916 (details: stern 6in gun, Iron Duke, 1914; superstructure, Iron Duke, 1918).

Above, Erin refitting in the floating dock at Invergordon in 1917–18. Note the three repair hulks to the left of the picture – from left to right, the disarmed battleship Mars and the old ironclad battleships Akbar (ex-Temeraire) and Algiers (ex-Triumph) (NMM).

Above left, in 1919, showing her distinctive mast with the tripod legs trailing forward. Note also that No. 3 turret is a deck higher than usual in British ships and that she has had aircraft platforms and searchlight towers added (NMM).

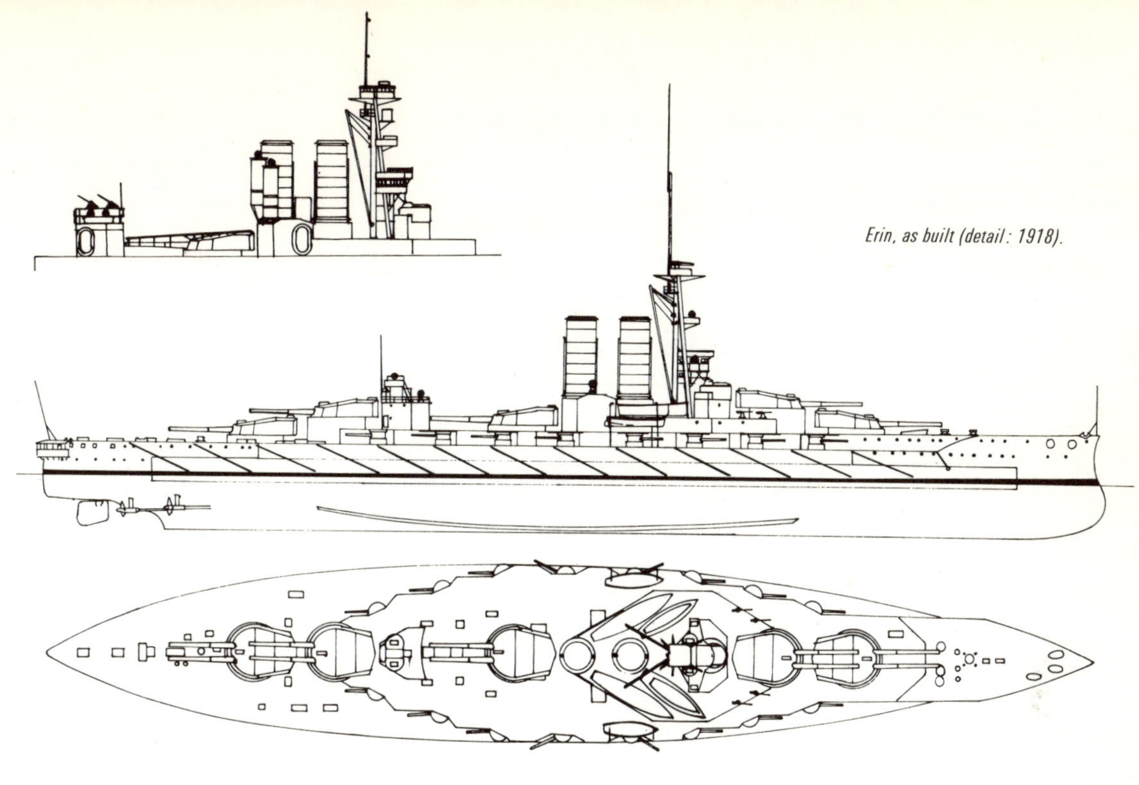

Erin, as built (detail: 1918).

Erin

Displacement: 22,780tons (normal load); 25,250tons (full load)
Dimensions: 525ft×91ft 7in× 28ft 8in
Guns: 10×13·5in 45cal (5×2) 16×6in (16×1) 6×6pdrs 2×3in A.A. (added during war)
Torpedo Tubes: 4×21in (submerged, beam)
Armour: 12–4in belt; 12–4in CT; 3–1½in decks
Machinery: 4-shaft Parsons turbines, 26,500hp = 21knots; 15 Babcock & Wilcox boilers
Coal Capacity: 900/2120tons
Oil Capacity: 710tons
Endurance: 5300miles at 10knots
Complement: 1070
Cost: approximately £2,000,000 ($8,000,000)

	Laid Down	Launched	Completed	Built/Engined
Erin (ex-Reshadieh)	1 Aug 1911	3 Sept 1913	Aug 1914	Vickers, Barrow

This fine unit had originally been ordered for the Imperial Ottoman Navy in 1911 with a sister, to be called *Reshad-i-Hamiss*. But after the Balkan War, in which the Turks were roughly handled by the Greeks, only one battleship was allowed to proceed on account of the poor financial position of the purchasing government. At the end of July 1914 the Turkish officers and seamen were standing by at Vickers to take over the *Reshadieh*, but as the Sarajevo Crisis showed no signs of diminishing the First Lord of the Admiralty, Winston Churchill, kept the Fleet assembled after the Test Mobilisation, and made secret contingency plans to take over this Turkish battleship and another building on the Tyne.

As soon as war broke out the Turkish crews were confined to their quarters and the two battleships were formally expropriated for use by the Royal Navy. There was indignation in Turkey at this high-handed action by Churchill, and shortly afterwards, when the German battle cruiser *Goeben* (*qv*) eluded the British and reached Turkish waters, the Turks threw in their lot with Germany against France and Great Britain. Churchill has been accused of a needless affront to a former staunchly pro-British Turkey, but the facts do not support this: from 1911 the Turkish involvement with Germany had become so great that it is very unlikely that anything could have prevented her from siding with Germany in 1914.

The design of the *Reshadieh* is interesting as an example of what British designers could do when freed from the restrictions of beam which so hampered the Director of Naval Construction. By increasing the beam of the *King George V* hull by 2ft 7in and shortening it by 30ft, Sir Richard Thurston was able to produce a battleship with the fighting qualities of the *Iron Duke* but displacing only 23,000tons. Although the shorter hull slightly reduced the coal capacity, there was no loss of freeboard or armour thickness. Furthermore, No. 3 turret was mounted a deck higher, which greatly improved its performance in a seaway.

Appearance: In profile the Erin differed from other British dreadnoughts by having a 'cleaver' bow in place of the customary ram type. Her tripod legs trailed forward instead of aft, and the funnels were rather smaller than those found in other ships. Although No. 3 turret was a deck higher it did not stand out as a recognition feature. By 1918 she had all the standard modifications of British dreadnoughts—aircraft platforms on No. 2 and No. 3 turrets, searchlight platforms and so forth.

Career

Lying at Barrow on outbreak of war in August 1914, awaiting completion as Turkish *Reshadieh*; taken over by the Royal Navy and renamed; joined 2nd Battle Squadron in September; fourth ship in line at Jutland, but suffered no casualities; 1919 Flagship of Nore Reserve at Sheerness; sold 19 December 1922 to Cox and Danks, Queenborough.

Agincourt

	Laid Down	Launched	Completed	Built/Engined
Agincourt	Sept 1911	22 Jan 1913	Aug 1914	Armstrong, Elswick/Parsons

Displacement: 27,500tons (normal load); 30,250tons (full load)
Dimensions: 632ft×89ft×27ft (mean)
Guns: 14×12in (7×2)
20×6in (20×1)
10×3in (10×1)
2×3in A.A. (added)
Torpedo Tubes: 3×21in (submerged, 1 stern, 2 beam)
Armour: 9–4in belt; 12–4in CT; 2½–1in decks; 12–8in turrets
Machinery: 4-shaft Parsons turbines, 34,000hp = 22knots; 22 Babcock & Wilcox boilers
Coal Capacity: 1500/3200tons coal
Oil Capacity: 620tons
Endurance: approx. 4500miles at 10knots
Complement: 1115 (as built); 1267 (by 1918)
Cost: £2,725,000 (price to Turkey in 1914) ($10,900,000)

Above left, Agincourt in 1915 with her after tripod still in position, although the flying bridge between the funnels has been removed (IWM).

Centre left, under way in 1917 with rig partially reduced. Not only has the flying bridge been removed, but the tripod main mast has been reduced to 1 leg. This was only a temporary measure and the entire mast was subsequently removed (NMM).

Below left, as she appeared in 1917–18 with the after tripod mast removed (IWM).

After all the praise lavished on the *Erin*, the *Agincourt* goes to the opposite extreme—a warship which, with her thin armour and outclassed guns, could not claim to be value for money even for her original owners, and certainly was a questionable asset to the Royal Navy. The *Agincourt* broke an imposing number of records, however: the longest battleship in the world; the largest number of guns afloat; the heaviest secondary armament; and finally the largest number of owners within one year.

This unique ship was laid down in 1911 during an outburst of what can only be described as 'battleship megalomania' among the three major republics of South America—Argentina, Brazil and Chile. With little regard for the limitations imposed by geography or economics, Brazil had ordered the powerful dreadnoughts *Minas Geraes* and *São Paulo* (twelve 12in guns) in 1907. Not to be outdone, Argentina ordered two similar ships from the United States, the *Moreno* and *Rivadavia*. Although these two were much delayed and finally entered service only in 1915, Brazil tried to ensure her supremacy by ordering an even larger dreadnought.

The extent of Brazilian fantasies can be gauged by noting that the designs under consideration went from a 27,500tonner with fourteen 12in guns to a 31,600tonner with twelve 14in, then to a similar sized ship with eight 16in and finally to the *Riachuelo*, a 31,250ton ship with ten 15in guns. After much argument it was decided to build the first design and the *Riachuelo* design, but only the former survived a not altogether unexpected financial crisis in Brazil. Finally, in January 1914 the incomplete *Rio de Janeiro* was sold to Turkey, and renamed *Sultan Osman I*.

Although her armour belt was thinner than her contemporaries in the Royal Navy, the *Agincourt* did have a 6in strake of armour carried to upper deck level, which was better than in the earlier British dreadnoughts, and her deck protection was up to contemporary British standards. Her main asset was considered to be the overwhelming volume of fire she could deliver, and although at one time it was held by some critics that she could not stand the shock of firing a full broadside of fourteen guns, at Jutland she fired full broadsides to confound her critics. According to eyewitnesses, the sheet of flame which resulted looked like a battle cruiser blowing up.

Appearance: With her widely spaced funnels and her flying deck for boats her profile was uniquely impressive. On being taken over in 1914 the flying deck was removed to avoid interference with the guns. In 1916 the after tripod was replaced by a short pole mast, but later this was suppressed and a light topmast was added to the derrick-pole. In 1918 the bridge was enlarged and searchlight towers were added around the second funnel.

Career:

Completed in July 1914, but various delays were indulged in by the authorities to prevent her from falling into Turkish hands until the international situation improved; taken over in August and renamed before joining the 4th Battle Squadron of the Grand Fleet on 7 September; at Jutland she was serving with the 6th Division of the 1st Battle Squadron (as her division mates were the *Marlborough*, *Revenge* and *Hercules* there were three gun calibres in one group, 15in, 13·5in and 12in, a unique mixture); fired 144 rounds of 12in, and suffered no hits or casualties; later transferred to 2nd Battle Squadron, and put on disposal list in 1919; recommissioned at Rosyth in 1921 for experimental work, and in 1922 began conversion to a depot ship; this involved the removal of all but No. 1 and No. 2 turrets, and the provision of fuel and ammunition stowage; work was stopped in the same year, and she was sold to the Rosyth Shipbreaking Co. on 19 December 1922 (a rumoured resale to Brazil did not materialise).

Agincourt, 1914 (details, 1918).

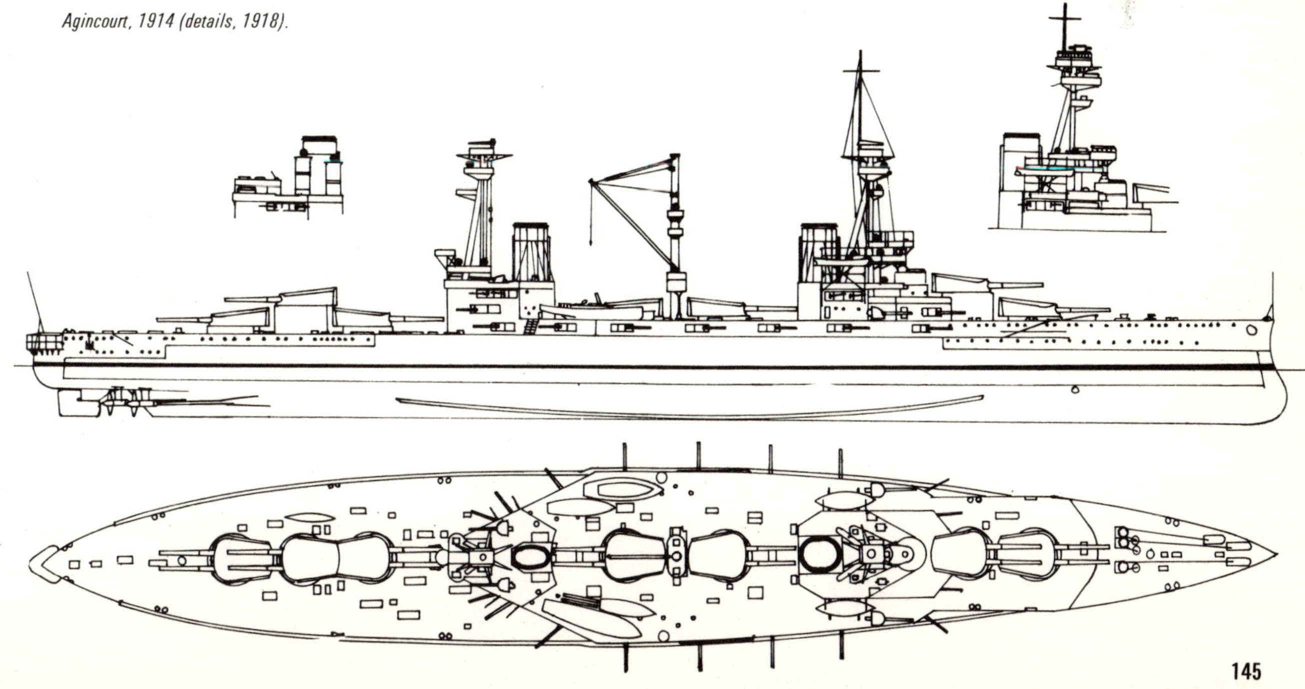

Displacement: 28,430tons (load draught), 35,160tons (full load)
Dimensions: 660ft×90ft 6in× 28ft 5in
Guns: 8×13·5in 45cal (4×2) 12×6in Q.F. (12×1) 2×3in A.A. (2×1) 4×3pdrs
Torpedo Tubes: 4×21in (submerged, beam)
Armour: 9–3in belt; 9in turrets; 10–3in CT; 3–1in decks
Machinery: 4-shaft Brown-Curtis turbines, 85,000hp = 28knots (see notes); 39 Babcock & Wilcox boilers
Coal Capacity: 450/3320tons
Oil Capacity: 450/3480tons
Endurance: Never officially quoted (see notes), but approx. 4650miles at 10knots
Complement: 1121
Cost: £2,593,100 ($10,372,400)

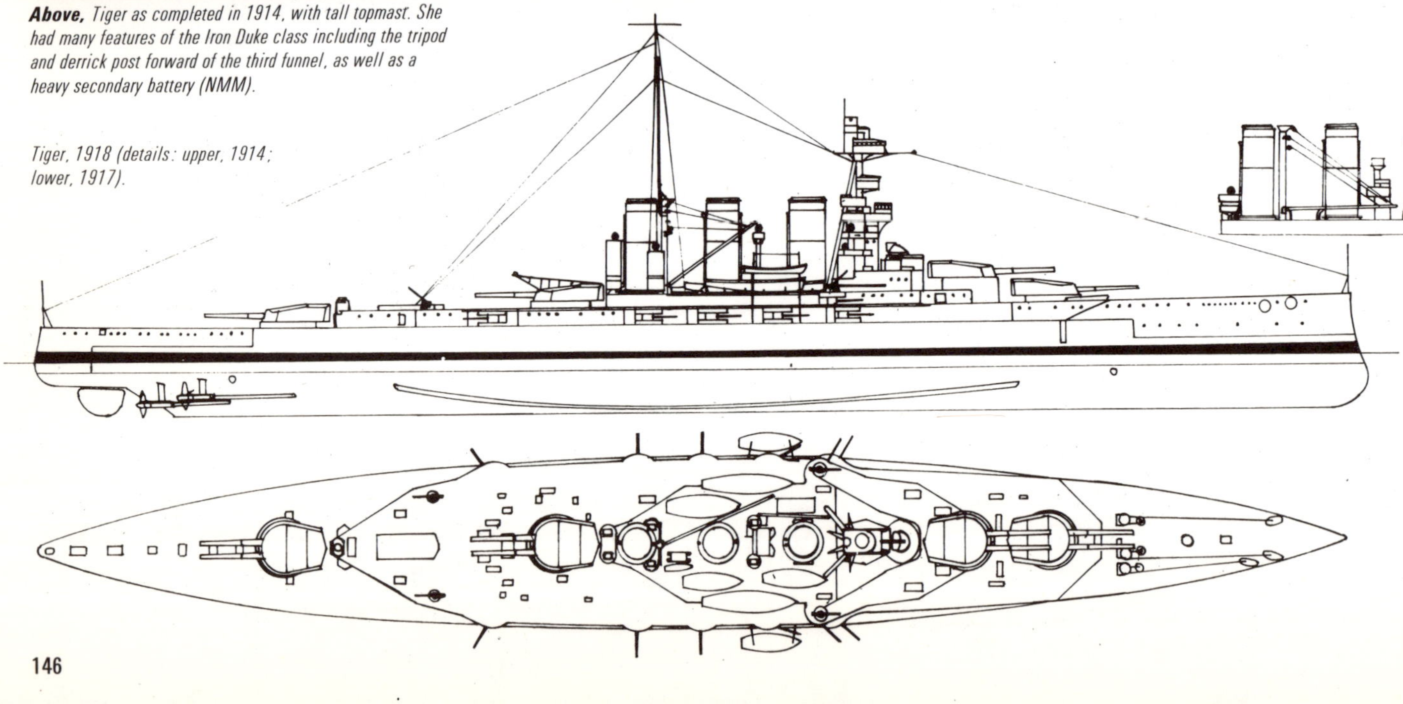

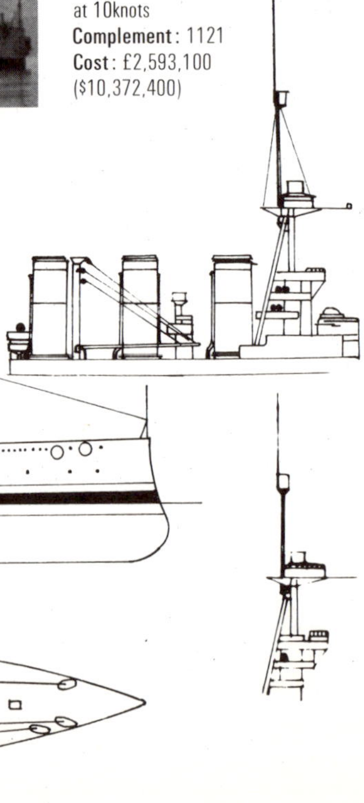

Above, Tiger as completed in 1914, with tall topmast. She had many features of the Iron Duke class including the tripod and derrick post forward of the third funnel, as well as a heavy secondary battery (NMM).

Tiger, 1918 (details: upper, 1914; lower, 1917).

Tiger

	Laid Down	Launched	Completed	Built/Engined
Tiger	20 June 1912	15 Dec 1913	Oct 1914	John Brown

Tiger was the battle cruiser equivalent of the *Iron Dukes*, and had the same style of 6in secondary armament, the same round slim funnels and so on. Although planned as the fourth ship of the *Lion* class (and meant to look like the *Queen Mary*) her design was strongly influenced by the Japanese battle cruiser *Kongo*. This fine ship had been launched a month before the *Tiger* was laid down, and as she had a vastly superior layout of her 14in guns, and a heavy secondary armament of 6in guns, as well as a superior disposition of armour, it would have been idiotic to build a fourth *Lion*.

The beam as altered was two feet greater than the *Lion's*, which increased draught by six inches. The horsepower was increased to 108,000 to give her 29–30knots, but as this involved a tremendous increase in coal consumption she had to be given the biggest coal capacity of any British warship. She burnt about 1245tons of coal daily to develop 59,500hp, with the result that her endurance was roughly the same as the *Lion* class.

Machinery: For the first time Brown–Curtis turbines were used. The Director of Naval Construction (Sir Eustace Tennyson d'Eyncourt) later pointed out that if small tube boilers had been adopted as the Germans had done with the *Derfflinger*, much of the weight allocated to machinery could have been allocated to armour or greater horsepower; he claimed that he could have made the *Tiger* and *Queen Elizabeth* capable of 32 and 28½knots respectively if his suggestion had been followed. On the other hand, there can be no doubt that the *Tiger's* German contemporary, the battle cruiser *Derfflinger* put the weight saved to better use, with 12in armour on the waterline.

Appearance: Easily the most handsome British capital ship for many years, the *Tiger* had a symmetrical, balanced beauty which still excites admiration. In 1918 the topmast was shifted to the top of the derrick-stump between the second and third funnels, which greatly spoiled her looks. During 1917–18 the usual alterations were made; heavier fire-control tops, aircraft platforms etc. In 1917 searchlight towers were added around the third funnel.

Career

Still building at Clydebank at outbreak of war; November 1914 joined 1st Battle Cruiser Squadron at Scapa Flow, less than a month after completion; Dogger Bank action January 1915, when she was hit on No. 2 turret and had 2 killed; in this action she was reported to have several workmen on board to rectify faults in the main armament; Jutland 31 May 1916, and received 21 hits in all (24 killed, 37 wounded); completed repairs 2 July 1916 and rejoined Battle Cruiser Fleet; served in Battle Cruiser Squadron of Atlantic Fleet 1919–22; seagoing gunnery training ship 1924–9, and then replaced *Hood* in Battle Cruiser Squadron from 1929–31; paid off 30 March 1931 at Devonport and sold March 1932 to be broken up under the Washington Treaty.

Above, *in 1918 with wartime modifications to her rig. Note that she has a topmast stepped on the derrick post between the second and third funnels, and an aircraft platform and hangar on No. 3 turret (NMM).*

Canada

Displacement: 28,600tons (load draught); 32,120tons (full load)
Dimensions: 625ft×92ft×29ft (mean)
Guns: 10×14in Mk. I 45cal (5×2)
18×6in; reduced to 16 in 1916 (see notes)
2×3in A.A.
4×3pdrs
Torpedo Tubes: 4×21in (submerged, beam)
Armour: 9–4in belt; 11–6in CT; 10in turrets; 4–1in decks
Machinery: 4-shaft Brown-Curtis (High pressure) and Parsons (Low pressure) turbines, 37,000hp = 22¾knots; 21 Yarrow type boilers (by John Brown)
Coal Capacity: 1150/3300tons
Oil Capacity: 520tons
Endurance: 4400miles at 10knots
Complement: 1167
Cost: approximately £2,000,000 ($8,000,000)

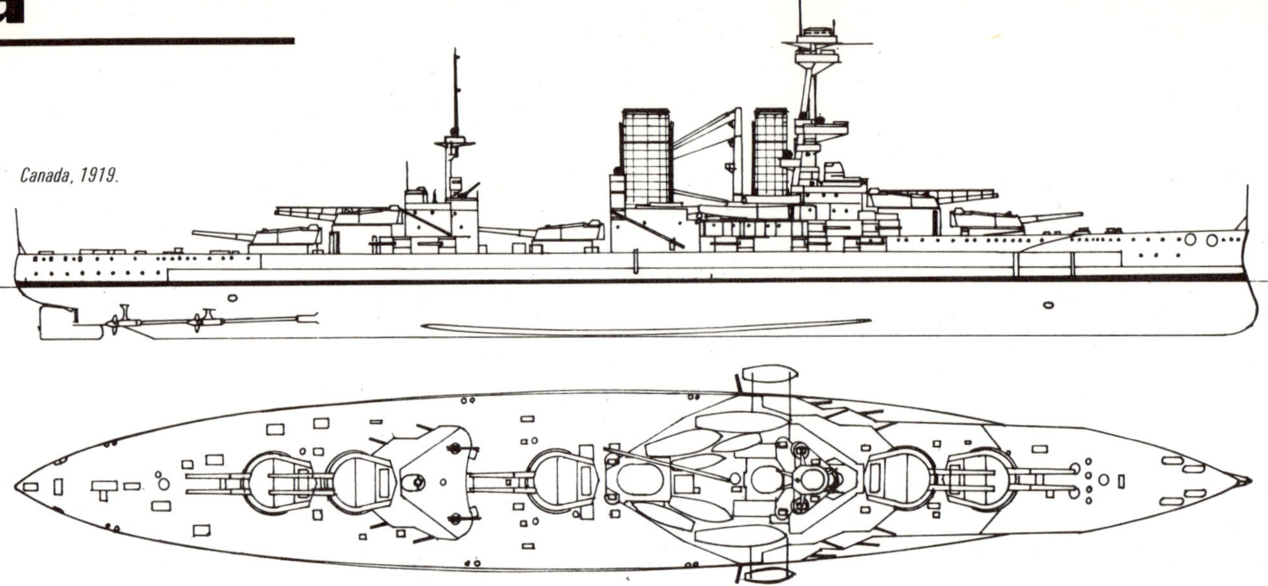
Canada, 1919.

	Laid Down	Launched	Completed	Built/Engined
Canada	27 Nov 1911	27 Nov 1913	Sept 1915	Armstrong, Elswick/
(ex-Almirante Latorre ex-Valparaiso)				
Eagle	22 Jan 1913	8 June 1918	Cancelled	Armstrong, Elswick/
(ex-Almirante Cochrane ex-Santiago)				John Brown

Chile, as the third of the major South American naval powers, was forced to lay down a pair of battleships to outclass the *Rio de Janeiro*, *Moreno* and *Rivadavia*. True to the Chilean tradition, these turned out to be the most practical answer to the problem with great emphasis on fighting power as opposed to the Brazilian and Argentinian designs (which were intended to overawe their rivals rather than beat them in action). Although far too large and expensive for the Chileans, they were magnificent ships, and when the *Canada* joined the Grand Fleet she was considered to be one of its best units.

The final design was a longer version of the *Iron Duke*, with more engine power and a beam slightly greater than the *Erin*. Being some hundred feet longer, her length-to-beam ratio was abnormally high (6·8:1), which gaver her a good turn of speed for virtually the same power. The new pattern Elswick 14in gun was adopted, firing a shell of the same weight as the improved 13·5in; with its slightly lower muzzle velocity it proved a first class weapon in service.

With her thinner armour, the *Canada* was lightly protected for her gunpower, but on a par with earlier British dreadnoughts and far superior to the *Agincourt*. Her normal coal capacity was the second highest in the Fleet, but the maximum stowage was 1000tons less than that of the *Iron Duke*.

Sister Ship: Both Chilean battleships were suspended at the outbreak of war, but work restarted on *Canada* in September 1914. An option to purchase *Almirante Cochrane* was not taken up until 1917, when she was converted to an aircraft carrier. The decision to purchase these two ships rather than expropriate them, as had been done to the Turkish dreadnoughts, is explained by the long tradition of friendliness between Chile and Great Britain—and by her possession of valuable deposits of nitrates.

Appearance: Resembling the *King George V* class, with large flat-sided funnels of unequal thickness, the heavy look and lofty tripod gave the *Canada* a majestic look. In 1916 the aftermost 6in guns in the forward battery were removed because of blast from No. 3 turret. Aircraft platforms were fitted to No. 2 and No. 4 turrets in 1918.

Career
Building for Chile in August 1914, and suspended; purchased for Royal Navy in September and fitting out restarted; joined 4th Battle Squadron, Grand Fleet in October 1915; at Jutland 31 May 1916 but suffered no casualties; returned to Chile in April 1920 and renamed *Almirante Latorre* 1 August 1920; served as flagship of Chilean Navy until 1958, the last major veteran of Jutland; sold May 1959 to Japanese shipbreakers, and arrived in Tokyo Bay 28 August 1959 for breaking up.

Above, Canada in 1918 with aircraft platforms on No. 2 and No. 4 turrets (NMM).

 Queen Elizabeth class

	Laid Down	Launched	Completed	Built/Engined
Barham	24 Feb 1913	31 Oct 1914	Oct 1915	John Brown
Malaya	20 Oct 1913	18 Mar 1915	Feb 1916	Armstrong/ Wallsend Slipway
Queen Elizabeth	21 Oct 1912	16 Oct 1913	Jan 1915	Portsmouth DY/ Wallsend Slipway
Valiant	31 Jan 1913	4 Nov 1914	Feb 1916	Fairfield
Warspite	31 Oct 1912	26 Nov 1913	Mar 1915	Devonport DY/ Hawthorn Leslie
Agincourt	1914	Cancelled 1914		Portsmouth DY

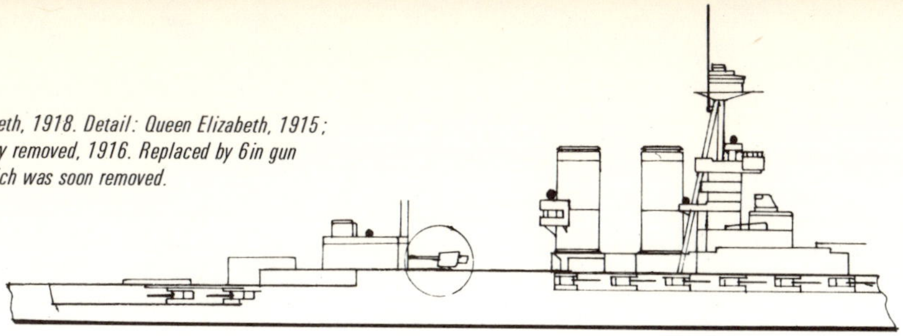

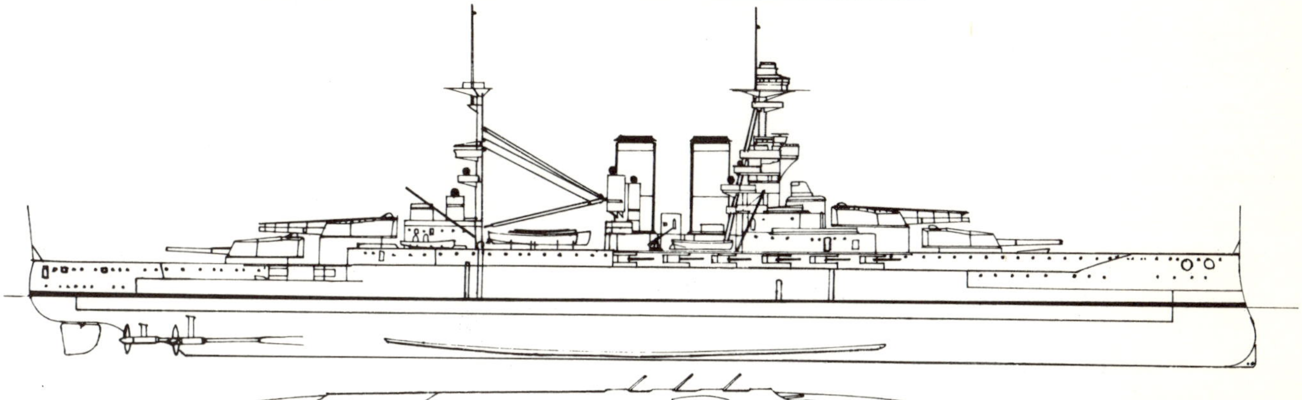

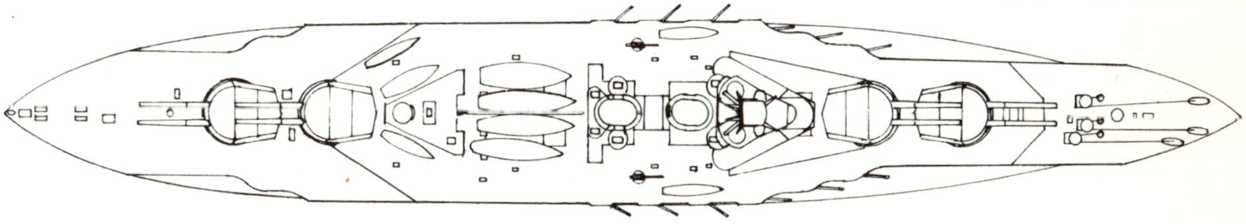

Displacement: 29,150tons (load draught, by 1917); 33,000tons (full load)

Dimensions: 600ft×90ft 6in×30ft 8in

Guns: 8×15in Mk. I 42cal (4×2) 16×6in Q.F. (16×1); reduced to 14 in Queen Elizabeth in 1915, while four later ships completed with 14; 1916–17 two 6in replaced by 3in A.A. guns 2×3in A.A. (2×1) added 1916–17 4×3pdrs

Torpedo Tubes: 4×21in (submerged, beam)

Armour: 13–6in belt; 13–11in turrets; 11in CT; 3–1in decks

Machinery: 4-shaft Parsons turbines (Brown-Curtis in Barham and Valiant), 75,000hp = 24knots; 24 Babcock & Wilcox boilers (24 Yarrow in Barham and Warspite)

Coal Capacity: Nil (see notes); 100tons carried for heating and cooking

Oil Capacity: 650/3400tons

Endurance: Not published, but approximately 4500miles at 10knots

Complement: 925–951

Cost: not published, but approximately £3,000,000 ($12,000,000)

The 1912 Programme allowed for the creation of a revolutionary 'Fast Squadron' of battleships which could perform all the battle tasks originally allotted to the battle cruisers. By giving them a margin of four knots over the battle fleet it was hoped that this 'fast wing' would be able to give a fleet commander greater tactical flexibility and help to bring a reluctant enemy to battle. Prewar exercises had shown more and more that line-of-battle tactics were becoming sterile and that higher speeds gave some chance of frustrating a turnaway by the opposing fleet.

The evolution of the *Queen Elizabeth* affords an interesting example of the compromises which make up any warship design. As first conceived, the *Iron Duke* was taken as the model, with the additional boilers substituted for No. 3 turret. This would have reduced the broadside to a mere eight guns, but as it was known that Armstrongs were developing a 15in gun, which promised to fire a shell of some 1900lb weight the decision was taken to give the new fast battleships eight of these guns, giving a total broadside weight of 15,000lb as against 14,000lb in the *Iron Duke*. In order to allocate the maximum weight to machinery without any sacrifice of protection, even further economies of weight had to be made, and the momentous decision was taken to adopt oil as the only fuel. There were many who attacked this step on strategic grounds, as the Royal Navy had the best steam coal in the world (in Wales) whereas oil had to be brought from the Persian Gulf, tankers had to be bought and storage depots had to be set up all over the world. Furthermore, it was held that coal bunkers afforded great protection against shell- and torpedo-hits, whereas an oil bunker offered no resistance to shells, and could be set on fire by torpedo explosions.

All the arguments against oil fuel had some point, and the argument about coal bunkers was probably the most valid, but they all ignored the chief advantages of oil. By saving weight on coal hundreds of tons could be devoted to an equivalent thickness of armour, and the speed of refuelling an oil-fired ship gave a tremendous advantage in wartime. The Grand Fleet used about 100,000tons of coal per week, and the efforts which had to be made to get this amount of coal up to the Orkneys put a tremendous strain on the British railway system. Enormous quantities of rolling stock and a huge fleet of colliers were kept busy simply ferrying coal to Scapa, and the effect on other sectors of the British war effort can be imagined. The strain on officers and men was very great, as each battleship took hours of hard physical labour to coal. The Grand Fleet carried out a large number of sweeps and was always at a high state of readiness, which meant that coaling went on continuously.

Machinery: Although the developed shaft horsepower was modest when compared to the *Tiger*, the rise of 150 per cent over the *Iron Duke* was outstanding among battleships. There were two high-pressure turbines ahead and two low-pressure turbines astern on the wing shafts, with two low-pressure ahead and astern coupled to each inner shaft, excluding cruising turbines on the wing shafts. The boilers were in two groups in eight boiler-rooms, and the working pressure was 235lb. Although the designed speed was 25knots; and all exceeded their designed horsepower on trials, the best reported speed was 24–24½knots, at 275rpm.

Armament: The 15in gun was a gamble, for the trials had not taken place when the *Queen Elizabeth* was laid down. However, it turned out to be the best British heavy mounting ever made, and possibly the finest mounting in any navy, taking into account reliability, accuracy, ruggedness and performance. The 'swash-plate' training machinery provided the right degree of 'creep', and the gun proved to have remarkable accuracy and lengthy barrel life, largely as a result of the lower muzzle velocity. The range at maximum elevation (20°) was 23,400yds using a full charge of 428lb of cordite, and developing 2450fps. It is interesting to note that German accounts of Jutland stress the phenomenal accuracy of the *Valiant*'s shooting.

The secondary armament was a slightly extended version of the *Iron Duke* arrangement, with the same errors of placing most of the guns too far forward and putting an extra pair in the ridiculous after position below No. 4 turret. *Queen Elizabeth* had been fitted with the four after guns before the adverse report on the *Iron Duke* was available, but they were just as quickly suppressed. Two were resited on the forecastle deck just abaft the second funnel where they proved to be the best 6in guns in the ship; this modification was extended to the others, and the ten spare 6in were allocated to five small monitors. In 1916–17 when anti-aircraft guns were needed to deal with the ever-present Zeppelins they were replaced by a pair of 3in guns.

Appearance: With their two broad funnels and well-planned silhouettes, the *Queen Elizabeth* class had the looks to match their power. Their looks were so unmistakable that Beatty purposely kept them at a respectable distance from his battle cruisers before Jutland in order to avoid any chance of the Germans spotting them before battle was joined. All had the usual wartime alterations to control tops, searchlight platforms, range clocks and so forth between 1917 and 1918. Flying-off platforms were added to No. 2 and No. 3 turrets in 1918.

Careers

Barham: Joined 5th Battle Squadron of Grand Fleet in October 1915; with the rest of the 5th B.S. temporarily attached to Beatty's battle cruisers shortly before Jutland; his six times at Jutland,

Above, Warspite in October 1920 (Admiralty).

Above right, Barham in 1917 with various wartime modifications including searchlights and control positions on the mainmast. Note that she is not fitted with aircraft platforms (NMM).

Below right, a 1919 view of Queen Elizabeth showing most of the wartime modifications to her and her sisters, including range clocks on the searchlight platforms around the after funnel and the control positions added on the mainmast (NMM).

with 26 killed and 37 wounded; repairs completed 4 July 1916; Flagship of 1st Battle Squadron, Atlantic Fleet 1920–4; Mediterranean Fleet 1924–7 and 1928–9 before returning to Atlantic Fleet; served in World War II, notably at Battle of Matapan and evacuation of Crete; torpedoed and blew up off Sollum 25 November 1941.

Malaya: This battleship was actually the sixth ship of the class, having been paid for by the Federated Malay States as an additional ship; as a result of this handsome gesture the fifth ship, *Agincourt*, was cancelled; joined 5th Battle Squadron February 1916, and spent the remainder of the war with the Grand Fleet; at Jutland, where she sustained eight hits and had 99 casualties, mainly from a hit in the starboard 6in battery; completed repairs on 4 July 1916; visited Cherbourg for Peace Celebrations April 1919, and conveyed the Allied Naval Commission to German ports for their inspection in 1920; served in Mediterranean and Atlantic Fleets 1921–39; served in World War II and sold in 1948.

Queen Elizabeth: Commissioned 22 December 1914 and sent to Mediterranean to support Dardanelles operations; joined February 1915 as Flagship, East Mediterranean Squadron; April 1915 sank a Turkish transport by indirect gunfire in three rounds; although her presence had great moral effect on the Allied troops, the dangers from mines and U-boats caused Lord Fisher to recall her, and she joined the Grand Fleet (5th Battle Squadron) in May 1915; in dockyard hands for refit at time of Jutland, and when she rejoined she took over from *Iron Duke* as Fleet Flagship when Admiral Sir David Beatty relieved Sir John Jellicoe; surrender of German Fleet signed on board 21 November 1918; postwar served in Atlantic and Mediterranean Fleets; reconstructed 1937–41 and served with distinction in World War II; sold June 1948.

Valiant: Joined 5th Battle Squadron, Grand Fleet in February 1916; undamaged at Jutland; service after Jutland as *Queen Elizabeth*; served in World War II, and sold in 1948.

Warspite: Completed March 1915 and joined 5th Battle Squadron, Grand Fleet; at Jutland she was hit in the steering gear by a heavy shell, and began to turn circles out of control; although under fire at one time from seven German battleships she emerged without serious damage; severely damaged on two occasions in 1915 and 1916 in collision with her squadron-mates; service postwar as *Queen Elizabeth*; taken in hand 1934 for reconstruction and recommissioned as Flagship of Mediterranean Fleet in 1937; in World War II acquired the longest battle record of any battleship, and sustained more damage than any other British battleship; although sold for scrapping in 1947, she went aground in Prussia Cove, Cornwall, and had to be broken up piecemeal over a period of years.

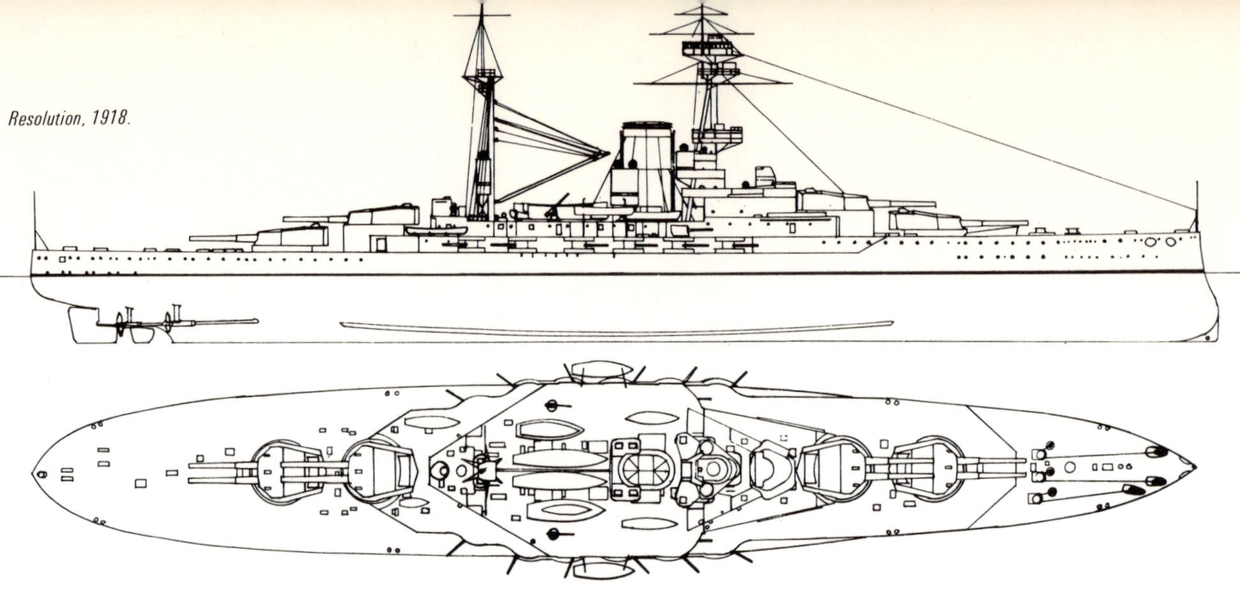

Resolution, 1918.

Revenge class

Displacement: 28,000tons (normal load); 31,200tons (deep load)
Dimensions: 580ft×88ft 6in×30ft
Guns: 8×15in 42cal (4×2)
14×6in (14×1): 16 guns as designed
2×3in A.A.
4×3pdrs
Torpedo Tubes: 4×21in (submerged, beam)
Armour: 13–11in belt; 3–1in decks; 11in CT; 13–4½in turrets
Machinery: 4-shaft Parsons tubines, 40,000hp = 21knots (as designed, see notes); 18 Babcock & Wilcox or Yarrow boilers
Coal Capacity: 140tons (for domestic use only, see notes)
Oil Capacity: 900/3400tons
Endurance: 4200miles at 10knots
Complement: 997
Cost: not published, but approximately £2,500,000 ($10,000,000)

	Laid Down	Launched	Completed	Built/Engined
Ramillies	12 Nov 1913	12 Sept 1916	Sept 1917	Beardmore
Resolution	29 Dec 1913	14 Jan 1915	Dec 1916	Palmer
Revenge	22 Dec 1913	29 May 1915	Mar 1916	Vickers, Barrow
Royal Oak	15 Jan 1914	17 Nov 1914	May 1916	Devonport DY/ Hawthorn Leslie
Royal Sovereign	15 Jan 1914	29 Apr 1915	May 1916	Portsmouth DY/ Parsons
Renown, Repulse completed as battle cruisers; Resistance cancelled			—	Fairfield

The last British dreadnoughts laid down before the war, these fine ships were not intended to join the *Queen Elizabeths* in a Fast Division but to serve in the battle line with the *Iron Dukes*. For this reason they were to be 21knot ships, with only half the horsepower of the previous class. As the Admiralty was by no means fully converted to the advantages of oil fuel for the whole of the Royal Navy, the decision was taken to make the *Revenge* class coal-burners.

Apart from the 15in gun armament, which was identical to the *Queen Elizabeth* class, the *Revenges* were improved *Iron Dukes* with heavier and better distributed armour. The original designs show that the 6in battery would have included four guns aft, abreast of No. 3 and No. 4 turrets, but this was dropped and as in the *Queen Elizabeths* two of these guns were mounted amidships. As a result of experience in the *Iron Dukes* the 6in guns were sited further aft to reduce interference from spray.

Modifications to the Design: When Lord Fisher returned to the Admiralty in August 1914, it was almost universally believed that the war would last only six months. As the Royal Navy had such a large margin of battleship strength over the Germans, it was decided to lay down no further big ships, and the last three of the eight projected *Revenges* were dropped from the building programme. Two of these were subsequently built as battle cruisers (*qv*), but the third was cancelled outright. As it turned out, the supply of guns and mountings was only just sufficient to complete the five and the *Ramillies* and *Resolution* were delayed when some of their turrets were diverted to monitors and battle cruisers.

Fisher's other modification was to alter the *Revenges*' propulsion from coal-fired to oil-burning. This caused a reduction in the load displacement, and raised speed to 23knots. However, *Ramillies* was fitted with anti-torpedo 'bulges' based on the experience with the old *Redoubtable* (*qv*), and this reduced her speed to 22knots. The bulges were modified, as compared with the *Redoubtable*, being much narrower, but they were subsequently enlarged and extended almost to upper deck level.

Appearance: For the first time in many years, a single funnel layout was possible, as there were only three boiler rooms. This made the *Revenges* unique in the Grand Fleet, but in other respects they resembled the *Queen Elizabeths*. The additional 6in guns were mounted level with the heel of the tripod mast on the forecastle deck, and the 3in anti-aircraft guns were sited on the shelter deck abreast of the boats.

Careers

Ramillies: At her launch in September 1916 she damaged her rudder, and had to be towed to Liverpool for repairs by Cammell Laird; as a result she did not join the Fleet until late in the war; 1st Battle Squadron, Grand Fleet 1917 to 1919; served postwar in Mediterranean, Atlantic and Home Fleets; served with distinction in World War II, and sold in 1948.

Resolution: Joined 1st Battle Squadron, Grand Fleet three months after Jutland; postwar service in Mediterranean and Home Fleets; served in World War II, and sold 1948.

Revenge: Joined 1st Battle Squadron, Grand Fleet in February 1916; at Jutland 31 May 1916, when she became the temporary flagship of Vice-Admiral Burney after torpedoing of *Marlborough*; from November 1916 flagship of Admiral Madden, Second-in-Command, Grand Fleet; served postwar in Mediterranean, Atlantic and Home Fleets; after much service in World War II sold in 1949.

Royal Oak: Joined *Revenge* in 1st Battle Squadron in time for Jutland; served postwar in Atlantic, Mediterranean and Home Fleets; on outbreak of World War II with 2nd Battle Squadron, Home Fleet, torpedoed in Scapa Flow by *U.47* 14 October 1939, the first capital ship to be sunk.

Royal Sovereign: Although completed in May 1916 she was still working up at the time of Jutland, and did not join her two sisters in the 1st Battle Squadron of the Grand Fleet until June 1916; postwar service as others of her class; served in various theatres during World War II, and in 1944 she was transferred to the Russian Navy as the *Arkhangelsk*, and served in Northern waters; returned by Russians on 4 February 1949 and sold immediately for breaking up.

Above right, *Royal Oak in 1918, virtually as she appeared at Jutland with the exception of the searchlight towers, which had been added in 1917 (NMM).*

Centre right, *Royal Sovereign in 1918 showing the addition of deflection scales on No. 1 and No. 4 turrets (NMM).*

Below right, *a dazzle-painted Revenge at Scapa Flow in 1918 (NMM).*

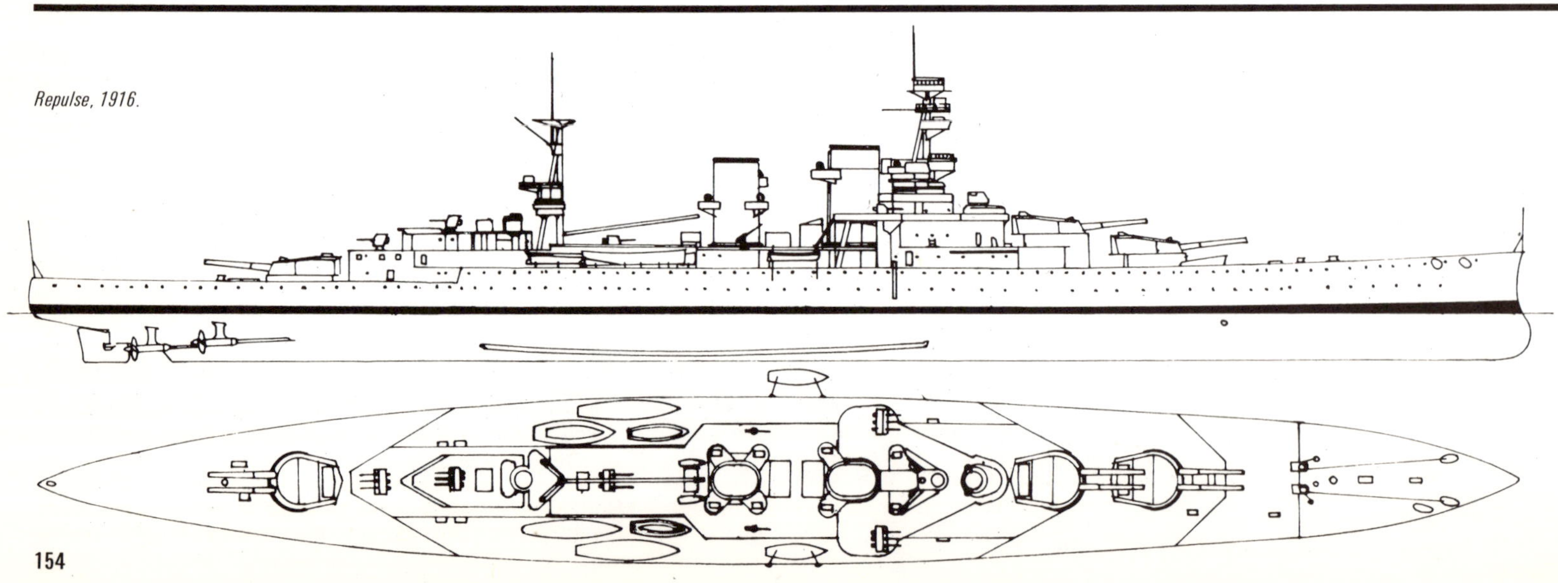

Above, *Royal Sovereign as completed, shown at Portsmouth dockyard in May 1916 (Admiralty).*

Repulse, 1916.

Right, two views of Renown at sea in 1917 by which time her forefunnel had been raised. Over her stern in the top picture can be seen either Lion or Princess Royal (NMM).

Renown class

	Laid Down	Launched	Completed	Built/Engined
Renown	25 Jan 1915	4 Mar 1916	Sept 1916	Fairfield, Govan
Repulse	25 Jan 1915	8 Jan 1916	Aug 1916	John Brown

Displacement: Renown 27,947tons (load draught); 32,727tons (full load) Repulse 27,333tons (load draught); 32,074tons (full load)

Dimensions: 750ft×90ft×27–27ft 6in

Guns: 6×15in 42cal (3×2) 17×4in Mk IX (5×3, 2×1) 2×3in A.A. 4×3pdrs

Torpedo Tubes: 2×21in (submerged, beam)

Armour: 6–1½in belt; 10in CT; 11–7in turrets; 3½–1in decks

Machinery: 4-shaft Brown-Curtis turbines, 112,000hp = 30knots (126,000 maximum hp = 32·6knots); 42 Babcock & Wilcox

Oil Capacity: 1000/4243tons

Endurance: 3650miles at 10knots

Complement: 967

Cost: £2,930,000 average $11,720,000)

With the building of the *Queen Elizabeths* it had seemed as if the battle cruiser had been superseded as a type by the fast battleship. But in August 1914 Lord Fisher, the arch-advocate of speed in place of armour, returned as First Sea Lord. When two of his original battle cruisers won their easy victory over Spee's obsolescent cruisers at the Battle of the Falklands in November 1914 Fisher immediately asked the Cabinet to rescind its suspension of further capital ship construction. Material for two of the cancelled *Revenge* class was allocated for a pair of very fast battle cruisers of abnormally light draught. Although Fisher harped on the value of battle cruisers for running down commerce-raiders, he wanted the two battle cruisers for his great Baltic invasion scheme, hence the shallow draught. The disastrous effect Fisher had on warship design can be seen to good advantage in these ships; eight years after the laying down of the *Invincible*, during which time gun calibres had risen from 12in to 15in, he revived the *Invincible*'s standard of armouring for a ship practically twice her size.

With the building time of the *Dreadnought* in mind, Fisher stipulated fifteen months as the time required to design and complete two ships with highly novel features. With 15in turrets already earmarked for two monitors, it was impossible to provide more than three for each ship within the time-limit. To save time the machinery of the *Tiger* was duplicated, but with extra boilers. Although five and six months respectively over Fisher's deadline, the building time for these ships remains a record achievement, and shows what British shipyards could do in the early part of the war.

The *Repulse* and *Renown* were the first ships to be completed with anti-torpedo bulge protection as an integral part of the hull. For the first time a triple mounting for the secondary guns was adopted. The five triple 4in mountings offered a good all-round defence on paper, but the mounting was too clumsy, and required a very large crew.

Although their arrival at Scapa Flow after Jutland was a welcome reinforcement, the knowledge that *Renown* and *Repulse* were armoured to the same puny scale as the lost *Invincible* and *Indefatigable* did not reassure the Fleet about their battle-worthiness. Jellicoe recorded his horror at seeing the two 'white elephants', with two rows of scuttles revealing for all to see the

155

fact that they had only a thin strip of waterline armour. Immediately they were taken in hand for some additional protection to magazines and turret roofs, while to add to their problems, *Renown*'s lightly built hull was strained during her gun trials; the two spent so much time in dockyard hands having minor improvements that they were christened *Refit* and *Repair*.

Appearance: Like all Fisher creations good looks could be guaranteed, and few ships could match their elegance, with the long flared forecastle, the 'cleaver' bow (adopted for the first time in a capital ship built for the Royal Navy) and massive funnels. As completed both had level funnels, but smoke interference caused the forefunnel to be raised 10ft during trials. At first, *Renown* could be distinguished by having a level searchlight platform, whereas *Repulse*'s was on two levels, but in 1918 both ships were given searchlight towers.

Careers

Renown: Joined the 1st Battle Cruiser Squadron, and served with the Battle Cruiser Force from September 1916 to the Armistice; used for Royal Tours in peacetime, and served with Atlantic Fleet; fully modernised between 1936 and 1939, and served with great distinction in World War II; sold in 1948.

Repulse: Served with 1st Battle Cruiser Squadron from August 1916; in action with German light cruisers in Heligoland Bight in November 1917; reconstructed 1919–22, and subsequently served with Atlantic Fleet; like *Renown* she was used for a Royal Tour, and went on a world cruise in 1923–4; modernised 1932–6, and served with Home Fleet from outbreak of World War II until 1941, when she went to the Far East to join *Prince of Wales*; sunk by Japanese air attack off coast of Malaya 10 December 1941.

Displacement: 18,600tons (normal); 22,690tons (full load)
Dimensions: 735ft×81ft×23ft 4in
Guns: 8×15in 42cal (2×2)
18×4in (6×3)
2×3in A.A. (2×1)
Torpedo Tubes: 2×21in (beam, submerged); after completion a further 12 were added (6×2, above water)
Armour: 3–2in belt; 1–¾in deck; 13in turrets; 10in C.T.
Machinery: 4-shaft Parsons all-geared turbines, 90,000shp = 31knots; 18 Yarrow small-tube boilers
Oil Capacity: 750/3160tons
Endurance: Not known
Complement: 840
Cost: Not known

Above, *Renown as she appeared in 1919 (Author's collection).*

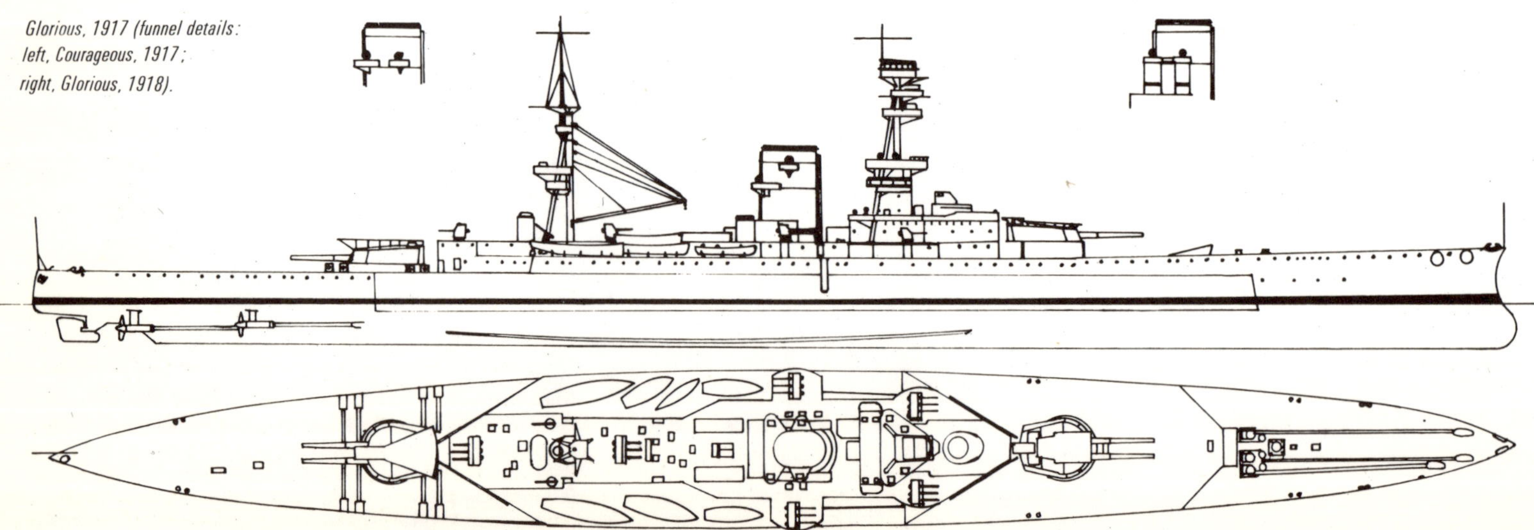

Glorious, 1917 (funnel details: left, Courageous, 1917; right, Glorious, 1918).

Courageous class

	Laid Down	Launched	Completed	Built/Engined
Courageous	May 1915	5 Feb 1916	Jan 1917	Armstrong, Elswick
Glorious	May 1915	20 Apr 1916	Jan 1917	Harland & Wolff

These ships were designed to meet Lord Fisher's requirements for fast shallow-draught cruisers with heavy armament to take part in his great Baltic invasion scheme. With their half-sister *Furious* they stand out as the most half-baked ideas ever produced by British naval architects, for they mounted 15in guns in an overblown light cruiser hull, protected by only 3in armour.

The weakness of the design lay in the enormous armament, for it was almost impossible to range accurately at a speed of 31knots with only two-gun salvoes from 15in turrets. If, on the other hand, as Fisher later claimed, they were intended for coastal bombardment in the Baltic, then four 15in-gunned monitors could have done the job at one-quarter the cost, and still be expendable. As cruisers they were a hopeless failure for the same reason; an armament of 6in guns would have made them far more effective, however wasteful it might be.

As Fisher left the Admiralty in 1915 his Baltic project was dropped, and we can only guess at what might have happened to his 'Spurious' and 'Outrageous' in the Baltic. When finally completed they proved white elephants, and had to be used to spearhead the light cruiser squadrons. They were able to out-strip destroyers in dirty weather with ridiculous ease, and were said to be a knot-and-a-half faster at deep load draught than at their legend draught. For a time *Courageous* served as a minelayer.

Machinery: They were the first big ships to have small-tube boilers, since they were given the same machinery as the small cruiser *Champion*, but with four shafts and eighteen boilers instead of eight.

Armament: The 15in turrets were spares made available as the result of cancelling the three additional *Revenge* class units. For the first time a triple 4in mounting was tried (see also *Renown*), but it did not prove a success. After completion both ships were given six pairs of 21in torpedo tubes, disposed abreast of the mainmast and abreast of the after turret. It proved impossible to fire torpedoes from the submerged tubes above 23knots without bending the firing bar. After conversion their 15in guns were stored until used to arm the battleship *Vanguard* in World War II.

Appearance: As first completed *Glorious* had her searchlight platforms on split levels, whereas those on *Courageous*' funnel were at the same level. Later both ships had 'coffee-pot' towers for the searchlights, which made them identical. As a minelayer *Courageous* had four sets of mine-rails discharging over her stern, which earned her the nickname of 'Clapham Junction'.

Careers

Courageous: Served with 3rd Light Cruiser Squadron and then with 1st L.C.S. of Grand Fleet; action off Heligoland 17 November 1917; paid off after Armistice and became gunnery training ship; converted to aircraft carrier 1924–8; torpedoed September 1939.

Glorious: Flagship of 3rd L.C.S. and 1st C.S., but otherwise service as *Courageous*; gunnery school at Devenport in 1919; converted to aircraft carrier 1924–30; sunk by gunfire of *Scharnhorst* and *Gneisenau* off Norway June 1940.

Right, a 1919 photograph of Courageous showing details of her No. 1 turret, tripod mast and bridgework (NMM).

Above, Glorious.

Left, Courageous in dock during the winter of 1917 undergoing conversion to a minelayer. The four sets of rails discharging over her quarterdeck gave rise to the nickname 'Clapham Junction' (NMM).

Furious

Displacement: 19,513tons (normal);
22,890tons (deep load)
Dimensions: 750ft ×88ft×24ft (max)
Guns: 2×18in 40cal (2×1) as designed;
1×18in as built
10×5·5in (10×1)
5×3in A.A.
4×3pdrs
Torpedo Tubes: 6×21in (4 above
water, beam and 2 submerged, beam)
Armour: As Courageous class
Machinery: 4-shaft Brown-Curtis
geared turbines 94,000shp = 31½knots;
18 Yarrow small-tube boilers
Oil Capacity: 750/3160tons
Endurance: Not known
Complement: 840
Cost: Not known

	Laid Down	Launched	Completed	Built/Engined
Furious	June 1915	15 Aug 1916	July 1917	Armstrong, Elswick

This ship was a slightly modified sister of the *Courageous* and *Glorious*. She had a slightly different hull form, and was intended to be armed with two single 18in guns, and a different secondary armament.

All the strictures heaped on the other two ships apply to the *Furious*, only more so. By Fisher's standards she was the perfect capital ship, with guns of the maximum range and speed to enable her to choose her own conditions for battle. Unfortunately a ship with only two 18in guns caught in misty conditions could easily find herself faced by an equally fast smaller ship which she could not hope to hit with two-gun or one-gun ranging salvoes.

Whatever the *Furious* would have been like as a battle cruiser, her future was settled at the Longhope Conference on naval aviation in 1917. As a large hull was needed for conversion to an aircraft carrier, the new ship fitting out at Elswick was chosen. Her forward 18in gun had not been installed, so the forward part of the ship was converted to a hangar and runway. After the war she underwent an even more drastic reconstruction as an aircraft carrier, and served with great distinction in World War II.

Armament: The 18in Mk. I gun (known for security reasons as the 15in 'B' Coastal Defence gun) was designed with a turret ring the same size as the 15in twin, so that if it had proved a failure, the *Furious* could have been converted to the *Courageous* standard. The gun weighed 150tons, and fired a shell of 3600lb nearly 30 miles. The 5·5in guns had been manufactured for the Greek *Salamis* (*qv*), and had a longer range than the Mk. XI 6in, and so the Admiralty was anxious to give them a trial.

Appearance: As designed she would have looked very like the *Courageous*, but with single guns, both main and secondary. Her appearance was totally altered during conversion, and then modified several times after that.

Career

Carried out numerous trials with aircraft and then joined the captive balloon section; heavily reconstructed postwar and served throughout World War II with great success.

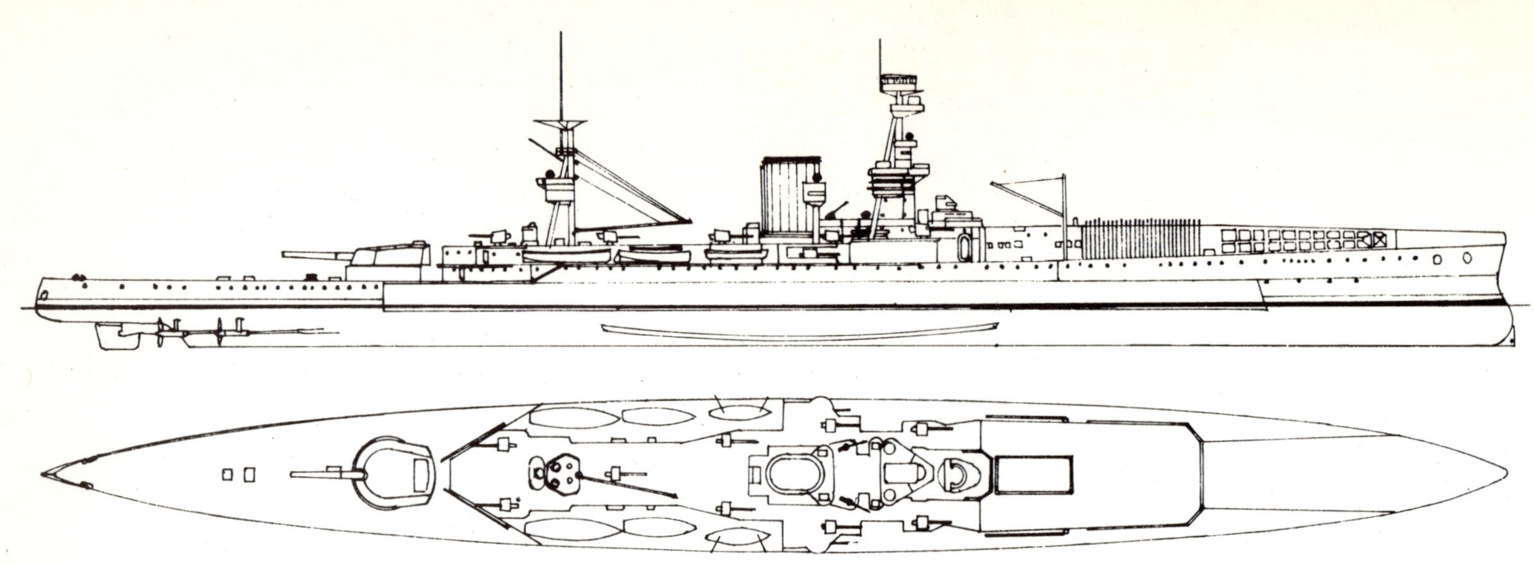

Below, *Furious in the closing stages of fitting out on the Tyne. The 18in gun can be seen aft, but the forward turret has already been replaced by the hangar and flying platform. Note the catwalk running from the forecastle deck down to the quarterdeck – this was adapted from the original shelf for torpedo nets (MoD).*

Hood class

Displacement: 36,300tons (increased to 41,200tons, Hood)
Dimensions: 810ft (pp)×104ft×29ft (maximum)
Guns: 8×15in (4×2) 16×5·5in (16×1); reduced to 12 in Hood 4×4in A.A. (4×1)
Torpedo Tubes: 2×21in (submerged); 4 above water/21in tubes added in Hood
Armour: 12–5in belt; 11–9in CT; 15in turrets; 3–1in decks (designed to have 8–9in belt)
Machinery: 4-shaft turbines (Brown-Curtis in Hood), 144,000hp = 32knots; 24 Yarrow small-tube boilers
Oil Capacity: 1200/4000tons
Endurance: 4000miles at 10knots
Complement: 1477
Cost: £5,843,039 (Hood): ($23,372,156)

	Laid Down	Launched	Completed	Built/Engined
Anson	? Apr 1916	Cancelled	—	Armstrong, Elswick
Hood	1 Sept 1916	22 Aug 1918	Mar 1920	John Brown
Howe	? Apr 1916	Cancelled	—	Cammell Laird
Rodney	? Apr 1916	Cancelled	—	Fairfield

To counter the proposed German battle cruisers of the *Mackensen* class, armed with 15in guns, the Board of Admiralty proposed the construction of four ships armed on a par with the *Queen Elizabeths* but capable of a speed of 32knots. Although the design was completed before the end of 1915 no orders were placed on account of the lack of suitable building berths. The initial design was comparable to the *Tiger* in having 9in belt armour, but the catastrophic loss of three battle cruisers cast grave doubts on the wisdom of this, and with Fisher no longer First Sea Lord more armour could be worked in.

As finally amended in 1917 the design of the *Hood* class was nearer to the *Queen Elizabeth* standard of a fast battleship, than to the concept of a battle cruiser such as the *Tiger*. With 12in armour and reasonable deck protection for the time, she seemed to be good value—but unfortunately a lot of weight was wasted in thin armour spread about in useless places. The proportion of armour to hull weight, only 33·6 per cent, places the *Hood*

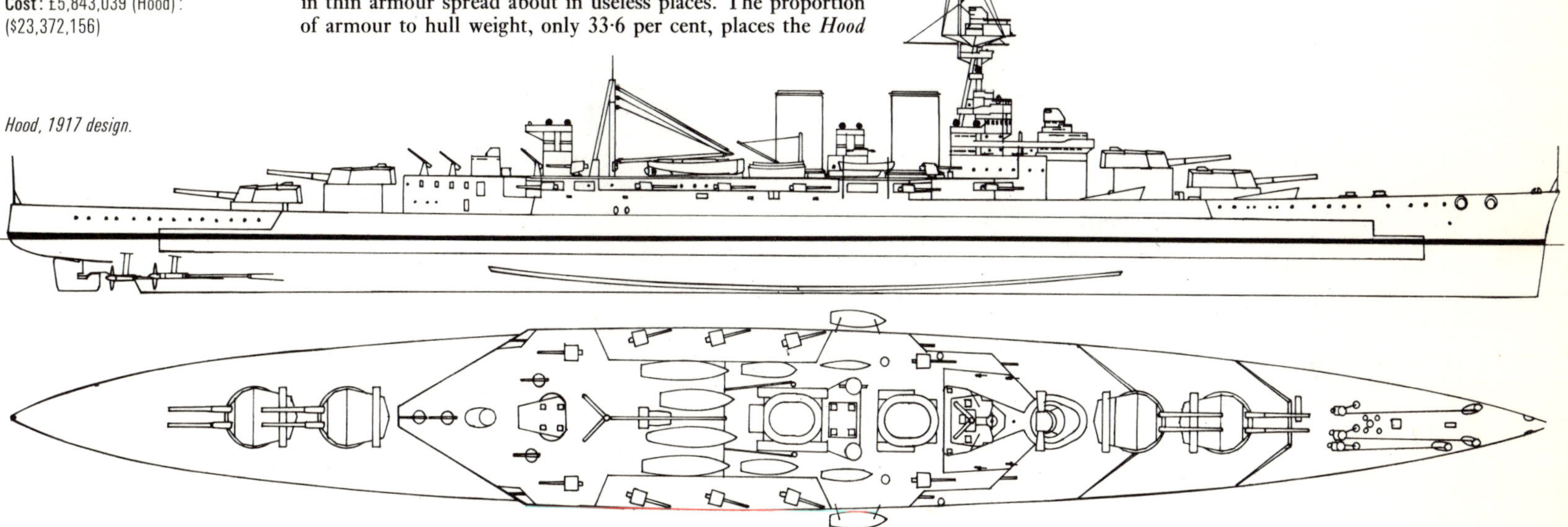

Hood, 1917 design.

firmly in the category of pre-Jutland protection standards, and she reflected very few new ideas, excepting the long overdue improvement of water-tube boilers which reduced the weight of machinery to only 13 per cent of the total.

The news in 1917 that the Germans had finally stopped all work on the *Mackensen* class resulted in *Anson*, *Howe* and *Rodney* being suspended in March. As very little material had been assembled (it was officially announced later that £860,000 had been spent on all three between 1916 and the Armistice) this was no great loss, and the hulls were dismantled to clear the slipways. Only *Hood* was sufficiently advanced to be worth continuing.

Career
Completed 1920 and retained after the Washington Disarmament Treaty, despite being well over the limit of displacement for capital ships; not modernised in any way between 1920 and 1939; saw considerable service in early years of World War II, and sunk by a magazine explosion during action against German battleship *Bismarck* 24 May 1941.

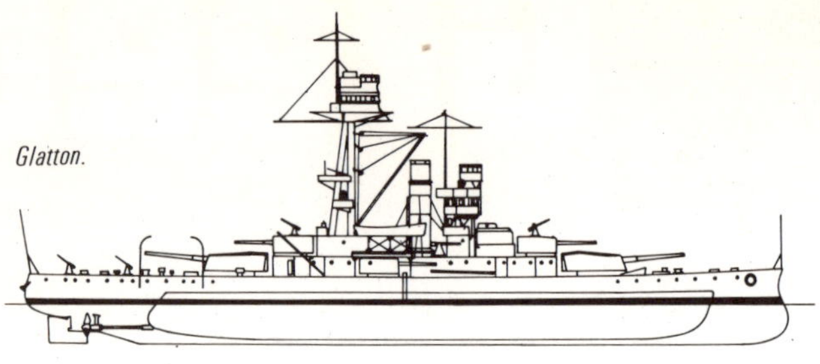

Glatton.

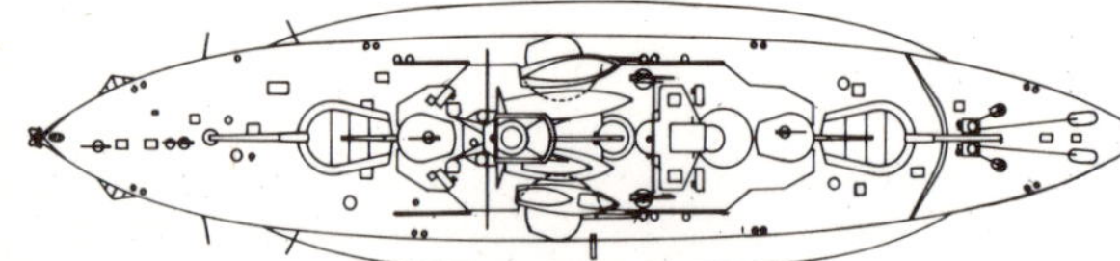

Gorgon class

Displacement: 4825tons (normal); 5700tons (full load)
Dimensions: 290ft×55ft (hull only)× 16ft 4in (mean) 73ft 7in (extreme)
Guns: 2×9·2in 50cal (2×1) 4×6in (4×1) 2×3in A.A. (2×1) 2×3pdr A.A. (2×1)
Armour: 7in belt; 2in deck; 8in turrets; 8in CT
Machinery: 2-shaft triple expansion, 4000ihp = 13knots; 4 Yarrow boilers (mixed firing)
Coal Capacity: 175/364tons
Oil Capacity: 175tons
Endurance: About 2500miles at 10knots
Complement: 323
Cost: Not known

	Laid Down	Launched	Completed	Built/Engined
Gorgon (ex-Nidaros)	11 June 1913	9 June 1914	July 1918	Armstrong, Elswick
Glatton (ex-Bjorgvin)	26 May 1913	8 Aug 1913	Sept 1918	Armstrong, Elswick

These interesting little ships were the smallest armoured ships to serve in the Royal Navy in the war. They had been laid down in 1913 for the Norwegian Navy as coast defence battleships, and construction had been suspended in 1914. However, the need for shore-bombarding vessels caused the Admiralty to purchase them on 31 January 1915. Work proceeded slowly until 1917.

The torpedo tubes were suppressed, and high-angle guns replaced the original 4in weapons. To protect the hull against torpedo attack, enormous 'bulges' were added, thus increasing the beam by nearly 24ft and reducing the draught.

Armament: The original 9·4in guns ordered had to be relined to take the standard British 9·2in shell. Actually, one gun had been completed, and had to be retubed, but the remaining three were completed as 9·2in.

Appearance: They were unique among British ships, with a tall funnel and a big tripod stepped abaft it. *Glatton* had a high-angle 3pdr gun on the forward 6in turret, but *Gorgon* had it on the after 6in gun.

Careers

Glatton: Served with Dover Patrol, but on 16 September 1918, not long after she joined, she caught fire in Dover Harbour; she was torpedoed three times by destroyers by order of Admiral Keyes to prevent the destruction of Dover, and sank; the fire had been caused by stokers piling hot clinker and ash against a magazine bulkhead; the wreck was raised on 16 March 1926 and broken up.

Gorgon: Joined the Dover Patrol and took part in several bombardments on the Belgian Coast; listed for disposal after paying off at Devonport in September 1919, but was retained for gunnery trials and experimental work at Portsmouth; paid off at end of 1927 and sold 28 August 1928 for breaking up at Pembroke Dock.

Left, Glatton in dry dock shortly before completion (IWM) and in 1918 after completion. Note the enormous bulge, and the paravane shoe fitted to her stem (IWM).

Greece

Introduction

The Royal Hellenic Navy was small, but it had shared in the reflected glory of the Army's success over Turkey in the Balkan War of 1912. Its units were a hotch-potch of foreign purchases, with three old French-built battleships suitable for nothing more than coast-defence, and two ex-American predreadnoughts purchased in 1914. The only big units were building in France and Germany, and the outbreak of war in August·1914 prevented them from being completed.

The government of Mr. Venizelos had been friendly towards the French and British, and in August 1914 negotiations were in progress with Britain to exchange Cyprus for base rights at Kephallenia. Had this become fact Greece might have been an ally of Britain and France in the first month of the war, but the talks were dropped. Despite assiduous wooing by both sides, the Greeks remained neutral; the internal division was between Venizelos, on the side of war, and the King favouring neutrality. The British and the French did their best to help the Venizelists to topple the monarchy, but the situation became confused as the King and his supporters inevitably began to intrigue with a view to frustrating these plans.

In 1915 Allied soldiers occupied Salonika, and in 1916 the French landed to secure Corfu as a refuge for the Serbians, but it was not until 27 June 1917 that Greece declared war on the Central Powers. For the Greek Navy this meant very little. The confused state of the country, with opinion still deeply divided over the war, meant that the Allies did not trust the Greek armed forces, and a large force of British and French ships kept close watch on their fleet. The two modern ships, the *Kilkis* and *Lemnos*, were kept at Piraeus as guardships, while the others remained at Poros on training duties.

Hydra class

Displacement: 5500tons (normal)
Dimensions: 320ft×51ft 10in×24ft (max)
Guns: 3×10·8in (2×36cal; 1×30cal) (3×1)
5×5·9in 45cal (5×1); Spetsai only 4
1×3·9in 50cal
8×65mm (8×1), 4×47mm, 16×37mm
Torpedo Tubes: 1×14·55in (bow, above water)
2×14in (submerged, beam)
Armour: 12–3in belt; 2¼in deck (2in only in Hydral); 12in CT
Machinery: 2-shaft vertical triple expansion, 6700hp=17knots (after reconstruction 1897–1900); cylindrical boilers (Belleville)
Coal Capacity: 400/600tons
Endurance: Not known
Complement: 440

	Laid Down	Launched	Completed	Built/Engined
Hydra	1887	15 May 1889	1891	Granville
Psara	1888	20 Feb 1890	1892	Granville
Spetsai	1887	26 Oct 1889	1891	St. Nazaire

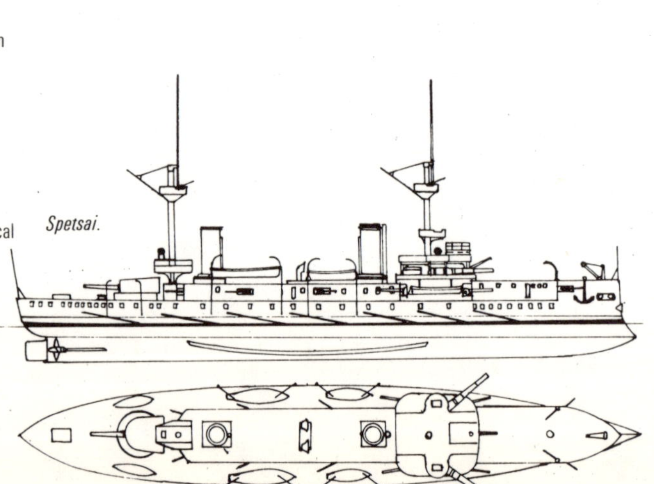

Spetsai.

These French-designed ships had a curious disposition of armament, with the forward guns in a barbette, over which they fired to port and starboard of the bridge; the short-barrelled gun aft was in a normal turret. With their antiquated guns, poor steaming and short endurance they were only fit for coast defence duties by 1914.

Appearance: *Psara* could be distinguished by having a heavy military mast with fighting top amidships. *Hydra* and *Spetsai* identical except for the existence of a small auxiliary funnel before the forefunnel in *Spetsai*; this is believed to have been removed either before 1914 or during the war.

Career

Hydra: Coast defence duties during war; navigational training ship at Poros 1920; discarded 1929 and broken up.

Psara: Had been a strokers' training ship from about 1910; coast defence duties during war; gunnery training ship at Poros from 1920; discarded 1928 and broken up.

Spetsai: Coast defence duties during war; refitted 1919 and became navigational training ship at Poros; discarded 1929 and broken up.

Kilkis/Lemnos

Displacement: 13,000tons
Dimensions: 375ft (wl)×77ft×24ft 9in
382ft (oa)
Guns: 4×12in (2×2); 8×8in (4×2);
8×7in (8×1); 12×3in (12×1)
Torpedo Tubes: 2×21in (submerged, beam)
Armour: Main belt 9in, ends 4in;
main turrets 12–8in; secondary
turrets 6in; casemates 7in
Machinery: 2 sets 4-cyl reciprocating;
10,000ihp = 17knots; ? Babcock
boilers

Coal Capacity: 600/1750tons
Endurance: 4000miles at 10knots

Complement: 725
Cost: Not known

	Laid Down	Launched	Completed	Built
Kilkis	12 May 1904	9 Dec 1905	1908	Cramp
(ex U.S.S. Idaho, BB24)				
Lemnos	12 May 1904	30 Sept 1905	1908	Cramp
(ex-U.S.S. Mississippi BB23)				

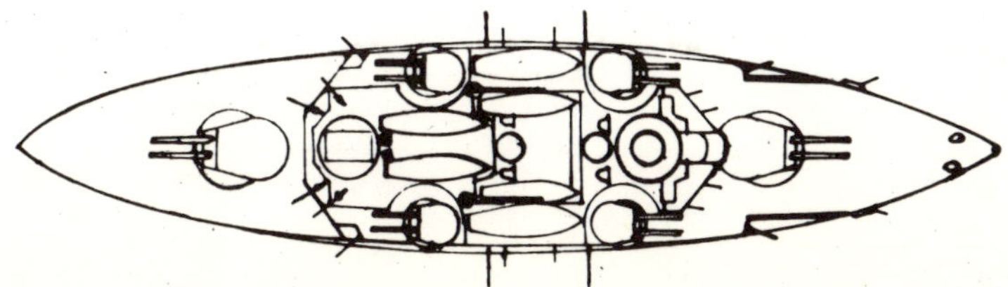

Kilkis.

Authorised by U.S. Congress in 1903, this pair of small battleships broke with the tradition of American battleships being as large and as well armoured as their European contemporaries. They were 3000tons smaller than the preceding *Connecticuts*, and had only two-thirds of their power, yet attempted to carry nearly as heavy an armament.

Not surprisingly the *Idaho* and *Mississippi* proved unsatisfactory in service, and when in 1914 the government of Greece wished to strengthen its navy with a view to meeting the threat of the Turkish predreadnoughts *Harreddin Barbarousse* and *Torgud Reis*, the U.S. Government responded with alacrity by offering them two six-year-old battleships. The pair were transferred without difficulty in July 1914 just time to avoid any diplomatic problems, and were commissioned in the Hellenic Navy as *Kilkis* and *Lemnos*.

Careers

Kilkis: Coast and harbour defence duties 1916–18; served until World War II, when she was sunk by Italian aircraft 10 April 1941.

Lemnos: As *Kilkis*; sunk 10 April 1941 by Italian aircraft.

Salamis

Displacement: Probably 19,500tons as finally designed (normal)
Dimensions: 564ft 5in (wl)×80ft 3in ×24ft 9in
Guns: 8×14in (4×2); 12×5·5in (12×1); 12×3in (12×1)
Torpedo Tubes: 3×19·5in (2 beam, 1 stern)
Armour: 9¾in belt; 3in ends
Machinery: 3-shaft AEG turbines; 40,000shp = 23knots; 18 Yarrow boilers (12 coal-firing, 8 oil-firing)
Fuel/Endurance: Not known
Complement: Not known
Cost: Not known

	Laid Down	Launched	Completed	Builder
Salamis	23 July 1913	11 Nov 1914	—	Vulkan, Stettin
(ex-Vasilefs Georgios)				

One of the enigmatic dreadnoughts of World War I, the *Salamis* had her origins in the Balkan War of 1912, when Greece and her allies had worsted Turkey. However, the rapid strides made by Turkey in 1913–14 in rebuilding her armed forces forced the Greeks to look to their defences. Cruisers and destroyers were ordered from Great Britain, and an armoured ship from Germany.

The original design evisaged something on the lines of the Japanese *Ibuki* type, a light battleship armament in a conventional armoured cruiser hull, but with the development of the battle cruiser type in England and Germany, the need for a proper capital ship was felt. Accordingly the design was expanded into a four-turret battleship or battle cruiser.

Armament: Nobody could accuse the Greek government of being unwilling to shop around, as the main armament was ordered from Bethlehem Steel in the U.S.A., while the secondary armament of 5·5in guns was ordered from the British Coventry Syndicate (a similar mark to the gun ordered for two Greek light cruisers). Delivery of both lots of guns was impossible after August 1914, but astute manoeuvring by the British ensured that the 14in guns, turrets and barbette armour were transferred from the United States to Britain, to be installed in a series of monitors.

Appearance: Much of the information about this ship is contradictory, and any attempt to describe her appearance must be pure speculation. She would in all probability have resembled the smaller Greek cruiser *Averoff*, with two tripods, and turrets arranged on the centreline fore and aft.

Work ceased on the ship as soon as war broke out in August 1914. Thereafter British intelligence continued to postulate that she might be completed with a new armament of 12in or even 15in guns! However, German problems of gun production made any project of this nature doubtful, and the ship was to all intents and purposes cancelled outright in 1915.

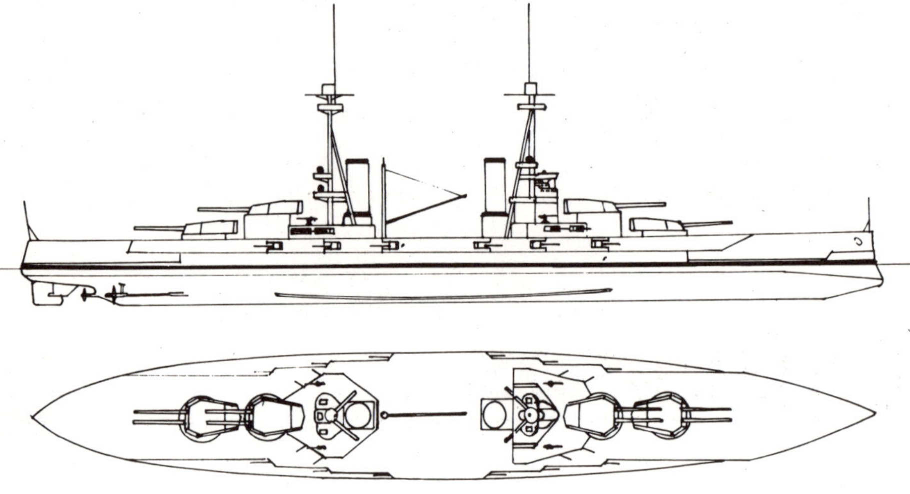

Vasilefs Konstantinos

	Laid Down	Launched	Completed	Builder
Vasilefs Konstantinos	July 1914	—	—	Ch. de Loire & Penhoet

The contract for this vessel was signed in 1914, and she was laid down in July 1914. The outbreak of war caused construction to be deferred immediately, since the French Government was unwilling to sanction work on any large naval units. Nevertheless there was talk of completing her as the *Savoie*, but this was never in fact considered, and the contract with the Greek Government was annulled.

After the renaming of the *Salamis* (*qv*) the *Vasilefs Konstantinos* was renamed *Vasilefs Georgios*. This resulted in widespread references to a pair of battleships building, but in fact only one was ordered (in April 1914).

Below, *Emanuele Filiberto at Fiume with British light forces in March 1919, by which time anti-aircraft guns had been mounted on the superstructure (IWM).*

Introduction

Italy was drawn into the war relatively late, being suspicious to a certain extent of French expansion. However, seizing the opportunity of regaining her lost provinces from the Austrians, she declared war on Austria at midnight, 23 May 1915. She did not declare war on Germany until 27 August 1916—the price she had to pay for increased Allied aid.

Given her war aims, Italy's naval problems were simple: to destroy or neutralise the Austrian Fleet in the Adriatic so that Italian troop movements could be made without hindrance.

Italy had, by the end of the nineteenth century, the industry to build and maintain a modern fleet, and in 1915 she had the *Andrea Doria* and *Caio Duilio* ready as well as four earlier dreadnoughts and eight effective predreadnoughts. She had also laid down four huge 15in-gun ships, modelled on the British *Queen Elizabeth* class, but like new construction in most other navies, work was suspended on them shortly after the war began. Italian designers were both competent and ingenious, and had been producing noteworthy ships for many years: having had a home-based shipbuilding and armament industry for fifty years they were able to turn out ships which were technically superior to the French, and at least the equal of the Austrians.

Dockyards and Bases

The main Italian naval base was at Taranto, under the 'heel' of Italy, but there were also Royal dockyards at Venice, Castellammare (near Naples) and La Spezia (near Genoa). The principal builders were as follows:

Abbreviated Name	Full Name and Location
Ansaldo	Cantieri Ansaldo, Genoa
Odero	Cantieri Odero, Genoa
Orlando	Cantiero Orlando, Livorno (Leghorn)

There were several novel features about the war in the Adriatic. Both Brindisi and Venice were bombed frequently by Austrian aircraft, a hazard almost unknown anywhere else, and although no damage was done to any big ships it confirmed the desire of the Italian Ministry of Marine to keep the main strength of the Fleet at Taranto. Another development was the high-speed motor torpedo-boat which became a potent weapon particularly suited to the individualistic Italian temperament. Lieutenant-Commander Luigi Rizzo was responsible for torpedoing and sinking two Austrian battleships, one at Trieste and another off Premuda, while lesser targets were attacked on many occasions.

Late in 1915 the Italian Fleet rendered valuable help in supplying the Serbian Army through the Albanian ports of Medua and Durazzo, and when eventually the Serbs were defeated the evacuation was carried out from these ports.

In 1916 the Allies collaborated with the Italians to lay the famous Otranto Barrage, an attempt to emulate the Dover Barrage, and pen the Austrian and German submarines in the Adriatic behind a barrage of mines. This proved very difficult, for the Otranto Straits are deep and wide, so the minefields could never be thickly sown. As with the Dover Barrage enemy light forces raided the patrol lines, but the capital ships based on Brindisi were never able to intervene.

The Army operations in Northern Italy in 1916 provided an opportunity to use the predreadnought battleships for shore bombardment. As a result the Fleet was reorganised:

Reorganisation of Italian Fleet in November 1916
1st Division
Conte di Cavour (flagship), Guilio Cesare, Dante Alighieri
2nd Division
Andrea Doria, Duilio
British Division
Queen, Prince of Wales, Venerable, Africa
Group 'C' (Valona)
3rd Division
Regina Elena (flagship), Vittorio Emanuele, Roma, Napoli
4th Division
Regina Margherita plus 2 armoured cruisers

Weapons

The Italians were well supplied with all types of naval guns, for the English firm of Armstrong had founded a factory at Pozzuoli in the previous century. As a result the Italians were well placed to make use of the latest British ideas in ordnance. British help was available when a 15in gun had to be designed for the new superdreadnought, and the latest Vickers weapons had also been supplied since 1908. Unfortunately the standard of cordite manufacture was not as good as the guns, and two ships were lost from internal explosions. The Italians were notable as the first designers to introduce triple turrets, in the *Dante Alighieri*.

Italian Guns

Calibre	Length	Muzzle Velocity	Elevation	Range	Notes
10in	40cal	2070fps	35°	22,500yds	St. Bon Class
12in	40cal	2550fps	25°	22,500yds	R. Margherita and R. Elena Classes
12in	46cal	2820fps	20°	28,900yds	D. Alighieri, Cavour and A. Doria Classes
15in	45cal	2296fps	20°	c.26,000yds	Carraiolo Class

Actions

There were no major actions, as the Austro-Hungarian Navy confined itself to hit-and-run tactics designed to hinder Italian and Allied ship movements. Accordingly the Italian battleships were left with little to do beyond shore bombardment and patrol duties. Despite the numerical advantage enjoyed by the Italians they had insisted before entering the war that they should be guaranteed not only the support of the French Fleet but also the actual presence of four British battleships under Italian command. As a result four ships swung around their buoys from

Disposition of Italian Fleet at the Outbreak of War (24 May 1915)
Taranto
Flagship of Commander-in-Chief
Conte di Cavour
1st Battle Squadron
Dante Alighieri (flagship), Guilio Cesare, Leonardo da Vinci
2nd Battle Division
Regina Elena (flagship), Vittorio Emanuele, Napoli, Roma
Brindisi
2nd Battle Squadron
Benedetto Brin (flagship), Regina Margherita
Venice
Sardegna (flagship), Emanuele Filiberto, Ammiraglio di St. Bon

1915 to 1918, and when in 1917 the Italians demanded more reinforcements the British were naturally unresponsive.

The *Regina Margherita* was sunk in 1916 when she strayed into an Italian minefield, while the only other actions of note took place in 1918 and were not battleship actions so far as the Italian Navy was concerned (an Italian motor boat torpedoed the *Szent Istvan*, and two men penetrated Pola Harbour and planted a mine under the *Viribus Unitis*).

Modifications and Colour Schemes

Nothing much was done to alter the appearance of Italian ships during the war, although light guns were altered on more than one occasion. The colour scheme was a medium grey overall.

Conclusion

The Italian Fleet was something of a showpiece during the war, as its most modern dreadnoughts lay at their moorings in Taranto, remote from the theatre of war. Had they been handled with more dash something might have been achieved, but the geographical conditions in the Adriatic put big ships at a disadvantage. The predreadnoughts, however, were put to good use and, like their counterparts in the Allied navies, they saw what action there was.

Disposition of Italian Fleet in November 1918
Battle Squadron
1st Division[1]
Andrea Doria (flagship), Duilio, Conte di Cavour, Guilio Cesare, Dante Alighieri
2nd Division[2]
Vittorio Emanuele, Roma, Napoli, Regina Elena
Northern Adriatic Naval Forces
Emanuele Filiberto, Ammigaglio di Saint Bon, Re Umberto

[1] All at Taranto, except Dante Alighieri at Brindisi.
[2] Vittorio Emanuele and Roma in Aegean, others at Taranto.

The following obsolescent battleships were used for local defence during the war. They formed no part of the main Italian strength, but have been included on account of the fact that they were armed for war purposes.

Name	Launched	Armament
Dandolo	1878	4×10in 40cal (2×2) 7×6in 40cal (7×1) 5×4·7in etc 4×17·7in TT
Italia	1880	3×17in 26cal (2×2) 1×17in 27cal 7×5·9in 26cal 4×4·7in 23cal etc 4×14in TT
Andrea Doria	1885	4×17in 27cal (2×2) 2×6in 32cal (2×1) 4×4·7in 32cal etc 2×14in TT
Re Umberto	1888	4×13·5in 30cal (2×2) 8×6in 40cal (8×1) 16×4·7in 40cal etc 5×17·7in TT

Careers

Dandolo: At the outbreak of war she was the floating oil tank vessel *GM.40*; served as harbour guardship at Brindisi and Valona 1915–18; laid up 31 December 1919; stricken from list 23 January 1920.

Italia: Had been laid up since June 1914, but reinstated on Navy List 23 May 1915, having been towed by the *St. Bon* to Brindisi 20 April to act as a floating battery in the outer harbour; left for La Spezia December 1917 to convert to grain carrier (armed with only 2×4·7in guns); laid up 13 January 1921 and stricken from list 16 November the same year for breaking up.

Andrea Doria: In use as depot ship at Taranto to outbreak of war, but had already, in February 1916, begun conversion to floating battery for harbour defence; named *GR.104* to avoid confusion with new dreadnought of the same name; towed to Brindisi 7 April 1915; after the war served as a floating oil tank until 1929, then broken up.

Re Umberto: Had been stricken from effective list 10 May 1914, but towed to La Spezia in June 1915 to act as depot ship during the completion of the new *Andrea Doria*; reinstated in Naval List 9 December 1915 as a floating battery; served at Brindisi March 1916–November 1917 and then Valona, November 1917–April 1918; converted to troop transport April–October 1918 and then modified as 'boom-breaker' for the projected assault on Pola, with 8×3in (8×1) and trench mortars; transferred to Venice for the Pola attack, which was cancelled when the war ended shortly afterwards; stricken 4 July 1920 and broken up.

In addition, two other elderly battleships, sisters of the *Re Umberto*, were also in service 1915–18. These were the *Sardegna* and *Sicilia* which served as depot ships without armament, and were stricken in 1923.

Right, Ammiraglio di Saint Bon about 1908/10 (Aldo Fraccaroli).

Right, Emanuele Filiberto seen in wartime about 1916. Note her tall funnels and low freeboard, particularly aft (Aldo Fraccaroli).

St. Bon class

Displacement: (in metric tons) 10,244tons, normal (Emanuele Filiberto 9800tons)

Dimensions: 344ft 6in×69ft×26ft (max)

Guns: 4×10in 40cal (2×2) 8×6in 40cal (8×1) 8×4·7in 40cal (8×1) 8×57mm and 2×37mm (St. Bon) 6×76mm and 8×47mm (Emanuele Filiberto)

Torpedo Tubes: 4×17·7in (beam, above water)

Armour: $9\frac{3}{4}$–4in belt; 3in decks; 6in turrets; 6in CT

Machinery: 2-shaft 3-cylinder triple expansion, 13,500hp=18knots; 12 cylindrical boilers

Coal Capacity: 600/1000tons

Endurance: 4000miles at 10knots

Complement: 537

Cost: £700,000 average ($2,800,000)

	Laid Down	Launched	Completed	Built/Engined
Ammiraglio di St. Bon	18 July 1893	29 Apr 1897	Sept 1900	Arsenale, Venice
Emanuele Filiberto	5 Oct 1893	29 Sept 1897	Apr 1902	Castellamare DY

These ships were a reaction against the giant Italian battleships of the 1880s. The Elswick pattern 10in gun was adopted to allow for an armour belt comparable to British and French contemporaries. The low freeboard and limited endurance were adequate for Mediterranean conditions, and both ships proved reliable, remaining in active service throughout the war.

Appearance: *St. Bon* differed from *Filiberto* in having short funnels, and in having both upper and lower fighting tops on her mast.

Careers

Ammiraglio di St. Bon: At Venice on outbreak of war in May 1915; Northern Adriatic 1916–18; removed from effective list 18 June 1920 and broken up.

Emanuele Filiberto: At Venice on outbreak of war; served with *St. Bon* in Northern Adriatic naval forces 1916–18; removed from effective list 29 March 1920 and broken up.

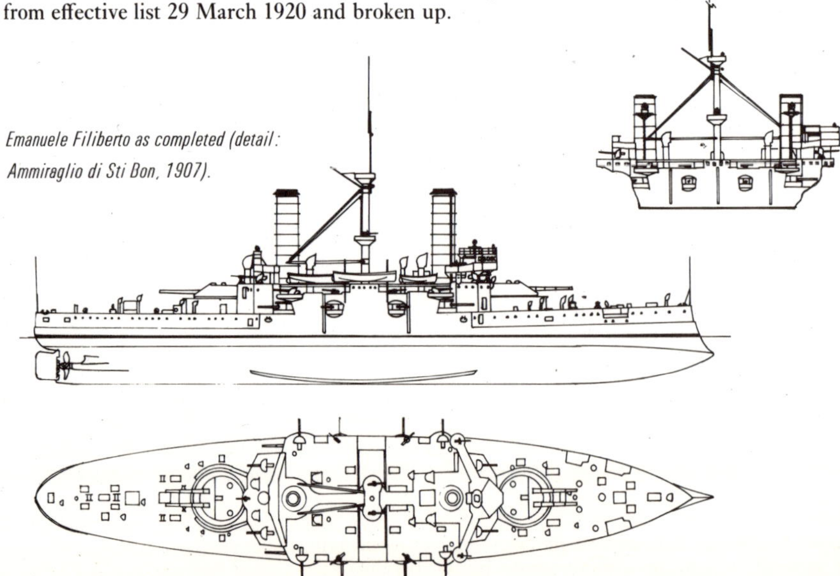

Emanuele Filiberto as completed (detail: Ammiraglio di Sti Bon, 1907).

Regina Margherita class

Displacement: (in metric tons)
Benedetto Brin: 13,400tons normal, 14,319tons full load
Regina Margherita: 14,319tons normal, 14,974tons full load
Dimensions: 426ft 6in×78ft×27ft 3in (mean)
Guns: 4×12in 40cal (2×2)
4×8in (4×1)
12×6in (12×1)
20×3in (20×1)
2×47mm
2×37mm
2×MGs
Torpedo Tubes: 4×17·7in (beam, submerged)
Armour: 6–2in belt; 3in deck; 12in CT; 8in turrets
Machinery: 2-shaft 4-cylinder triple expansion, 20,000hp = 20knots; 26 Belleville boilers (Niclausse in Regina Margherita)
Coal Capacity: 1000/2000tons
Endurance: 5000miles at 10knots
Complement: 1170
Cost: £1,150,000 average ($4,600,000)

	Laid Down	Launched	Completed	Built/Engined
*Benedetto Brin	30 Jan 1899	7 Nov 1901	Sept 1905	Castellamare DY
*Regina Margherita	20 Nov 1898	30 May 1901	Apr 1904	Arsenale, Spezia

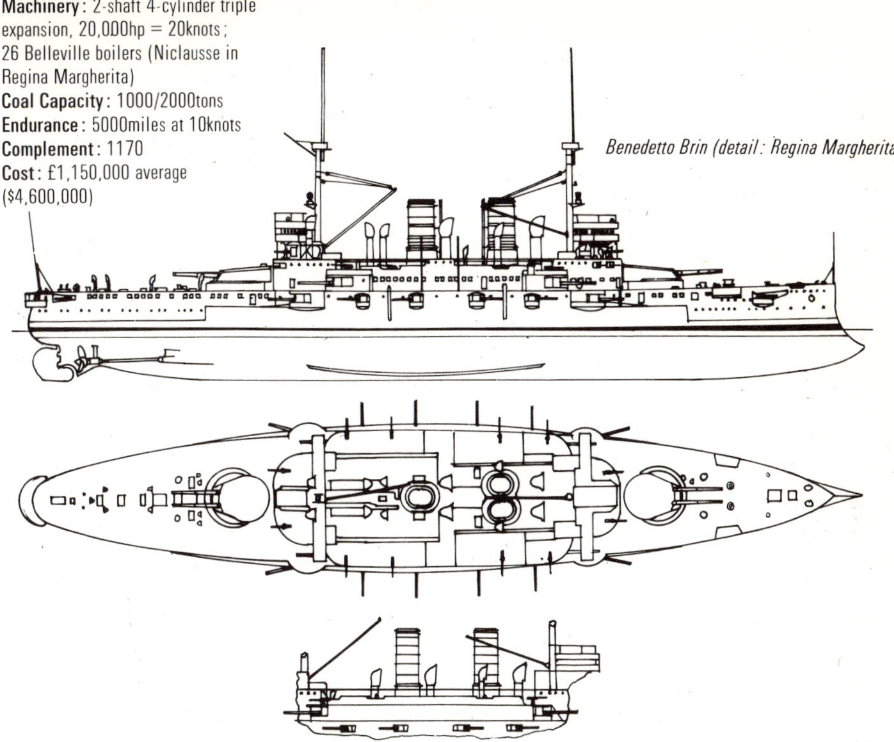

Benedetto Brin (detail: Regina Margherita).

These ships had been designed by the great naval architect Benedetto Brin, although modified after his death (much as the British *King Edward VII*s were modified after the death of Sir William White). With more than 7ft more freeboard they were more seaworthy than the *St. Bon* type, but protection was reduced to cruiser standard to allow for high speed. In this sense they can be regarded as one of the steps in the evolution of the battle cruiser, but also reflecting the trend towards a battery of powerful medium-calibre guns so typical of late predreadnoughts.

Appearance: Their unusual arrangement of funnels, two side-by-side and one on the centreline, was not easily identified if the ships were viewed from the beam. *Brin* had shorter funnels than *Margherita*.

Careers

Benedetto Brin: Flagship of 2nd Battle Squadron, and also flagship 3rd Division, at Brindisi on outbreak of war; destroyed in Brindisi by magazine explosion 27 September 1915 (probable cause was defective cordite).

Regina Margherita: At Brindisi on outbreak of war; sank off Valona 11 December 1916 after striking two mines laid by German submarine *UC.14*.

Below left, Benedetto Brin in 1908 (Aldo Fraccaroli).
Below right, Regina Margherita in 1908 with the armoured cruiser Guiseppe Garibaldi in the distance. Note the unusual layouts of the funnels (Aldo Fraccaroli).

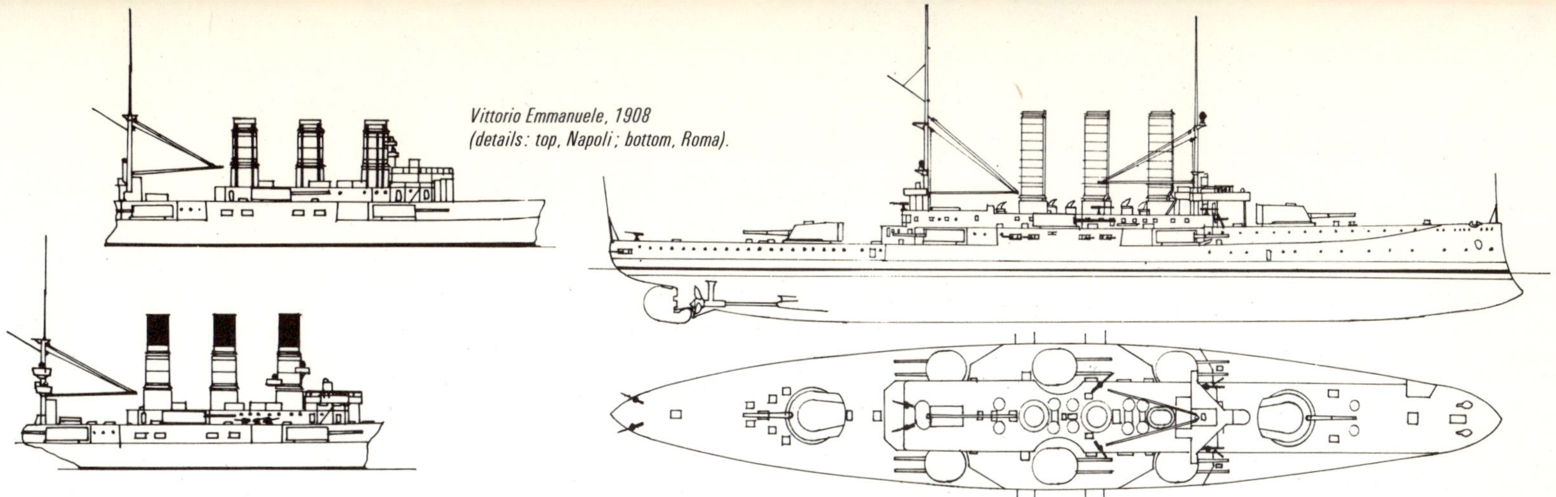

Vittorio Emmanuele, 1908
(details: top, Napoli; bottom, Roma).

Regina Elena class

Displacement: (in metric tons)
12,752–12,861 tons normal, 14,028–14,137 tons full load
Dimensions: 435ft×73ft 6in×28ft 3in
Guns: 2×12in 40cal (2×1)
12×8in 45cal (4×2)
24×3in (Regina Elena and Vittorio Emmanuele 16×3in)
Torpedo Tubes: 2×17·7in (beam, submerged)
Armour: 10–4in belt; 2¼in deck; 8in turrets; 10in CT
Machinery: 2-shaft 4-cylinder vertical triple expansion, 20,000hp=21knots; 28 Belleville boilers (Babcock & Wilcox in Napoli and Roma)
Coal Capacity: 1000/2000 tons
Endurance: Not known
Complement: 710 (727 as flagships)
Cost: £1,000,000 average ($4,000,000)

	Laid Down	Launched	Completed	Built/Engined
Regina Elena	27 Mar 1901	11 June 1904	June 1907	Arsenale, Spezia
Napoli	21 Oct 1903	10 Sept 1905	Sept 1908	Castellamare DY
Roma	20 Sept 1903	21 Apr 1907	Dec 1908	Arsenale, Spezia
Vittorio Emmanuele	18 Sept 1901	12 Oct 1904	Aug 1908	Castellamare DY

These ships were designed by General Cuniberti for high speed, and may in that sense be regarded as a step in the direction of the battle cruiser concept. Like the preceding class, the *Benedetto Brins*, they sacrificed main armament and protection for higher speed, but the heavy 8in battery was intended to provide weight of fire as compensation.

Cuniberti made considerable use of high-tensile steel in the structure of the *Napoli* and *Roma* in an attempt to reduce weight even more than in the other two, and in all four the lines were made as fine as possible.

Appearance: All four were distinguished by their high freeboard and clean hulls, with the 8in battery recess running in a gentle flare from the forecastle. *Napoli* and *Roma* had much shorter capped funnels, and lacked the foremast of *Vittorio Emanuele* and *Regina Elena*. *Roma* differed from *Napoli* in having a searchlight platform on her mainmast.

Careers

Napoli: Serving in 2nd Battle Division at Taranto on outbreak of war in May 1915; remained with Southern Adriatic and Ionian Sea forces 1916–18; removed from effective list 3 September 1926; broken up at Savona 1927–8.

Regina Elena: Flagship 2nd Battle Division, Taranto on outbreak of war; headquarters ship for Group 'C' at Valona 1916; with Southern Adriatic and Ionian Sea forces (Taranto) 1917–18; laid up 16 February 1923 and broken up.

Roma: With her sisters at Taranto on outbreak of war; with 3rd Division at Valona 1916; Southern Adriatic and Ionian Sea forces 1917–18 (2nd Division); in Aegean late 1918; laid up 1 September 1927; served as harbour training ship to 1932 and broken up.

Vittorio Emanuele: With her sisters at Taranto on outbreak of war; 3rd Division, Group 'C' at Valona 1916; Southern Adriatic and Ionian Sea forces 1917–18; with 2nd Division in Aegean late 1918; laid up 1 April 1923 and later broken up.

Above left, Vittorio Emmanuele as she appeared in 1908 (Aldo Fraccaroli).

Below left, Roma at Taranto on 9 June 1917 (IWM).

Above right, Regina Elena on trials in May 1907 (Aldo Fraccaroli).

Below right, Napoli at speed in April 1910. Note how her rig and funnels differ from the Regina Elena (Aldo Fraccaroli).

Below, *Dante Alighieri as she appeared on the outbreak of war. Note the widely spaced funnels reminiscent of the Russian dreadnoughts (Aldo Fraccaroli).*

Dante Alighieri

	Laid Down	Launched	Completed	Built/Engined
Dante Alighieri	6 June 1909	20 Aug 1910	Jan 1913	Castellamare DY

Displacement: (in metric tons) 19,552tons normal (21,600tons full load)

Dimensions: 519ft 6in×87ft 3in×29ft

Guns: 12×12in 46cal (4×3) 20×4·7in 50cal (20×1) 13×3in 50cal (13×1)

Torpedo Tubes: 3×17·7in (1 stern, 2 beam, all submerged)

Armour: 9½in belt; 1½in deck; 9in turrets; 12in CT

Machinery: 4-shaft Parsons geared turbines, 32,000hp = 22¾knots; ? Blechynden boilers

Coal Capacity: 920/3000tons

Endurance: 4800miles at 10knots

Complement: 981

Cost: Not known

This unusual ship showed that Italian designers had lost none of their flair for creating unorthodox warships. The *Dante Alighieri* was not only the first Italian dreadnought but also the first battleship in the world to have her main armament in triple turrets, and the first with light guns in turrets. She was also the first Italian ship to have Parsons turbines and four screws.

Machinery: She was designed for 35,000hp (23knots), although she did not quite reach this target on her trials.

Armament: The layout of four triple 12in turrets reflected the thinking of General Cuniberti, whose ideas helped to shape the British *Dreadnought*. All other considerations were sacrificed to gain maximum broadside fire, and the superstructure and funnels were kept to a minimum. As with other Italian designs, this feature was permissible for Mediterranean conditions, but

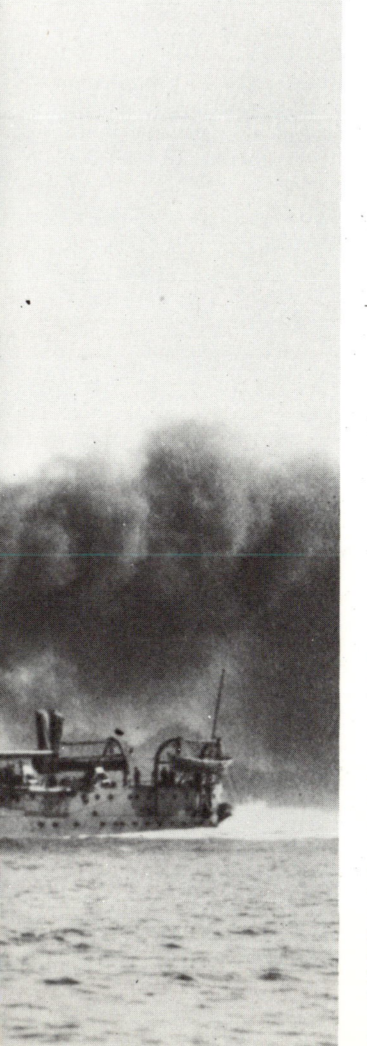

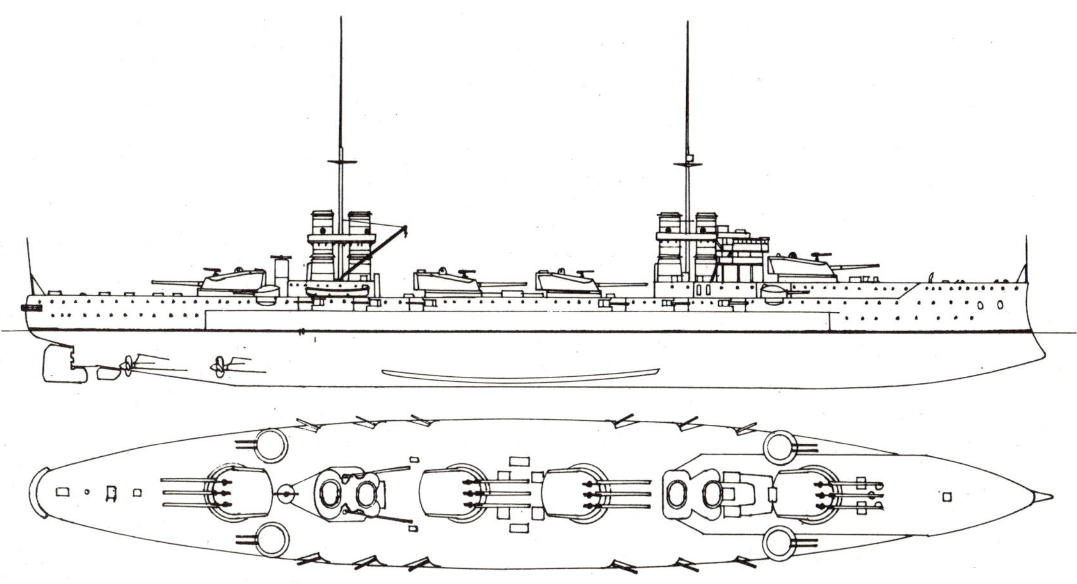

the *Alighieri* would have been badly placed for fighting in average Atlantic conditions.

Eight of the 4·7in guns were mounted in small twin turrets abreast of No.1 and No.4 turrets. As blast and spray would have rendered exposed guns almost useless in battle this was a very sound move, some years ahead of other navies; compare the dubious value of the remaining 4·7in guns at upper deck level, and the 3in guns on turret-tops.

Appearance: Her layout gave a unique silhouette, with two groups of funnels widely separated by the midships turrets, and a hull devoid of the normal conning-tower, searchlight platforms and so on. Her bow was of the 'cleaver' type.

Careers

Flagship of 1st Battle Squadron at Taranto at outbreak of war in May 1915; with 1st Division at Taranto (Group 'A') at Taranto 1916; with Southern Adriatic and Ionian Sea forces 1917–18; at Brindisi late in 1918; laid up 1 July 1928 and broken up.

Conte di Cavour class

Displacement: (in metric tons) 22,800tons normal.-(24,300tons full load)

Dimensions: 554ft 8in×91ft 10in×28ft 7in

Guns: 13×12in 46cal (3×3, 2×2) 18×4·7in 50cal (18×1) 13×3in 50cal (13×1); Leonardo da Vinci 14×3in

Torpedo Tubes: 3×17·7in (1 stern, 2 beam, all submerged)

Armour: 9·8in belt; 1½in deck; 9·8in turrets; 11in CT

Machinery: 4-shaft Parsons geared turbines, 30,000hp = 22½knots; ? Blechynden boilers (Babcock in Guilio Cesare)

Coal Capacity: 1000/2500tons

Endurance: 4800miles at 10knots

Complement: 1197/1200

Cost: Not known

	Laid Down	Launched	Completed	Built/Engined
Conte di Cavour	10 Aug 1910	10 Aug 1911	Apr 1915	Arsenale, Spezia
Guilio Cesare	24 June 1910	15 Oct 1911	May 1914	Ansaldo, Genoa
*Leonardo da Vinci	18 July 1910	14 Oct 1911	May 1914	Odero, Sestri

Following the lead set with the *Dante Alighieri*, Italian designers continued the development of centreline armament in this class, with a novel combination of triple and twin turrets. Superimposed turrets were adopted to allow an extra three 12in guns without increasing length unduly. The result was a handsome class, with a logical arrangement of main armament. Unfortunately for the Italians the time taken to authorise and build the three ships meant that they were outclassed by the 13·5in and 14in gunned ships built by other navies, but as they were intended to match the Austrian *Viribus Unitis* class this was not important.

As the main Austro-Hungarian fleet was never brought to action there was no chance to test the design in battle; however, as with so many Italian ships, armour was sacrificed for gun-power and speed, and the *Cavour* might have been unlucky against the *Viribus Unitis*. Problems with cordite might have combined to cause some unpleasant surprises.

Machinery: They failed to reach more than 22knots on trials, despite exceeding the designed horsepower.

Armament: The guns were from Armstrongs' Pozzuoli works, but technical help was given with the triple and twin 12in mountings by their Elswick works. The 4·7in guns were mounted at upper deck level, excepting four which were a deck higher, unprotected.

The 3in guns had been intended to be mounted on the roofs of turrets and in embrasures at the stern, but after the trials of *Cesare* and *da Vinci* in 1914 these guns were resited in groups on the forecastle, abreast of the superstructure and on the quarterdeck.

Appearance: The 'cleaver' bow was continued, but the class was given two large funnels and tripod masts similar to British ships, separated by the No. 3 turret. The legs of the forward tripod trailed forward.

Careers

Conte di Cavour: Flagship of the C-in-C, at Taranto on the outbreak of war in May 1915; Flagship of Group 'A' at Taranto 1916; Southern Adriatic and Ionian Sea Forces 1917; 1st Division 1918; underwent complete transformation during modernisation 1933–7; torpedoed at Taranto by British aircraft 1940; refloated but still under repair when sunk by bombs 1945; wreck broken up 1947–52.

Guilio Cesare: At Taranto at outbreak of war; 1st Division (Group 'A') at Taranto 1916; Southern Adriatic and Ionian Sea Forces 1917–18; modernised as *Cavour* 1933–7; handed over to Russia as reparations 1948, and renamed *Novorossiisk*; her subsequent fate is not clear, as there are conflicting reports that she was mined in the Black Sea in 1955 or merely laid up for scrapping in the same year.

Leonardo da Vinci: At Taranto at outbreak of war; she blew up at her moorings there on 2 August 1916 (248 men killed); the Italians have always blamed saboteurs, but it is possible that the true reason was defective ammunition; salvaged 17 September 1919 with a view to refitting her for service, but the hull was eventually sold for breaking up 22 March 1923.

Above, *Conte di Cavour at Taranto in June 1917. Note that the midships turret (No. 3) is a deck higher than in the Andrea Doria class, and that the forefunnel is before the tripod mast (IWM).*

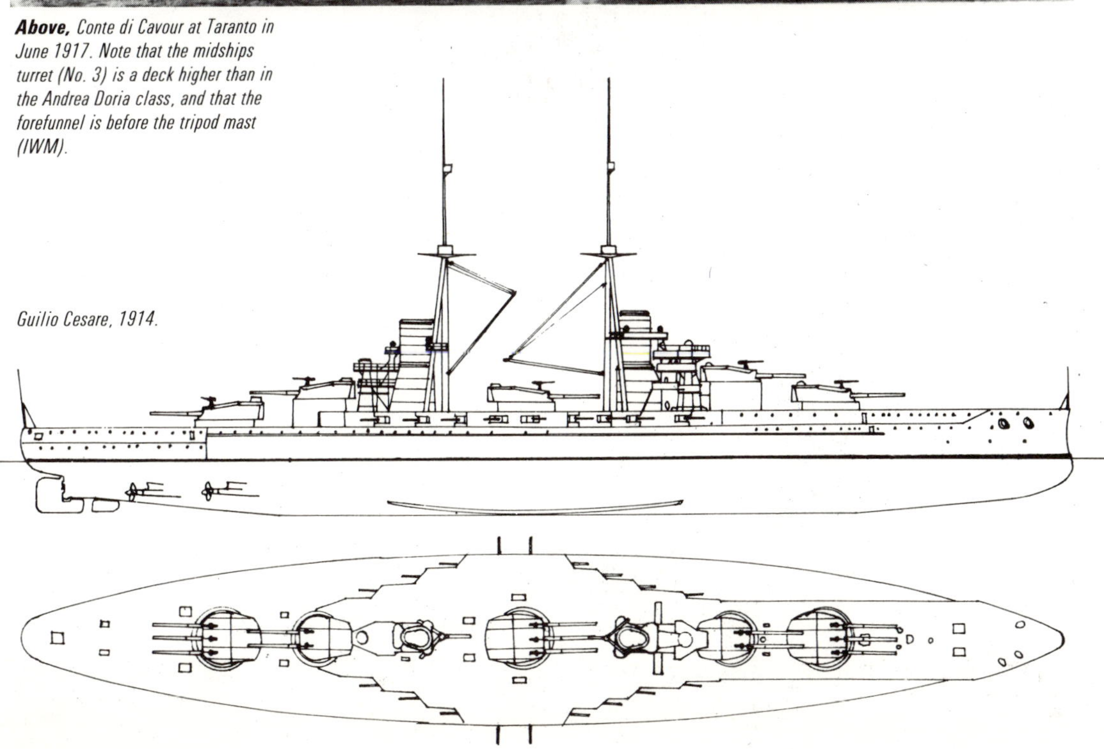

Left, *Guilio Cesare seen at Taranto after the Armistice. Note that her torpedo nets have been removed (IWM).*

Andrea Doria.

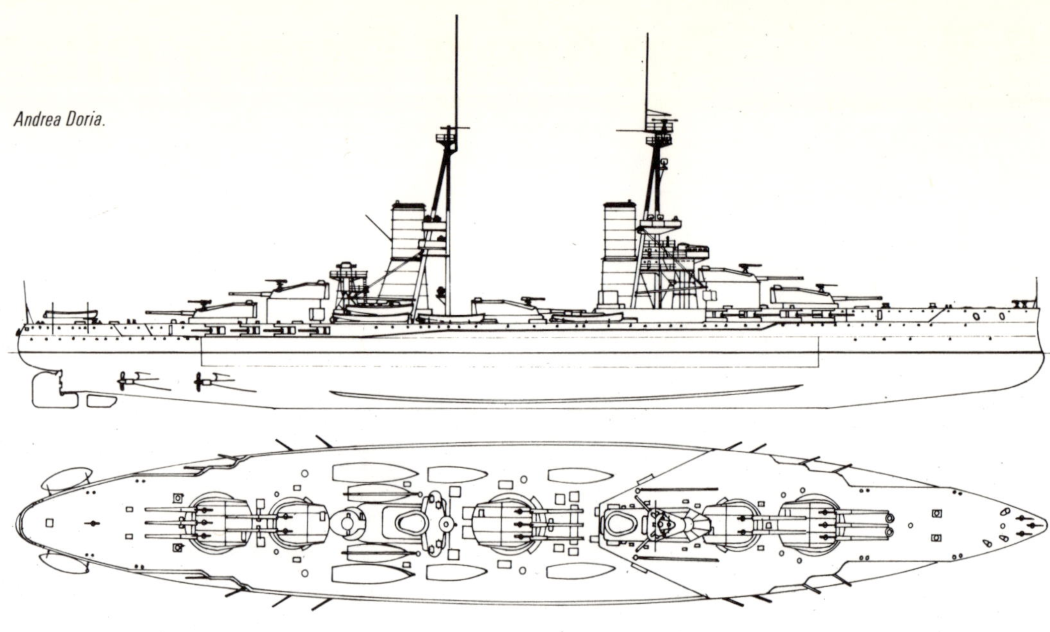

Below, *Caio Duilio as she appeared in April 1916 (Aldo Fraccaroli).*

Below right, *Andrea Doria shortly after the Armistice. Note the anti-aircraft gun mounted on the crown of the after superimposed turret (No. 4) and the tall funnels arranged abaft the tripod masts which distinguished this class from the Cavours (IWM).*

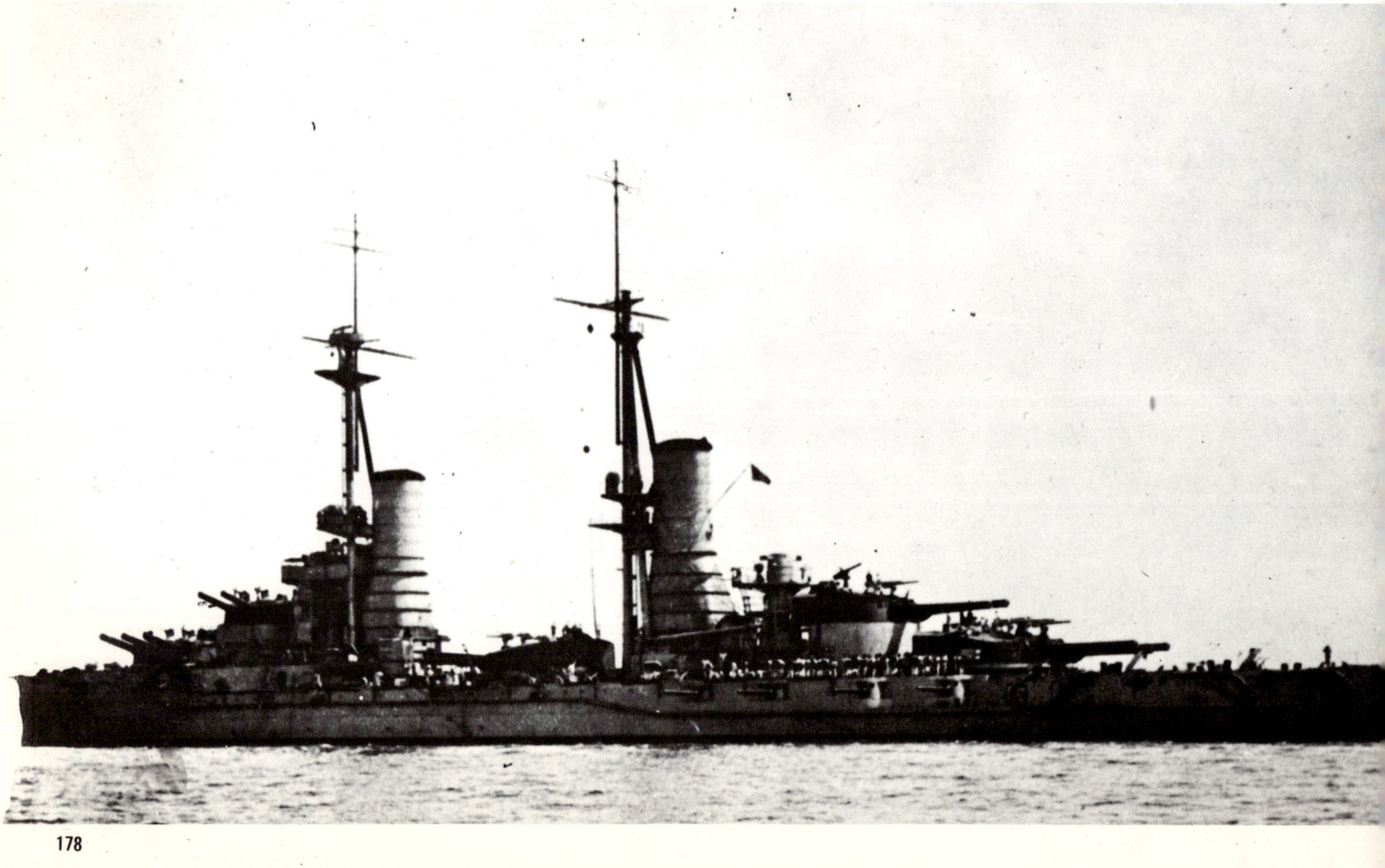

Andrea Doria class

	Laid Down	Launched	Completed	Built/Engined
Andrea Doria	24 Mar 1912	30 Mar 1913	Mar 1916	Arsenale, Spezia
Duilio	24 Feb 1912	24 Apr 1913	May 1915	Castellamare DY

This class had the same dimensions as the *Cavours*, but with slightly greater horsepower. To keep pace with foreign battleships the 6in gun was adopted in place of the 4·7in gun for close-range defence. To offset the increased weight of the 6in battery the midships 12in turret (No. 3) had to be positioned a deck lower, which cannot have improved its shooting in bad weather.

In other respects they were virtually repeats of the *Cavour* design, but for some reason the protection of the turrets was slightly reduced, while the thickness of the conning tower armour was slightly increased.

Machinery: As with the *Cavours* the designed speed of 22knots was not attained on trials, despite the fact that they developed more than the designed horsepower. The highest mean speed on trials was 21·3knots.

Armament: The distribution of armament did not compare with the *Cavours*. For technical reasons already mentioned it was necessary to have the midships turret at upper deck level, with all the attendant problems of interference from spray. Also, in common with the designers of other navies, the Italians spread the 6in battery too far forward and aft, below the forecastle and abreast of turrets No. 4 and 5, where they would be worst affected by blast and spray.

Appearance: Although basically similar to the *Cavours*, with two large funnels and tall tripods, they could be distinguished from the earlier class by having their tripods before each funnel. Also the lower midships turret and different distribution of secondary guns was distinctive. Both ships ran trials with 3in guns on turret tops, but these were resited shortly afterwards on the forecastle and elsewhere.

Careers

Andrea Doria: Joined 2nd Division of Group 'A' at Taranto 1916; with Southern Adriatic and Ionian Sea forces 1917–18; Flagship 1st Division 1918; totally reconstructed as *Cavour* and *Cesare* 1937–40; removed from effective list 1 November 1956 and broken up.

Duilio: Joined 2nd Division at Taranto 1915; Group 'A' 1916; Southern Adriatic and Ionian Sea forces 1917–18; with 1st Division 1918; rebuilt as *Doria* 1937–40; removed from effective list 15 September 1956.

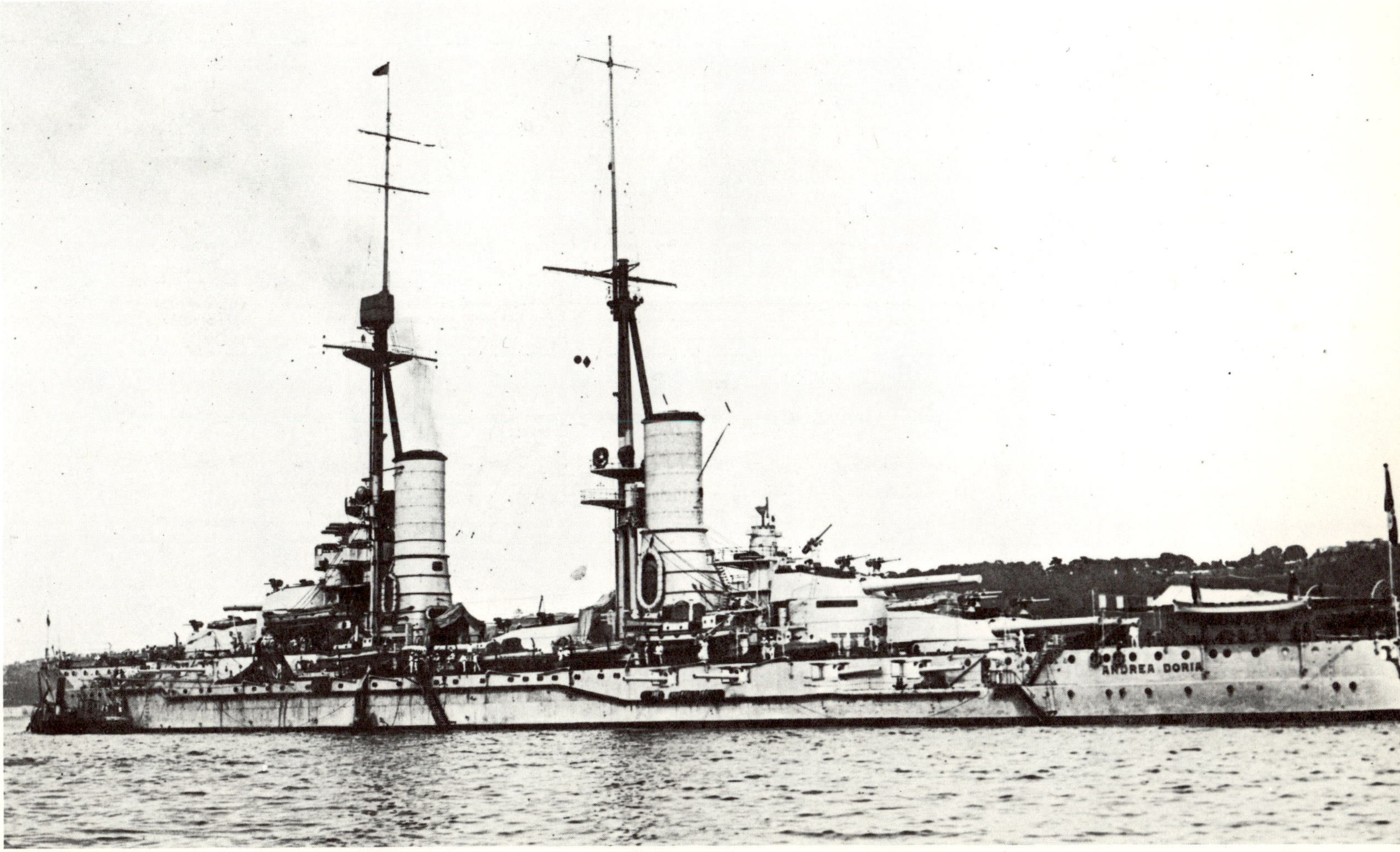

Carraciolo class

Displacement: 34,000tons (metric) normal
Dimensions: Not known
Guns: 8×15in 40cal (4×2)
12×6in 45cal (12×1)
12×2pdr pom-poms (12×1)
Torpedo Tubes: Nil
Armour: Not known
Machinery: 4-shaft Parsons geared turbines, 105,000hp = 28knots;
? boilers
Oil Capacity: Not known
Coal Capacity: Not known
Endurance: 8000miles at 10knots
Complement: Not known
Cost: Not known

	Laid Down	Launched	Completed	Built/Engined
Francesco Carraciolo	16 Oct 1914	12 May 1920	—	Castellamare DY
Cristoforo Colombo	14 Mar 1915	—	—	Ansaldo Genoa
Marcantonio Colonna				

This class of 'super dreadnoughts' was modelled on the British *Queen Elizabeth* class, but with the usual Italian emphasis on speed. Designed by Engineer–General Ferrati, they would have been handsome ships and would have been more than a match for anything envisaged by the Austro-Hungarian Navy. However, like so many battleships projected in 1914, they were suspended in order to concentrate shipyard resources on smaller craft.

The main points of interest were the absence of torpedo tubes, and the flush-decked hull. The arrangement of the 6in battery a deck higher was a great improvement over the *Cavour* and *Duilio* classes.

Three were suspended in 1915, but work continued on *Francesco Carraciolo* until March 1916, when about 9000 metric tons of material had been worked into her hull. Work recommenced on her in October 1919, and she was launched in 1920, but the grave state of Italian finances caused her to be sold on 25 October 1920 to the Navigazione Generale Italiana for conversion to a liner. This scheme collapsed and the hull was later scrapped.

Work was recommenced on the remaining three in 1919, but the financial crisis already mentioned resulted in their scrapping; they were stricken on 2 January 1921 and the material was removed from the slips.

Gunnery: The 15in gun was similar to the British weapon but slightly lighter, and had been developed by Armstrong Whitworth at Elswick. Apparently all design and proving was to be done in England, but the guns were to be made at Armstrongs' Pozzuoli works; some of the guns were completed and installed in monitors for coastal bombardment.

Appearance: They would have been radically different from preceding classes, with a spoon bow and a flush deck. The 6in battery was well arranged, with good command for all guns. As originally designed they would have had two short funnels, but both masts and funnels were to be raised.

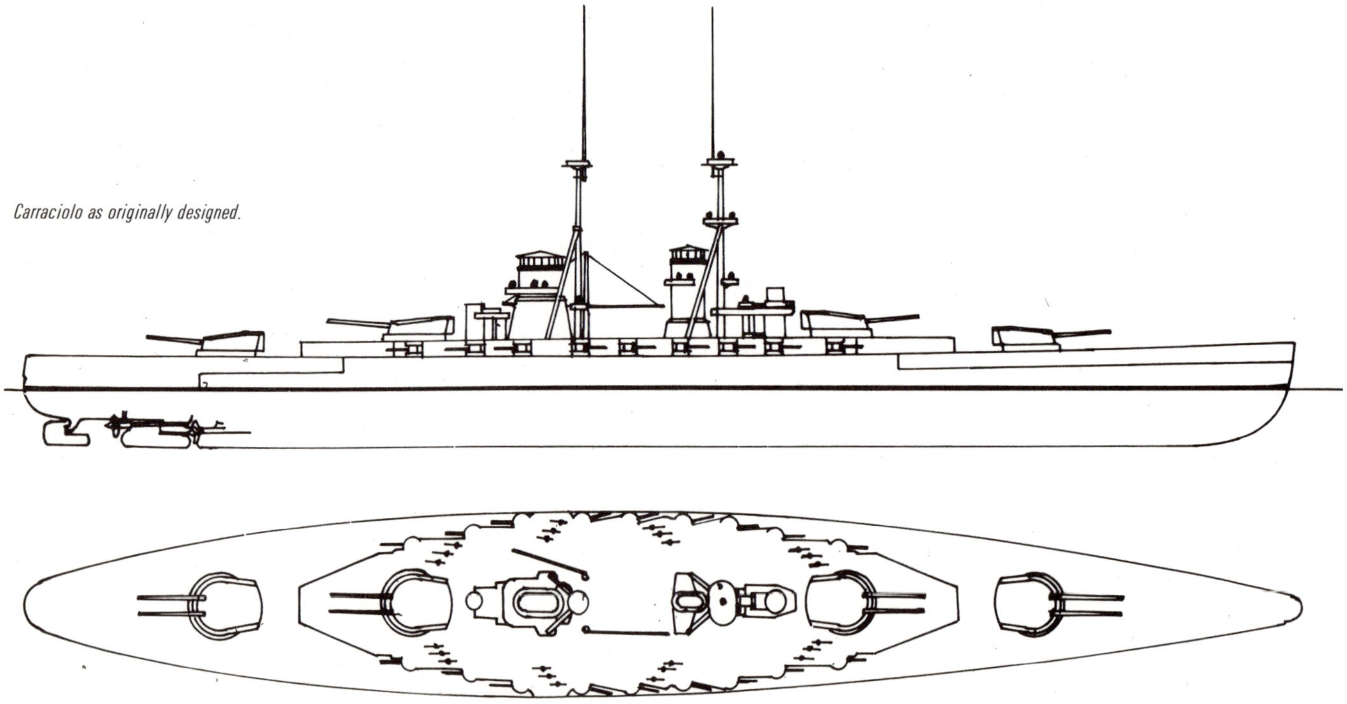

Carraciolo as originally designed.

Below, *Fuji shown prewar showing to good advantage the Imperial chrysanthemum on the bow (Admiralty).*

Introduction

The modern Imperial Japanese Navy had been founded in 1868, and was thus the most modern of the major navies. However, the Japanese military tradition went back many centuries, and it was hardly surprising that the Japanese proved to be the most vigorous naval power in the Far East. After the restoration of the Emperor in 1867 and the Civil War, shipyards were established, but until the twentieth century battleships continued to be built abroad.

The first sign of Japan's rising aspirations as a naval power were seen in the Sino-Japanese War of 1894, when the modern armament of Japanese ships gave them an easy victory over two obsolescent Chinese battleships and two other armoured vessels. The Anglo-Japanese Alliance of 1901 gave the Japanese the backing they needed before they could embark on a war to expel Russia from Manchuria, as they needed British technical assistance to build a modern fleet quickly.

The Russo-Japanese War of 1904–5 left the Japanese as the unopposed masters of the Far East, having destroyed Russian opposition by capturing Port Arthur and then sinking or capturing virtually their entire Baltic Fleet at the Battle of Tsushima. By now Japanese industry had expanded to the point where battleships could be built in Japanese shipyards, and from now on there was less and less reliance on Western technology.

When the war broke out in August 1914 Japan honoured her treaty obligations by declaring war on Germany. Her most important contributions were the reduction of the German colony and naval base at Kiaou Chao (Tsingtao), and the provision of cruisers to hunt down German commerce-raiders in the Pacific. The Kiaou Chao operations were successfully concluded, British naval units assisting. The availability of several powerful Japanese cruisers in the Western Pacific made British problems of convoying and hunting for German cruisers much easier.

Japanese capital ships did not serve outside the Pacific during the war; the British Cabinet made overtures to Japan to allow the four *Kongo* class to serve with the Grand Fleet or to borrow them for the duration of hostilities, but the Japanese Government decided against such a move.

With the laying down of the hybrid battleship-cruisers *Ikoma* and *Tsukuba*, and the battleship *Satsuma* in 1905, Japan became independent of Western shipyards, and henceforward capital ships were to be built in Japan. The only exception was the battle cruiser *Kongo*, ordered in 1911 from the English firm of Vickers to give Japanese designers experience in the latest techniques. Although three sisters of the *Kongo* were built in Japanese yards much material had to be imported, and in the *Haruna* this amounted to as much as 31 per cent.

All previous heavy units had been built at the two dockyards, Kure and Yokosuka, but in 1912 the big private firms of Kawasaki (Kobe) and Mitsubishi (Nagasaki) came to the fore.

Weapons

Apart from Russian weapons in the prizes, the principal weapons were supplied by the English firms of Vickers and Armstrong. The Vickers 14in type supplied for the *Kongo* class was copied and produced by the Japanese Kamegakubi ordnance works for the *Fuso* and *Ise* classes, and thereafter Japanese heavy ordnance followed its own line of development.

The lessons learned in 1905 all stressed the importance of gunpower, and so the Japanese increased gun calibre from 14in to 16in guns during the war, and tested the world's only 19in gun in 1919.

The '8–8' Programme

Japan prospered during the war, with her shipyards and armament industry steadily expanding to meet the demands of her allies, and yet with only a modest commitment of ships and men. It was not surprising, therefore that Japanese thoughts turned to expansion. In 1915 there was a clash with the United States over a Japanese attempt to force demands on China, and it was decided to build up the Imperial Japanese Navy with a view to attaining at least parity with the U.S. Navy in the Pacific.

Disposition of Japanese Navy at the Outbreak of War
China Station
1st Standing Squadron
Settsu (flagship), Satsuma, Iwami, Suwo, Kongo, Tsukuba
Yokosuka
Kawachi, Katori, Sagami, Asahi (gunnery and torpedo training ship), Iki (attached to naval barracks), Kurama
Kure
Aki, Fuji (seamen's training ship), Tango (attached to naval barracks), Ikoma, Ibuki
Sasebo
Shikishima, Hizen, Okinoshima (attached to naval barracks)
Maizuru
Mikasa, Kashima, Mishima (attached to naval barracks)

Disposition of Japanese Fleet in October 1918
1st Fleet
Fuso, Yamashiro, Hyuga, (Ise refitting)
2nd Fleet, (3rd Squadron)
Kongo, Hiei, Kirishima
3rd Fleet (5th Squadron)
Katori (flagship) and Kashima (at Nikolaievsk), Hizen (flagship at Vladivostock), Kurama
Yokosuka
Asahi, Suwo (gunnery training ship), Haruna (refitting), Ikoma (gunnery and torpedo training ship)
Kure
Ise, Aki, Settsu, Fuji, Iwami, Ibuki (refitting)
Sasebo
Satsuma, Shikishima, Okinoshima

The '8–8' Fleet Law was modelled on the German Navy Laws, and provided for a strength of eight modern battleships and eight battle cruisers by 1927. As will be seen under the individual classes, progress on this programme was slow, and most of the units were cancelled to comply with the Washington Treaty of 1922.

Dockyards and Shipbuilders

The main dockyard was at Yokosuka, and had been established in the 1860s. Other bases were at Maizuru, Kure and Sasebo, all in the southern part of the country and well placed for watching the old Russian base in Manchuria, Port Arthur. In 1914 work was proceeding on Port Arthur, but it was not ready as a fleet base.

Iki

Displacement: 9960tons
Dimensions: 326ft 5in (oa)×66ft 10in ×26ft 6in (max)
Guns: 2×12in 40cal (1×2)
6×6in 35cal (6×1)
6×4·7in (6×1)
16×3pdrs (16×1)
4×1½pdrs (4×1)
Torpedo Tubes: 6×14in (above water, 1 bow, 1 stern, 4 beam)
Armour: 14–4in belt (compound); 2½in deck; 10in turret; 10in CT
Machinery: 2-shaft 3-cyl triple expansion, 8000hp=approx 12knots; 16 Belleville boilers
Coal Capacity: 850/1000tons
Endurance: 4900miles at 15knots
Complement: 611

	Laid Down	Launched	Completed	Built/Engined
Iki (ex-Imperator Nicolai I)	July 1886	20 May 1889	July 1893	Franco-Russian Works St. Petersburg

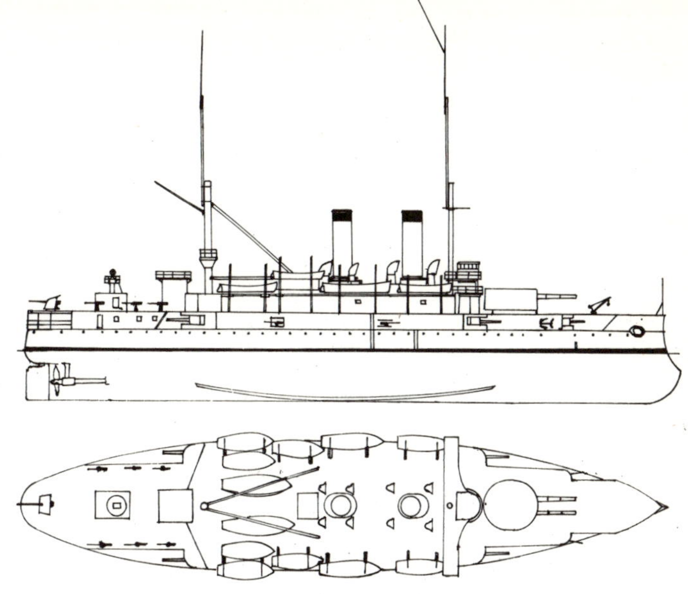

This vessel and the two *Okinoshima* class which follow were of virtually no fighting value, but are included for the sake of completeness. As far as is known none of them played any active part in the war.
Sister ship: Russian *Imperator Aleksander II* (q.v.)
Career
Used as training ship at Yokosuka 1910–15; target ship 1915–18; stricken late 1918 and broken up in 1922.

Okinoshima class

Displacement: 4270tons
Dimensions: 265ft×52ft 6in×17ft
Guns: Okinoshima: 3×10in 45cal (2×1, 1×1)
6×4·7in 45cal (4×1)
10×3pdrs (10×1)
12×1½pdrs (12×1)
Mishima: 4×9in (2×2); reduced to 2×9in in 1918 (1×2)
6×4·7in etc as Okinoshima
Torpedo Tubes: 4×18in (above water)
Armour: 10–8in belt; 8in turrets
Machinery: 2-shaft triple expansion, 5700hp=approx 12knots; ? cylindrical boilers
Coal Capacity: 400tons
Endurance: 3000miles at 10knots
Complement: 404/406
Cost: Not known

	Laid Down	Launched	Completed	Built/Engined
Okinoshima (ex-General-Admiral Apraxin)	1895	12 May 1896	1898	Baltic Works, St. Petersburg
Mishima (ex-Admiral Senyavin)	1892	22 Aug 1894	1895	New Admiralty Yard

These two ships were ex-Russian prizes taken in the Russo-Japanese War of 1904–5.
Careers
Mishima: Stricken 1928 (harbour service 1914–18 at Maizuru).
Okinoshima: Training ship at Sasebo 1905–15; partly disarmed and served as accommodation ship; stricken 1926.

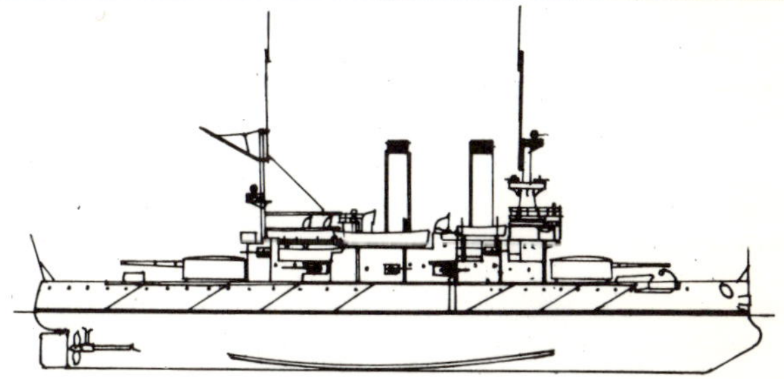

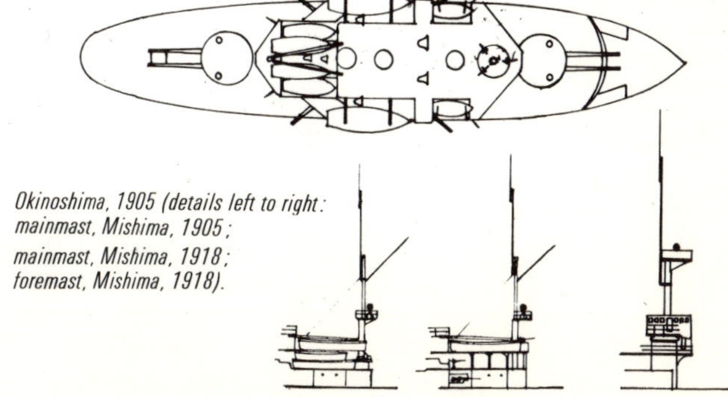

Okinoshima, 1905 (details left to right: mainmast, Mishima, 1905; mainmast, Mishima, 1918; foremast, Mishima, 1918).

Tango

Displacement: 11,135tons
Dimensions: 367ft (wl)×69ft×28ft (max)
Guns: 4×12in 40cal (2×2)
12×6in 45cal (12×1)
16×3pdrs, 12×1½pdrs
Torpedo Tubes: Not known
Armour: 15in belt (compound); 10in turrets
Machinery: 2-shaft, 3-cyl triple expansion, 10,600hp=approx 13knots; 16 Miyabara boilers
Coal Capacity: 1050tons (max)
Endurance: 4000miles at 10knots

	Laid Down	Launched	Completed	Built/Engined
Tango (ex-Poltava)	1 May 1891	6 Dec 1894	1898	New Admiralty Yard,

This was the former Russian *Poltava*, which was sunk at Port Arthur in 1904, but salvaged by the Japanese and incorporated into the Imperial Japanese Navy. Of virtually no fighting value, but retained for prestige purposes.
Sister ship: *Petropavlovsk* and *Sevastopol* sunk 1904–5.
Career
Served as coast defence ship and gunnery training ship 1909–15; returned to Russia 5 April 1916 and renamed *Chesma*.

Fuji

Displacement: 12,300tons (normal)
Dimensions: 374ft (pp)×73ft 9in×29ft (max)
Guns: 4×12in 40cal (4×2)
10×6in 40cal (10×1)
16×12pdrs (16×1')
4×2½pdrs (4×1)
Torpedo Tubes: 5×18in (1 above water in bow, 4 beam submerged)
Armour: 18–8in belt (compound); 2½in deck; 6in turrets; 14in CT
Machinery: 2-shaft 4-cylinder vertical triple expansion, 13,690hp = approx 13knots (by 1914); cylindrical boilers
Coal Capacity: 700/1300tons
Endurance: 4000miles at 10knots
Complement: 741
Cost: Not known, but approx £1,000,000 ($4,000,000)

	Laid Down	Launched	Completed	Built/Engined
Fuji	1894	31 Mar 1896	Aug 1897	Thames Ironworks

This unit was the oldest effective battleship in the Japanese Navy, but by 1914 she was too slow for any but subsidiary duties. Hull basically similar to British *Revenge* but main armament similar to the later *Formidable*.
Appearance: Very similar to British predreadnoughts, with equal-sized funnels and pole masts.
Sister ship: *Yashima* was mined and sunk in the Russo-Japanese War 1904.
Career
Served as gunnery training ship before 1914; spent entire war at Kure; laid up and disarmed; stricken 1923 but retained as training hulk in Yokosuka until 1945; broken up 1948.

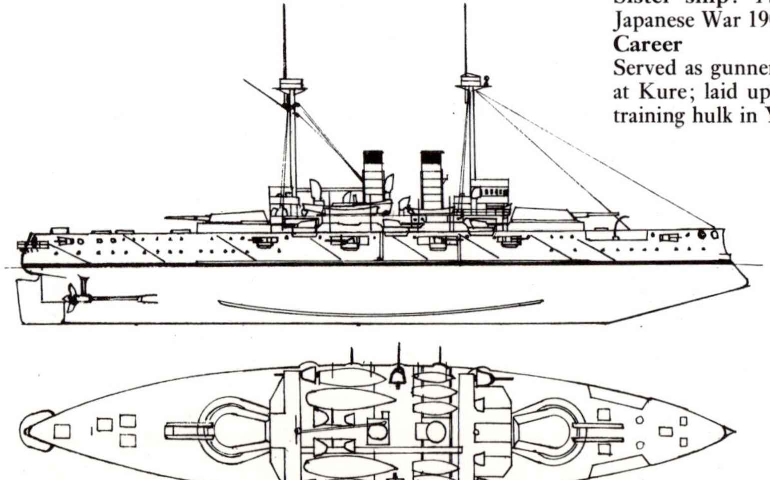

Right, Fuji (Admiralty).

 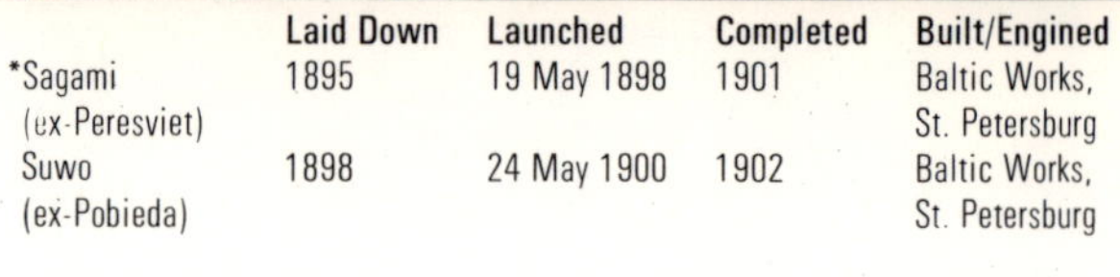

Sagami class

Displacement: 13,500tons (normal)
Dimensions: 424ft (wl)×71ft 6in×27ft 3in
Guns: 4×10in 45cal (2×2)
10×6in 45cal (10×1)
16×12pdrs (16×1)
21×3pdrs
8×1½pdrs
Torpedo Tubes: 2×18in (submerged, facing aft at 20°)
Armour: 9–6in belt; 2¾in deck; 10in turrets; 10in CT
Machinery: 3-shaft 3-cylinder vertical triple expansion, 14,500hp=approx 16knots (by 1914); 30 Miyabara boilers
Coal Capacity: 1060/2056tons
Endurance: 6000miles at 10knots (Suwo 10,000miles)
Complement: 732/775
Cost: Originally £1,000,000 ($4,000,000)

	Laid Down	Launched	Completed	Built/Engined
*Sagami (ex-Peresviet)	1895	19 May 1898	1901	Baltic Works, St. Petersburg
Suwo (ex-Pobieda)	1898	24 May 1900	1902	Baltic Works, St. Petersburg

The *Pobieda* and *Peresviet* were scuttled at Port Arthur during the Russo-Japanese War and were salvaged by the Japanese after the fall of Port Arthur in 1905. Reconstructed 1908–9, when a bow-mounted 6in gun was removed.

Protection: Although sister ships, their protection differed in that *Sagami* had a belt of Harvey steel which stopped short thirty feet from bow and stern, whereas *Suwo* had a complete waterline belt of Krupp non-cemented armour.

Appearance: Distinctive silhouette with high freeboard and three equal funnels. The slab-sided appearance of the 6in battery was unique.

Careers

Sagami: Coast defence duties 1914–16; returned to Russia March 1916 and renamed *Peresviet*; lost after transfer (see Russian section).

Suwo: Serving as training ship for engineers and cadets on outbreak of war; 1st Standing Squadron August 1914; Flagship of 2nd Squadron (2nd Fleet) 1915–16; became gunnery training ship at Yokosuka 1917–18; disarmed at Kure in 1922; capsized during this disarming on 13 July 1922 and was later hulked; survived until 1945.

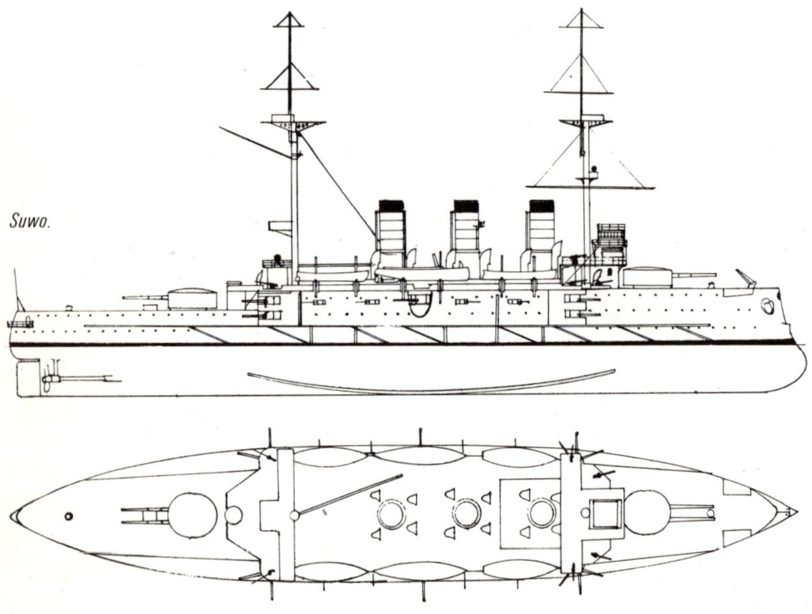

Suwo.

***Right**, Sagami as she appeared in 1913 (P. A. Vicary).*

Right, Mikasa just before the Russo-Japanese War when funnel bands were still in use. Note her similarity to the British Formidable group (IWM).

Right, an early photograph of Shikishima showing well the general overall resemblance to British pre-dreadnoughts with the exception of her 3 funnels (IWM).

Asahi class

Displacement: 15,200 tons (normal)

Dimensions: 415ft(wl) 76ft (Mikasa 75ft 6in)×28ft 3in

Guns: Asahi and Shikishima: 4×12in 40cal (2×2) 14×6in 40cal (14×1) Mikasa: 4×12in 45cal (2×2) 14×6in 45cal (14×1) All: 20×12pdrs (20×1)

Torpedo Tubes: Shikishima: 5×18in (4 beam, submerged and 1 above water, bow) Others: 4×18in (submerged, beam)

Armour: 9–4in belt; 3in deck; 10–8in turrets; 14in CT

Machinery: 2-shaft 3-cylinder vertical triple expansion, 15,000hp=approx 15knots (by 1914); 25 Belleville boilers

Coal Capacity: 700/1600tons (Mikasa and Asahi 1000/2000tons)

Endurance: 9000miles at 10knots (Shikishima 5000miles)

Complement: 741/770 (Mikasa 935)

Cost: Not known, but approximately £1,000,000 ($4,000,000)

	Laid Down	Launched	Completed	Built/Engined
Asahi	July 1897	13 Mar 1899	July 1900	Clydebank
Mikasa	1899	8 Nov 1900	Mar 1902	Vickers, Barrow
Shikishima	Jan 1897	1 Nov 1898	Jan 1900	Thames Ironworks

Very similar to the British *Formidable* and *Canopus* classes, but with an extra 6in casemate amidships (at main deck level in *Mikasa*, and a deck higher in others). Although sister ships, they differed in detail from one another in detail, and *Mikasa* had been reconstructed after being sunk at Sasebo by a magazine explosion in September 1905. Although good sturdy ships they were quite unsuited for any front line service, and had been outclassed by newer Japanese construction.

Armament: During her 1907–8 reconstruction *Mikasa* was rearmed with newer pattern 12in and 6in guns. All guns were British pattern, supplied by Armstrong, Whitworth and Vickers.

Appearance: *Mikasa* and *Asahi* looked similar to contemporary British predreadnoughts, but *Shikishima* had three thin funnels instead of two thick ones, as in the other two. Differed from the older British ships in having no fighting tops on their masts.

Careers

Asahi: Served in home waters throughout the war; gunnery training ship; reclassified as 1st Class coast defence ship in September 1921; served to July 1923 and then stricken; retained as submarine repair and training ship, being fitted with lifting frames; torpedoed by U.S. submarine 25 May 1942:

Shikishima: Served at Sasebo 1914–15; 2nd Squadron 1916; 5th Squadron 1917–18; reclassified as 1st Class coast defence ship in 1921; 1921–3 training ship for submarine crews; stricken 1923 but retained as hulk at Sasebo until 1945; broken up 1948.

Mikasa: Served on coastal defence duties at Maizuru 1914–15; 2nd Div., 2nd Squadron 1915–16, 5th Squadron 1917; Maizuru 1918; operations off Vladivostok in 1921 supporting Japanese intervention in Siberia; stricken 1923 and preserved as a relic at Yokosuka until 1945; repaired and reinstated as a memorial to Admiral Togo and Battle of Tsushima in 1960.

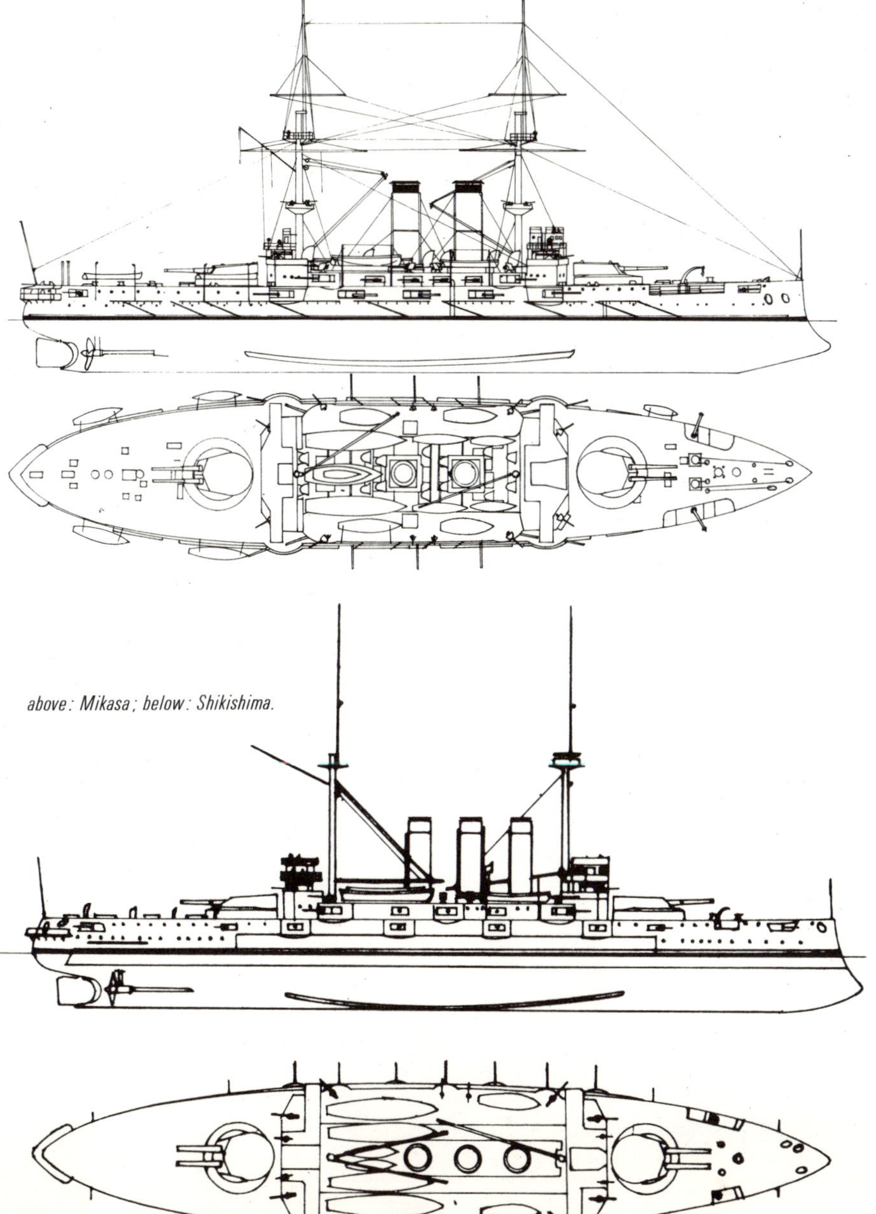

above: Mikasa; below: Shikishima.

Above, a pre-1914 photograph of Asahi showing her fore turret trained to starboard. The chrysanthemum emblem was borne on the bows of all Japanese ships (IWM)

189

Displacement: 16,400tons (Katori 15,950) normal
Dimensions: Kashima: 425ft× 78ft 1¼in×26ft 7½in (mean) Katori: 420ft×78ft ¼in×27ft
Guns: 4×12in 45cal (2×2) 4×10in 45cal (4×1) 12×6in 45cal (12×1) 12×14pdrs (12×1)
Torpedo Tubes: 5×18in (submerged; 4 beam, 1 stern)
Armour: 9–6½in belt; 9in turrets; 6in battery; 3in decks; 9in CT
Machinery: 2-shaft 4-cyl vertical quadruple-expansion, 17,000hp = 18½knots; ? Niclausse boilers
Complement: 864
Coal Capacity: 750/2000tons
Endurance: 9000miles at 10knots
Cost: Approximately £1,500,000 each ($6,000,000)

Left, Kashima as completed (IWM)

Displacement: 13,750tons (normal); 15,150tons (full load)
Dimensions: 440ft×74ft 9in×26ft
Guns: 4×12in 45cal (2×2) 12×6in 45cal (12×1) 12×4·7in 50cal (12×1) 2×14pdrs (76mm) 4×3pdrs
Torpedo Tubes: 3×18in (1 above water, stern, two submerged, beam)
Armour: 7–4in belt; 2in deck; 7in turrets; 8in CT
Machinery: 2-shaft vertical triple-expansion, 20,500ihp = 20½knots; 20 Miyabara boilers
Coal Capacity: 600/1700tons
Endurance: Not known
Complement: 817
Cost: Not known

Left, Ikoma as completed. Note the Japanese-style clipper stem and the overall resemblance to a capital ship (IWM)

Kashima class

	Laid Down	Launched	Completed	Built/Engined
Kashima	Feb 1904	Mar 1905	Mar 1905	Armstrong Humphreys
Katon	Feb 1904	July 1905	(1906	Vickers

These ships were very similar to the British *King Edward VII* class, but the 10in Elswick gun was adopted in place of the 9·2in. Apart from a slight increase in beam the Japanese ships were very similar in many details, but worked in an extra 6in gun amidships by having a double-storied casemate.

Appearance: By 1914 both ships had small fire-control tops fitted to their masts. *Kashima* had 2 port anchors, 1 starboard, whereas *Katori* had 1 port and 2 starboard.

Careers

Kashima: At Maizuru 1914–15; 2nd Squadron 1915–16 (Flagship 2nd Division); 5th Squadron 1916; Flagship 2nd Squadron 1917; Flagship 5th Squadron mid-1918, and sent to Nikolaevsk; disarmed at Maizuru; stricken 1923 and broken up by Mitsubishi at Nagasaki in 1923–4.

Katori: At Yokosuka DY 1914–15, and then to Maizuru for ordnance refit, which lasted from 1915 to late 1916; 2nd Squadron 1917; Flagship 5th Squadron 1917–18; late 1918 Flagship of C-in-C at Nikolaevsk; disarmed *c.*1921 and broken up at Maizuru in 1924–5.

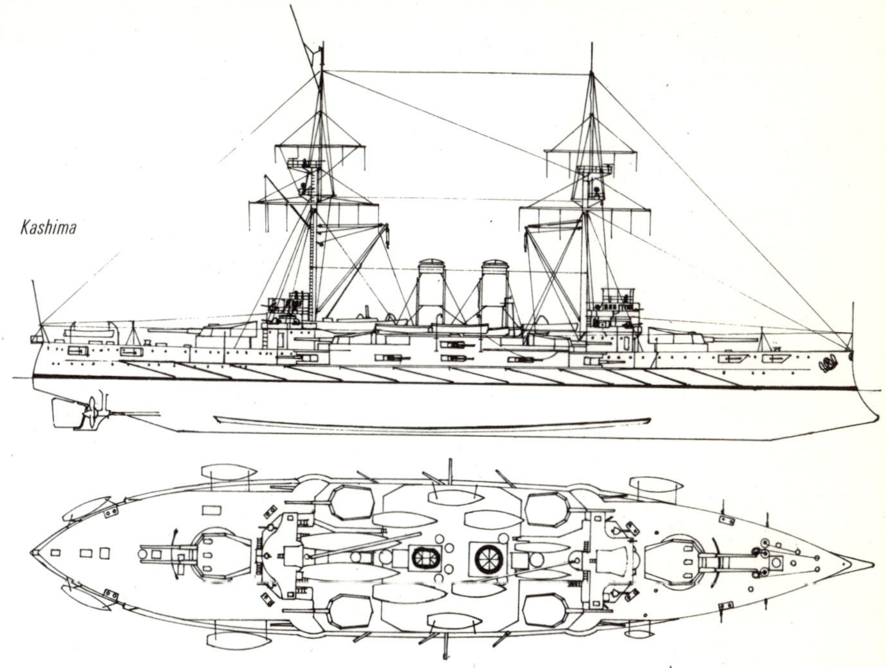
Kashima

Tsukuba class

	Laid Down	Launched	Completed	Built/Engined
*Tsukuba	14 Jan 1905	26 Dec 1905	Jan 1907	Kure DY
Ikoma	15 Mar 1905	9 Apr 1906	Mar 1908	Kure DY

These hybrid ships were laid down during the Russo–Japanese War to take advantage of Japan's existing capacity to manufacture 7in armour plate, and at the same time provide 12in gunned ships. They were rated at 1st Class armoured cruisers until 1912, and were without parallel in any other navy, with the possible exception of the *Vittorio Emmanuele* type in Italy. Like so many other interesting experimental designs of that period they were completely overshadowed by the *Dreadnought*, but were nonetheless powerful ships for their displacement.

Appearance: They looked more like battleships than cruisers, with clipper bows and 6in guns in casemates.

Careers

Ikoma: At Kure on outbreak of war; joined 1st South Seas Squadron November 1914 in search for German Pacific Squadron (Spee); 2nd Squadron 1917; gunnery and torpedo training ship at Yokosuka in October 1918, having been rearmed; disarmed 1922 at Sasebo; stricken 1923 and broken up 1924–5.

Tsukuba: In 1st Standing Squadron in August 1914; with *Kurama* and cruiser *Asama* sailed from Yokosuka in November 1914 to search for Graf Spee's squadron; joined by *Ikoma* at Suva, Fiji, 2 December 1914; gunnery and torpedo training ship at Yokosuka in 1916; destroyed by magazine explosion in Yokosuka harbour 14 January 1917.

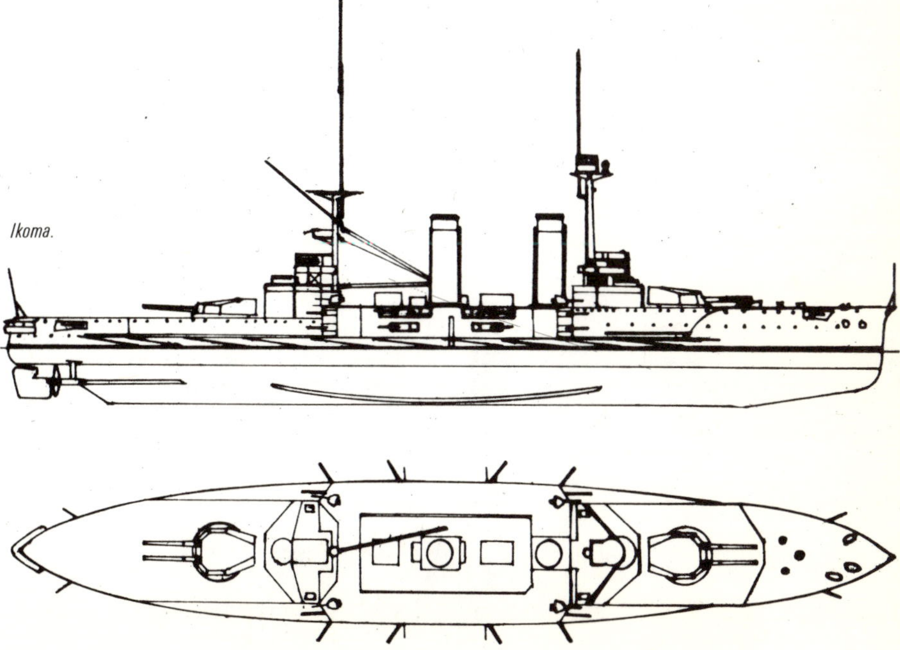
Ikoma.

Hizen

Below, *Hizen in 1902 when she was the Russian Retvizan. The Japanese did little to change her appearance after capture (IWM).*

Displacement: 12,700tons (normal), 12,902tons (full load)
Dimensions: 376ft×72ft×26ft
Guns: 4×12in 40cal (2×2)
12×6in 45cal (12×1)
20×3in (20×1)
4×2½pdrs (42mm)
Torpedo Tubes: 2×18in (above water, bow and stern)
Armour: 9–2in belt; 3–2in deck; 10in turrets; 10in CT
Machinery: 2-shaft vertical triple-expansion, 16,000ihp = 18knots (as built); 24 Niclausse boilers
Coal Capacity: 1000/2000tons
Endurance: Approx 9000miles at 10knots
Complement: 750
Cost: Not known

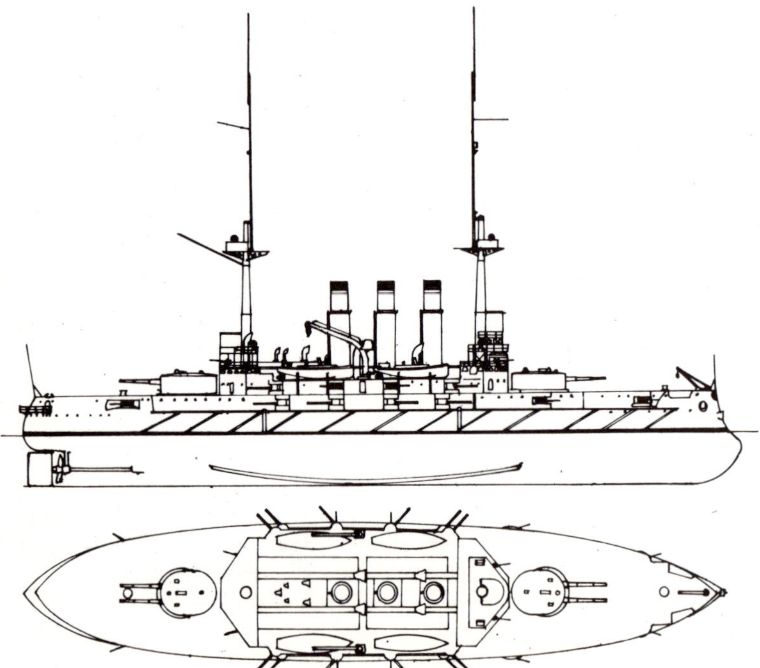

	Laid Down	Launched	Completed	Built/Engined
Hizen (ex-Retvizan)	Dec 1899	10 Oct 1900	1902	Wm. Cramp, Philadelphia

This vessel was the best of the ex-Russian prizes taken into the Imperial Japanese Navy after capture. She had been completed only two years before the Russo–Japanese War broke out, and was similar in general design to the American *Maine*, although her armament was Russian. Being built on American lines, the *Retvizan* presented a workmanlike appearance far removed from the towering silhouettes of earlier Russian ships.

After her salvage at Port Arthur she was refloated in September 1905 and repaired at Sasebo from January 1906 to November 1908. On completion of her repairs she was commissioned as the Japanese *Hizen*. A tribute to the qualities of her design was the fact that virtually no major alterations were made to her, apart from removal of her fighting tops. Furthermore, when the time came in 1916 to return various ex-Russian prizes the *Hizen* was not among them.

Appearance: She was unique among three-funnelled battleships in having her funnels cased up to the level of the control tops, in a manner reminiscent of some French vessels.

Career

At Sasebo on outbreak of war; flagship of Special Squadron sent to United States early in 1915, but recalled in February; with 2nd Division of 2nd Squadron 1916; 5th Squadron (3rd Fleet) 1916–18, including service at Vladivostock; rerated as 1st Class coast defence ship 1 September 1921 and disarmed at Sasebo in April 1922; stricken 1923 and sunk as a target in the Inland Sea in July 1924.

Iwami

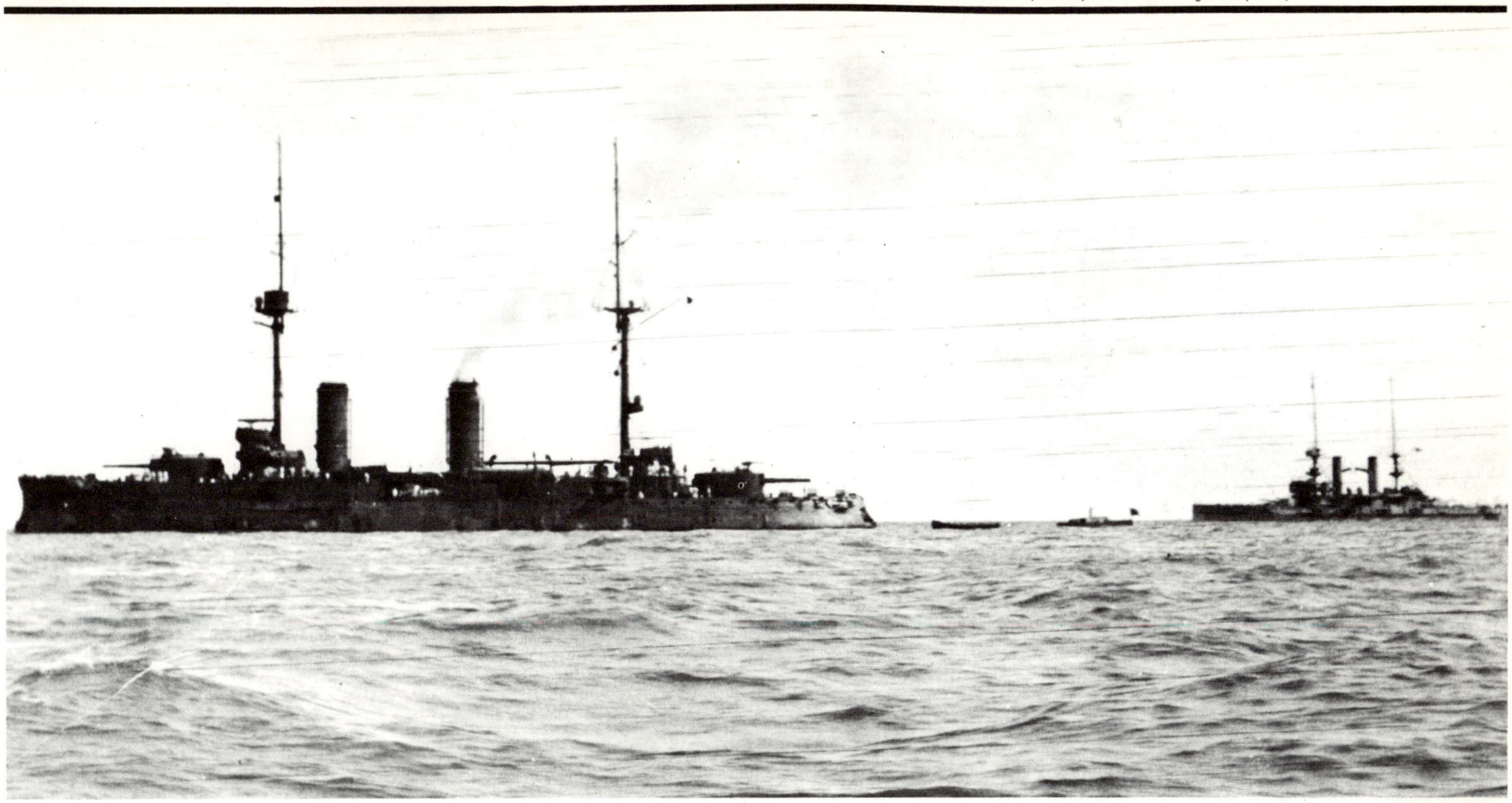

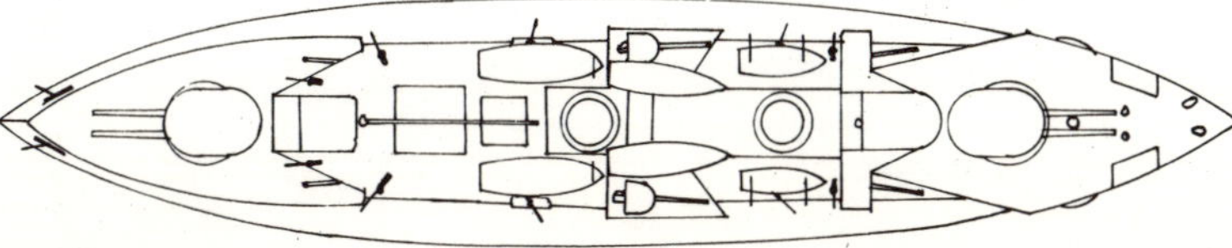

Displacement: 13,516tons (normal), 15,275tons (full load)
Dimensions: 376ft 6in×76ft 1in× 26ft 2in (mean)
Guns: 4×12in 45cal (2×2)
6×8in 45cal (6×1)
16×3in (16×1)
4×25mm (saluting)
Torpedo Tubes: 4×18in (submerged, beam)
Armour: $7\frac{1}{2}$–4in belt, $2\frac{3}{8}$–$1\frac{3}{4}$in decks; 10in main turrets; 8in CT
Machinery: 2-shaft vertical 4-cylinder triple-expansion, 15,800ihp = 18knots; 20 Belleville boilers

Coal Capacity: 800/1580tons
Endurance: 6624miles at 10knots

Complement: 825
Cost: Not known

	Laid Down	Launched	Completed	Built/Engined
Iwami (ex-Orel)	June 1900	19 July 1902	Sept 1904	Galernii Is. Works

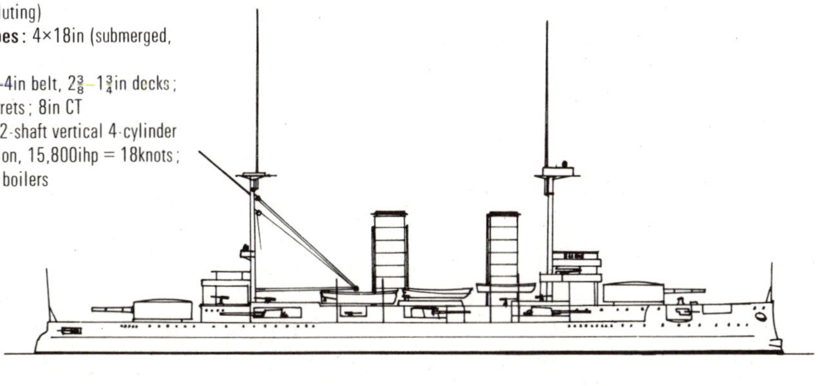

This ship was a prize taken at Tsushima. It is a significant comment on her margin of stability that the Japanese immediately set about removing topweight. In place of the great weight of twin 8in turrets, they mounted single 8in guns (Elswick pattern) in shields, and plated up all the lower deck 3in ports.

Armament: The 12in guns were the original Obuchov pattern, but the other guns were all replaced by Japanese pattern. The 3in (12pdrs) were resited out in the open along the superstructure.

Appearance: Completely changed from her original appearance (compare *Slava*, her Russian sister).

Career

Arrived Sasebo 30 May 1905 and reconstruction completed June 1907; 8in turrets removed, funnels shortened, and structure reduced; $4\times2\frac{1}{2}$pdr saluting guns on bridge; beam torpedo tube retained; rerated 2nd Class coast defence ship 1 September 1912; disarmed April 1921, depot ship; stricken 1923; Flagship Japanese Intervention Squadron, Vladivostock.

Kurama class

Displacement: 14,636tons (normal); approx 16,000tons (full load)
Dimensions: 450ft×75ft 6in×26ft
Guns: 4×12in 45cal (2×2)
8×8in 45cal (4×2)
14×4·7in 50cal (14×1)
8×14pdrs (76mm) 4×MGs

Torpedo Tubes: 3×18in (1 above water stern, 2 submerged, beam)
Armour: As Tsukuba class, but 6in on secondary turrets
Machinery: Kurama: 2-shaft vertical triple-expansion, 22,500ihp = 21½knots; 28 Miyabara boilers

Ibuki: 2-shaft Curtis turbines, 24,000shp = 22½knots; 18 Miyabara boilers
Coal capacity: 600/7000tons
Endurance: not known
Complement: 844
Cost: not known

	Laid Down	Launched	Completed	Built/Engined
Kurama	23 Aug 1905	21 Oct 1907	Feb 1911	Yokosuka DY
Ibuki	22 May 1906	21 Nov 1907	Nov 1909	Kure DY

These ships were improved *Tsukubas*, with more power and a secondary armament of 8in guns. *Ibuki* was the first major Japanese warship with turbines. Laid down as 1st Class armoured cruisers but rerated in 1912.

Appearance: *Ibuki* had pole masts, while *Kurama* had prominent tripods. Both ships looked much longer than the *Tsukubas*, due to the shorter funnels, but the two classes were almost the same size.

Careers

Ibuki: At Kure on outbreak of war, but joined Admiral Jerram's British squadron at Singapore, and took part in search for *Emden* in the following month; on 1 November sailed for Colombo as escort for big troop convoy from New Zealand to Australia; although she asked permission to go to Cocos-Keeling Is. in answer to an S.O.S. about the German *Emden*; permission was refused as she was the most powerful unit of the escort, and H.M.A.S. *Sydney* was sent in her place; with 2nd Squadron in 1917; refitted at Kure in 1918, and still in dockyard hands at Armistice; disarmed 1922 and stricken 1923; broken up 1923–5 at Kobe.

Kurama: At Yokosuka in August 1914; sailed with *Tsukuba* in 1st South Seas Squadron 14 November 1914 to hunt Graf Spee's squadron; 2 December 1914 at Suva, Fiji; Flagship of 2nd Squadron 1917; with 5th Squadron 1918; 1922 disarmed at Sasebo and stricken 1923; broken up at Kobe 1924–5.

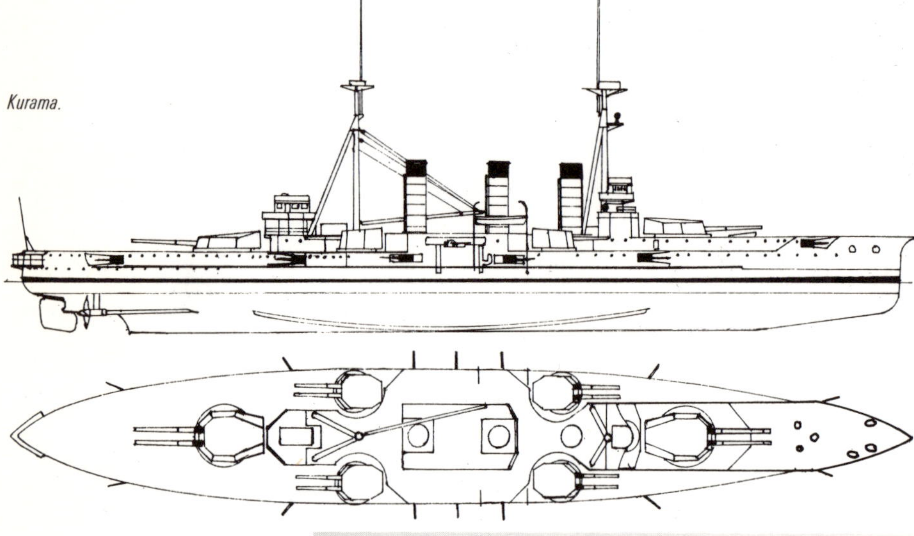

Kurama.

Right, *Kurama as she was in 1911 after the removal of her torpedo nets (NMM).*

Satsuma class

Aki

Displacement: 19,800 tons (normal);
approx 21,000tons (load condition)
Dimensions: 460ft (pp)×83ft 8in×
28ft 9in (max)
Guns: 4×12in 45cal (2×2)
12×10in 45cal (6×2)
8×6in 45cal (8×1)
12×12pdrs (12×1)
Torpedo Tubes: 5×18in (submerged;
4 beam and 1 stern)
Armour: 9–4in belt; 8in turrets; 2in
deck
Machinery: 2-shaft Curtis turbines
(built by Fore River Co. USA),
25,000hp = 20knots; 15 Miyabara
boilers
Coal Capacity: 900/2,500tons
Endurance: Approx 9100miles at
10knots
Complement: 800
Cost: Approximately £1,750,000
($7,000,000)

Satsuma

Displacement: 19,370tons (normal);
approx 21,000tons (load conditions)
Dimensions: 450ft×83ft 6in×28ft 9in
Guns: 4×12in (as Aki)
12×10in (as Aki)
12×4·7in 50cal (12×1)
4×12pdrs (4×1)
Torpedo Tubes: As Aki
Armour: As Aki
Machinery: 2-shaft vertical triple-
expansion, 17,300hp = 18¼knots;
20 Miyabara boilers
Coal Capacity: 1000/2000tons
Endurance: Approx 9100miles at
10knots
Complement: 800
Cost: As Aki

Above, *Aki* as completed (Musée de la Marine).

	Laid Down	Launched	Completed	Built/Engined
Satsuma	15 May 1905	15 Nov 1906	Mar 1909	Yokosuka DY
Aki	15 Mar 1905	15 Apr 1907	Mar 1911	Kure DY

These two interesting ships could have been the first 'all big gun' battleships in the world, as they were originally intended to have an armament of twelve 12in guns, in four twin turrets and four singles. However, as with Fisher's sketch designs for the *Dreadnought*, the cost of such monsters would have been enormous. Japan was in the middle of a war with Russia at the time, and the cost of such a ship would have strained her finances too much. As it was, with considerable British technical assistance, and the provision of gun-mountings by Armstrong, Whitworth, the ships took four and six years to build, respectively.

The extent of British technical assistance can be seen by the close resemblance to the *Lord Nelson* layout of armament. As both Japanese ships were laid down at almost exactly the same time as the *Lord Nelson* and *Agamemnon*, it is almost certain that Japanese constructors were allowed to see their plans. It is also significant that the Japanese ships adopted the extra two guns amidships which had been proposed for the *Lord Nelson*s but ruled out on grounds of size and cost.

The two ships were experimental in many ways, as the wide variation in data shows. Many improvements were incorporated in the *Aki*, and as her completion was delayed she reflected some change in Japanese ideas on disposition of secondary armament.
Appearance: Totally different from one another, *Aki* having three irregularly spaced short funnels, and *Satsuma* having two wider spaced tall funnels. Both ships had the distinctive Japanese-type clipper bow, and a light pole rig, similar to contemporary British predreadnoughts.
Careers
Aki: At Kure 1914; 1st Squadron of 1st Fleet 1915–17; 2nd Squadron 1918; stricken from effective list 1922 and broken up 1924.
Satsuma: With 1st Standing Squadron in August 1914; Flagship of 2nd (Southern) Squadron 1915; 1st Squadron of 1st Fleet 1915; refitted at Sasebo 1916; 1st Squadron 1917–18; stricken 1922 and used for a time as a target; broken up 1924.

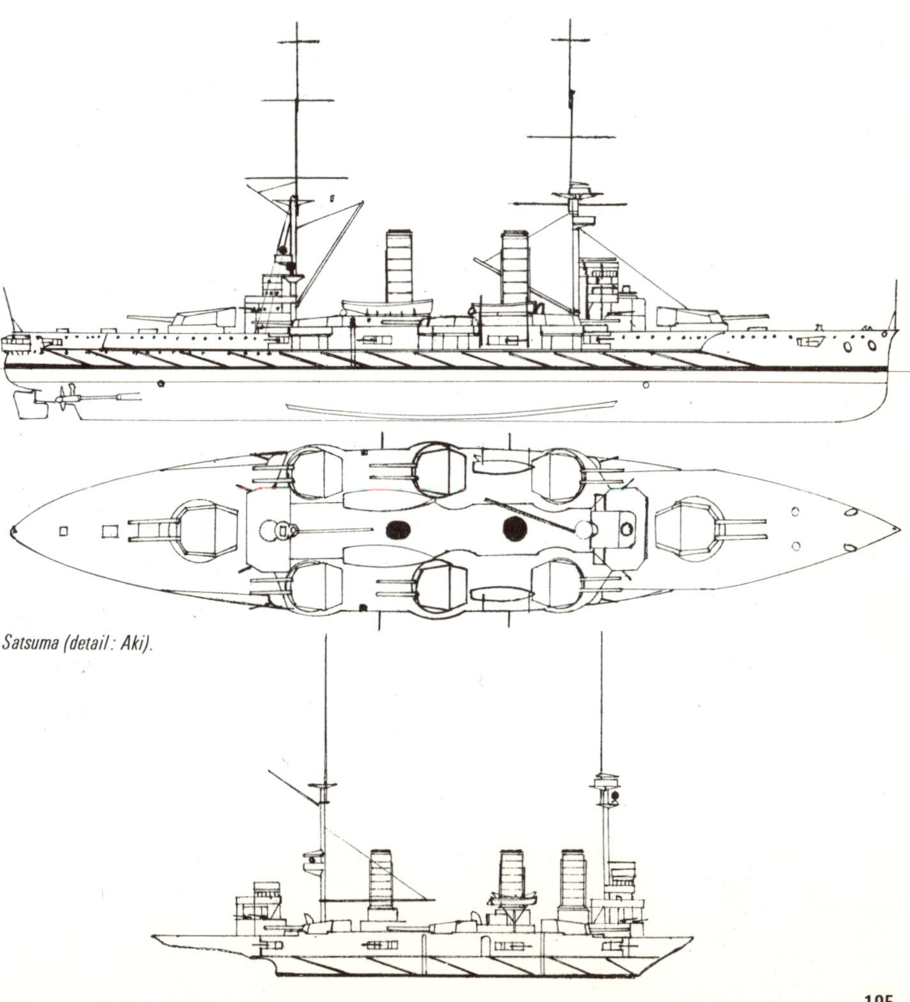

Satsuma (detail: Aki).

Kawachi class

Displacement: 21,420tons (normal); approx 23,000tons (load conditions)
Dimensions: 500ft×84ft×28ft 3in (max)
Guns: 12×12in (6×2)
10×6in (10×1)
8×4·7in (8×1)
12×14pdrs (12×1)
Torpedo Tubes: 5×18in (submerged); 4 beam, 1 stern)
Armour: 12–5in belt; 11in turrets
Machinery: Kawachi: 2-shaft Curtis turbines, 25,000hp = 21knots; 16 Miyabara boilers
Settsu: 4-shaft Parsons turbines, 25,000hp = 21knots; boilers as Kawachi
Coal Capacity: 1000/2500tons
Oil Capacity: 176tons
Endurance: 2700miles at 10knots
Complement: 990
Cost: Approximately £1,750,000 ($7,000,000)

Above, *Settsu on trials in 1911 (NMM).*

	Laid Down	Launched	Completed	Built/Engined
*Kawachi	1 Apr 1909	15 Oct 1910	Mar 1912	Kure DY
Settsu	18 Jan 1909	30 Mar 1911	July 1912	Yokosuka DY

These ships were the first true dreadnoughts built in Japan. After the building of the *Aki* and *Satsuma* Japanese constructors realised that their next step should be a cautious one, and it is significant that four years elapsed between the laying down of the two classes. The design closely follows that of the second German dreadnought class, the *Helgolands*, both in layout and general appearance.

Their experience of what armoured cruisers with medium calibre guns (8in and 10in) could do to crippled battleships led the Japanese to reject the Fisher principle of sacrificing the secondary armament. The *Kawachi* and *Settsu* carried a very heavy battery of 6in and 4·7in guns when compared to other dreadnoughts, without sacrificing weight of protection.

Appearance: Introduced the tripod mast in Japanese battleships, with widely spread legs. *Settsu* had the characteristic Japanese-type clipper bow, but *Kawachi's* was of the 'cleaver' type found in British ships built at Elswick (see British *Agincourt*, *Erin* and *Canada*).

Careers

Kawachi: At Yokosuka DY August 1914; 1st Squadron 1915–17; refitted 1917; 2nd Squadron 1918; destroyed by an internal explosion (defective cordite) in Tokuyama Bay 12 July 1918.

Settsu: 1st Standing Squadron 1914; 1st Squadron 1915–16; refitted Kure 1917; 2nd Squadron 1918; laid up in 1921, and declared for disposal under Washington Treaty in 1922; converted to target ship 1924, and underwent various modifications; damaged at Kure by air attack July 1945 and sank; broken up 1947.

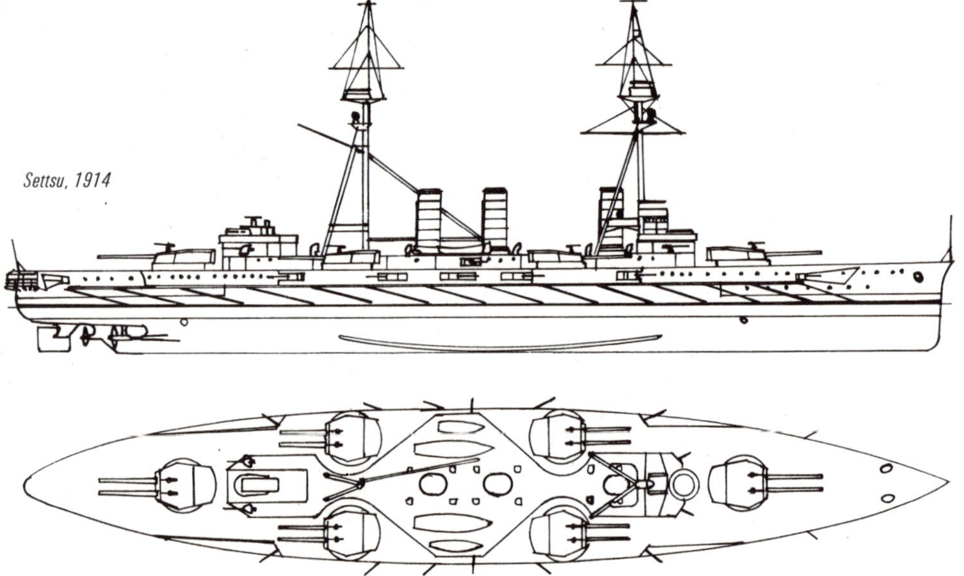

Settsu, 1914

Right, *Kongo running trials in 1913 (P. A. Vicary).*

Kongo class

Displacement: 26,320tons normal;
27,500tons in load condition (Haruna
and Kirishima 27,613tons)
Dimensions: 653ft×92ft×27ft 6in
Guns: 8×14in 45cal (4×2)
16×6in 50cal (16×1)
16×14pdrs (16×1)
Torpedo Tubes: 8×21in (submerged,
beam)
Armour: 9–5in belt; 9in turrets;
10in CT
Machinery: 4-shaft Parsons turbines
(Brown-Curtis in Haruna), 64,000hp =
27½knots; 36 Yarrow boilers (Miyabara
boilers in Japanese-built ships)
Coal Capacity: 1000/4200tons
Oil Capacity: 1000tons
Endurance: Approx 10,000miles at
10knots
Complement: 1221
Cost: £2,500,000 ($10,000,000),
Kongo

	Laid Down	Launched	Completed	Built/Engined
Kongo	17 Jan 1911	18 May 1912	Aug 1913	Vickers, Barrow.
Hiei	4 Nov 1911	21 Nov 1912	Aug 1914	Yokosuka DY
Haruna	16 Mar 1912	14 Dec 1913	Apr 1915	Kawasaki, Kobe
Kirishima	17 Mar 1912	1 Dec 1913	Apr 1915	Mitsubishi,

In 1910 the Imperial Japanese Government ordered the first of four powerful battle cruisers to follow the two *Kawachis*. The first was to be built in an English yard, but the remainder were to be built in Japanese yards, with gun-mountings supplied by Vickers and Armstrongs. The big Japanese shipyards were now able to undertake construction of the largest warships, a remarkable rate of progress when it is remembered that they had built only two dreadnoughts previously. The supply of gun-mountings was still difficult, but Japanese enterprise was equal to the problem, and the 14in guns for the *Kongo* class were the last to be ordered from England.

Although nominally equivalent to the British *Lions*, the *Kongo* was so obviously superior to them, both in protection and in distribution of main armament, that she made a great impression when she appeared. As we have seen, the design of the fourth *Lion* was drastically modified to include all the features of the *Kongo*. The British thought so highly of the class that in 1915, when the margin of capital ship superiority over the Germans was slender, the Japanese Government was asked to consider the loan of all four to the Royal Navy. The loan was refused on the grounds that the Japanese taxpayers would be highly indignant at seeing the ships which they had paid for to defend the homeland, lent to an ally.

Armament: The heavy secondary armament of the previous class was retained, but with only one calibre, better distributed. *Hiei* was completed in 1914 without 14pdrs scattered on turret roofs and on the forecastle deck, as in *Kongo*, and the remaining three followed suit. The Japanese continued to have faith in the value of torpedoes fired by battleships, and the scale of torpedo armament in this class is easily the heaviest in any navy.

Appearance: As completed *Kongo* was a very handsome ship, with three level-topped funnels and two well-spaced tripod masts. *Hiei* and her two Japanese built sisters had the forefunnel raised, which altered the balance of the profile, but kept smoke away from the bridgework. Only *Kongo* had 14pdr guns on her turrets and on the forecastle deck, and these were removed during the war.

Careers

Haruna: 1st Squadron 1915; 3rd Squadron 1916–17; while operating in Southern Pacific in mid-1917 she was damaged by a mine, probably laid by the German raider *Wolf*; repaired at Sasebo; retained under Washington Treaty, but completely

reconstructed for service in World War II; sunk in shallow
water at Kure after air attack in March 1945; broken up 1945–6.
Hiei: 1st Squadron 1915–16; 3rd Squadron 1916; refitted 1917;
Flagship of 3rd Squadron 1918; 'demilitarised', as training ship
to conform to Washington Treaty, but modernised for service
in World War II; sunk 13 November 1942 in Battle of Guadal-
canal.
Kirishima: 2nd Squadron 1915; 1st Squadron 1916; 3rd
Squadron 1916–18; retained in postwar fleet under Washington
Treaty, and modernised before World War II; sunk in action
with American battleships *Washington* and *South Dakota* off
Savo Island, 15 November 1942.
Kongo: 1st Standing Squadron 1914; 1st Squadron 1915–16;
refitted 1916; 3rd Squadron 1917–18; retained in postwar fleet
under Washington Treaty, and totally reconstructed for service
in World War II; torpedoed off Formosa 21 November 1944 by
U.S. submarine *Sea Lion*.

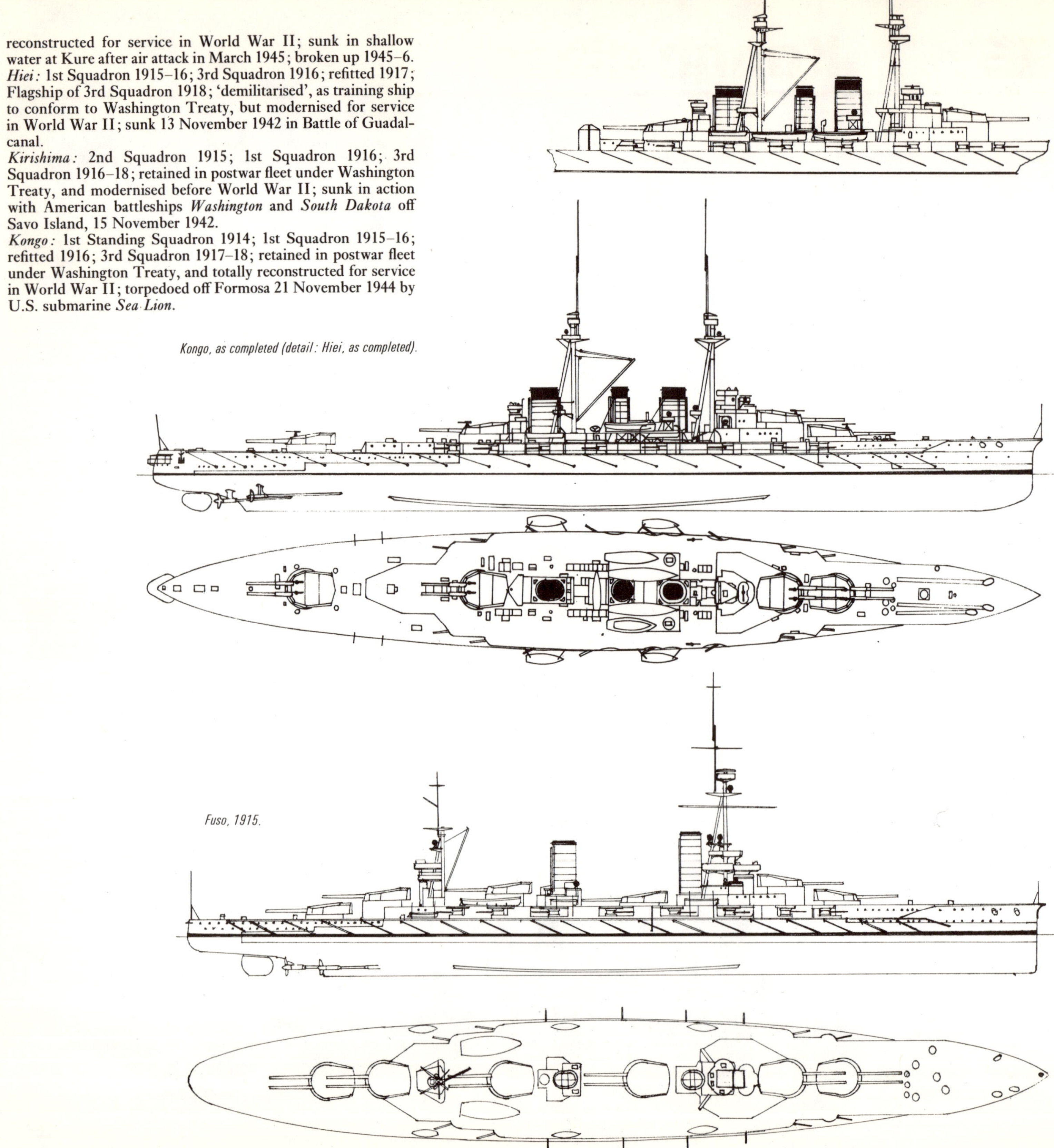

Kongo, as completed (detail: Hiei, as completed).

Fuso, 1915.

Right, Yamashiro in 1923 with a cap to her forward funnel and much extended bridgework (P. A. Vicary).

Right, Fuso (P. A. Vicary).

Fuso class

Displacement: 29,326tons (normal); 30,600tons (load condition)
Dimensions: 630ft×94ft×28ft 6in (max)
Guns: 12×14in 45cal (6×2) 16×6in 50cal (16×1)
Torpedo Tubes: 6×21in (submerged, beam)
Armour: 12–4in belt; 1¼in deck; 12in turrets; 13¾in CT
Machinery: 4-shaft Brown-Curtis turbines, 40,000hp = 23knots; 24 Miyabara boilers
Coal Capacity: Approx 1000/5022tons
Oil Capacity: 1026tons
Endurance: 8000miles at 14knots
Complement: 1193
Cost: Approximately £2,500,000 ($10,000,000)

	Laid Down	Launched	Completed	Built/Engined
Fuso	11 Mar 1912	28 Mar 1914	8 Nov 1915	Kure DY
Yamashiro	20 Nov 1913	3 Nov 1915	31 Mar 1917	Yokosuka DY

Laid down to rival the American *New York* and *Texas*, with an additional pair of 14in guns, these ships reflected the growing industrial might of Japan. Although an overt bid for naval supremacy in the Far East was yet to come, the laying down of four superdreadnoughts showed that the Imperial Japanese Navy was rapidly becoming a major factor in Far Eastern affairs.

One outstanding feature of the *Fuso* class was their speed, which was two knots above service speeds of foreign dreadnoughts. By comparison with the *New York*, the *Fuso* was 110ft longer, and had more than 40 per cent more horsepower.

The armament was for the first time entirely manufactured in Japan, although the heavy mountings were based on the Vickers and Armstrong mountings supplied for the *Kongo* class. The arrangement of turrets No.3 and 4 was unique, with the forward mounting at forecastle deck level and the after mounting a deck higher. Although the official model showed small guns, probably 14pdrs, on the turret tops, these were not mounted in either ship on completion, as Japanese opinion against these light guns out in the open seems to have hardened around this time (compare the *Kongo*). The 6in battery suffered from being too far forward, and no attention was paid to the problems of blast affecting the guns abreast of No.3 turret, but as we have seen in other navies, this was a common failing.

Sister ships: 'C' and 'D' were cancelled and redesigned as the *Ise* and *Hyuga*.

Appearance: Very striking ships, with a tall, bare tripod forward and widely spaced funnels. Designed with the fore-funnel higher in order to reduce smoke interference on the bridges.

Careers

Fuso: 1st Squadron 1916; Flagship of 1st Squadron 1917–18; totally reconstructed before World War II; sunk by gunfire of American battleships *Mississippi*, *Maryland*, *West Virginia*, *Tennessee*, *California* and *Pennsylvania* and others during the Battle of Surigao Strait, 25 October 1944.

Yamashiro: 1st Division, 1st Squadron 1917–18; modernised before World War II; torpedoed by U.S. Navy destroyers in Battle of Surigao Strait, 25 October 1944.

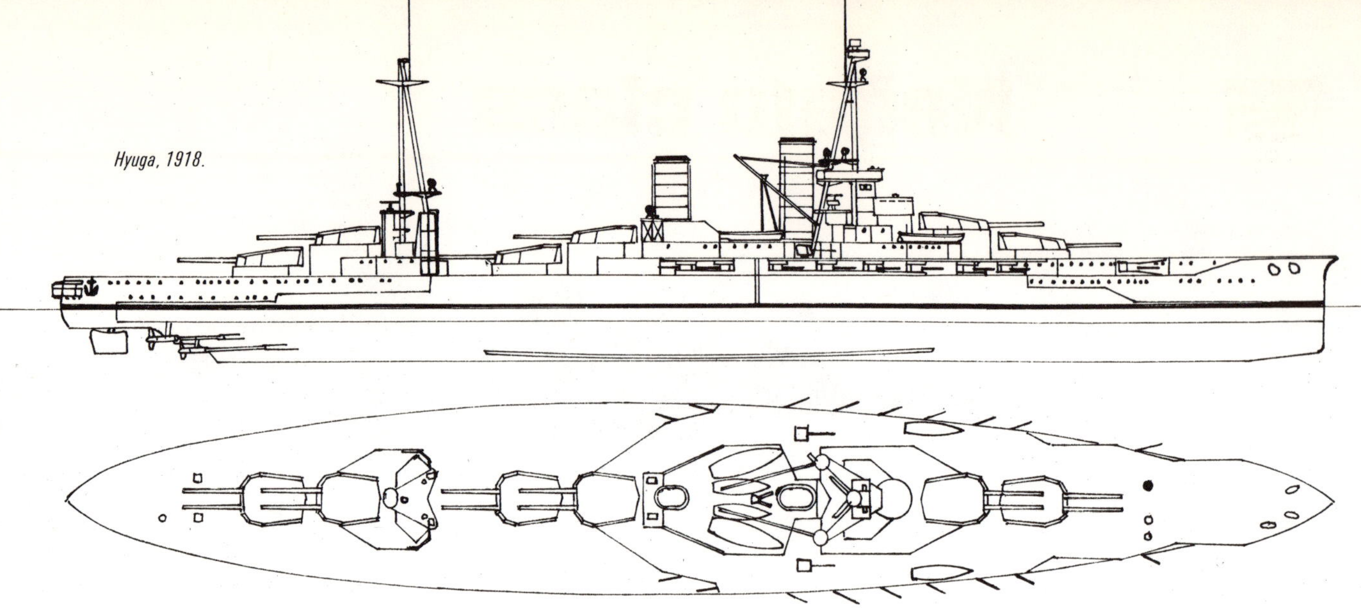

Hyuga, 1918.

Hyuga class

Displacement: 29,980tons (normal); 31,260tons (load condition)
Dimensions: 640ft×94ft×28ft 4in
Guns: 12×14in 45cal (6×2) 20×5·5in 50cal (10×2)
Torpedo Tubes: 6×21in (submerged, beam)
Armour: 12–3in belt; 2in and 1¼in decks; 12in turrets; 12in CT
Machinery: 4-shaft Parsons turbines (Brown-Curtis in Ise), 45,000hp = 23knots; 24 Kansai boilers
Coal Capacity: 4607tons max
Oil Capacity: 1411tons
Endurance: 9680miles at 14knots
Complement: 1360
Cost: Approx £3,000,000 ($12,000,000)

	Laid Down	Launched	Completed	Built/Engined
Hyuga	6 May 1915	27 Jan 1917	Apr 1918	Mitsubishi, Nagasaki
Ise	10 May 1915	12 Nov 1916	Dec 1917	Kawasaki, Kobe

Originally projected as the third and fourth ships of the *Fuso* class, these two incorporated so many improvements that they emerged as a completely separate class.

The layout of the main armament was made more logical, with turrets No.3 and 4 concentrated abaft the funnels. This arrangement resembled that of the American *Arkansas* and *Wyoming*, but the arrangement of main and after superstructure was more reminiscent of contemporary British ships.

Armament: A new type of gun was adopted in this class, a 50calibre 5·5in, similar to the Coventry Ordnance Works weapon supplied for the Greek *Salamis*. To provide a heavier volume of fire the number of guns had to be increased. A pair of guns was placed under the forecastle, ahead of No.1 turret, where it would have been virtually useless in rough weather.

Appearance: Similar to the *Fuso* class, but had their funnels closer together. The tripod mainmast was similar in height to the foremast, and the legs trailed forward.

Careers

Hyuga: 1st Squadron 1918; completely reconstructed before World War II; while lying damaged at Kure, sunk in shallow water by air strike from U.S. carrier *Ticonderoga* 28 July 1945; salvaged and broken up 1946.

Ise: 1st Squadron 1917–18; modernised for service in World War II; sunk by American air attack from carrier *Lexington* while lying damaged at Kure, 28 July 1945; wreck salvaged and broken up 1946.

Right, Ise in 1927 (NMM).

Nagato class

Displacement: 32,720tons (normal); 33,800tons (load condition)
Dimensions: 660ft 9in×95ft×29ft 9in
Guns: 8×16in 45cal (4×2) 20×5·5in 50cal (20×1)
Torpedo Tubes: 4×21in (submerged, beam)
Armour: 12–4in belt; 1in and 1½in decks; 14in turrets; 14½in CT
Machinery: 4-shaft Gihon turbines, 80,000hp = 26¾knots; 21 Kanpon boilers (16 oil-firing, 5 coal-firing)
Coal Capacity: 1600tons max
Endurance: 5500miles at 16knots
Oil Capacity: 3400tons
Complement: 1333
Cost: Not known, but exceeded £5,000,000 ($20,000,000)

	Laid Down	Launched	Completed	Built/Engined
Nagato	28 Aug 1917	9 Nov 1919*	Nov 1920	Kure DY
Mutsu	1 June 1918	31 May 1920	Oct 21	Yokosuka DY

*built in dry dock

These two ships were the Japanese equivalent of the *Queen Elizabeth* class, but with eight 16in guns, making them the first battleships of any nation to adopt this calibre. In other respects they were improved *Hyugas*, without the midship turrets. They were also the first Japanese battleships to adopt the famous 'pagoda' mast structures which became such a well-known Japanese feature.

Careers

As they were completed long after the end of the war their careers can be summarised briefly. After massive reconstruction both ships fought in World War II: *Nagato* survived to be expended in the atom bomb tests at Bikini in July 1946, but *Mutsu* blew up while at anchor in Hiroshima Bay, 8 June 1943, when her magazines exploded.

Nagato.

Tosa class

Displacement: 38,500tons (normal); 39,330tons (load condition)
Dimensions: 715ft×100ft×30ft 9in
Guns: 10×16in 45cal (5×2) 20×5·5in 50cal (20×1)
Torpedo Tubes: 8×24in (beam, above water)
Armour: 11–10in belt; 6½in and 4in decks, turrets probably 14in CT
Machinery: 4-shaft Brown-Curtis turbines, 91,000hp = 26½knots; 12 Kanpon boilers (8 coal-firing, 4 oil-firing)
Coal Capacity: 1700tons max
Oil Capacity: 3600tons
Endurance: 5000miles at 16 knots
Complement: Approx 1500
Cost: Not known

	Laid Down	Launched	Completed	Built/Engined
Tosa	16 Feb 1920	18 Dec 1921	—	Mitsubishi, Nagasaki
Kaga	19 July 1920	17 Nov 1921	—	Kawasaki, Kobe

In 1918 the Japanese approved designs for the first of their '8–8 Plan', so called because it was part of a programme of new construction designed to provide the fleet with eight modern battleships and eight battle cruisers. Apart from the two battle cruisers of the *Amagi* class the remainder of the programme falls outside the scope of this book, but it can be summarised as follows:
Built: 2 *Fuso* Class; 2 *Hyuga* Class; 2 *Nagato* Class.
Planned: 2 *Kaga* Class; 4 *Owari* Class; 4 (No. 13–16, all to be laid down by January 1927).
Built: 4 *Kongo* Class.
Planned 4 *Amagi* Class (all 4 to be laid down by January 1927).

The '8–8 Plan' was a response to the enormous increase in American battleship strength which had been authorised in 1916. American ambitions in the Pacific had not gone unnoticed, and the big 1916 programme of sixteen ships was seen as a direct challenge by the Japanese. Their ships were designed specifically to counter the *Colorado*, *South Dakota* and *Lexington* classes, and this knowledge did much to convince the Americans that the only sane solution was to convene a disarmament conference to negotiate a reduction in naval strength.

Had the American and Japanese programmes gone ahead as planned, the British would have built their replies, and a naval arms race would have begun only two or three years after the Armistice. Almost certainly a war between Japan and the United States could have followed within ten years.

The *Tosa* class were 'fast battleships' and were an expansion of the *Nagato*. There were many novel features in the design, including a flush deck similar to the U.S.S. *New York* and *Texas*, an inclined armour belt which was continued behind the bulge as an anti-torpedo bulkhead, and a heavy armament of the new 24in torpedo in above water positions. For battleships of their generation the scale of protection seems meagre, and they could well be classed as battle cruisers.

Appearance: As projected they would have had a 'pagoda' foremast, a single funnel and a tripod mainmast. The after turrets were unusually arranged, with No.4 superimposed between Nos.3 and 5, No.3 being immediately abaft the mainmast.

Careers

Kaga and *Tosa* were both cancelled under the Washington

Disarmament Treaty and were to be broken up. *Tosa* was used as a target ship for extensive experiments, and was finally sunk by gunfire in the Bungo Strait 9 February 1925. When the hull of the *Amagi* was damaged beyond repair in the great earthquake of 1923 the hull of the *Kaga* was substituted for conversion to an aircraft carrier. In this new guise she proved very successful, and was one of the principal units in the attack on Pearl Harbor in 1941. Sunk by air attack during the Battle of Midway 5 June 1942.

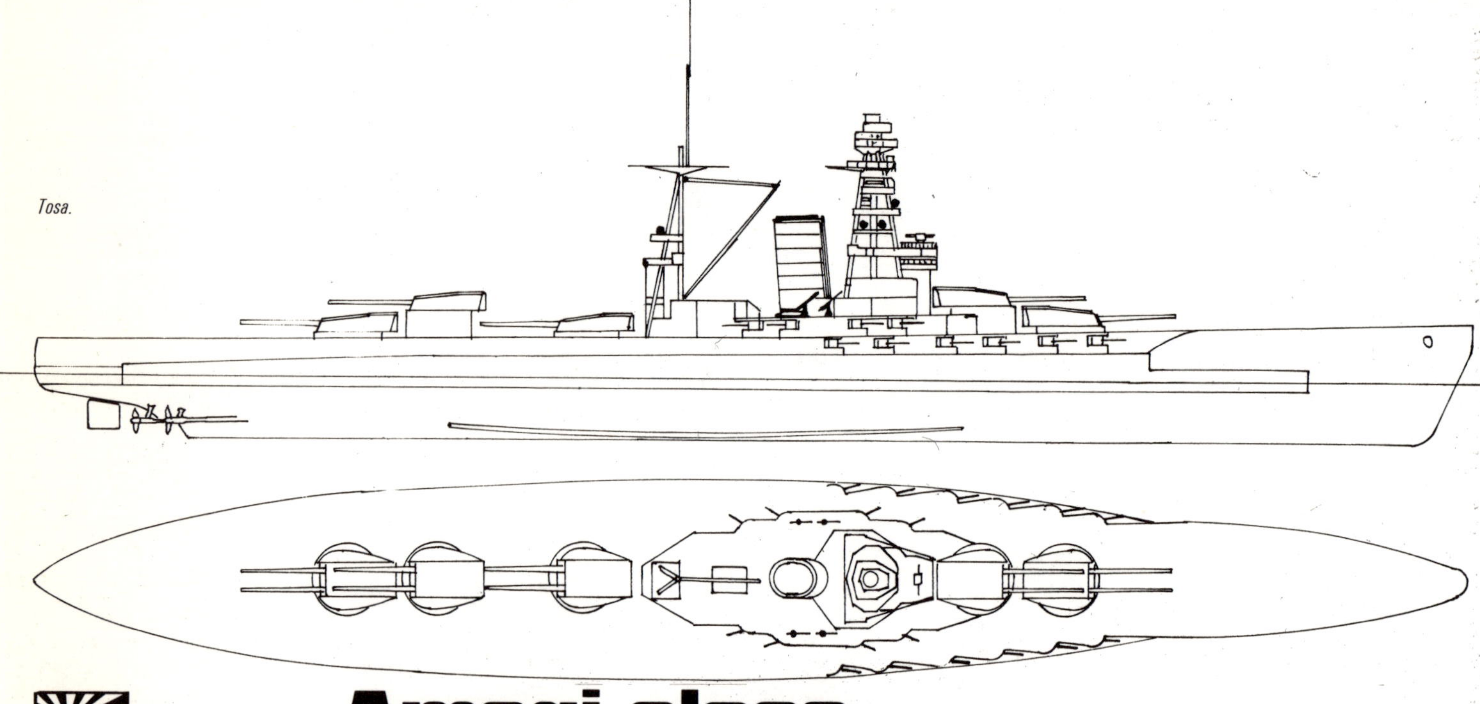

Tosa.

Amagi class

Displacement: 40,000tons (normal);
41,217tons (load condition)
Dimension: 770ft×101ft 31ft
Guns: 10×16in 45cal (5×2)
16×5·8in 50cal (16×1)
4×4·7in A.A. (4×1)
Torpedo Tubes: 8×24in (beam, above water)
Armour: As Tosa class, but maximum thickness 10in on belt
Machinery: 4-shaft Gijutsu Honbu geared turbines, 131,200hp=30knots; 19 Kanpon boilers (8 coal·firing, 11 oil-firing)
Coal Capacity: 2000tons max
Oil Capacity: 4000tons
Endurance: Not stated
Complement: Approx 1600
Cost: Not known

	Laid Down	Launched	Completed	Built/Engined
Amagi	16 Dec 1920	—	—	Yokosuka DY
Akagi	6 Dec 1920	—	—	Kure DY
Atago	22 Nov 1921	—	—	Kawasaki, Kobe
Takao	19 Dec 1921	—	—	Mitsubishi

Battle cruiser versions of the *Tosa* class, these ships and the similar *Owari* class which were to follow them, were very similar to the *Tosa* class in layout and distribution of armour. The principal difference lay in the increased horsepower needed for 30 knots.

Appearance: As projected, they were two-funnelled editions of the *Tosa*, with the same layout of turrets, and the same flush-decked hull with its distinctive bullnosed bow.

Sister ships: *Amagi* and *Akagi* were suspended under the Washington Treaty, and were to be converted to aircraft carriers as counterparts of the *Lexington* and *Saratoga*, but as the hull of *Amagi* was badly damaged during an earthquake the hull of the cancelled *Kaga* was substituted, and her remains were broken up on the slipway. *Akagi* completed her conversion to a carrier, and was one of the principal carriers in the attack on Pearl Harbor in 1941. Sunk by Japanese forces after heavy damage from American carrier-aircraft during Battle of Midway in June 1942. The other two were cancelled in February 1922 and broken up.

Russia

Left, *Tsesarevich in 1914 (Boris Lemachko).*

Introduction

The problems of the Imperial Russian Navy were many, for it had a vast coastline to protect. Its fleets had to be divided between the Baltic, the Black Sea, the White Sea and the Pacific, and it was almost impossible to transfer forces from one theatre to another. Furthermore, Russia was so backward both industrially and politically that her Imperial Navy never reflected her great potential strength.

When the war broke out in August 1914 Russia was in the process of rebuilding her Navy after the appalling disasters of the Russo-Japanese War in 1904–5. In this débâcle the despised Japanese had first captured the great base at Port Arthur and then destroyed with incredible swiftness the avenging Baltic Fleet sent out to the Far East. The degree of ineptitude shown by the Russian Government had dismayed even the Russians, and the result had been widespread unrest in the Service.

Russian design was heavily influenced by French ideas of protection and layout, but these ideas were so slowly executed that the ships were always out of date by the time they were launched. Thus could a ship like the *Andrei Pervozvanni* be laid down in 1903, altered to incorporate war lessons, and still not be completed until 1910. Many Russian ideas, such as turrets for secondary armament and electric ammunition hoists, were introduced many years before they appeared in other navies. Nobody could deny that Russian designers were talented and ingenious, but the inertia of the state bureaucracy made it difficult for these ideas to be exploited.

In 1909 the first dreadnoughts were laid down for the Baltic Fleet, followed two years later by similar ships for the Black Sea. Under the energetic direction of Admiral Girgorovitch much was done to improve the dockyards, and foreign firms and designers were consulted in order to improve the quality of Russian shipbuilding. Unfortunately a large amount of equipment, particularly machinery for various ships, was on order from Germany and never reached Russia.

Dockyards and Shipbuilders

In the Baltic there was the main fleet base at Kronstadt (near modern Helsinki) which had been established for centuries. Shipyards existed at St. Petersburg (renamed Petrograd after the outbreak of war to avoid a Germanic name for the capital). The New Admiralty Yard, the Galernii Yard and the Baltic Works were all on the River Neva. There were a number of operating bases in the Baltic, notably Libau (now Libaja), Reval (now Tallinn) and Helsingfors (now Helsinki).

The main Black Sea Base at Sevastopol was again long-established, but the main building yard was at Nikolaiev. Odessa was a commercial port, but was used throughout the war as a fleet anchorage, as Nikolaiev was too shallow.

During the war no heavy forces were based on Vladivostock, on the Pacific coast, although the ships returned by the Japanese were handed over there. The only battleship in the White Sea, the *Chesma*, was stationed at Murmansk as a depot ship.

Weapons

Most Russian guns came from the Obukhov works. The Russians were among the first to experiment with triple turrets, although some technical assistance was provided by the British firm of Armstrong in their development.

The Baltic Fleet

When the war broke out two new dreadnoughts were complete, and the others were nearing completion. However, opportunities to use them were rare, for the Germans made good use of their submarines and mines. The dreadnoughts were thought to be too valuable to risk, so most of the patrol and convoy duties had to be undertaken by the four predreadnoughts. In 1915 and again in 1917 German land forces were supported by units of the High Seas Fleet, but there was no attempt to use the four dreadnoughts to counterattack. The German units were boldly handled, and thus offset their numerical inferiority without much trouble.

Throughout the war there was serious discontent among the Baltic Fleet battleships, and mutinies broke out as early as 1915. In 1917 the sailors at the main fleet base, Kronstadt (now Kallinin), helped to turn the tide in favour of Lenin's Bolsheviks and established the Communists in Petrograd (now Leningrad). The entire Navy was put on a 'voluntary' basis on 13 February 1918, meaning that all orders given by officers had to be authorised by the ship's soviet. Under conditions like this efficiency rapidly sank to zero level, and in 1918 the Fleet was lying virtually immobilised at Kronstadt.

The Black Sea Fleet

The Black Sea Fleet had traditionally been weaker than the Baltic Fleet, but in 1904–5 the Baltic Fleet had been stripped to provide reinforcements for the Far East. The disaster at Tsushima upset this balance and until the completion of the *Gangut* class of four dreadnoughts the Black Sea Fleet was considerably stronger than the Baltic Fleet. However, in 1910 it was learned that the Turks were about to order dreadnought battleships, and so the decision was taken to increase the strength of the Black Sea Fleet almost to the level of the Baltic Fleet, and four dreadnoughts similar to the *Ganguts* were laid down in 1911.

The Turkish dreadnoughts were taken over by the British in July 1914, but the unexpected arrival of the *Goeben* in Turkey gave the Black Sea Fleet a doughty opponent. There were several brushes with the ex-German battle cruiser, in which even the older Russian ships acquitted themselves very well. Russian ships were fitted with long-base rangefinders, with the result that their long-range gunnery provided some unpleasant surprises for Admiral Souchon.

By comparison with the Baltic battleships, the Black Sea Squadron was energetically handled, and many sorties were made. The loss of the *Imperatritsa Maria* was another example of what negligent handling of ammunition could do, although at the time it was inevitably blamed on sabotage. No ships were lost by enemy action.

The revolutions of February and October 1917 affected the discipline and effectiveness of the Black Sea Fleet, just as they had destroyed the morale of the Baltic Fleet. On 3 March 1918 the Soviet Government concluded the Treaty of Brest-Litovsk with Germany, but German forces immediately began a drive on Sevastopol and the Ukraine. Odessa was occupied on 13 March, Nikolaiev fell two days later and

Russian Guns

Calibre	Length	Wt. of Shell	Muzzle Velocity	Notes
10in	45cal	490lb	2500fps	Peresviet
12in	35cal	731lb	2200fps	G. Pobiedonosetz
12in	40cal	724lb	2600fps	Imp. Pavel Cl etc
12in	52cal	—	—	Gangut Cl etc

Disposition of Russian Fleets in August 1914
Baltic:
Battle Squadron (at Kronstadt)
Gangut (flagship), Sevastopol, Cesarevitch (flagship), Imperator Pavel I, Andrei Pervozanni, Slava
Training Division
Imperator Aleksandr II
Black Sea:
Battleship Squadron (at Sevastopol)
Evstafi (flagship), Ioann Zlatoust, Panteleimon, Tri Sviatitelia
Training Division
Rostislav, Georgi Pobiedonosetz (port guardship)

The following old battleship existed during the war, but only as a hulk, having been struck off the effective list in 1911:

Dvenadtstat Apostolov (1889), as harbour service hulk No. 81 she was retained, and not broken up until 1922.

Sevastopol was taken on 4 May. Many ships fell into German hands, and others were taken to Novorosiisk, but lack of repair facilities prevented anything being done to these units, and the most valuable of them were scuttled. Of the remaining ships, all were badly damaged by the Germans and by both sides in the Civil War which followed. Intervention by British and French naval contingents led to further damage, and by 1920 the Black Sea Fleet battleships were virtually useless.

Ships Returned by Japan

In 1915 the Russian Government began negotiations with the Japanese for the return of some old battleships and cruisers. This was partly to remedy a shortage of ships, but partly for prestige reasons, although the need to find officers and ratings to man them was probably more trouble than it was worth. However, the Japanese also had more ships than crews to man them, they proved amenable, and in the event they had the best of the bargin; they kept the better Russian ships and returned those that were in poor condition.

Colour Schemes and Alterations to Appearance

The former livery of black hull and buff funnels with black tops had been discarded after the Russo-Japanese War, and dark grey overall remained standard during the war. Funnel bands were retained.

There were few major changes to battleships during the war. Torpedo nets were removed from some ships, but *Andrei Pervozvanni*, for example, still had them in 1916, having had them added after the outbreak of war. This ship and her sister *Imperator Pavel I* were unusual in having the only lattice masts seen outside the U.S. Navy, but in 1915–17 these were cut down to stumps.

Disposition of Russian Fleet in October 1917
Baltic Fleet Battle Squadron
1st Division:
Poltava, Petropavlosk, Gangut, Sevatopol
2nd Division:
Respublica, Grazdhanin, Andrei Pervozvanni, Slava
Black Sea Battle Squadron
1st Division:
Svobodnaya Rossia, Volya
2nd Division:
Evstafi, Ioann Zlatoust, Borets za Svobodu
3rd Division:
Tri Sviatitelia (port guardship, Odessa), Rostislav, Sinope
White Sea
Chesma (guardship, Murmansk)

Displacement: 9244tons (normal); 10,244tons (full load)
Dimensions: 346ft 7in (oa)×67ft×25ft 9in
Guns: 2×12in 30cal (2×1)
1×8in 45cal (1×1)
10×6in 45cal (10×1)
4×4·7in
4×47mm
8×MGs
Torpedo Tubes: 6×18in (surface, 1 bow, 1 stern and 4 beam)
Armour: 14–4in belt (compound); 2½in deck; 10in turret; 10in CT
Machinery: 2-shaft vertical compound 3-cylinder engines, 8000ihp = 15knots; 16 Belleville boilers
Coal Capacity: 1200tons
Endurance: 3985miles at 10knots
Complement: 648
Cost: Not known

	Laid Down	Launched	Completed	Built/Engined
Imperator Aleksandr II	Nov 1885	26 July 1887	1889	New Admiralty Yard

This old unit was the survivor of a pair of battleships built in the 1880s, when end-on fire was the vogue in all European navies. She was of little military value, but was kept in commission during the war as a gunnery training ship.
Sister ship: *Imperator Nicolai I* captured by Japanese after the Battle of Tsushima in 1905, and became the Japanese *Iki*.
Nomenclature: Renamed *Zaria Svobody* ('Dawn of Freedom') after the February 1917 Revolution.

Career
When war broke out she was the Flagship of the 2nd Reserve of the Baltic Fleet, and in commission as gunnery training ship; she continued in this humble but important service until 1917; her crew took part in the October Revolution, and in 1919 she was damaged during the British C.M.B. (Coastal Motor Boat) attack on Kronstadt; either as a direct result of this, or subsequently she sank, but was salvaged in 1921 and broken up 1922.

Displacement: 12,540tons (normal), 13,318tons (full load)
Dimensions: 370ft 8in×73ft×28ft 5in (max)
Guns: 4×12in 40cal (2×2)
14×6in 45cal (14×1)
4×47mm
Torpedo Tubes: Removed
Armour: 18–14in belt (Harvey steel); 3–2in decks; 16in turrets; 12in CT
Machinery: 2-shaft vertical triple-expansion, 11,400ihp = 16knots; 14 cylindrical boilers
Coal Capacity: 750/900tons
Endurance: 3980miles at 10knots
Complement: 744
Cost: Not known

Displacement: 10,500tons (normal); 11,032tons (full load), but Sinope 11,230tons (full load)
Dimensions: 339ft 6in×69ft×29ft (max)
Guns: Sinope (1914):
4×8in 50cal
12×6in 45cal
2×47mm
2×MGs
Georgi Pobiedonosetz:
6×12in 35cal (3×2)
8×47mm (8×1)
18×37mm (18×1)
Torpedo Tubes: Sinope: none
Armour: 16–10in belt (compound); 2½in decks; 2in turrets; 12in CT
Machinery: 2-shaft vertical triple-expansion, 10,600hp = 16½knots; 16 cylindrical boilers (Sinope 20 Belleville)
Coal Capacity: 700/1050tons
Endurance: 2000miles at 10knots
Complement: 665
Cost: Not known

These two ships were obsolete when war broke out in 1914, and two earlier sister ships had already been scrapped some years before. Both ships had attracted attention abroad in their day having an unusually heavy main battery. In addition *Sinope* had the distinction of being the first warship in the world to have triple-expansion machinery, while *Georgi Pobiedonosetz* was the first to have electrically worked turrets and hoists.
Armament: *Sinope* had been rearmed in 1910, but her sister retained her original armament until 1919.
Sister ships: *Imperatritsa Ekaterina II* sunk in 1907, and *Chesma* scrapped in 1910.

Careers
Georgi Pobiedonosetz: Returned fire of *Goeben* 29 October 1914; became floating headquarters of C-in-C's staff for the Black Sea Fleet at Sevastopol; incorporated into Red Fleet after October 1917 Revolution; captured by White Russian Army December 1918, and machinery wrecked 25 April 1919; around this time her guns were removed to strengthen the land defences; November 1920 towed with the remainder of General Wrangel's fleet to Bizerta and interned by the French; sold for scrap by French Government 1936.
Sinope: At Sevastopol on outbreak of war, but sent to Odessa as guardship September 1914; provided fire support for Russian and Rumanian troops at the mouth of the Danube 1916; escorted troop convoys in North West part of the Black Sea; disarmed at Sevastopol June 1917 on orders of Vice-Admiral

	Laid Down	Launched	Completed	Built/Engined
Sinope	Apr 1883	20 June 1887	1889	Ropit, Sevastopol
Georgi Pobiedonosetz	July 1889	9 Mar 1892	1894	

Kolchak; machinery wrecked 25 April 1919 by British interventionist forces; discarded 1922 by Soviet Navy and scrapped 1923–4.

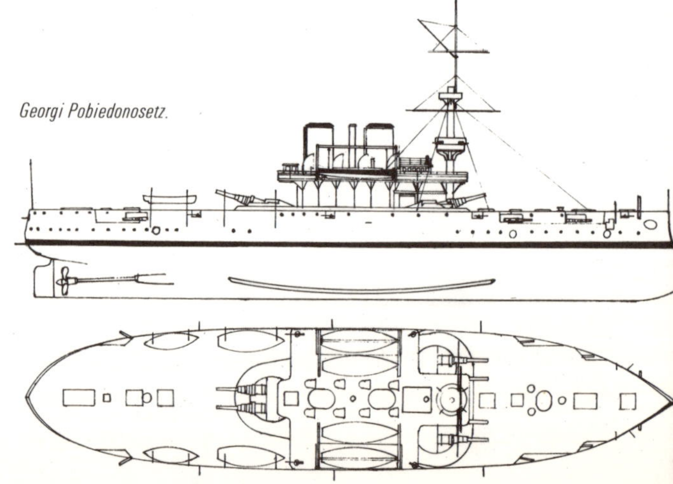

Georgi Pobiedonosetz.

Tri Sviatitelia

	Laid Down	Launched	Completed	Built/Engined
Tri Sviatitelia	14 Aug 1891	31 Oct 1893	1895	Nikolaiev DY

This elderly unit of the Black Sea Fleet was a low freeboard turret ship similar to the old British *Nile* and *Trafalgar*. She had been extensively modernised in 1911–12, and remained in front-line service until the new dreadnoughts were ready.

Appearance: During the 1911–12 refit the old 'military' masts were replaced by a light pole rig. Additional 6in guns were added in place of the old 4·7in guns at the corners of the super-structure, and an extra position on either side at the after end of the battery.

Career

At Sevastopol on outbreak of war; covered minelaying operations off Bosphorus 4 November 1914 and carried out shore bombardments subsequently; in action against the *Goeben* and *Breslau* 18 November; on 12 August 1915 joined *Evstafi*, *Ioann Zlatoust*, *Panteleimon* and *Rostislav* in Third Battleship Group, which remained in partial reserve. In April 1916 convoyed troops to Novorossiisk, but as her machinery and guns were in poor shape she was laid up at Sevastopol in the winter of 1916–17; captured by Austro-German forces in April 1918, but fell into White Russian hands in December 1918; her machinery was wrecked by British forces on 25 April 1919 and her armament removed; fell into Soviet hands in November 1920, by which time the old ship was a useless hulk; she was condemned in 1922 and scrapped in 1923–4.

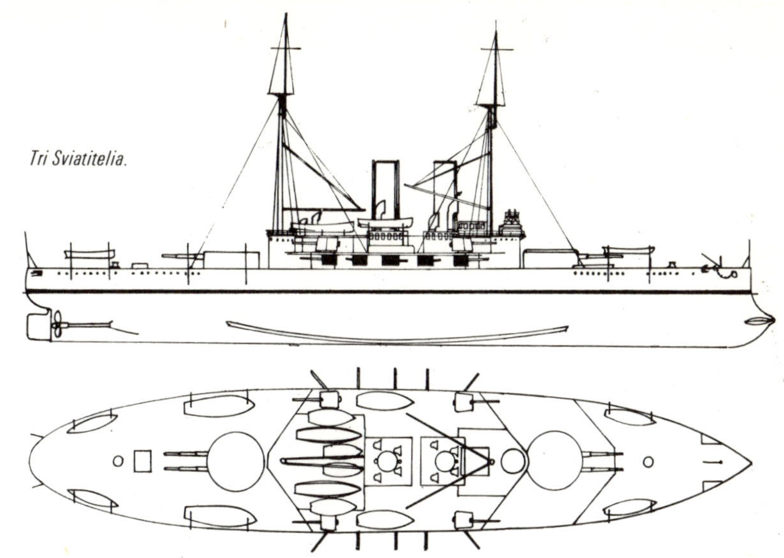

Tri Sviatitelia.

Ex-Japanese prizes

These ships had been captured during the Russo-Japanese War in 1904–5, and were incorporated into the Japanese Navy. In April 1916, as the Japanese were having manning problems with so much new construction coming forward, they allowed two battleships and the cruiser *Varyag* to be returned to the Russians. They had always been misfits in the Japanese fleet organisation, which relied largely on British equipment, and had been retained mainly for prestige; in 1916 such a gesture would relieve the Japanese of the burden of finding spares, and possibly bolster up an unsteady ally.

The transfer was effected in March 1916, but as the ships were in poor shape they did little to strengthen the Russians. Indeed, by further straining their fleet manning and supply organisation they proved more trouble than they were worth. Little or nothing was done to alter the armament after their return.

Careers

Chesma: Transferred to Russian control at Vladivostock 5 April 1916; transferred to White Sea as Flagship of Rear-Admiral Bestoujev-Roumin arrived in Kola Gulf 3 January 1917; after 1917 Revolution laid up at Murmansk; immobilised by Anglo-American forces and broken up in 1922.

Peresviet: Sold to Russia in March 1916 and handed over at Vladivostock 5 April 1916; stranded 23 May 1916, and not refloated until July; transferred to Northern Fleet for service in the White Sea, and set out via the Indian Ocean and the Suez Canal; after repairs to her machinery she left Port Said 4 January 1917, but when about ten miles north of Port Said she struck two mines laid by *U.73* (one forward and one abreast of the boiler room); after being swept by fire she sank (167 lives lost).

Below, *Chesma seen at Murmansk in 1920 before she fell into the hands of the Reds (P. A. Vicary).*

Panteleimon

Displacement: 12,582tons (normal); 12,600tons (full load)
Dimensions: 370ft 8in×73ft×27ft (mean)
Guns: 4×12in 40cal (2×2)
16×6in 45cal (16×1)
14×3in
6×47mm
2×MGs
Torpedo Tubes: 5×18in (submerged, 4 beam and 1 stern)
Armour: 9–6in belt; 10in turrets; 3–2½in decks; 9in CT
Machinery: 2-shaft vertical triple-expansion, 10,600hp = 16knots; 22 Belleville boilers
Coal Capacity: 776/1070tons
Oil Capacity: 580tons
Endurance: 3400miles at 10knots
Complement: 741
Cost: Not known

	Laid Down	Launched	Completed	Built/Engined
Panteleimon	Dec 1898	9 Oct 1900	1904	Nikolaiev
(ex-Knaz Potemkin Tavrichevsky)				

This ship has been immortalised by the Eisenstein film, *The Battleship Potemkin*, as it was she that had been taken over by her crew in June 1905, and eventually interned at Constanza.

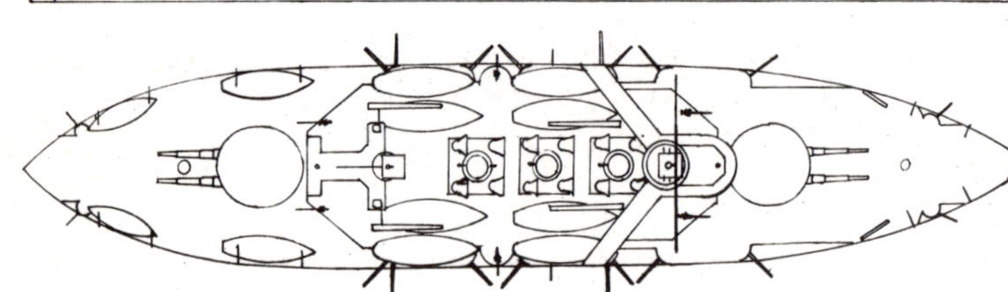

As she was returned to Russian ownership on the feast day of St. Panteleimon (9 August, which was also the anniversary of the great battle of Gangut) she was renamed *Panteleimon* to expunge the record. However, the Provisional Government of February 1917 renamed her *Potemkin* as a democratic gesture.

Although too slow and weakly protected, the *Panteleimon* and other Russian predreadnoughts in the Black Sea were more than a match for any Turkish ships, until the arrival of the *Goeben* at the end of 1914.

Nomenclature: After being renamed *Potemkin* in March 1917, she was again renamed on 11 May 1917; this time she became *Boretz Za Svobodu* ('Fighter for Liberty').

Appearance: Similar to the *Evstafi* class, but could be distinguished by her heavier 'military' masts, with prominent fighting tops, and 3in guns in sponsons under the forecastle and right aft below the upper deck. She also had prominent goosenecked cranes at both ends of the superstructure.

Career

Joined the new 'flying squadron' at Sevastopol on outbreak of war; took part in bombardment of Bosphorus 26 April 1915, and in ensuing action she scored two 12in hits on the *Goeben*; carried out several shore bombardments in May 1915; on 10 August she was transferred to the 3rd Manoeuvring Group, comprising old battleships held in reserve for shore bombardment; shelled Varna 20–22 October 1915, and attacked unsuccessfully by *UB.7* on 25 October; April 1916 stationed at Trebizond to give gunfire support to Russian Army; June 1916 transferred to Batum for patrol duties and enforcement of Anatolian coast blockade; laid up at Sevastopol late in 1916, and deserted by her crew after the Russo–German armistice in December 1917; her engines were disabled by British forces in April 1919, and she was finally recaptured by Soviet forces in November 1920; during 1921–2 the old hulk was used for the making of the film, *The Battleship Potemkin*, and was finally broken up 1922–4.

Right, Slava as she appeared in 1914 (Musée de la Marine).

Slava

Displacement: 13,516tons (normal);
14,400tons (full load)
Dimensions: 376ft 6in×76ft 1in×
26ft 2in
Guns: 4×12in 40cal (2×2)
12×6in 45cal (6×2)
20×3in 60cal (20×1)
4×47mm
8×MGs
Torpedo Tubes: 2×18in (submerged,
beam)
Armour: 9–2½in belt (Krupp); 4–2in
deck; 10in turrets; 8in CT
Machinery: 2-shaft vertical 4-cylinder
triple-expansion, 15,800hp = 18knots;
20 Belleville boilers
Coal Capacity: 800/1580tons
Endurance: 6624miles at 10knots
Complement: 825
Cost: Not known

	Laid Down	Launched	Completed	Built/Engined
*Slava	4 Oct 1902	29 Aug 1903	1905	Baltic Works

This ship was the sole survivor of five ships built 1899–1905, as Russian versions of the French-built *Tsesarevich*. They closely followed contemporary French ideas, and had a pronounced 'tumblehome', in an effort to combine topweight with high freeboard. As in the *Rostislav* the 6in guns were all in turrets, but in twin turrets, yet another example of Russian designers' ingenuity.

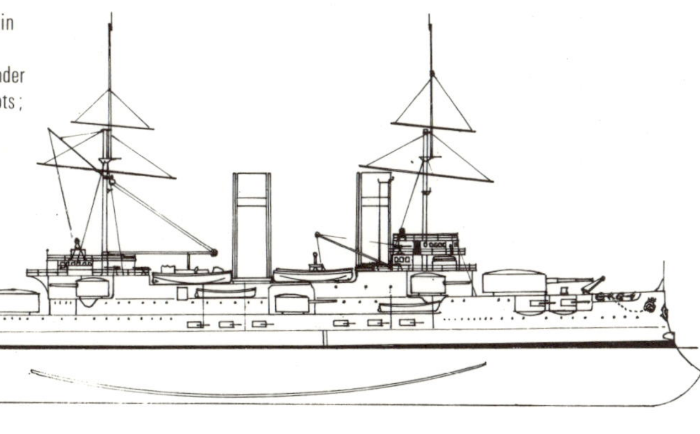

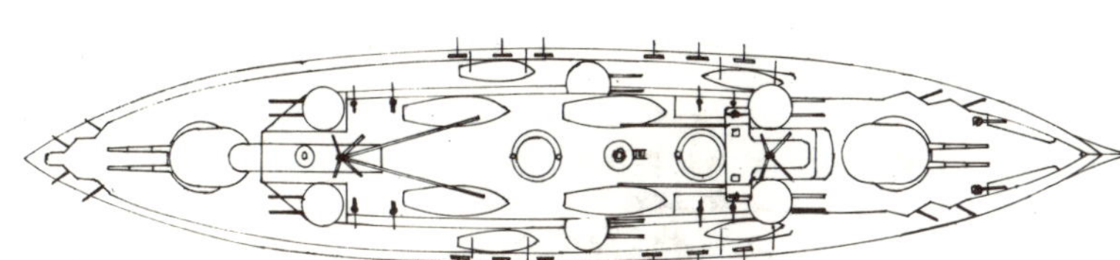

The *Borodinos* all had unlucky histories, and they became known as 'jinx-ships' after a series of mishaps. All proved too topheavy in service, and unseaworthy, due to the great weight of the secondary turrets carried high up. Conversely, the 3in guns were carried too low to be of any use at sea, and absorbed an undue proportion of the displacement without adding to the fighting power.

Sister ships: *Imperator Aleksandr III*, *Borodino* and *Kniaz Suvorov* were sunk in action at Tsushima 1905, and *Orel* was captured at the same battle, and became the Japanese *Iwami*.

Appearance: Looked very similar to the *Tsesarevich*, with two large, widely spaced funnels, but could be distinguished by the larger number of 3in ports at main deck level, and the casemates under the forecastle. Fighting tops had been removed in 1906.

Career

With 2nd Battleship Squadron, Baltic Fleet, on outbreak of war; ordered to Gulf of Riga in July 1915; in action with German battleships August 1915, and hit by German shore batteries in September; slightly damaged by bomb from German aircraft April 1916; replaced at Riga by *Tsesarevich* September 1916, and sent to Helsingfors; the *Slava* was one of the few ships not affected by unrest after the Revolution, and September 1917 she was sent once more to the Gulf of Riga to support the Russian right flank; after a spirited action with the German battleships *König* and *Kronprinz* on 17 October off Moonsund, she was hit by several shells and disabled; as a result of flooding she now drew too much water to escape through the dredged channel, and Admiral Bachirev ordered her to be scuttled in the fairway; she was scuttled at the entrance to the Moonsund Channel and torpedoed by the destroyer *Turkmenets-Stavropolsky*; the wreck remained in an upright position, with the upperworks showing, and the Germans later salvaged some material; broken up 1935 by Estonian ship-breakers.

Right, *Slava beached and burnt out in October 1917 after her heroic action in the Moonsund Channel. Note the anti-aircraft gun on No. 1 turret (P. A. Vicary).*

Rostislav

Displacement: 8800tons
Dimensions: 345ft×69ft×25ft (mean)
Guns: 4×10in 45cal (2×2)
8×6in 45cal (8×1)
12×47mm
4×37mm
Torpedo Tubes: 2×18in (submerged, beam)
Armour: 16·4–12·5in belt (Harvey steel); 10in turrets; 2–3in decks; 6in CT

Machinery: 2-shaft vertical triple-expansion, 8500ihp = 16knots; 12 cylindrical boilers (4 double-ended, 4 single-ended)

Oil Capacity: 500/800tons
Endurance: 3000miles at 10knots
Complement: 641
Cost: Not known

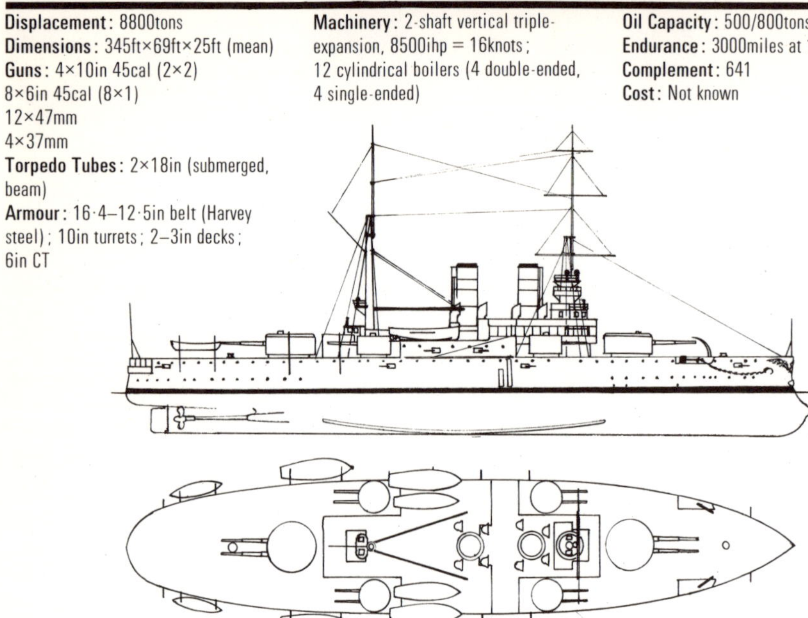

	Laid Down	Launched	Completed	Built/Engined
Rostislav	1894	20 Aug 1896	1899	Nikolaiev

This unit, although obsolescent in 1914, was remarkable for being the first oil-fired battleship in the world. Like the *Petropavlosk* class, she followed the trend towards higher freeboard in Russian ships of the period, and was remarkable for having her 6in guns in twin turrets, thirty years before this feature emerged in other navies.

Appearance: She underwent virtually no change during the war.

Career

In reserve at Sevastopol on outbreak of war, but commissioned for active service; between 1914 and 1917 she took part in all the patrols and sorties of the Black Sea Fleet, including the bombardments of Zunguldak and Trebizond; hit by a bomb from a German seaplane in September 1916 with only slight damage; captured April 1918 at Sevastopol by German forces and used by them as an accommodation ship; her engines were destroyed by the British and French interventionist forces in April 1919, but this did not prevent the White Russians towing her to the Sea of Azov, where they used her as a floating battery; finally run aground and had the breech-blocks removed from her guns 16 November 1920; scrapped by Soviet Government order in 1922.

Nomenclature: At the time of the Revolution the name *Edinenie* ('Union') was chosen for this ship, but she was not renamed.

Tsesarevich

Displacement: 12,912tons (normal); 13,380tons (full load)
Dimensions: 388ft 9in (oa)×76ft 1in ×28ft 3in (max)
Guns: 4×12in 40cal (2×2)
12×6in 45cal (6×2)
14×3in
4×47mm
2×37mm
Torpedo Tubes: 3×18in (2 submerged, beam and 1 bow, surface)
Armour: $9\frac{3}{4}$–$4\frac{3}{4}$in belt (Krupp); main turrets 10in, secondary turrets 6in; $2\frac{1}{4}$–$1\frac{1}{2}$in decks; 10in CT
Machinery: 2-shaft vertical 4-cylinder triple-expansion, 15,300ihp = 18 knots; 20 Belleville boilers
Coal Capacity: 800/1350tons
Endurance: 5500miles at 10knots
Complement: 774
Cost: Not known

	Laid Down	Launched	Completed	Built/Engined
Tsesarevich	May 1899	23 Feb 1901	Aug 1903	La Seyne, Toulon

This ship marked an attempt by the Imperial Russian Government to acquire a battleship embodying all the latest French ideas, at a time when Franco-Russian relations were particularly codial. Unfortunately, the prototype displayed all the vices inherent in contemporary French battleships, being heavily overloaded for her displacement and tending to heel unduly when turning. With her heavy secondary armament in twin turrets she set a new standard for offensive power, but this was offset by having her 3in guns so close to the waterline that they could never have been used without endangering the ship.

The most alarming feature was the tendency to shift her centre of gravity rapidly under certain conditions, and this contributed to the loss of the Russian ships built as copies of the *Cesarevitch*, the *Borodino* class (see *Slava*). As a result of war experience in 1904–5, she was drastically modified, and had as much of the top-hamper removed as possible.

She was unique as the only battleship to escape the disaster of Tsushima as in 1904 she had been inadvertently interned at the German colony of Kiaou Chao.

Appearance: As originally built she embodied French ideas of 'fierce-face', with massive masts and fighting tops, and an exaggerated tumblehome side bristling with guns of all sizes. The rig was greatly simplified after 1906, when light pole masts were substituted, and some tertiary guns were removed. Very similar to *Slava* in appearance, but could be distinguished by her large luffing boat cranes between the funnels.

Nomenclature: After the February 1917 Revolution she was given the democratic name of *Grazdhanin* ('Citizen').

Career

At Kronstadt with the Baltic Fleet on outbreak of war; her deep draught restricted her usefulness in local operations, and she was only able to take part in the 1917 Gulf of Riga actions after the Moonsund Channel had been specially deepened; hit twice in action with German battleships *Kronprinz* and *König* 17 October 1917; her final disposal is rather obscure, but it seems that she was broken up by German ship-breakers in 1922–4.

Below, two photographs of Tsesarevich showing her exaggerated tumblehome and the enormous funnels which gave her a strong resemblance to contemporary French ships. Top, a 1901 photograph (P. A. Vicary). Below, as she appeared in 1914 (Boris Lemachko).

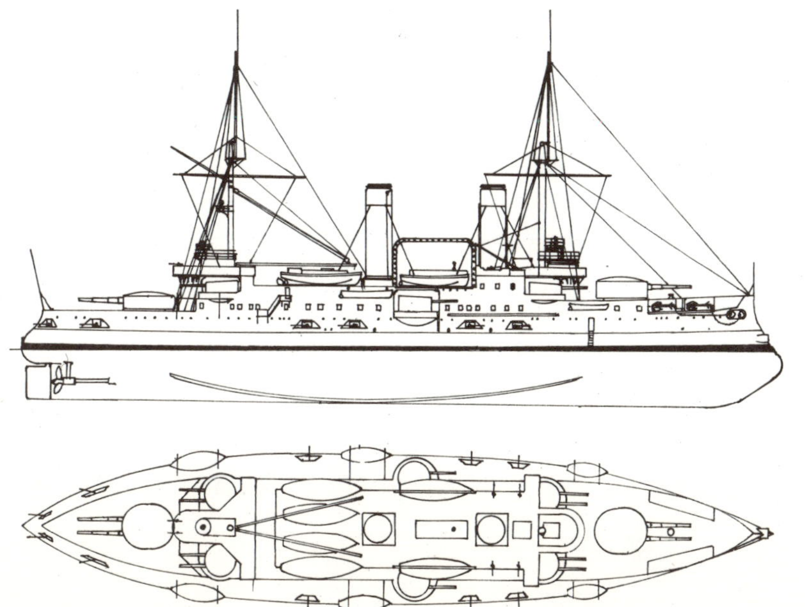

Evstafi class

Displacement: 12,840tons (normal), 13,000tons (full load)

Dimensions: 372ft×74ft×27ft (mean)

Guns: 4×12in 40cal (2×2)
4×8in 50cal (4×1)
12×6in 45cal (12×1)
14×3in
6×47mm

Torpedo Tubes: 3×18in (submerged, 1 stern and 2 beam)

Armour: 9–6in belt (Krupp); 10in turrets; 3–1½in decks; 9in CT

Machinery: 2-shaft vertical triple-expansion, 10,600hp = 16knots; 22 Belleville boilers

Coal Capacity: 670/800tons

Oil Capacity: 580tons

Endurance: 4500miles at 10knots

Complement: 879

Cost: Not known

	Laid Down	Launched	Completed	Built/Engined
Sviatitoi Evstafi	Nov 1903	3 Nov 1906	1910	Nikolaiev
Ioann Zlatoust	Nov 1903	14 May 1906	1910	Sevastopol DY

These two ships were laid down before the outbreak of the Russo-Japanese War, and incorporated some alterations to the design in the light of war experience. The heavy secondary armament of 8in guns reflected the trend in other major navies towards medium calibre guns as well as 6in guns, (compare the British *King Edward VII*, German *Deutschland* etc.).

These ships were the most powerful units of the Russian Black Sea Fleet until the new dreadnoughts appeared, and gave a good account of themselves in action. Unfortunately, like all the Russian predreadnoughts, they were slow, and poor maintenance tended to magnify this defect. The guns were carried at a reasonable height above water, with the 8in carried at the corners of the superstructure.

Appearance: Similar to the *Panteleimon*, with three funnels, but had only light pole masts.

Careers

Sviatitoi Evstafi: Joined the new 'flying squadron' of the Black Sea Fleet on outbreak of war; as flagship of the Commander-in-Chief, Admiral Eberhard, she covered minelaying operations and carried out shore bombardments on several occasions; on 18 November 1914 she and her squadron met the ex-German battle cruiser *Goeben* off Sarych Point; she scored at least one hit on the Turkish ship, out of the total of fourteen, and received four hits in return (33 dead, 25 wounded); in action with cruisers *Breslau* and *Hamidieh* January 1915, and had her foreturret disabled; in August 1915 she was transferred to the 3rd Manoeuvring Group, with *Ioann Zlatoust* and *Panteleimon*, to carry out shore bombardments; demobilized in March 1918 after the Russo-German armistice, but fell into German hands the following month; when Sevastopol was recaptured by White Russian forces in December 1918 she changed hands once again, but her machinery was destroyed by Anglo-French forces in April 1919 to deny her to Soviet forces; broken up 1922–4 by Soviet Government.

Ioann Zlatoust: Served in 'flying squadron' with *Sviatitoi Evstafi* and others from outbreak of war; action with *Goeben* 18 November 1914, and suffered no damage; 3rd Manoeuvring Group August 1915; demobilized March 1918, by which time both she and *Sviatitoi Evstafi* were badly worn out by constant steaming; captured by German forces April 1918, and by White Russians December 1918; machinery destroyed by Anglo-French interventionist forces April 1919; broken up 1922–4 by Soviet authorities.

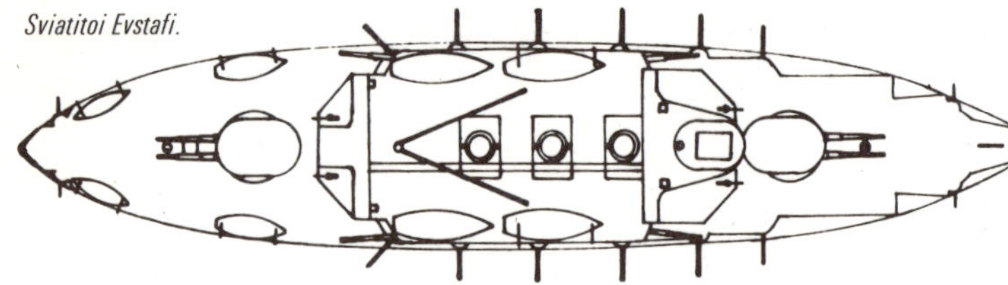

Sviatitoi Evstafi.

Right, Andrei Pervozvanni in 1918, showing how her lattice masts had been cut down in 1916–17. Note that she still has torpedo nets and booms (IWM).

Imperator Pavel 1 class

Displacement: 17,400tons (normal), 18,580tons (full load)
Dimensions: 454ft×80ft×27ft (mean)
Guns: 4×12in 40cal (2×2)
14×8in 50cal (4×2, 6×1)
12×4·7in 50cal (12×1)
4×47mm
8×MGs
Torpedo Tubes: 3×18in (submerged, 1 stern and 2 beam)
Armour: $8\frac{1}{2}$in–$3\frac{1}{2}$in belt; $2\frac{1}{4}$–$1\frac{1}{4}$in decks, main turrets 8in, secondary turrets 6in; 8in CT
Machinery: 2-shaft vertical triple-expansion, 17,000ihp = 18knots; 25 Belleville boilers
Coal Capacity: 1600/3100tons
Endurance: 7000miles at 10knots (approximate)
Complement: 933
Cost: Not known

	Laid Down	Launched	Completed	Built/Engined
Imperator Pavel I	Jan 1903	7 Sept 1907	Sept 1910	Baltic Works
Andrei Pervozvanni	Sept 1903	20 Oct 1906	Aug 1910	Galernii Is. Works

These two ships were the most powerful and modern units of the Black Sea Fleet in 1914, although laid down in 1903. They approximated in nominal power to the British *Lord Nelson* class, and had been drastically modified as a result of war experience.

Apart from the heavy secondary armament, with its twin turrets and additional guns in the battery, the after 12in turret was unusually far aft, leaving a clear arc for the 8in turrets. Lattice masts were adopted, although smaller and narrower than the American pattern.

Although the armour was light by contemporary standards, it had been spread over the whole of the hull. This was a result of the Battle of Tsushima, when heavily laden ships had foundered after water found its way into the hull through splinter holes or even gun-ports. However, in their zeal to prevent this from recurring the Russian constructors gave the new ships a hull absolutely devoid of scuttles, making them extremely unhealthy.

During the war neither ship fired a shot in anger, although *Andrei Pervozvanny* did open fire briefly during the Civil War.
Appearance: During 1916–17 both ships had their lattice masts cut down to stumps, and stepped a lighter rig of pole masts in their place. In addition *Andrei Pervozvanny* (and possibly *Imperator Pavel I*) carried torpedo nets and booms.
Nomenclature: After the February 1917 Revolution the *Imperator Pavel I* was renamed *Respublika*.

Careers

Imperator Pavel I: At Kronstadt on outbreak of war; carried out various patrol and convoy operations without incident; affected by mutinous behaviour of crew October 1915; outright mutiny broke out on the Tsar's abdication, with the death of five officers; fell into a state of disrepair after the February 1917 Revolution, and was laid up in Kronstadt; broken up at Leningrad in 1922.
Andrei Pervozvanny: Was undergoing repairs at Kronstadt in August 1914, after running aground; minor patrol and convoy operations as *Imperator Pavel I* 1915–16; after some insubordination the ship was taken over by the Soviets in October 1917 at Helsingfors; with other ships of the Baltic Fleet she was moved to Kronstadt in April 1918, and fired on Krasnaya Gorka and Sevaya Loda forts during the Civil War; torpedoed by British C.M.Bs. 18 August 1919, and sank in shallow water; salvage completed early in 1920, but the Soviet Government was too impoverished to spare money for her refit, and she was broken up at Leningrad in 1922.

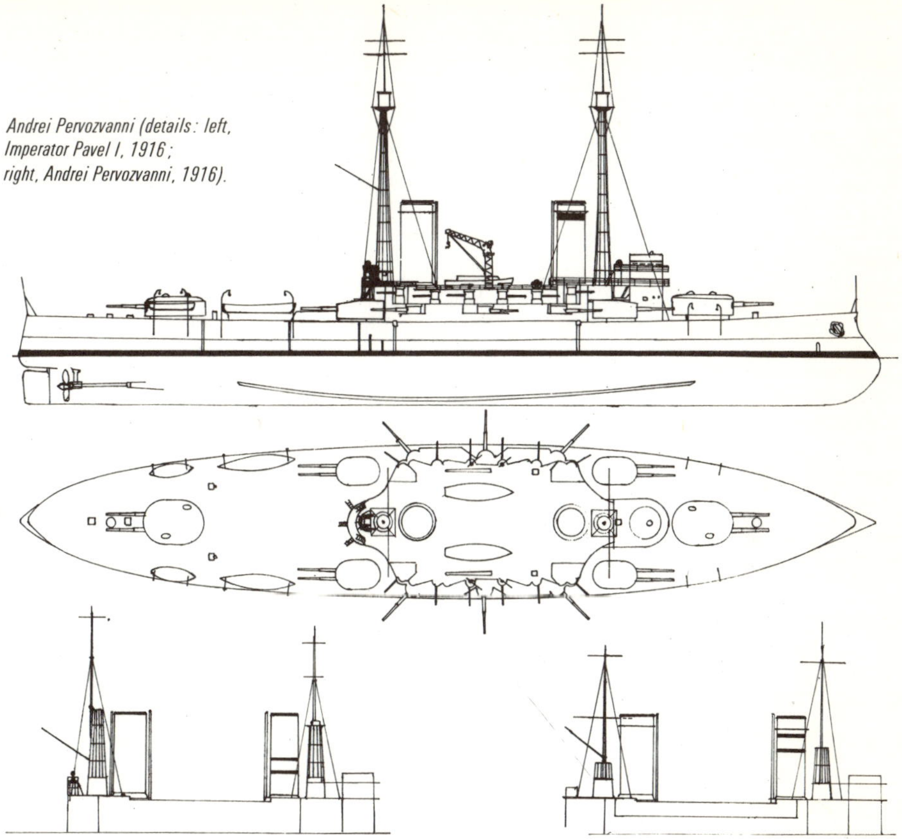

Andrei Pervozvanni (details: left, Imperator Pavel I, 1916; right, Andrei Pervozvanni, 1916).

Right, *Andrei Pervozvanni in 1914 with her original masts (Boris Lemachko).*

Gangut class

Displacement: 23,400tons (normal), 25,850tons (full load)

Dimensions: 600ft (oa)×80ft×27ft 3in (mean)

Guns: 12×12in 52cal (4×3)
16×4·7in 55cal (16×1)
4×47mm
8×MGs

Torpedo Tubes: 4×18in (submerged, beam)

Armour: 11–4in belt; 3–1½in decks; 12–10in turrets; 10in CT

Machinery: 4-shaft Parsons turbines, 42,000shp = 23knots; 25 Yarrow boilers

Coal Capacity: 1000/3000tons

Oil Capacity: 1170tons

Endurance: Approx 5000miles at 10knots

Complement: 1125

Cost: Not known

	Laid Down	Launched	Completed	Built/Engined
Petropavlovsk	13 July 1909	9 Sept 1911	Jan 1915	Baltic Works
Gangut	13 July 1909	7 Oct 1911	Jan 1915	Galernii Is. Works
Sevastopol	13 July 1909	29 June 1911	Nov 1914	Baltic Works
Poltava	13 July 1909	10 July 1911	Dec 1914	Galernii Is. Works

These ships were laid down as the first instalment of an enormous replacement programme for the period 1909–30 which would have restored the Imperial Russian Navy to the rank of a 1st Class naval power. The Baltic Fleet was to include 20 battleships and four battle cruisers, but only the *Ganguts* and the *Borodinos* got beyond the planning stage.

Although the Russians strenuously denied the influence of the Italian General Cuniberti on the design of the *Ganguts*, a comparison with the *Dante Alighieri* will show the same arrangement of triple turrets and the same simple layout of super-structure, devoid of all but the minimum of bridgework. What is certain is that the Russian constructors sought a great deal of help abroad, from Italy, Germany and Great Britain. As in each case the firms concerned had no desire to enter into contracts for building in Russian yards, these schemes all came to nothing. However, in the process Russian constructors looked at a number of interesting designs, and Engineer Krilov was able to embark on an 'original' Russian design which relied strongly on Cuniberti's ideas.

The principal new ideas incorporated into the Krilov design were:

1. The use of high-tensile steel throughout;

Right, Poltava at speed in the Baltic. 1914–15 (IWM).

Right, Petropavlovsk as she appeared in 1915 (IWM).

2. The addition of an inner belt of 4in armour eleven feet inboard and above the main belt;
3. The reduction of the main belt by 4in and discarding of the torpedo-bulkheads;
4. High-powered machinery;
5. Ice-breaking bows.

Unfortunately, the cumulative effect of these alterations was to make the class obsolescent, for Krilov's inexplicable insistence on high-tensile steel (normally only required for destroyers) delayed their completion by three years, and the novel arrangement of armour gave no measure of protection against long-range fire. Furthermore the extra weight devoted to machinery produced no increase in speed or endurance, and the reported lack of efficient ventilation would have decreased their efficiency.

The choice of triple turrets was a bold one, at a time when the Italians had only just laid down the *Dante Alighieri*. The 12in guns were the longest in the world, and were reputed to make very good shooting at maximum range. The design of the hull called for complete symmetry, and the main turrets were exactly 116ft apart. The positioning of the 5·1in guns would have made some of them unusable in rough weather, but in this the Russian constructors erred in good company.

Appearance: *Gangut* differed from the other three in having her ensign gaff low down on the mainmast, instead of at funnel height. All four could be distinguished from the Black Sea dreadnoughts by their thicker funnels and having their secondary guns split up into groups of two, level with each 12in turret. All appear from photographs to have been fitted with torpedo-nets and booms during the war, but these were not permanent features.

Nomenclature: Not renamed after the February 1917 Revolution, but in 1920 they were renamed *Marat, Oktyabrskaya Revolutsia, Parishkaya Kommuna* and *Mikhail Frunze* respectively. In 1942, by a special order from Moscow, the three survivors were given their original names.

Careers

Gangut: Carried out her gunnery trials in December 1914 and commissioned in January 1915 in 1st Brigade of Baltic Fleet; by command of the Russian Stavka (Military High Command) she and the other dreadnoughts were not to be risked, so their service was limited to the Gulf of Finland; affected by acts of insubordination October 1915; covered minelaying operations on 10 November 1915 and again on 5–7 December, but thereafter she remained at Helsingfors; left Helsingfors 12 April 1918 with remainder of Red Fleet and withdrew to Kronstadt; as *Oktyabrskaya Revolutsia* saw much service in World War II, being damaged by air attack; broken up 1956–7.

Petropavlovsk: Commissioned January 1915 and became Flagship of 1st Brigade of Baltic Fleet at Helsingfors; with *Gangut* escorted *Slava* into the Gulf of Riga July 1915; under the command of Rear-Admiral L. B. Kerber she and *Gangut* covered minelaying operations in November and December 1915; three officers executed by 'Ship's Committee' in August 1917; with other ships at Helsingfors she was demobilised on 29 January 1918, but in April 1918 she and the other ships of the Baltic Fleet were evacuated from Helsingfors to Kronstadt; during the Civil War she fired on Krasnaya Gorka and Seraya Loshad forts, which had defected to the White Russians in June 1918, and caused them to surrender; torpedoed by British C.M.Bs. at Kronstadt 18 August 1919, and sank in shallow water; salvaged and returned to service in 1920; as *Marat* served with distinction in World War II, and lost her bow after a direct hit from German bombers during siege of Leningrad; laid up 1942 and scrapped in 1953.

Poltava: Commissioned January 1915 and joined 1st Brigade at Helsingfors; apart from patrols in the Gulf of Finland, played little active part, and was finally withdrawn to Kronstadt in April 1918; renamed *Mikhail Frunze* in 1920, and was almost totally destroyed by fire while lying in the River Neva; after removal of her 12in guns she was scrapped in 1923.

Sevastopol: Arrived at Helsingfors 22 November 1914 and joined 1st Brigade of Baltic Fleet; service as *Poltava*, but survived as *Parishkaya Kommuna* to play a distinguished part in World War II; broken up 1956–7.

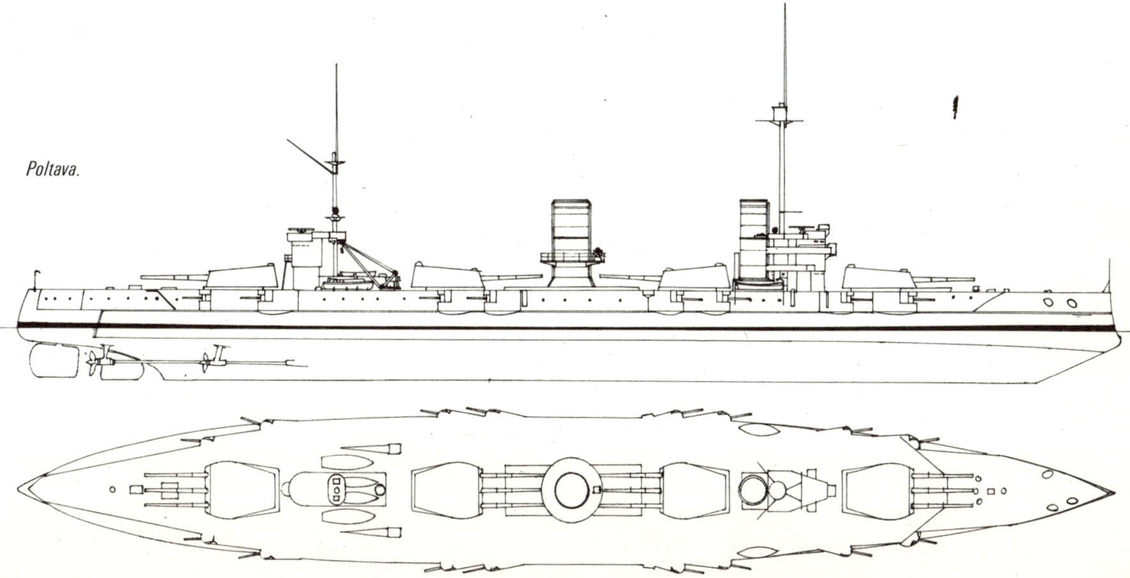

Poltava.

Imperatritsa Maria class

Displacement: 22,800tons (normal), 24,000tons (full load)
Dimensions: 551ft 3in (oa)×89ft 6in× 27ft 3in (mean)
Guns: 12×12in 52cal (4×3) 18×5·1in 55cal (18×1)
4×3in
4×3in A.A.
4×47mm
4×MGs
Torpedo Tubes: 4×18in (submerged, beam)
Armour: 12–4in belt; 3–1½in decks; 12in turrets; 12in CT
Machinery: 4-shaft Parsons turbines (Brown-Curtis in Imp. Aleksandr III); 26,500shp = 21knots; 20 Yarrow boilers
Coal Capacity: 1200/3000tons
Oil Capacity: 720tons
Endurance: Not known
Complement: 1252
Cost: Not known

	Laid Down	Launched	Completed	Built/Engined
*Imperatritsa Maria	Oct 1911	1 Nov 1913	July 1915	Russud, Nikolaiev
*Imperatritsa Ekaterina II	Sept 1911	6 June 1914	Oct…1915	Nikolaiev
Imperator Aleksandr III	Oct 1911	13 Apr 1914	June 1917	Russud, Nikolaiev

These three dreadnoughts were based on the *Gangut* class building for the Baltic Fleet, and were authorised by the Duma (Russian Parliament) in 1911 as a counter to the revitalised Turkish Navy. The Turks had ordered the *Reshadieh* and *Reshad-I-Hamiss* from English yards, and it was felt that three dreadnoughts would maintain the balance of naval power in Russian favour.

The layout and armament of the Black Sea dreadnoughts was closely modelled on the Baltic type, but armour thickness was increased by 2in, speed reduced by 2knots, and a heavier secondary battery was mounted.

Nomenclature: *Imperatritsa Ekaterina II* lost her 'Tsarist' name on 29 April 1917, when the Kerensky Provisional Government ordered her to be renamed *Svobodnaya Rossia*, ('Free Russia'). *Imperator Aleksandr III* was renamed *Volya* in the summer of 1917, on completion, but was again renamed when in White Russian hands, becoming *General Alexeiev*.

Appearance: Distinguished from the *Ganguts* by their generally lighter appearance and by the arrangement of the secondary guns. These were in two groups, the forward group of sponsons facing towards the bow, and the group abaft the after superstructure facing towards the stern. *Imperatritsa Maria* had a long lattice boom attached to her bows early in her career, but there is no information as to its use.

Careers

Imperatritsa Maria: On completion sailed under heavy escort for Sevastopol on 23 July 1915; joined 1st Manoeuvring Group August 1915 and was actively employed on convoy and patrol duties, mainly covering the old predreadnoughts while carrying out shore bombardments; sunk by internal explosion at Sevastopol 20 October 1916 (thought to be sabotage at the time, but more likely to have been due to unstable ammunition); raised 1918, but proved to be beyond repair; broken up 1926–7.

Imperatritsa Ekaterina II: Joined 2nd Manoeuvring Group on completion; indecisive action with *Goeben* 7 January 1916; 7 February escorted *Rostislav* from Caucasian coast back to Sevastopol; 3 April in action with *Breslau*, and again on 25 June 1917; her crew mutinied in November during her last operational sortie, and took her back to Sevastopol; when the Germans advanced on Sevastopol in defiance of the Treaty of Brest-Litovsk, she and other units were moved to Novorossiisk 14 April 1918; to avoid her capture by the Germans Leon Trotsky (then War Commissar) ordered her to be sunk, and she was torpedoed by the destroyer *Kerch* four times in deep water to the east of Novorossiisk, on 18 June 1918.

Imperator Aleksandr III: On completion in the summer of 1917 she joined the Sevastopol fleet; took part in the November 1917 operation which had to be cancelled when *Svobodnaya Rossia* (ex-*Imperatritsa Ekaterina II*) mutinied; sent to Novorossiisk in April 1918 with other units, but her commander refused to scuttle his ship; on her return to Sevastopol she was taken over by the Germans, who planned to commission her as the *Wolga*, but failed to do so, most probably for lack of trained ratings; she passed once more into White Russian and then British hands; in April 1919 the British Naval Command had her sent to Izmid, in Turkey, to keep her out of Soviet hands; she was returned to White Russian control 17 October 1919 as the *General Alexeiev*; after the collapse of White Russian resistance she carried a large number of refugees, and the cadets and midshipmen of the Naval Academy to exile on 31 October 1920; from Constantinople she and other ships (including *Georgi Pobiedonosetz*) went to Bizerta, where the French Government interned them; when her St. Andrew's ensign was hauled down on 29 October 1924 she was the last operational battleship of the old Imperial Russian Navy; she was slowly dismantled between 1926 and 1937.

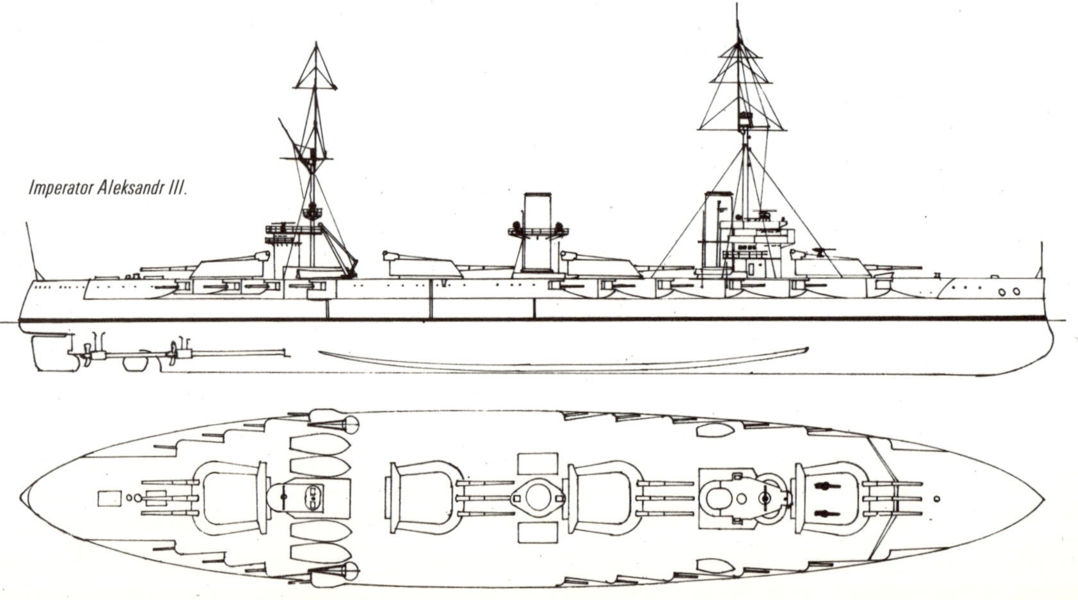

Imperator Aleksandr III.

Above, *Imperator Aleksandr III as she appeared in 1918 (P. A. Vicary).*

Imperator Nikolai I

Displacement: 27,300tons
Dimensions: 597ft (oa)×95ft×29ft 6in
Guns: 12×12in 52cal (4×3)
20×5·1in 55cal (20×1)
Approximately 16 smaller weapons
Torpedo Tubes: 4×18in (submerged, beam)
Armour: As Imperatritsa Maria class
Machinery: 4-shaft Brown-Curtis turbines, 29,700tons = 21knots
Coal Capacity, Endurance and Complement: As Imperatritsa Maria class

	Laid Down	Launched	Completed	Built/Engined
Imperator Nikolai I	June 1914	18 Oct 1916	—	Russud

This was an additional dreadnought authorised in May 1914 for the Black Sea Fleet when it was learned that Turkey was trying to buy dreadnoughts abroad. She was in most respects similar to class, but had greater horsepower, and a slightly heavier secondary battery. The horsepower figures should be treated with caution, as the great increase in hull dimensions suggests a rather greater speed than 21knots. Indeed, most particulars of this ship are suspect, even her launch date, as some authorities claim that she was launched in 1915—a record for a Russian battleship! Other authorities claim that she was only 30 per cent complete in April 1918, which would mean that she was still on the building slip.

It is known that the hull was launched, on or about the date given (possibly 5 or 31 October), and that the Germans and White Russians each inflicted damage to prevent her falling into the other's hands. Although for many years *Brassey's Naval & Shipping Annual* and *Flottes de Combat* listed her as still in existence (as late as 1933), it seems certain that the damaged incomplete hull was broken up by the Soviets in 1922–3.

Nomenclature: She was renamed *Demokratiya* ('Democracy') in April 1917. For a time it was rumoured that she had been renamed *Ivan Grozny* ('Ivan the Terrible'), but this was unfounded.

Borodino class

Displacement: Approx. 30,000tons (normal), 32,500tons (full load)
Dimensions: 728ft 3in (oa)×98ft× 28ft 9in
Guns: 12×14in 52cal (4×3)
24×5·1in 55cal (24×1)
4×3·9in A.A.
4×47mm
4×MGs
Torpedo Tubes: 6×18in (submerged, beam)
Armour: 12–4in belt; 2·6in decks; 12in turrets; 12in CT
Machinery: 4-shaft Parsons turbines, 68,000shp = 26½knots; 25 Yarrow boilers (16 mixed firing, and 9 oil-fired)
Coal and Oil Capacity: Not known
Endurance: Approx. 5000miles at 10knots
Complement: 1250 (approximate)
Cost: Not known

	Laid Down	Launched	Completed	Built/Engined
Borodino	19 Dec 1912	7 July 1915	—	Galernii Is. Works St. Petersburg
Navarin	19 Dec 1912	11 Nov 1916	—	Baltic Works, St. Petersburg
Ismail	19 Dec 1912	22 June 1915	—	Galernii Is. Works St. Petersburg
Kinburn	19 Dec 1912	30 Oct 1915	—	Baltic Works, St. Petersburg

These ships were authorised by the Duma in June 1912, and although described as battle cruisers, they should be called fast battleships, as their armouring was to be equal or superior to the *Ganguts*. The layout was very similar, but the calibre of the main armament was increased from 12in to 14in, as this was rumoured to be happening in the German Navy.

Unfortunately the Russians had tried to expedite construction of the *Borodinos* by ordering machinery abroad, the *Navarin's* turbines from Vulkan, Germany, and either *Ismail's* or *Kinburn's* from Parsons, in England. The German turbines were never delivered and were used for two minelaying cruisers, S.M.S. *Brummer* and *Bremse*.

Work on all four was stopped from shortage of materials and labour problems, shortly before the February 1917 Revolution, when the *Borodino* and *Ismail* were more than half complete. As their names commemorated great Russian victories they were not renamed, but the Soviet Navy found that they were not worth completing by 1922. *Borodino*, *Navarin* and *Kinburn* were sold in 1923 to German shipbreakers and broken up at Bremen, Hamburg and Kiel respectively in 1924–5, while *Ismail* was broken up at Leningrad at the same time.

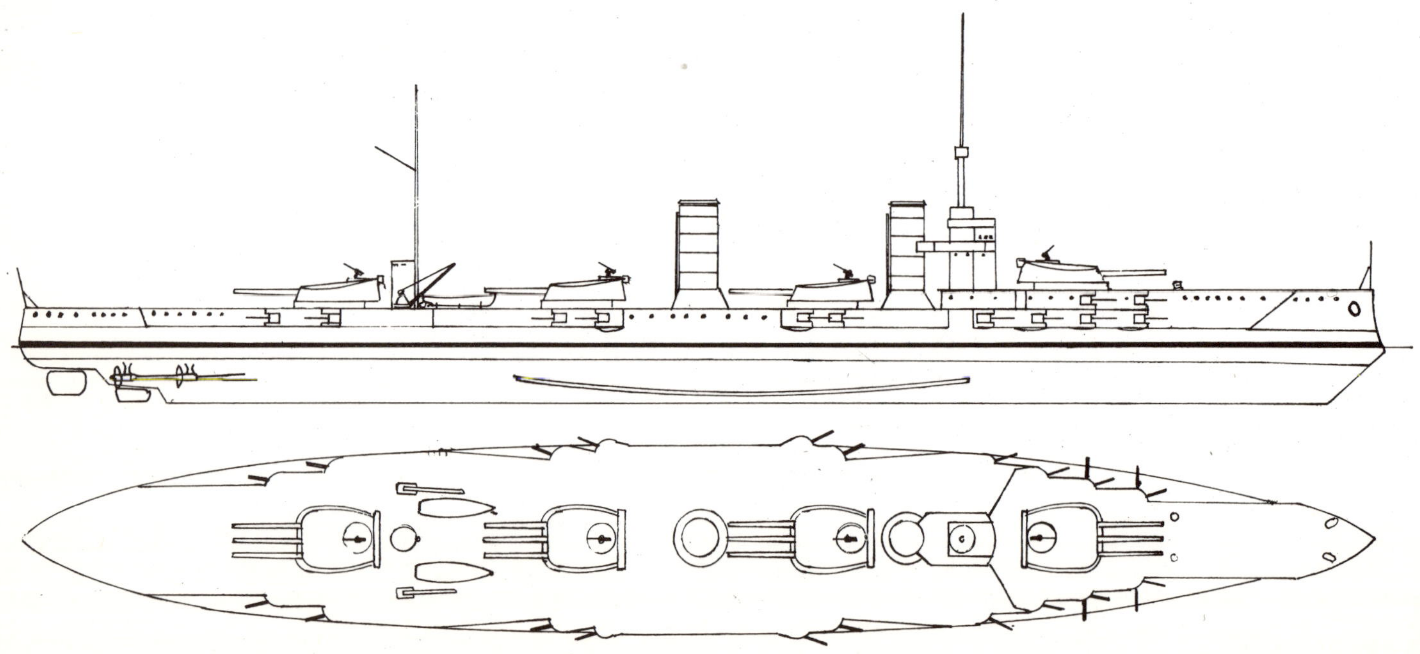

Below, Yavuz Sultan Selim, shown here as S.M.S. Goeben before her transfer to the Turkish Navy (IWM).

Introduction

Turkey had suffered a great decline from a relatively strong position in the mid-nineteenth century. In the 1860s and 1870s the British policy of bolstering the 'sick man of Europe' as a bulwark against Russia meant that Turkey had a number of reasonably modern front-rank ships. From the 1880s, however, British interest in Turkey waned, and the Navy was allowed to rot away.

The Germans were not slow to see the value of a Turkish alliance, and from 1911 their naval advisers replaced the British at Constantinople. With the sale of two elderly predreadnoughts the Germans were soon well-established, and able to begin the slow process of rebuilding the Turkish Navy, but little had been achieved by August 1914. The arrival of the *Goeben* changed all this, and in a sense the story of the Turkish naval effort from 1914 to 1918 is the story of the *Goeben*. The full details are given under that ship's career, as the only 'Turkish' capital ship to see any action of importance.

The Turkish collapse in 1918 meant the end of their naval effort, and Allied warships passed through the Dardanelles—nearly four years after their abortive attempt to force their way past the Narrows forts.

Muin-I-Zaffer

Displacement: 2400tons (normal)
Dimensions: 229ft (wl)×36ft×16ft 6in (mean)
Guns: 4×6in 40cal (4×1)
6×3in (6×1)
10×6pdrs (57mm)
2×1pdr
Armour: 6–3in battery; 5in bulkheads
Machinery: 1-shaft horizontal compound, 2200hp = 12knots; cylindrical boilers
Coal Capacity: 250tons
Endurance: Unknown, but very low
Complement: 220
Cost: Not known

	Laid Down	Launched	Completed	Built/Engined
Muin-i-Zaffer	1867	1869	1874	Samuda, Poplar

Even more than the *Messudieh*, this ship was more of a curiosity than a fighting ship, being an ancient iron corvette reconstructed by Ansaldo at Genoa in 1904–7. This modernisation was far less radical than that given to *Messudieh* as it left her central battery and even her venerable horizontal machinery, and was restricted to providing new Krupp guns and modern boilers.
Armament: The 6in guns were placed in the old 'box battery', with the 3in guns between them in ports at the rear of the casemates, and on either side of the conning tower. The 6pdrs were placed on the stern and forecastle, and on the forecastle deck amidships, while two 1pdr guns were carried in the fighting top.
Appearance: The exaggerated ram bow and central battery betrayed her mid-Victorian design, and her original hull was virtually unchanged, but without the original full rig.
Career
Laid up during war, as no use could be found for her; broken up *c*.1922.

Messudieh

Displacement: 9250tons (metric)
Dimensions: 331ft 5in×59ft×27ft (max)
Guns: 2×9·2in 40cal (2×1): see notes
12×6in 45cal (12×1)
14×12pdrs (14×1)
10×6pdrs (10×1)
2×3pdrs (2×1)
Torpedo Tubes: Nil
Armour: 12in belt (iron); 1½in deck; 3in barbettes; 9–6in turrets
Machinery: 2-shaft inverted 4-cylinder triple-expansion, 11,000hp = 17½knots (in 1902); 16 Niclausse water-tube boilers
Coal Capacity: 600tons
Endurance: 2200miles at 10knots
Complement: 600 (640 as flagship)
Cost: Not known

	Laid Down	Launched	Completed	Built/Engined
*Messudieh	1872	28 Oct 1874	1876	Thames I.W.

This interesting vessel had begun life as an ironclad frigate, but in 1898–1903 she was totally reconstructed at Genoa. This involved the replacement of the antiquated broadside armament of muzzle-loading guns with modern 9·2in guns and bargettes supplied by Vickers, and new machinery. However, the original wrought-iron armour was retained, with additional protection to the steering.

Were it not for the fact that this vessel took an active, although short-lived part in the Dardanelles operations in 1915 she would hardly rate more than a mention in this book, but she is nevertheless a good example of how far small navies were prepared to go to keep old tonnage in some degree of readiness for coast defence.
Armament: The secondary guns were disposed as follows: 6in guns in the upper deck battery, 12pdrs in a battery at forecastle deck level and in ports at bow and stern, 6pdrs a deck above the 12pdrs and on either side of the forward and after superstructure, and two 3pdrs in the fighting top.

The 9·2in guns were not delivered in time by Vickers, and in 1903 the ship sailed from Genoa with wooden dummy guns in the turrets. German advisers found late in 1914 that these wooden guns were still in position, although the guns were in Turkey. As she was in very poor condition the Germans gave up any idea of refitting her, and she was stationed in Sari Sigla Bay, opposite Chanak, where her 6in guns might offer some defence for the upper end of the Narrows.
Career
Stationed above the Narrows of the Dardanelles on 1 December 1914, at anchor, when she was torpedoed by the British submarine *B.11*; she was hit by a single 18in torpedo, rolled over and sank in ten minutes.

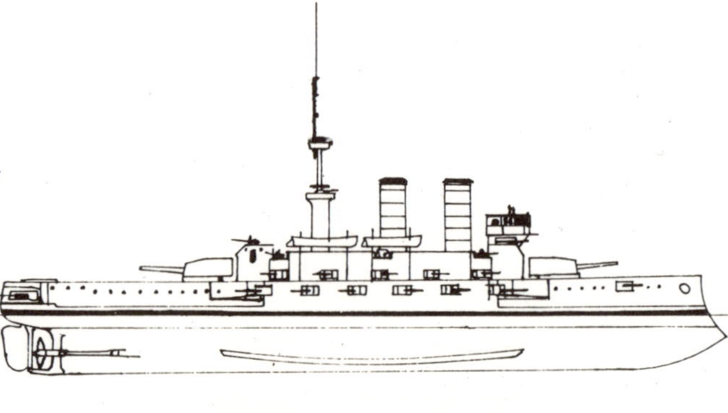

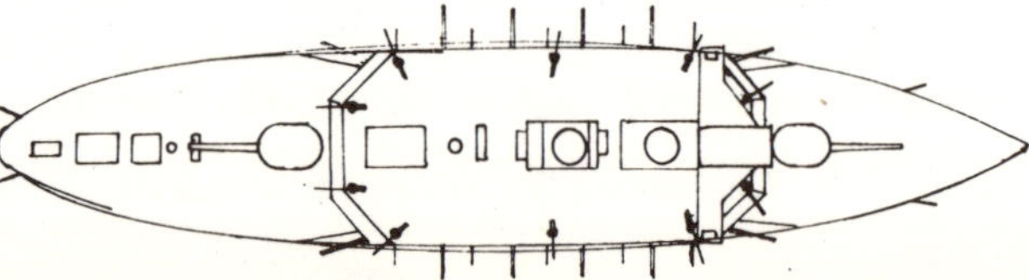

Ex-German type

Displacement: 10,060tons (normal) 10,727tons (full load)
Dimensions: 340ft 10½in (wl)× 64ft 9in×25ft 4in (mean)
Guns: 6×9·4in (2×2 40cal and 1×2 35cal)
8×4·1in 35cal (8×1)
8×3·4in (8×1)
12×37mm (12×1)
Torpedo Tubes: 3×17·7in (1 bow, above water and 2 beam, submerged)

Armour: 15¾–11¾in belt; 2–3in deck; 5–9in turrets; 11¾in CT
Machinery: 2-shaft vertical triple-expansion, 3-cylinder, 10,000hp = 17knots (in 1905); 12 cylindrical boilers
Coal Capacity: 650/1050tons
Oil Capacity: 110tons
Endurance: 4500miles at 10knots
Complement: 591
Cost: Not known

	Laid Down	Launched	Completed	Built/Engined
*Hairreddin Barbarousse (ex-Kurfürst Friedrich Wilhelm)	1890	30 June 1891	Apr 1894	Wilhelmshaven DY
Torgud Reis (ex-Weissenburg)	1890	14 Dec 1891	June 1894	Vulkan, Stettin

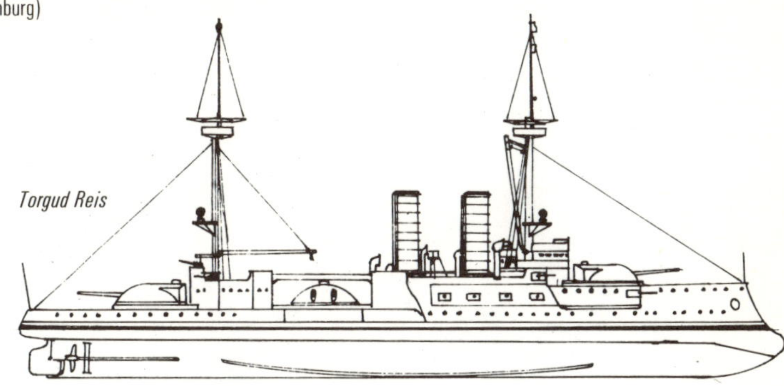
Torgud Reis

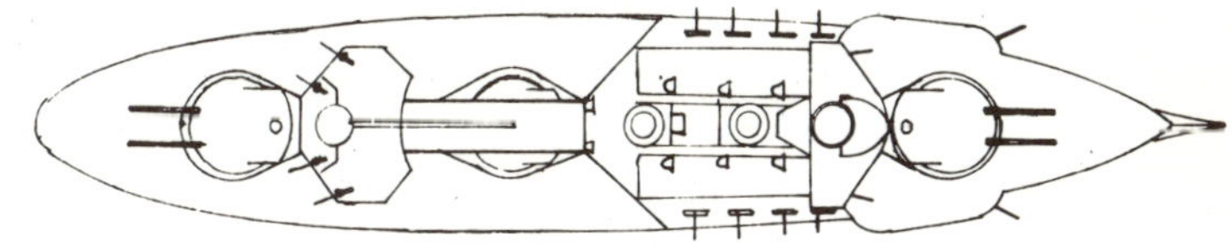

These two elderly ships were purchased from Germany on 12 September 1910 as part of a programme to replace even older Turkish warships which dated back as far as 1870. Their main value was political, although originally they were intended to counter the Greek coast-defence ships.
Sister ships: Identical to their sisters *Wörth* and *Brandenburg* in the German Navy.
Careers
Hairreddin Barbarousse: Based on Constantinople 1914–15 and fired at *Queen Elizabeth*; torpedoed in Sea of Marmora by British submarine *E.11* while transporting Army ammunition to Gallipoli, 8 August 1915.
Torgud Reis: Based on Constantinople 1914–18; in 1919 was allocated to Japan as reparations, but not taken over; converted to training ship 1924, and remained in Bosphorus until broken up in 1938.

Yavuz Sultan Selim

Displacement: 22,979tons (normal)
Dimensions: 610ft×96ft 9in×30ft 3in
Guns: 10×11in 50cal (5×2)
12×5·9in 45cal (12×1)
8×3·4in 45cal (by 1914); reduced to 4 and replaced by 4×3·4in A.A. (4×1); all removed 1917
Torpedo Tubes: 4×19·7in (beam, submerged)
Armour: 10½–3¾in belt; 8in turrets; 8in CT; 3–1in decks
Machinery: 4-shaft Parsons turbines, 70,000hp = 25knots; 24 Schulz-Thornycroft boilers
Coal Capacity: 1000/3100tons
Oil Capacity: 100tons
Endurance: Approx 3000miles at 10knots
Complement: 1081
Cost: Not known

	Laid Down	Launched	Completed	Built/Engined
Yavuz Sultan Selim (ex-S.M.S. Goeben)	Aug 1909	23 Mar 1911	July 1912	Blohm & Voss

It has been said of this ship that she caused more suffering and disaster than any other ship in history. Even if we do not accept this sweeping statement, as the German battle cruiser S.M.S.

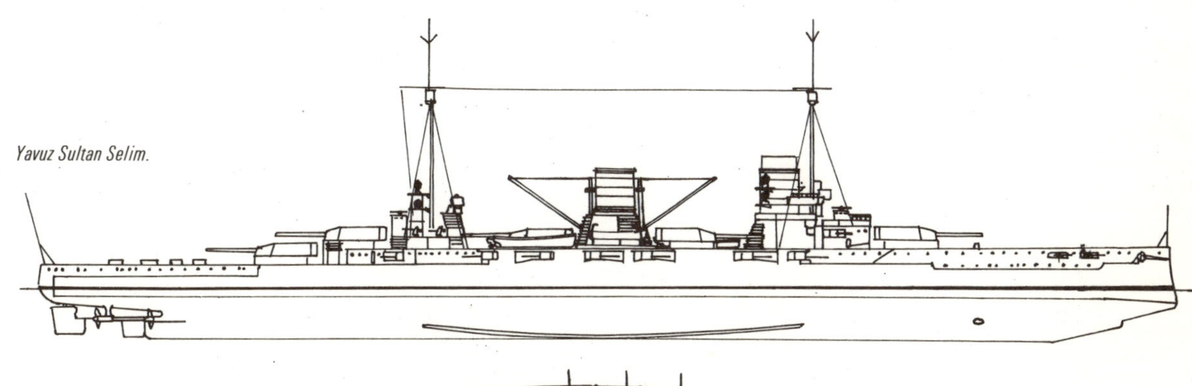
Yavuz Sultan Selim.

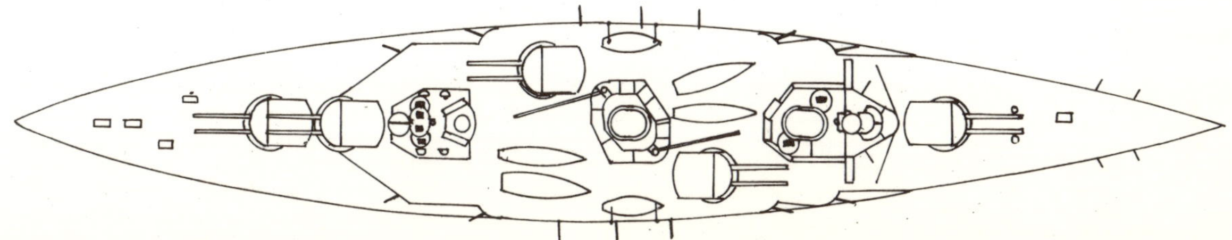

Goeben she was instrumental in bringing Turkey into World War I as an ally of the Central Powers, which in turn made the British embark on their disastrous Gallipoli campaign. The failure of the British and French to force the Dardanelles made it impossible to provide Russia with the essential war material which she needed, and while this did not of itself cause the 1917 Revolution, that event might have been postponed if Russian civilian and army morale had been bolstered by supplies from the West. The saga of the *Yavuz Sultan Selim* is well known, but the sequence of diplomatic manoeuvring would not be out of place. After escaping from the British battle cruisers, the German battle cruiser and her escorting cruiser, the *Breslau*, made for the Dardanelles, hoping that the Turkish Government would co-operate, despite official German fears of a sudden change of allegiance.

Admiral Souchon in the *Goeben* sent a collier ahead to make the necessary arrangements, with the result that the two ships arrived off Cape Helles on the afternoon of 11 August 1914. When the three days allowed by International Law to a belligerent warship had expired the Turkish Government surprised the world by announcing that the *Goeben* and *Breslau* were to be purchased 'to overawe Greece'.

As Turkey was still neutral the two warships remained idle for some time, but on 28 October Admiral Souchon put to sea and carried out a surprise attack on the Russian Fleet off Sevastopol the next day. From the Germans' point of view the results justified the risks taken, for an embarrassed Turkey was forced to declare war on Great Britain, France and Russia as an ally of the Central Powers.

Armament: The four 3·4in guns mounted in ports under the forecastle had been removed before 1914. Late in 1915 the four 3·4in (88mm) guns in the after superstructure were replaced by anti-aircraft guns, and in June 1917 all the remaining 3·4in were removed. Two 5·9in guns were damaged in 1915 and not remounted.

Appearance: Originally identical to the *Moltke* in the German Navy. The torpedo nets were removed during her mid-1917 refit.

Class: Formerly sistership of the *Moltke* in the German Navy.
Career
Arrived at Constantinople 11 August 1914 and purchased by Turkey 16 August; bombarded Sevastopol 29 October and was hit by two 12in shells from Russian shore battery; action with *Evstafi, Ioann Zlatoust, Panteleimon, Tri Sviatitelia* and *Rostislav* 18 November; mined in Bosphorous 26 December, and had both wing turrets put out of action; fired on by *Queen Elizabeth* 27 April 1915; action with Russian battleships *Tri Sviatitelia* and *Ioann Zlatoust* 10 May, during which she was hit twice; owing to coal shortage, the remainder of the year was spent in limited patrolling; 8 January 1916 engaged the Russian battleship *Imperatritsa Ekaterina II* but suffered no damage; escaped from *Imperatritsa Maria* September 1916; refitted January to June 1916; with *Breslau* left the Dardanelles to attack Mudros, 20 January 1918, and during her sortie she destroyed the British monitors *Raglan* and *M.28*; having driven off all opposition she was just about to begin firing at Mudros when the *Breslau* hit a mine; while trying to tow her the *Yavuz* struck a mine herself, and then another; by this time British aircraft had begun to drop bombs, and then she ran aground off Nagara Point; eventually after the heaviest bombing any ship suffered in the war, she was towed off by the old battleship *Torgud Reis* on 26 January and returned to Constantinople; repaired in time to take the Russo–German Armistice commission to Odessa in March; refitted at Nikolaiev Dockyard with Soviet approval in May; on 2 November to comply with the Mudros Armistice ending Turkey's part in the war, she was finally handed over to a fully Turkish crew, although the Germans took away all plans, instruments and gun-sights; interned at Ismid 5 October 1918, where she sank in shallow water as a result of previous hull damage; although ceded to Great Britain as reparations in 1920, the Treaty of Sèvres was rejected by Kemal Ataturk, and as the British Government was anxious to conciliate Kemal's government, in 1923 the Treaty of Lausanne permitted the *Yavuz Sultan Selim* to remain in the Turkish Navy; completely overhauled and modernised at Ismid by a French firm 1926–30; scrapped 1971.

USA

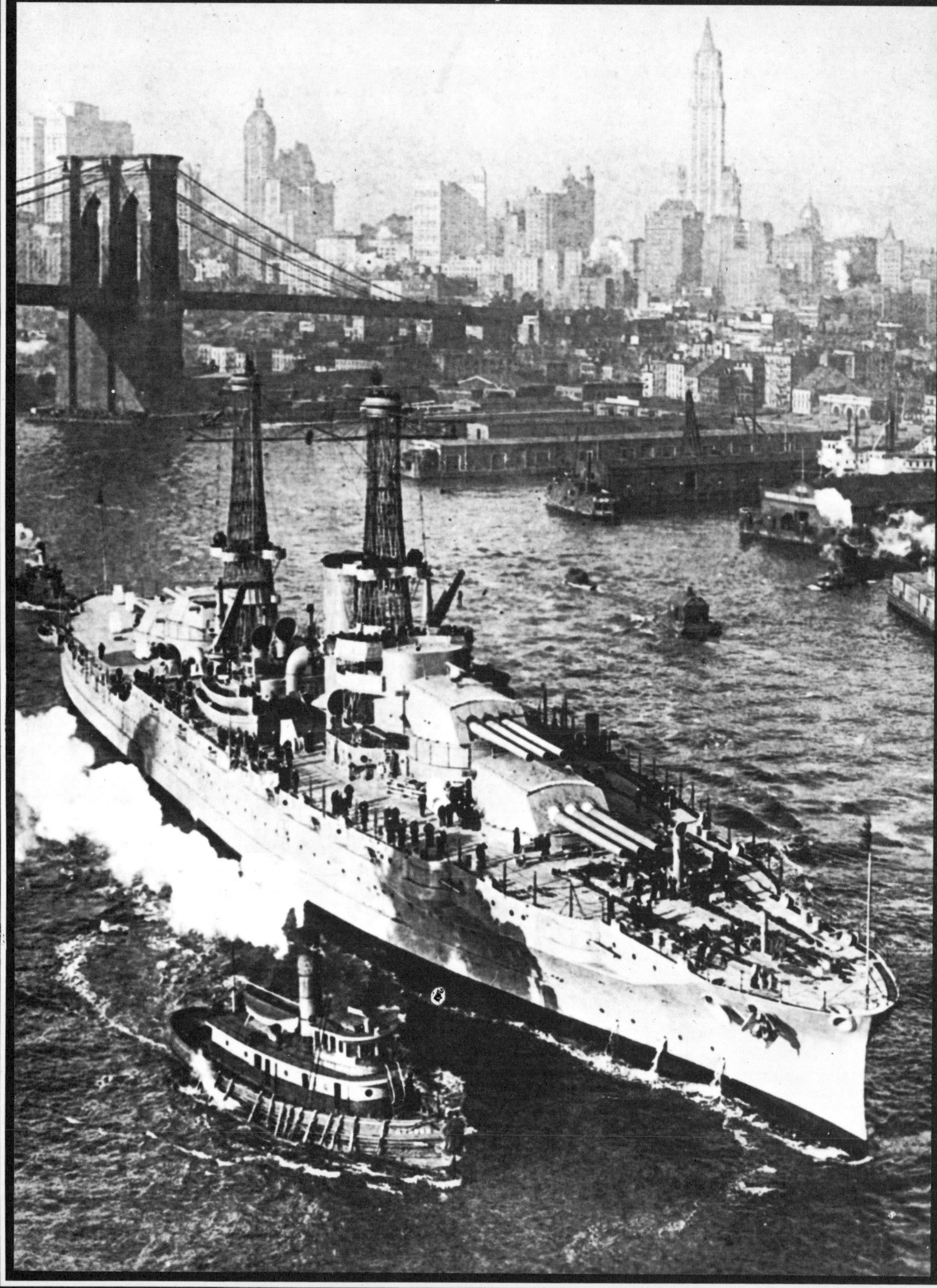

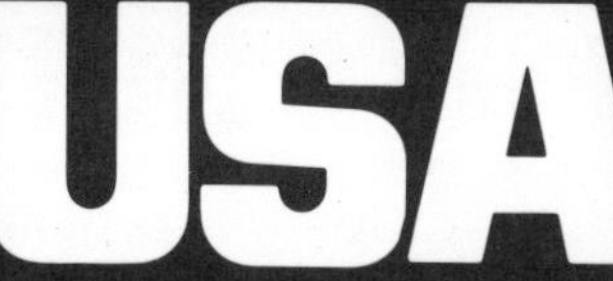

Left, *Nevada seen on her triumphal return to New York at the end of 1918 (IWM).*

Introduction

The United States Navy expanded at a rate only equalled by the German Navy. Although it had enjoyed a good reputation in the decade following the Civil War (1861–5) the need to expand and develop her vast internal resources had led the United States to neglect her navy. As Great Britain and the Royal Navy were guarantors of her freedom from interference by European naval powers, she built nothing but a series of useless monitors for coast defence. Until the 1890s there was no attempt to provide a truly ocean-going navy, but all this was changed when in 1896 the *Iowa* was launched. She and the ships that followed her had the freeboard and gunpower necessary to fight on the high seas. From this date American battleships were noted for their protection and gunpower, neither of which was sacrificed in favour of speed.

The Spanish-American War of 1898 provided the impetus for the development of the U.S. Navy, and a steady stream of powerful ships joined the Fleet between 1900 and 1914. American guns and ship designs enjoyed a high reputation abroad, and their best ideas, such as the centreline turrets of the *South Carolina* class and the 'all-or-nothing' protection of the *Nevada*, quickly became the standard for all navies. In other ways the U.S. Navy was probably over-complacent as a result of its easy victories over obsolescent Spanish ships in 1898, and there is plenty of evidence to prove that American officers were profoundly worried by the disparity between the equipment of the Grand Fleet and their own in 1917. Although their ammunition was of high standard, handling was careless—for example there were unduly large numbers of ready-use charges kept in turrets in order to speed up the rate of fire.

The lattice or 'basket' masts were peculiar to American ships (although copied by the Russians for two ships). The idea was to provide a sturdy structure which could sustain a considerable number of heavy shell hits without collapsing, and they came into vogue around 1908. In practice they proved too light, and the vibration threw off fire control instruments; in addition the light lattice structure was liable to be damaged by bad weather, and the British heavy tripod proved superior in both respects.

The United States had a geographical problem akin to the Russians, in that their continent required two fleets to protect it. In the nineteenth century British sea power, however much resented in the United States, had been the main guarantee against any attack on either the Eastern or Western coastlines. But towards the end of the century a growing sense of nationalism as well as uneasiness about the tensions in Europe made it necessary to build a fleet which could be deployed in either the Pacific or the Atlantic. To make this possible the United States Government built the Panama Canal across the isthmus linking North and South America and when this opened in 1914 the U.S. Navy at last had strategic mobility—battleships could be transferred at a few days' notice from one ocean to the other.

The United States stood aloof from the war in Europe from 1914 to 1917, although supplying vast quantities of war material to the British and French. As a powerful neutral she had a vested interest in trade with all the belligerents, but the British blockade prevented all but a tiny trickle of contraband from reaching Germany. Although the blockade caused friction between America and Great Britain the Americans remained broadly sympathetic to the Allied cause, and German acts such as the sinking of the liner *Lusitania* and the unrestricted U-boat campaign reinforced this sympathy. Finally, when it was learned that the Germans had been negotiating with Mexico and had 'offered' them Arizona, Texas and California as a price for cooperation, the United States declared war on Germany on 6 April 1917.

The first naval reinforcements from America were destroyers to help in the battle against the U-boats, but in November 1917 the 4th Squadron of battleships was sent to join the Grand Fleet; at first only coal-burners were sent on account of the acute oil-shortage in Britain. This squadron, under Admiral Rodman, became the 6th Battle Squadron of the Grand Fleet and was completely integrated into the British organisation: British methods of signalling and fire control were adopted, and every attempt was made to coordinate at a tactical level.

The 1916 Programme

In 1916 the 'big navy' interests in Washington were able to persuade Congress to vote money for an enormous expansion of the U.S. Navy, on the grounds that the United States needed a navy which was equal to any other—but in both the Pacific and the Atlantic. It was this programme that sparked off the Japanese '8–8' programme, and ultimately led to the Washington Disarmament Conference; but in 1916 it was seen as an attempt to overtake the British while they were embroiled in the war, and to overawe the Japanese in the Pacific. Up to this point the U.S. Navy had not built any battle cruisers, but the 1916 programme included six battle cruisers, as well as twelve of the largest battleships the world had ever seen. Like the Japanese ships, very few were completed, and the rest were abandoned under the conditions of the Washington Treaty.

Dockyards and Shipbuilders

The traditional dockyards on the East coast were at Boston, Brooklyn (New York), Norfolk, Philadelphia and Charleston. On the Pacific coast there was San Diego, Bremerton (Seattle) and Mare Island (San Francisco). Most of the private ship-building resources were concentrated on the East coast, as can be seen from the table of private yards:

United States
Shipbuilders

East Coast		West Coast	
Name	Location	Name	Location
Wm. Cramp & Son	Philadelphia	Union Ironworks	San Francisco
Fore River Engine Co.	Quincy, Mass.	Moran & Co.	Seattle
Newport News Co.	Newport News		
New York Shipbuilding Co.	Camden, N.J.		

Weapons

American guns were built up, and not wire-wound like the British guns. They had a good reputation for length of barrel-life and accuracy, and did not suffer from 'droop' in the way that wire-wound guns did. The quality of ammunition, following the *Maine* disaster in 1898, had been steadily improved, and there were no accidents involving propellants after 1905.

Several American ships had tried out the revolutionary idea of double-storied turrets, with a twin 8in turret placed coaxially on the roof of a 12in turret: this innovation lasted from 1895 to 1900, and in theory offered greater all-round arcs of fire without too much weight. But in practice the problems of ammunition supply and blast outweighed the advantages.

With the *Nevada* class triple mountings were introduced, but as the guns were in a single sleeve they were somewhat cumbersome in operation and when the 16in gun was introduced in 1916 the twin turret was readopted. From the *Delaware* class onwards the 6in gun was replaced by the 51cal 5in gun as the standard secondary gun.

American Guns

Calibre	Mark	Weight	Length	Range (max)	Elevation	Notes
8in	Mk.IX	19·7tons	55cal	28,000yds	35°	
7in	Mk.I, II	13·3tons/ 12·7tons	45cal	16,500yds	15°	
13in	Mk.I, II	61·5tons	35cal	12,100yds	15°	Indiana etc
12in	Mk.V, Mk.VI	52·9tons 53·6tons	45cal	21,600yds 22,000yds	15°	BBs 18–29
12in	Mk.VII	57·2tons	50cal	23,500yds	15°	BBs 32–33
14in	Mk.I	63·5tons	45cal	21,000yds	15°	BBs 34–39
14in	Mk.IV	81·7tons	50cal	35,500yds	30°	BBs 40–44
16in	Mk.II	119·6tons	50cal	27,200yds	20°	South Dakota Class and Lexington Class
16in	Mk.I	105tons	45cal	34,000yds	30°	Maryland Class

Machinery

American machinery manufacturers had difficulty in meeting the specifications for turbines, and so for some years American ship machinery lagged behind British and German developments. As the *South Carolina* class had been designed before the details of the *Dreadnought* were known, it was impossible to give them turbines, but the *Delaware* class, authorised in 1906–7 had triple-expansion machinery. Four-shaft turbines followed, but when the *Wyoming* class was authorised in 1909 they were intended to have a combination of reciprocating machinery and turbines. Matters came to a head when the *New York* and *Texas* were ordered in 1910, as the builders refused to accept Navy Department specifications, and the U.S. Navy was forced to go back to triple-expansion machinery in order to force their hand.

The *New Mexico*, authorised in 1914, broke new ground in adopting turbo-electric drive, with her turbines driving large electric motors. This system was adopted for the next class and for the ships of the 1916 programme, but it proved to be more trouble than it was worth, and it was never repeated.

Colour Schemes and Alterations of Appearance

American battleships were the only ones to approach the British in the number and variety of wartime modifications to their rig. The older ships

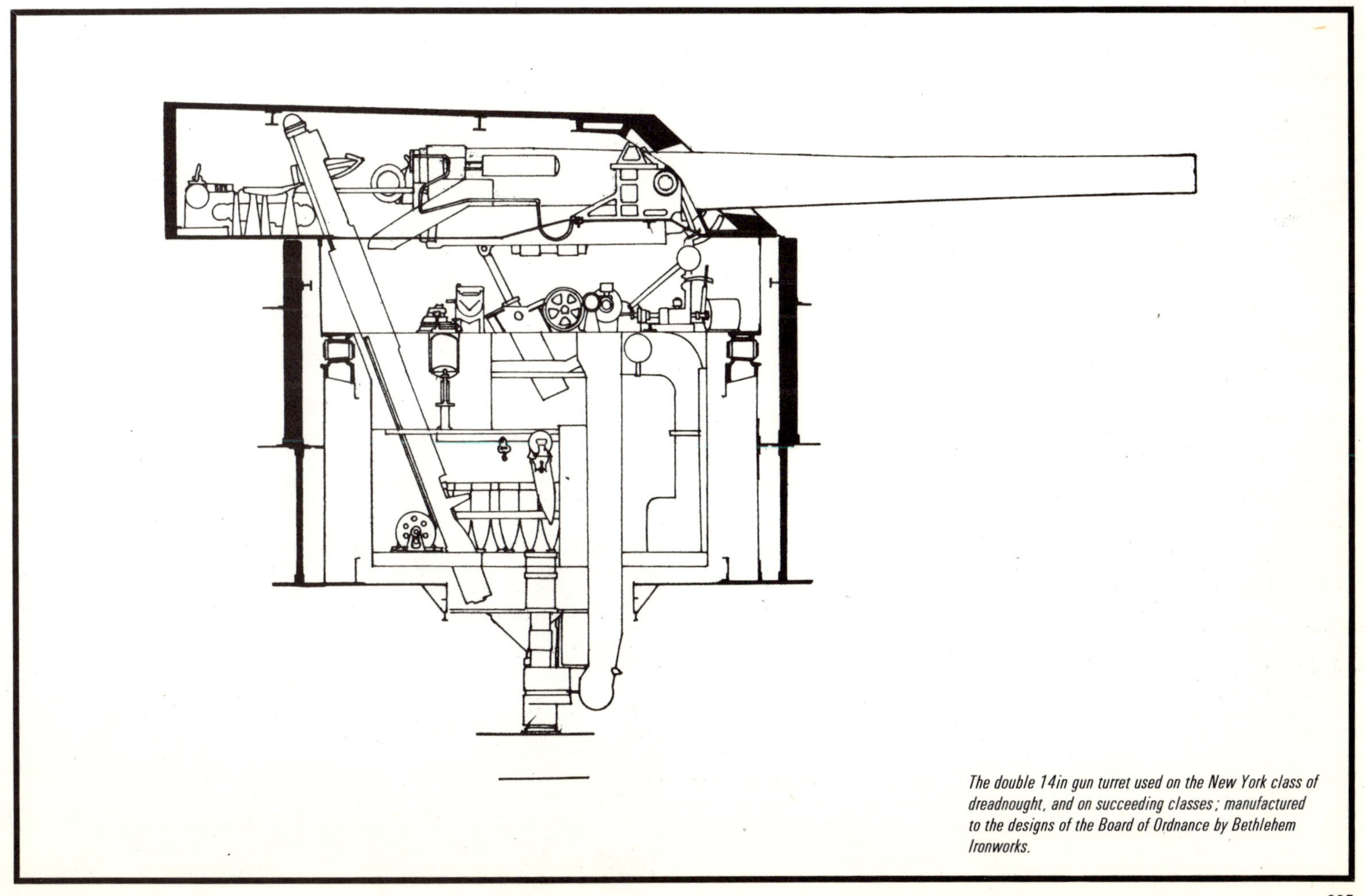

The double 14in gun turret used on the New York class of dreadnought, and on succeeding classes; manufactured to the designs of the Board of Ordnance by Bethlehem Ironworks.

lost a number of light guns in 1917–18, usually to arm merchant ships. Some 6in and 7in guns were removed in the later predreadnoughts to reduce topweight, and in some cases removed entirely. Anti-aircraft guns were added, usually on top of the large crane-posts, and in 1918 some ships were dazzle-painted.

The deflection scales and range clocks used in the Grand Fleet were adopted, at first by the 6th B.S., but later by other dreadnoughts. The normal colour scheme was a medium grey overall. Stockless anchors replaced the older type in the predreadnoughts.

Disposition of United States Navy April 1917
Pacific Reserve Fleet (San Pedro, California)
Oregon
Atlantic Fleet
Fleet Flagship
Pennsylvania
3rd Squadron, 5th Division
Connecticut, Michigan, South Carolina
3rd Squadron, 6th Division
New York, Delaware, Oklahoma, Texas
4th Squadron, 7th Division
Arkansas, Florida, Utah
4th Squadron, 8th Division
Wyoming, Nevada, Arizona
Atlantic Reserve Fleet (Philadelphia)
Alabama, North Dakota, Kansas, Louisiana, Ohio (receiving ship), New Jersey, Rhode Island, Minnesota, Georgia, Kearsage, New Hampshire, Virginia, Maine, Vermont, Kentucky, Missouri, Wisconsin, Nebraska
Mexican Waters
Illinois
Vessels not in Commission (all at Philadelphia)
Indiana, Iowa, Massachusetts

Disposition of United States' Fleet in October 1918
Atlantic Fleet
Fleet Flagship
Pennsylvania (normally with 4th Squadron)
Battleship Force I
1st Squadron, 1st Division
Alabama, Illinois, Kentucky, Kearsage
1st Squadron, 2nd Division
Missouri, Ohio, Maine, Wisconsin
2nd Squadron, 3rd Division
Virginia, New Jersey, Rhode Island, Nebraska, Georgia
2nd Squadron, 4th Division
Minnesota, Louisiana, Kansas, New Hampshire
Battleship Force II
3rd Squadron, 5th Division
Connecticut, Michigan, South Carolina, Vermont
3rd Squadron, 6th Division
Utah, Oklahoma, Nevada (all at Queenstown, Ireland), North Dakota
4th Squadron, 8th Division
Pennsylvania (Fleet Flagship), Arkansas (with 6th Battle Squadron, Grand Fleet), Arizona, Mississippi, New Mexico
4th Squadron, 9th Division
New York, Wyoming, Florida, Texas (all with 6th Battle Squadron, Grand Fleet), Delaware
Coast Defence Forces
Atlantic Coast Division
Iowa, Indiana, Massachusetts
Pacific Fleet
Oregon (flagship)

Indiana, after modernisation.

Indiana class

Displacement: 10,288tons (normal)
Dimensions: 348ft (wl)×69ft 3in×24ft (mean)
Guns: 4×13in (2×2)
8×8in (4×2)
12×3in (12×1); reduced to 4×3in in 1918
20×6pdrs (20×1)
Torpedo Tubes: 6×18in (4 beam, 1 bow and 1 stern, all submerged)

Armour: 18in belts; 15in turrets; 10in CT
Machinery: 2-shaft vertical triple-expansion, 9000hp = 15knots
Coal Capacity: 400/1567tons
Endurance: About 3000miles at 10knots
Complement: 473
Cost: £631,528 average ($2,526,112) excluding guns

	Laid Down	Launched	Completed	Built
BB1 Indiana	7 May 1891	28 Feb 1893	Nov 1895	Cramp
BB2 *Massachusetts*	5 June 1891	10 June 1893	June 1896	Cramp

Low freeboard coast-defence battleships, the first vessels of the United States Navy which approached their foreign contemporaries in fighting power. All three served in the Spanish-American War of 1898 and *Oregon* distinguished herself. With their low freeboard they were not suitable for Atlantic duties, and they were relegated to secondary duties during World War I.

The *Indianas* were authorised in 1890, and their protection was designed to equal the British *Royal Sovereign* class (see H.M.S. *Revenge*). Although intended to have ordinary nickel steel armour, they were given some of the latest Harvey steel, which only became available after they had been laid down. The secondary 8in guns had $8\frac{1}{2}$in of armour and initiated a new phase of heavy secondary armaments in all navies.

In addition to the 8in guns, the *Indianas* also carried four 6in guns in casemates at forecastle deck level, but inevitably this weight of armament on a displacement of only 10,000tons meant that the guns were too close together. Blast from the 8in guns interfered with the 13in guns' crews, and in turn 13in gun blast affected the crews of the 6in guns. For this reason the 6in guns were replaced in 1911 by 3in.

Armament: Both 8in and 13in turrets had all-round loading, which was in advance of contemporary European designs, but as they were not balanced the main turrets tended to make the ship heel when trained abeam. On one occasion in this class a forward turret broke adrift in a heavy gale.

In 1918 eight 3in guns were removed.

Appearance: During their modernisation in 1909–11 all three had the famous 'cage' or 'basket' type mast fitted in place of the pole mainmast.

Careers

Indiana: Paid off in May 1914 at Philadelphia, but recommissioned 24 May 1917 as gunnery training ship on East Coast, based on York River, Virginia until decommissioned in January 1919; reclassified as *Coast Battleship No.1* to release her name for a new battleship, and sunk as a target 1 November 1920; hull raised and sold for scrap in 1924.

Massachusetts: Paid off in May 1914 but recommissioned 9 June 1917 at Philadelphia Navy Yard to serve as gunnery training ship at Newport from October 1917 to May 1918; repaired at Philadelphia followed by further training duties with 'A' Division of Battleship Force I, U.S. Atlantic Fleet; decommissioned March 1919; reclassified 29 March 1919 as *Coast Battleship No. 2* to release the name for a new battleship; lent to War Department for use as a target and sunk by gunfire from coastal batteries off Pensacola Bar, Florida 22 November 1920.

Oregon: Commissioned 7 April 1917 as Flagship, Pacific Fleet; during 1918 and 1919 she escorted transports for U.S. expedition to Siberia under General Graves; decommissioned 16 June 1919 but recommissioned 21 August of that year as Presidential reviewing ship for review of Pacific Fleet at Seattle, and paid off once more on 4 October at Bremerton Navy Yard; although scheduled for scrapping under the Washington Treaty in 1922, the old ship's record in the Spanish-American War led to public agitation for her preservation, and the citizens of Oregon finally made the U.S. Navy tranfer the *Oregon* on loan in June 1925; she lay at Portland peacefully until the outbreak of World War II in 1941, when she was re-acquired for naval use as a hulk, numbered *IX.22*; towards the end of the war she was towed to Guam to act as an ammunition hulk, and was finally sold in 1956 after stranding.

Left, *Oregon in August 1919 (USN).*
Above right, *Indiana as completed (Marius Bar).* **Below right,** *Massachusetts as completed (Marius Bar).*

Iowa

	Laid Down	Launched	Completed	Built/Engined
BB4 Iowa	5 Aug 1893	28 Aug 1896	June 1897	Cramp

Displacement: 11,410tons
Dimensions: 360ft (wl)×72ft 3in×24ft
Guns: 4×12in (2×2)
8×8in (4×2)
10×4in (10×1); reduced to 4×4in in 1918
4×6pdrs (4×1)
Torpedo Tubes: Removed (1911)
Armour: 15in belt; 15in turrets; 10in CT
Machinery: 2-shaft vertical triple-expansion, 11,000hp = 16knots
Coal Capacity: 625/1795tons
Endurance: 3000miles at 10knots
Complement: 486–520
Cost: £618,514 ($2,474,056) excluding guns

This vessel was an improved *Indiana* armed with a lighter main armament and higher freeboard. Although modernised in 1911 the improvements were confined to her secondary armament and fire-control, and she was no longer suitable for frontline duties by the outbreak of war.

Iowa, 1911.

The restriction of size had hampered the designers of the *Indianas*, who had therefore produced ships which were wet and overloaded. By allowing the *Iowa* nearly 1500tons more and reducing the weight of armament, her efficiency was much improved. Although the 8in guns were retained the main battery was reduced to 12in guns and the 6in guns were omitted. In the light of later experience it could be said that the *Iowa* should have had 6in guns in turrets, and sacrificed the 8in to give her a quicker-firing secondary armament, but it must be remembered that in 1896 a battleship was designed to smother her opponent at ranges not exceeding 4000yds.

With improved armour now available it was possible to reduce the thickness of the belt and extend its length to cover 77·5 per cent of the waterline.

Armament: Balanced turrets were introduced for the first time in American battleships, with moving weights balanced around the axis of rotation. The blast problems encountered in the *Indiana* class were met by spacing the 8in guns well clear of the main turrets.

Appearance: Resembled the *Indiana* class, with two widely spaced funnels. The 1911 refit gave her a 'basket' main mast in place of the old military type.

Career

Recommissioned 1917 and served in training role; decommissioned at Philadelphia 31 March 1919; redesignated *Coast Battleship No. 4* April 1919 to release her name for a new battleship; numbered *IX.6* in 1920; sunk by battleships' gunfire as a target 22 March 1923 (name officially stricken 27 March) and wreck sold the same month.

Above, *Iowa in October 1911 after the addition of a cage mainmast (USN).*

Kearsarge class

Displacement: 11,540 tons
Dimensions: 368ft (wl)×72ft 3in× 23ft 6in
Guns: 4×13in (2×2)
4×8in (2×2)
18×5in (18×1); reduced to 8×5in in 1918
2×3in A.A. (added 1918)
4×6pdrs (4×1)
Torpedo Tubes: 1×18in (one above water, Kearsarge only)
Armour: $16\frac{1}{4}$–$9\frac{1}{4}$in belt; 17–15in turrets; 10in CT
Machinery: 2-shaft vertical triple-expansion, 10,000hp = 16knots
Coal Capacity: 410/1590 tons
Endurance: 3000 miles at 10knots
Complement: 554–690
Cost: £462,345 ($1,849,380) excluding guns

	Laid Down	Launched	Completed	Built/Engined
BB5 Kearsarge	30 June 1896	24 Mar 1898	Feb 1900	Newport News
BB6 Kentucky	30 June 1896	24 Mar 1898	May 1900	Newport News

In 1896 the Naval War College had recommended that future American battleships should have an extreme deep load draught of not more than 23ft. This would enable ships to operate with greater freedom off the coast of Mexico, for instance. This restriction did not last long, but it was a dominant factor in the design of the *Kearsarge* class, leading to the peculiar double turrets in an attempt to save weight.

In this class moderate freeboard was necessary as the 13in gun was used once more with a heavy secondary and tertiary battery. The most original feature was the double-storey turret arrangement, with twin 8in turrets placed on top of the 13in turrets. The idea was to gain maximum fire on the broadside, without paying the weight penalty of four 8in turrets, but the disadvantages seem to have outweighed the advantages. Blast effects

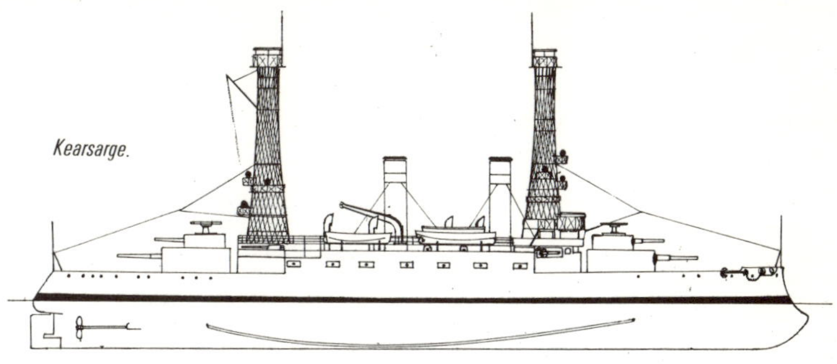
Kearsarge.

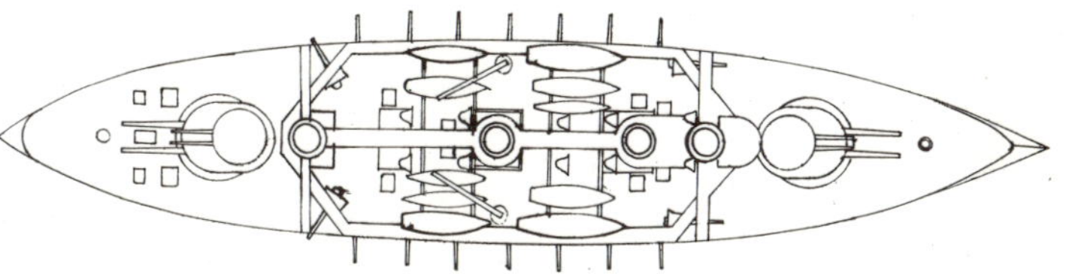

were severe, and an unlucky hit could knock out two turrets at once; no reports on the ammunition supply have been examined, but a joint 8in and 12in hoist was in all probability unduly complex.

Armament: The 8in turret was an integral part of the 13in turret, and could not be trained independently. The 8in hoists were arranged well clear and forward of the breeches of the 13in guns, in the fore part of the secondary turret.

For the first time the now-standard 5in gun was mounted, as the largest calibre using 'fixed' ammunition. The fourteen (later eighteen) 5in guns were arranged in a novel midships battery, with internal splinter screens. The battery proved wet in service, due to the restricted freeboard, and all but eight guns were removed in 1918.

Appearance: The double-storey turrets were conspicuous and the general effect of widely spaced funnels and the long uniform 5in battery made these ships a handsome pair. The tertiary battery was reduced in 1918, and two anti-aircraft guns were added. Both masts were originally of the military type, but these were changed to the 'basket' type in 1909.

Careers

Kearsarge: Having been relegated to training duties before war broke out, she was assigned to engineers' training duties on the East Coast, based on York Bay, Virginia; on the day war broke out she was lying in Boston, and her boarding parties took possession of five German merchant ships; at New York on 26 December 1918 for Presidential review of U.S. 6th Battle Squadron on its return from Scapa Flow; training duties continued in 1919, and finally decommissioned at Philadelphia 10 May 1920; converted to a crane-hulk, *AB-1*, which served until 1955 (she retained her battleship name until 1941, when it was required for a new aircraft-carrier).

Kentucky: Undergoing repairs at New York NY on outbreak of war; from May 1917 took up duties as training ship for stokers and so forth on the East Coast; paid off at Philadelphia August 1919 and decommissioned May 1920; sold for breaking up 23 January 1924.

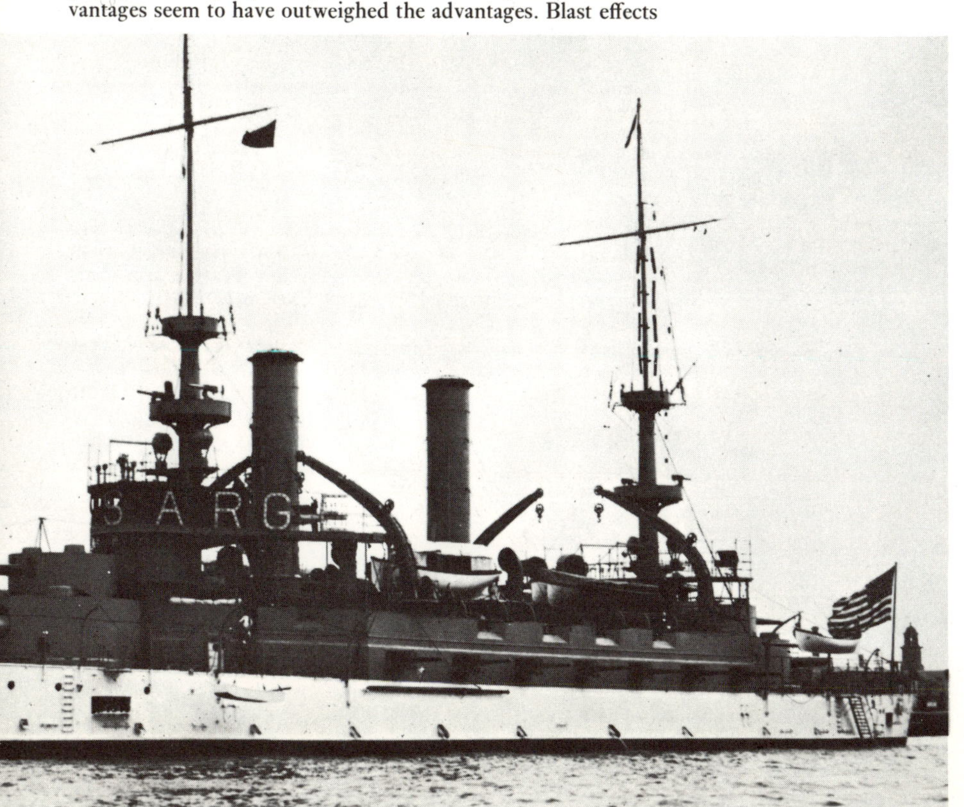
Above, *Kearsarge pre-1914 showing her pole masts and prominent midships secondary battery (IWM).*

Illinois class

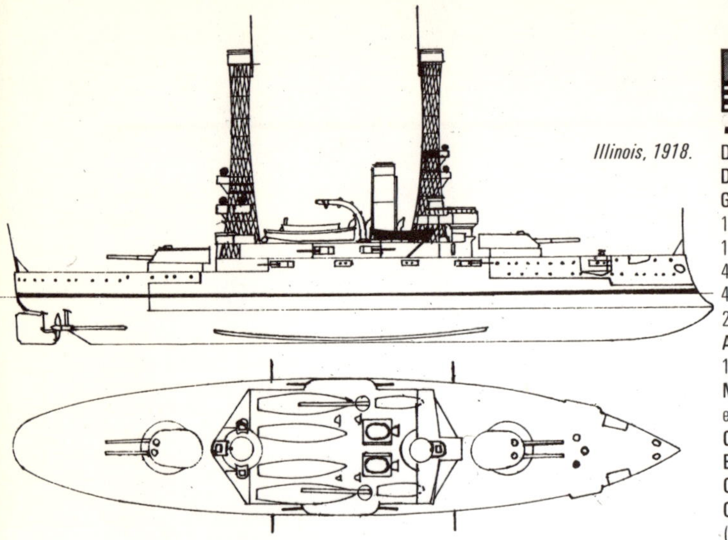

Illinois, 1918.

Displacement: 11,565tons
Dimensions: 368ft×72ft 3in×23ft 6in
Guns: 4×13in (2×2)
14×6in (14×1); reduced to 8×6in 1917–18
4×3in (4×1)
4×6pdrs (4×1)
2×3in A.A. added in 1917–18
Armour: 16–9¼in belt; 14in turrets; 10in CT
Machinery: 2-shaft vertical triple-expansion, 10,000hp = 16knots
Coal Capacity: 800/1275tons
Endurance: 3000miles at 10knots
Complement: 592–686
Cost: £542,480 average ($2,169,920) excluding guns

	Laid Down	Launched	Completed	Built/Engined
BB7 Illinois	10 Feb 1897	4 Oct 1898	Sept 1901	Newport News
BB8 Alabama	2 Dec 1896	18 May 1898	Oct 1900	Cramp
BB9 Wisconsin	9 Feb 1897	26 Nov 1899	Feb 1901	Union Ironworks

This class was strongly influenced by Sir William White's *Majestic* class, as can be seen from their profiles. The double-storey turret idea of the *Kearsarge* class was not repeated, and the freeboard was higher. Not employed on frontline duties in 1917–18 on account of their age.

Although officially described as 'seagoing coastline battle-ships' the designers were able to produce a seaworthy ship by the simple expedient of omitting the 8in armament. It had been decided by a special Board of the U.S.Navy that intermediate calibre guns achieved little beyond complicating the ammunition supply.

All three ships were good steamers, and exceeded 17knots on trials. The boilers were arranged in longitudinal stokeholds, back-to-back against the centreline bulkhead, which gave easy access and ensured a constant supply of coal from the bunkers.
Armament: The 6in gun reappeared, as it was felt that something heavier than the 5in was needed if the 8in gun was not mounted. In 1917–18 the forward and midships 6in guns at upper deck level were removed, leaving only the battery guns level with the bridge and the mainmast, and those in the super-structure.

The 13in gun appeared for the last time in this class. For the first time heavy guns were mounted in 'hooded barbettes' as opposed to old-fashioned turrets.
Appearance: The original military masts had been replaced by 'basket' masts in 1909–11, and during the war the upper deck casemate 6in guns amidships were removed and the positions were plated over.
Careers
Alabama: In Atlantic Reserve Fleet on outbreak of war, and recommissioned at Philadelphia 5 April 1917; as Flagship, Division I, Atlantic Fleet Battle Force; based on Norfolk, and carried out training duties; decommissioned 7 May 1920 and transferred to War Dept. 15 Sept 1921 for use as target; sunk by bombing 27 September 1921 in Chesapeake Bay; wreck later raised and broken up in dry dock at Baltimore.
Illinois: Laid up Philadelphia Navy Yard on outbreak of war, and used as accommodation ship from 1917–19, when she was laid up once more; lent to New York State Naval Militia 23 October 1921; 14 February 1924 listed as incapable of combat duty, and subsequently fitted out as floating armoury; redesignated as hulk *No. IX-15* in 1941, and renamed *Prairie State*; stricken from Navy List 26 March 1956 and sold for breaking up in Baltimore.
Wisconsin: In reserve at Philadelphia on outbreak of war in 1917; recommissioned 24 April 1917 for service with Coast Patrol Squadron; training ship for engine room personnel 1917–18, and went to New York for the fleet review at New York on 26 December 1918; training cruise to Caribbean in 1919, and decommissioned at Philadelphia 15 May 1920; sold for breaking up 26 January 1922.

Below left, Alabama late in 1918 with only eight 6in guns and closed control tops (USN).

Above left, Wisconsin in 1909/10 before her cage mainmast had been added (USN).

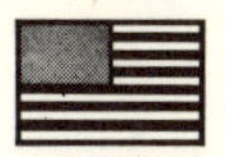

Maine class

Displacement: 12,500tons
Dimensions: 388ft (wl)×72ft 3in×24ft
Guns: 4×12in (2×2)
16×6in (16×1); reduced to 8×6in 1917–18
6×3in (6×1); replaced by 2×3in A.A. in 1918
4×6pdrs; removed 1918
Torpedo Tubes: 2×18in (beam, submerged)
Armour: 11–7½in belt; 12–8in turrets; 10in CT
Machinery: 2-shaft vertical triple-expansion, 16,000hp = 18knots
Coal Capacity: 1000/1800tons
Endurance: 3000miles at 10knots
Complement: 799
Cost: £593,787 average ($2,375,148) excluding guns

	Laid Down	Launched	Completed	Built/Engined
BB10 Maine	15 Feb 1899	27 July 1901	Dec 1902	Cramp
BB11 Missouri	7 Feb 1900	28 Dec 1901	Dec 1903	Newport News
BB12 Ohio	22 Apr 1899	18 May 1901	Oct 1904	Union Ironworks

These were the first U.S. battleships with submerged torpedo tubes and also the first to steam at 18knots. As they were laid down at the time of the Spanish-American War, they were modified during construction to take advantage of war experience and they set up the pattern for the next three classes.

To achieve another two knots' speed the length of hull was increased by twenty feet, but in other respects the main features of the *Illinois* class were repeated. Krupp armour was introduced, and the thickness of the belt could thus be reduced to twelve inches, while the new pattern of 12in gun had the same penetrative power as the old 13in.

The secondary battery was again in the form of a battery on two levels, and all guns were protected by a uniform thickness of 6in armour. American designers continued their preference for splinter screens between the guns in the battery, as compared with the casemates found in Sir William White's ships in the Royal Navy.

Although very good ships for their day they suffered from wetness in rough weather. Their 6in guns tended to be washed out in heavy seas, as they were placed too low and too far forward. This tendency continued in U.S. battleships until the end of the war.

Machinery: As displacement was increased at the same time as the weight of armour was reduced, it was possible to provide a greater coal-supply. The *Maine* was given large-tube Niclausse boilers, but her two sisters were fitted with Thornycroft small-tube boilers. These did not prove satisfactory, and service opinion was prejudiced against them for some years.

Armament: In 1917–18 eight 6in guns were removed, leaving only the guns on the forecastle deck amidships and the guns at either end of the battery.

Appearance: The first three-funnelled U.S. battleships, all three had been remasted with 'basket' masts in 1909–11. Eight 6in guns were removed from the upper deck battery in 1918.

Careers

Maine: Had been in reserve from 1914–16, but after repairs at Philadelphia Navy Yard she commissioned in January 1917 as training ship for reservists; after a refit at New York Navy Yard, March-August 1917 she was anchored in the York River as engineering training ship; 1918–19 serving in 1st Squadron, U.S. Atlantic Fleet, and on training duties; reserve 1919–20 and paid off for disposal May 1920; sold for breaking up 22 January 1922.

Missouri: Serving with Naval Academy Practice Squadron in 1917, and joined Atlantic Fleet at Yorktown on outbreak of war; spent the entire war in the Chesapeake Bay area, training guard crews for merchant ships; after the Armistice served as troop transport, making four round trips to France to repatriate American Expeditionary Force (carried 3278 soldiers); paid off September 1919 and sold for breaking up 26 January 1922.

Ohio: In reserve at Philadelphia Navy Yard at outbreak of war, but then recommissioned for service at Norfolk as engineering and gunnery training ship; June-August 1918 served as training ship for midshipmen, but paid off November 1918 and was placed in reserve January 1919; in 1921 refitted as control ship for the wireless-controlled target ship *Iowa*; echo-sounding trials in March 1922, but paid off May that year, and sold for breaking up 23 March 1923.

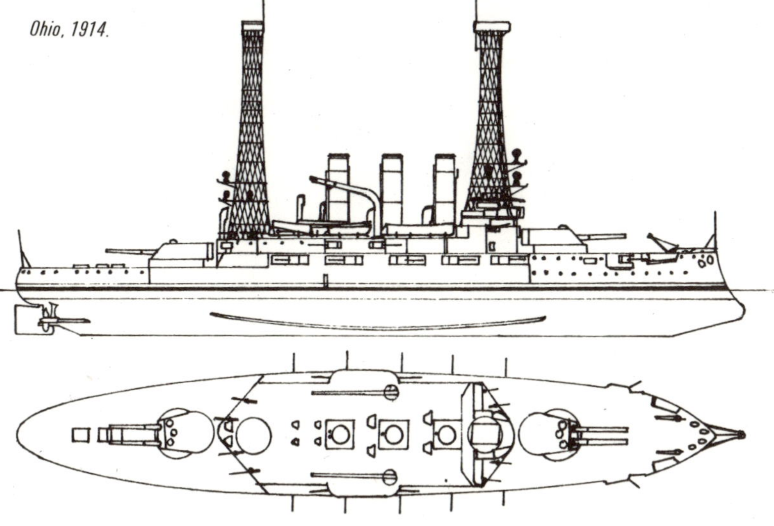

Ohio, 1914.

Right, *Ohio* as she appeared in 1911 (IWM).

Virginia class

Displacement: 14,948tons (normal)
Dimensions: 435ft (wl)×76ft 3in× 23ft 9in (mean)
Guns: 4×12in (2×2); 8×8in (4×2); 12×6in (12×1); 12×3in (12×1) (as built) 4×12in; 8×8in; 6×3in; 2×3in HA (2×1) (as rearmed 1917–18)
Torpedo Tubes: 4×21in (submerged, beam)
Armour: Main belt 8–11in, 4in ends; main turrets 10–11in; secondary turrets 6in; conning-tower 9in
Machinery: 2 sets 4-cyl reciprocating; 19,000ihp = 19knots
Coal Capacity: 900/1900tons
Endurance: 4000miles at 10knots
Complement: 905
Cost: £728,395 average ($2,913,580) excluding guns

	Laid Down	Launched	Commissioned	Built
BB13 Virginia	21 May 1902	5 Apr 1904	May 1906	Newport News
BB14 Nebraska	4 July 1902	7 Oct 1904	July 1907	Moran Bros.
BB15 Georgia	31 Aug 1902	11 Oct 1904	Sept 1906	Bath I.W.
BB16 New Jersey	2 Apr 1902	10 Nov 1904	May 1906	Fore River
BB17 Rhode Island	1 May 1902	17 May 1904	Feb 1906	Fore River

This class was authorised in 1898 at the time of the Spanish-American War, but not completed until 1906–7, owing to alterations and additions to the design. As finally completed they were similar to the British *King Edward VII* class in having heavier calibre guns to supplement the standard 6in secondary guns. In this case, the calibre chosen was 8in, and American designers revived the double-storey turret to accommodate it—a twin 12in position surmounted by twin 8ins.

Like other American ideas on gun disposition at this time, the double turret offered far more on paper than in practice. In theory the high command for the 8in guns was gained economically, since the structure of the 12in barbette could be made stronger while the weight was saved elsewhere; but in practice the two mountings suffered from mutual blast and the extra topweight made the *Virginias* roll badly.

The *Virginia* class were fine ships in their day, with good armour protection, but their rolling and their cumbersome double turrets would have left them at a disadvantage against the ships they were intended to match, ie: the *King Edward VII* class. As it was, by the time they could be tested in action in 1917 they were outclassed by the dreadnoughts and were restricted to second-line duties. In 1917–18 their weaknesses in seakeeping were finally admitted, and their entire 6in battery was suppressed.

Armament: The 8in gun owed its reintroduction to the good work done by guns of this calibre at the Battle of Santiago in 1898. Unfortunately the designers chose to revert to the double-storied turret, in order to avoid any sacrifice of 6in guns. The result was an overgunned ship, and all the tertiary guns had to be removed during the war.

Machinery: Once again the designers had to increase the length in order to gain higher speed. For the first time Babcock & Wilcox large-tube boilers were introduced in some ships.

Appearance: They were built with pole masts, but cage masts were substituted 1910; tops were added to the masts in 1918, and the mast-structures were strengthened.

Careers

Georgia: Serving as receiving ship at Boston prior to outbreak of war in 1917, but recommissioned for active service 6 April 1917 (3rd Division, Battleship Force); convoy escort duties with Cruiser Force Atlantic, September 1918; 10 December 1918 joined Cruiser and Transport Force and made five trips to Brest repatriating American troops until June 1919; paid off July 1920 and sold 10 November 1923; broken up at Oakland, California 1924.

Nebraska: Attached to 3rd Division Battleship Force on outbreak of war in April 1917, but undergoing repairs at Boston Navy Yard; exercises and training duties to January 1918, followed by further repairs at Boston, and at Norfolk Navy Yard in April; took body of Uruguayan Ambassador to Montevideo May–July 1918; escorted two fast convoys to U.K. October–November; transport duties between Brest and U.S.A. December 1918–June 1919; joined 2nd Division Squadron 1 of Pacific Fleet until paid off July 1920; stricken 9 November 1923 and sold shortly afterwards for breaking up, which was completed in 1924.

New Jersey: Stationed on East coast at outbreak of war in 1917; training duties 1917–18; transport service between Brest and U.S.A. December 1918–June 1919; paid off at Boston 6 August 1920; stricken 1922; sunk as target in Mitchell tests off Cape Hatteras 5 September 1923.

Rhode Island: Service with Atlantic Fleet prior to outbreak of war, but completed repairs at Boston Navy Yard March 1917; training and convoy duties to December 1918 and then served as transport between Brest and U.S.A. to July 1919; while en route to West coast via Panama Canal, forced to undergo emergency repairs at Balboa; paid off at Mare Island, San Francisco, 30 June 1920; stricken 1 November 1923 and broken up 1924.

Virginia: In reserve and undergoing refit at Boston Navy Yard on outbreak of war, but the ship supplied a landing party to board the interned German merchantmen in Boston; refit completed August 1917 and joined 3rd Division, Battleship Force, Atlantic Fleet; gunnery training ship 1917–18, and during December 1917 acted as temporary Flagship of 1st Division; Flagship 3rd Division same month until refitted at Boston for convoy escort duties September 1918; escorted two convoys to Europe, and then served as troop transport December 1918–July 1919; paid off at Boston August 1920; stricken 12 July 1922 and sunk in Mitchell bombing tests 5 September 1923.

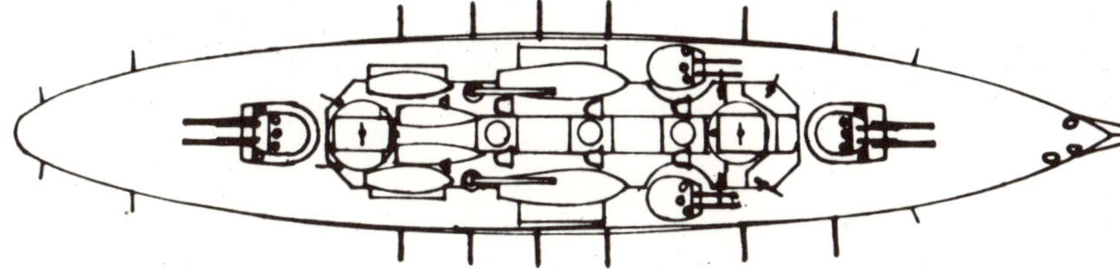

New Jersey, 1914.

Above left, a pre-1914 view of Georgia at Brest (Musée de la Marine).

Below left, Virginia as she appeared shortly before the war (USN).

Connecticut class

Displacement: 16,000tons (normal); (18,000tons full load)

Dimensions: 450ft (wl)×76ft 9in×24ft 6in

Guns: 4×12in (2×2); 8×8in (4×2); 12×7in (12×1); 20×3in (20×1) (as built) 4×12in, 8×8in, 12×3in (12×1); 2×3in HA (as rearmed 1917–18)

Torpedo Tubes: 4×21in (submerged, beam)

Armour: 9–11in belt, with 4in ends; casemates 7in; main turrets 8–12in; secondary turrets 4–6½in; 9in conning tower

Machinery: 2 sets 4-cyl reciprocating; 16,500ihp = 18knots (18·8 maximum); 12 Babcock boilers

Coal Capacity: 900/2400tons

Endurance: 5000miles at 10knots

Complement: 827–880

Cost: £839,500 ($3,358,144) average +approximately £760,500 ($3,042,000) for guns

	Laid Down	Launched	Commissioned	Built
BB18 Connecticut	10 Mar 1903	29 Sept 1904	Sept 1906	New York NY
BB19 Louisiana	7 Feb 1903	27 Aug 1904	June 1906	Newport News
BB20 Vermont	21 May 1904	31 Aug 1905	Mar 1907	Fore River
BB21 Kansas	10 Feb 1904	12 Aug 1905	Apr 1907	New York NY
BB22 Minnesota	27 Oct 1903	8 Apr 1905	Mar 1907	Camden N. News
BB25 New Hampshire	1 May 1905	30 June 1906	Mar 1908	New York NY

This class was an improved version of the *Virginias*, laid down at the time of the Russo-Japanese War. The secondary armament was greatly strengthened when compared to the preceding *Virginia* class, with a heavy 7in battery at upper deck level comparable to the *Lord Nelson* in the Royal Navy. It is an interesting comment on the different tempo of construction in British and American yards—the *Agamemnon* was laid down a fortnight after the *New Hampshire*, had both 12in turrets, turntables and barbettes diverted to enable *Dreadnought* to complete early, but was still only two months later in completing than the *New Hampshire*.

Like their fellow 'intermediate dreadnoughts' abroad, they were too powerful to be relegated to subsidiary duties, but as they were totally outclassed by the later dreadnoughts no wartime employment could be found for them outside American waters. By later standards they were overgunned for their displacement, and furthermore the 7in guns were carried at upper deck level where they would be washed out or masked by spray in ordinary North Atlantic conditions. The twin turrets for the 8in guns were obviously a more practical disposition than the two-storey turrets in the *Virginias*, but the value of the turrets might have been greater if they had contained lighter and faster-firing guns.

These weaknesses seem to have been realised when the ships undertook Atlantic patrols in the winter of 1917, for they were taken in hand immediately: the 7in positions were plated over, eight useless 3in guns were removed, and two high-angle guns

added. In 1919 the ships were all used as troop transports to repatriate the A.E.F. from Europe.

Armament: In this class the double-storey turret was finally abandoned, but in an attempt to augment the tertiary armament a new mark of 7in gun was introduced. It is difficult to see the logic of this change, as it made the tertiary armament almost equal to the secondary in power, but at the expense of handiness, for the 6in gun was universally known to be the largest which could be conveniently handloaded.

Machinery: Once more the length was increased, by fifteen feet as compared with the *Virginias*. As a result horsepower was actually reduced without loss of speed.

Appearance: All were built with pole masts, but 'basket' masts were substituted in 1910–11; control tops were added in 1917–18.

Careers

Connecticut: Flagship of 5th Division, Atlantic Fleet, on outbreak of war; based on York River, on training duties 1917–18; October 1918 assigned to 4th Division of 2nd Squadron; sailed from Hampton Roads 6 January 1919 to begin repatriation of U.S. troops; in three trips she carried over 3,000 troops from Brest to Hampton Roads; reverted to Flagship of 2nd Battleship Squadron in June 1919; training duties 1919–21, and became Flagship of Pacific Train at San Pedro October 1921 to December 1922; sold 1 November 1923 and scrapped at San Francisco.

Kansas: In dockyard hands at Philadelphia on outbreak of war; joined 4th Division for training stokers and engineers; sailed from Norfolk 10 December 1918 on the first of five repatriation trips to Brest, and carried over 6000 U.S. soldiers home from France; refitted for training duties 1919–20 and became Flagship of 4th Division, 2nd Battleship Squadron, in September 1920; decommissioned at Philadelphia December 1921, stricken 24 January 1923 and sold for scrapping 23 January 1924.

Louisiana: On training duties on East Coast when war broke out; joined 4th Division 19 March 1917 as gunnery and engineering training ship; escorted convoy to Halifax in September 1918, and then made four repatriation trips to Brest, bringing home 7000 soldiers; decommissioned at Philadelphia 20 October 1920 and stricken 24 August 1923; sold 1 November 1923 and scrapped at Baltimore.

Minnesota: Flagship of Reserve Force, Atlantic Fleet, on outbreak of war; joined 4th Division of 2nd Squadron on training duties 1917–18; while proceeding from Hampton Roads to Philadelphia Navy Yard, on 29 September 1918 she was badly damaged by a mine; after repairs she joined the Cruiser and Transport Force for three repatriation trips to Brest; training 1919–21; decommissioned 1 December 1921 and dismantled in 1923; sold 23 January 1924 for scrapping.

New Hampshire: Under repair at Norfolk Navy Yard on outbreak of war; training duties 1917–18 but also sailed as part of the escort of troop convoys to France in September and October 1917; trooping duties from December 1918 to June 1919, bring home 8500 soldiers; refitted 1919–20 for service in Caribbean; decommissioned 11 May 1921 and stricken 24 August 1923; sold 1 November and scrapped at Baltimore in 1924.

Vermont: Entered Philadelphia Navy Yard for refit two days before outbreak of war; and did not enter service until August 1917; joined 3rd Division on engineering training duties in Chesapeake Bay; carried body of Chilean Ambassador from Norfolk to Valparaiso in May 1918; refitted November 1918 for service as a troop transport and made four repatriation trips to Brest from January to June 1919; decommissioned at Mare Island June 1920, stricken 10 November 1923 and sold 30 November for scrapping.

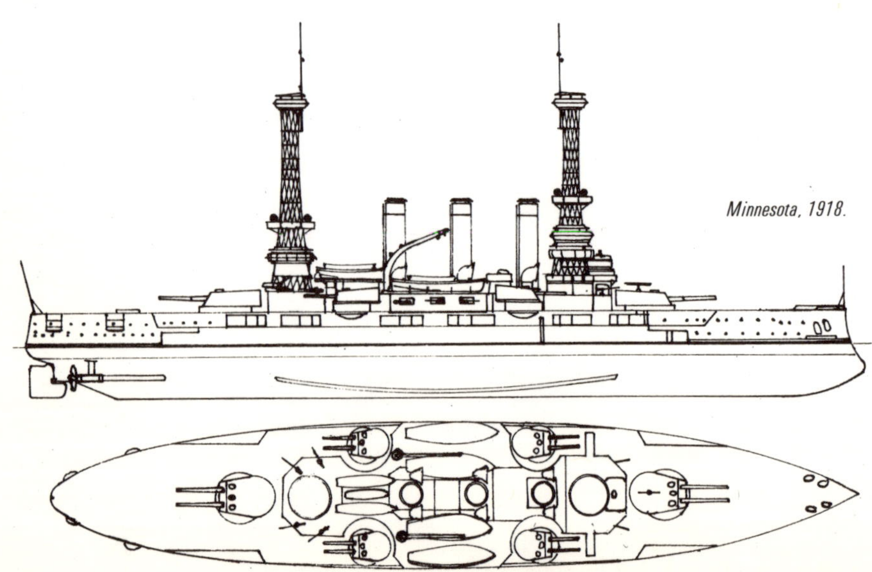

Minnesota, 1918.

Left, New Hampshire c. 1914 (USN).

Left, Vermont with wartime modifications, including a large rangefinder over the bridge and enclosed control tops (USN).

Left, Minnesota c. 1918 at Philadelphia Navy Yard. Note that the guns have been removed from the main deck battery (USN).

South Carolina class

Displacement: 16,000tons (normal); 17,900tons (full load)

Dimensions: 450ft (wl)×80ft 3in× 24ft 6in

Guns: 8×12in 45cal (4×2) 22×3in 50cal (22×1); reduced to 14×3in 1917 2×3in A.A. added 1917 4×1pdrs (4×1)

Torpedo Tubes: 2×21in (beam, submerged)

Armour: 12–9in belt; 12–8in turrets; 12in CT

Machinery: 2-shaft vertical triple-expansion, 16,500hp = 18½knots

Coal Capacity: 900/2380tons

Endurance: Approx 5000miles at 10knots

Complement: 869

Cost: £700,000 ($2,800,000) excluding guns

	Laid Down	Launched	Completed	Built/Engined
BB26				
South Carolina	18 Dec 1906	11 July 1908	Mar 1910	Cramp
BB27 Michigan	17 Dec 1906	26 May 1908	Jan 1910	New York SB Co.

These two ships were precursors of the *Dreadnought*, and were in fact the first 'all big-gun' battleships in the world. With the *Lord Nelsons*, the Japanese *Aki* and *Satsuma* and other contemporaries, they were the outcome of the increasing efficiency of long-range gunnery. The Russo-Japanese War having proved that naval battles would be fought at ranges of 7000yards and more, it was logical to increase the volume of long-range fire in order to make ranging by salvoes possible.

Had approval of the naval appropriations not been delayed, and had the Royal Navy not been able to build the *Dreadnought* in a year, the *Michigan* or the *South Carolina* might have given their name to a new type of battleship, for they embodied a huge jump in offensive power. Their chief virtue lay in the logical layout of the armament—all the main guns on the centre-line with the inner turrets superfiring. This meant that they had the same broadside as the *Dreadnought*, but without the penalty imposed by having wing turrets, thus doing away with the need for a fifth gun position. On the other hand, the U.S. Navy was not able to gamble on the Parsons turbine, and the conventional reciprocating machinery was retained. Like the *Dreadnought* herself, reliance was placed on a large battery of very light guns for defence against torpedo-craft. These guns were placed a deck higher than in other American ships of the same era, with obvious advantages in rough weather.

The displacement of this class had been restricted by Congress to 16,000tons. As valuable weight had been devoted to the superimposed 12in guns, it was necessary to compensate for this elsewhere. As a result the freeboard aft was reduced to 10ft, being equivalent to the loss of height of one deck when compared to the *Dreadnought*.

Armament: The approximate arc of fire for all guns was 270°. Before the ships were laid down experiments had been carried out with a 12in gun fired over the turret of a monitor. This had proved conclusively that blast would not interfere unduly with the lower turret, but in this the U.S.Navy was lucky in having turrets with the sighting hoods at the rear. Other navies, particularly the British, had turrets with sighting hoods at the front, which meant that superimposed guns could not fire straight ahead.

Appearance: The silhouette of these two ships was unique, with prominent caps on the funnels, two 'basket' masts, and the secondary battery at forecastle deck level between the turrets. In 1917–18 both carried two 3in anti-aircraft guns on the crowns of the after derrick-posts (replacing searchlights).

Careers

Michigan: Serving with Atlantic Fleet on outbreak of war, and attached to Battleship Force II; refitted at Philadelphia Navy Yard July 1917 and then served on training duties in Chesapeake Bay; refitted once more August–September 1918 and returned to training duties until February 1919; sailed for France as transport 4 February 1919 and repatriated soldiers until July; stricken 17 October 1923 and scrapped at Philadelphia NY in 1924.

South Carolina: Following a refit at Philadelphia Navy Yard completed January 1917, served in Guantanamo Bay area until outbreak of war; April 1917 became gunnery training ship in Chesapeake Bay area; left Tompkinsville, N.Y. as unit of the ocean escort for a troop convoy in September 1918, and returned a week later for repairs; returned to gunnery training duties in the York River until the Armistice; served as troop transport from February to July 1919, making four runs between Hampton Roads and Brest and carrying 4500 soldiers; Annapolis midshipmen's cruise to Pacific 1920, and to West Indies and foreign ports 1921; paid off at Philadelphia Navy Yard 15 December 1921; stricken 13 January 1924 and scrapped.

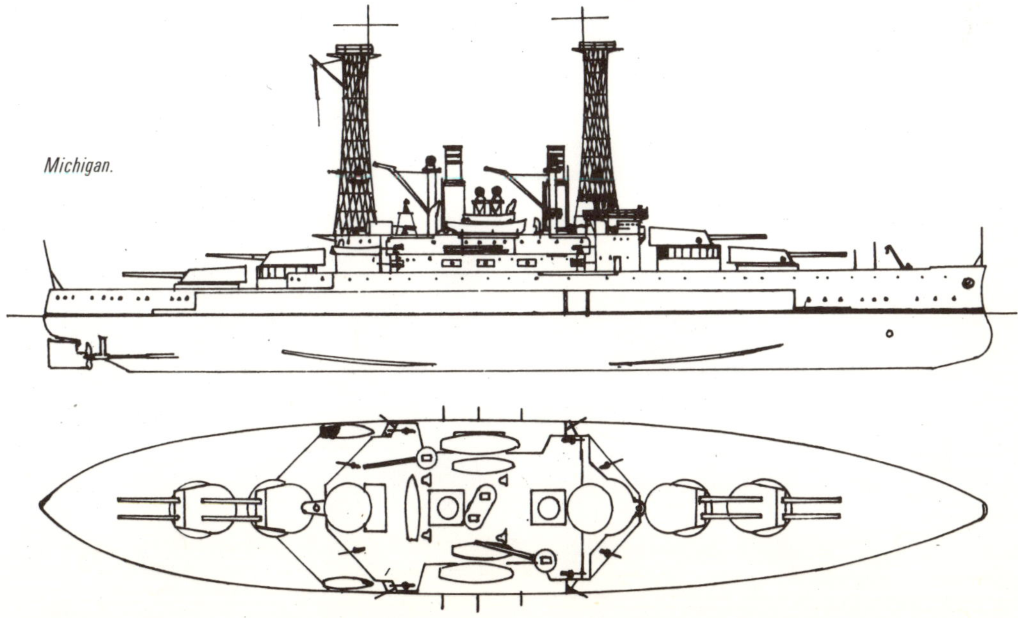

Michigan.

Above left, *Michigan on full-power trials, showing to good advantage her cleanliness and balanced layout (IWM).* **Below left,** *a prewar view of Michigan (IWM).*

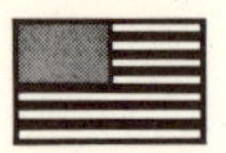

Delaware class

Displacement: 20,000tons (Delaware 20,380tons) normal : 22,400tons in load condition
Dimensions: 510ft (wl)×85ft 3in×27in
Guns: 10×12in 45cal (5×2)
14×5in 50cal
2×3in A.A. (2×1) added 1917
Torpedo Tubes: 2×21in (beam, submerged)
Armour: 1i–9in belt ; 12–8in turrets ; 12in CT
Machinery: Delaware : 2-shaft vertical triple-expansion, 25,000hp = 21knots ; North Dakota : 2-shaft Curtis turbines, 25,000hp = 21knots (re-engined with Parsons turbines 1916–17) ; 14 Babcock boilers in both
Coal Capacity: 1930/2670tons
Oil Capacity: 380tons
Endurance: About 6000miles at 10knots
Complement: 933
Cost: £858,400 ($3,433,600) excluding guns

	Laid Down	Launched	Completed	Built/Engined
BB28 Delaware	11 Nov 1907	6 Feb 1909	Apr 1910	Newport News
BB29 North Dakota	16 Dec 1907	10 Nov 1908	Apr 1910	Fore River

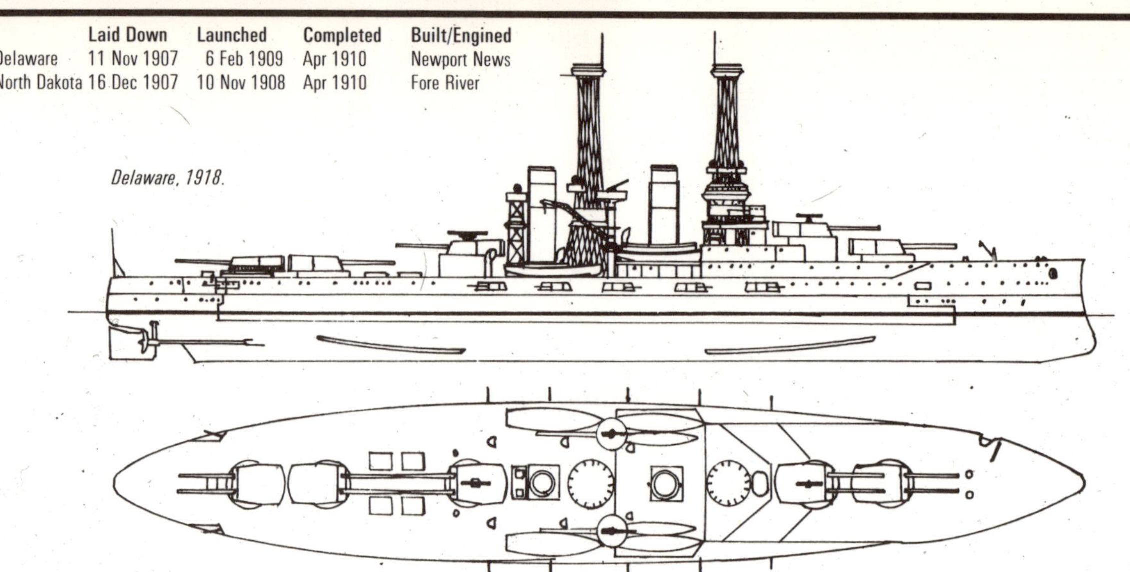

Delaware, 1918.

The *Delawares* showed the influence of the British dreadnoughts in the increased battery of 12in guns. Because of the great increase in size over the *South Carolina* class (25 per cent) freeboard had to be reduced somewhat and the secondary armament was carried lower. *North Dakota* was the first American battleship with turbines, but difficulties with possible suppliers forced the Bureau of Ships to design *Delaware* with reciprocating machinery.

The heavy secondary battery of 5in guns is in marked contrast to their British contemporaries, although not as heavy as in German battleships. They adopted a novel disposition of heavy armament, with No. 3 turret superimposed but Nos. 4 and 5 back-to-back and a deck lower. Some of the guns in the secondary battery were too far forward and aft to be of much use in a seaway.

Armament: In this class the 5in gun was again adopted, for the first time since 1900. The main armament was mounted on the centreline, as in the preceding class.

Appearance: Resembled the British *Bellerophon* class in having a mast stepped before each funnel. By 1918 both ships had range clocks on masts and deflection scales on turrets.

Careers

Delaware: Serving with U.S. Atlantic Fleet on outbreak of war in 1917; assigned to training duties in Chesapeake Bay, and trained 5in gun crews for armed merchantmen; refitted Boston Navy Yard before joining Battleship Division 9 in November 1917; sailed 25 November with *New York, Wyoming* and *Florida* for Scapa Flow and joined the British Grand Fleet 17 December 1917, forming the 6th Battle Squadron; convoy and support duties, covering operations between Firth and Forth and Scapa; while covering a convoy from Norway in February 1918 *Delaware* was unsuccessfully attacked by a U-boat; returned to U.S.A. for refit at Boston Navy Yard in July 1918; commissioned June 1919 for training duties and finally decommissioned November 1923; stricken 19 November 1923 and sold to Boston Iron and Metal Co. 5 February 1924 for scrapping at Philadelphia NY.

North Dakota: Had been in reserve at Philadelphia until two months before the outbreak of war in April 1917, but had been recommissioned in February for working up, following the renewal of her main machinery; gunnery and engineering training duties 1917–18, based alternately on York River and New York; 1919 sailed with 3rd Squadron of Battleship Division 1 to Mediterranean; training cruise in Caribbean and West Indies 1920; U.S. Atlantic Fleet and training duties 1921–3; paid off at Norfolk Navy Yard November 1923; target duties from May 1924; stricken 7 January 1931 and sold at Boston for breaking up 16 March 1931.

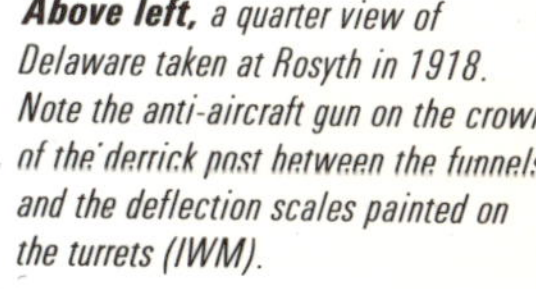

Far left, Delaware in October 1912 during the Naval Review (USN).

Above left, a quarter view of Delaware taken at Rosyth in 1918. Note the anti-aircraft gun on the crown of the derrick post between the funnels and the deflection scales painted on the turrets (IWM).

Below left, Delaware as seen from her kite balloon, while lying in the Firth of Forth in 1918 – clearly demonstrating the square control tops on the mastheads (IWM).

Above, two views of Florida in 1918 – left, with an experimental colour scheme of stripes on the bow and funnels; right, at Rosyth. Note the aerial spreaders on the lattice masts and the rangefinders on No. 2 and No. 3 turrets, and the anti-aircraft gun on the derrick post visible between the funnels (both IWM).

Florida class

Displacement: 21,825tons (normal);
23,400tons (load)
Dimensions: 518ft 9in (wl)×88ft 3in
×28ft 3in
Guns: 10×12in 45cal (5×2)
16×5in 51cal (16×1); reduced to
12×5in in 1918
2×3in A.A. added 1918
Torpedo Tubes: 2×21in (submerged,
beam)
Armour: 11–9in belt; 12–8in
turrets; 12in CT
Machinery: 4-shaft Parsons turbines,
28,000hp = 21knots; 12 Babcock
boilers
Coal Capacity: 1930/2500tons
Oil Capacity: 400tons
Endurance: 6720miles at 10knots
Complement: 1000
Cost: £1,046,750 ($4,187,000)
average, excluding guns

	Laid Down	Launched	Completed	Built/Engined
BB30 Florida	9 Mar 1909	12 May 1910	Sept 1911	Brooklyn NY
BB31 Utah	16 Mar 1909	23 Dec 1910	Aug 1911	New York NY

Improved *Delawares* with 3ft more beam, they featured a changed layout of masts and funnels. These two ships were the first in the U.S. Navy to have four propeller shafts. Although originally intended to have eight 14in guns in a *South Carolina* layout, the delay in supplying guns and mountings of a new type was unacceptable, and they were given the same type of 12in turrets as the *Delawares*. Even so, trouble with delivery of turbine casings delayed their completion.

Like the British, the Americans found that the easiest way to keep abreast of their rivals in the dreadnought race was to duplicate the previous design. The only alteration to the *Florida* class was to simplify the layout by putting the funnels between the masts, but even so, they exceeded their contract delivery date. Had the original armament been fitted these delays might have been far more serious, and even in 1909 the U.S. Navy was aware of the danger of falling behind the other naval powers.

Armament: As in the previous class the 5in guns were mounted in a battery at main deck level. When anti-aircraft guns were added in 1917–18 they were mounted on circular platforms at the head of the crane posts between the funnels, surely the most uncomfortable site for any gun's crew.
Appearance: Although generally similar to the *Delaware* class, the mainmast was abaft the second funnel. In 1918 both ships had the normal alterations common to British and American dreadnoughts, ie: range clocks on masts and deflection scales on turrets; 3in anti-aircraft guns were added on top of the stump masts supporting the boat cranes abreast the second funnel. As in other American dreadnoughts, prominent auxiliary rangefinders were carried on Nos. 2, 3 and 4 turrets.
Careers
Florida: Serving in Battleship Division 9, Squadron 4 of U.S. Atlantic Fleet on outbreak of war; training duties in Chesapeake Bay until November 1917, when she sailed with *New York*, *Wyoming* and *Delaware* to join the British Grand Fleet; with other American ships of the 6th Battle Squadron she was present at the surrender of the German High Seas Fleet, 21 November 1918; sailed from Portland (England) 12 December 1918 to

Florida, 1918.

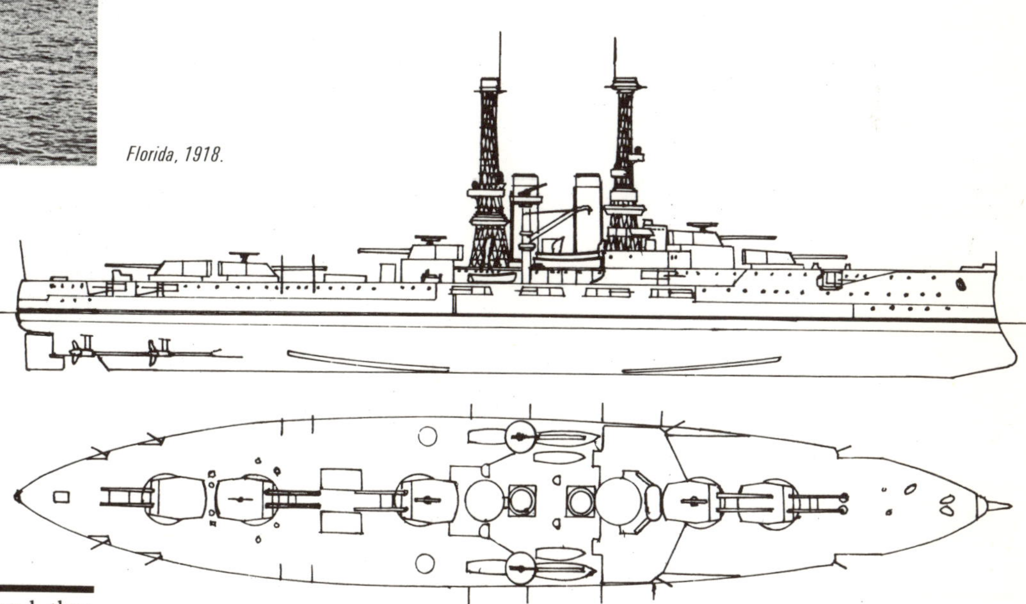

escort liner carrying President Wilson to Brest, and then returned to U.S.A.; served with U.S. Atlantic Fleet and on various duties 1920–4; modernised 1924–6; Battleship Division 2, Scouting Fleet 1928–30; paid off at Philadelphia Navy Yard February 1931, stricken under London Naval Treaty 6 April 1931, and breaking up completed 30 September 1932.

Utah: Serving on East coast on outbreak of war; gunnery and engineering training ship April 1917–August 1918; sailed for United Kingdom as Flagship of Vice-Admiral Mayo, Commander-in-Chief of the U.S. Atlantic Fleet; arrived Bantry Bay, Ireland 10 September 1918, and became Flagship of Rear-Admiral Rodgers, commanding Battleship Division 6; September-November 1918 covered Western Approaches convoys; December 1918 escorted liner carrying President Wilson to France (see *Florida*) and then returned to Boston Navy Yard to refit; 1921–22 Flagship U.S. Naval Forces in European Waters, and then joined Scouting Fleet; modernised 1926–8; stricken from effective list under London Naval Treaty, but converted to wireless-controlled target ship; mistaken by Japanese pilots for a commissioned battleship at Pearl Harbor, and sunk at her moorings 7 December 1941.

Wyoming class

Displacement: 26,000tons (normal);
27,700tons (load condition)
Dimensions: 554ft (wl)×93ft 3in×
28ft 6in
Guns: 12×12in 50cal (6×2)
21×5in 51cal (21×1); reduced to
16×5in in 1917
Torpedo Tubes: 2×21in (submerged,
beam)
Armour: 11–9in belt; 12–9in
turrets, 12in CT
Machinery: 4-shaft Parsons geared
turbines, 28,000hp=20½knots;
12 Babcock boilers
Coal Capacity: 1990/2660tons
Oil Capacity: 400tons
Endurance: 8000miles at 10knots
Complement: 1063
Cost: £964,000 ($3,856,000),
excluding guns

	Laid Down	Launched	Completed	Built/Engined
BB32 Wyoming	9 Feb 1910	25 May 1911	Sept 1912	Cramp
BB33 Arkansas	25 Jan 1910	14 Jan 1911	Sept 1912	New York NY

The *Wyomings* were designed as enlarged *Floridas*, with extra
beam and greater length to allow space for an additional turret.
They adopted a new hull form, flush-decked but with freeboard reduced aft. Although originally intended to have a combination of turbines and reciprocating machinery they were given
Parsons turbines.

Armament: For these ships a new pattern of longer 12in
gun was adopted as an interim measure before the introduction
of a new 14in gun. This weapon was already late in development
(see the *Florida* class), and the Bureau of Ships decided to
increase the volume of fire as an alternative.

In common with other navies at this time the U.S. Navy was
entering a phase of increasing the number of secondary gun
positions without much regard for practical problems such as
arcs of fire, spray interference or blast effect. The *Wyomings*
had a 5in gun placed right aft under the poop, and another pair
abreast of No. 1 turret. These were removed in 1917 after
proving quite useless, along with another pair out in the open
alongside No. 2 turret.

Appearance: Generally similar to the *Florida* class, they were
distinguished by the different turret arrangement aft. In 1917-18
the gun positions under the forecastle abreast of No. 1 turret
and right aft at the stern were blanked off. Other alterations
included range clocks on masts and deflection scales on turrets.

Careers

Arkansas: With Battleship Division 7 when war broke out;
assigned to training duties, training gun crews for armed
merchantmen; sailed for United Kingdom July 1918 to relieve
Delaware, and docked at Rosyth 28 July before joining the
U.S. 6th Battle Squadron, Grand Fleet; at surrender of High
Seas Fleet 21 November, and then sailed to Portland to join
President Wilson's escort before returning to New York in
December 1918; after many years of service, including complete
modernisation and reconstruction in 1925-6, she survived to
serve in World War II; after arduous convoy escort duty in
the North Atlantic she formed part of the Normandy Invasion
bombarding force, and then went to the Pacific for the Okinawa
landings; finally expended as a target during the Bikini atomic
bomb tests, 25 July 1946.

Wyoming: Serving on East coast on outbreak of war; served as
engineering training ship in Chesapeake Bay April–November
1917, and then sailed for Scapa Flow with Battleship Division 9;
served with 6th Battle Squadron, Grand Fleet December 1917–
November 1918, and was present at surrender of German Fleet;
hoisted flag of Rear-Admiral W. S. Sims U.S. Navy and
escorted liner carrying President Wilson to Brest for Peace
Conference, December 1918; returned to U.S.A. the same
month; after peacetime service on various stations she was
disarmed to comply with the London Naval Treaty, and was
renamed *A.G.17* in April 1932; stricken September 1947 and
broken up at Kearney, N.J. in 1947-8.

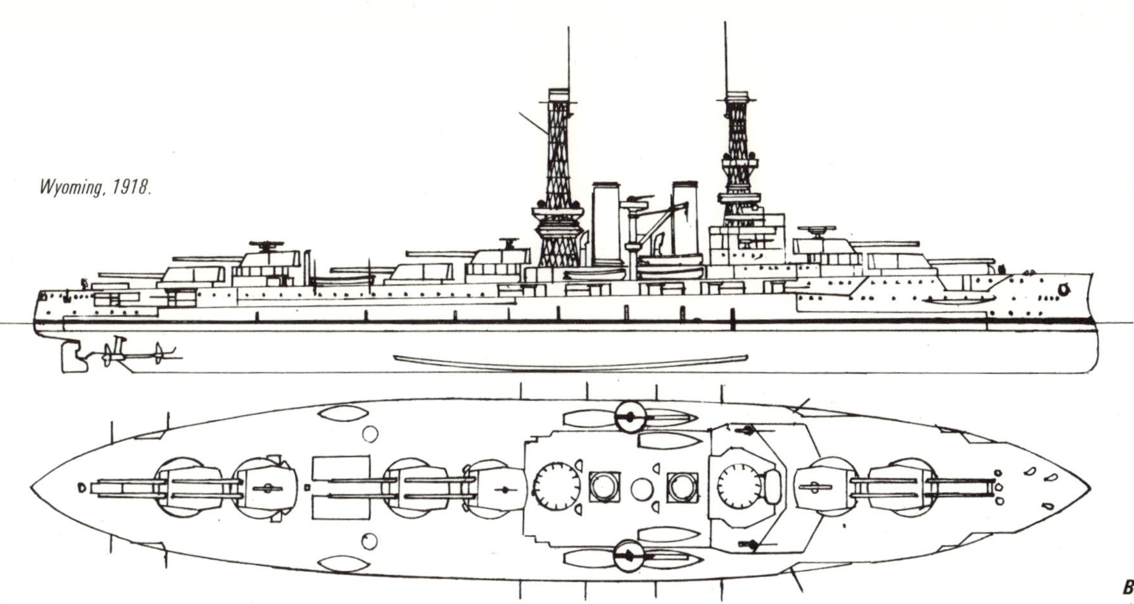

Wyoming, 1918.

Below, Arkansas as completed in 1912. Note the flush deck sloping aft and the light bridgework (IWM).

New York class

Displacement: 27,000tons (normal): 28,400tons (load condition)
Dimensions: 565ft (wl)×95ft 3in×28ft 6in
Guns: 10×14in 45cal (5×2) 21×5in 51cal (21×1)
Torpedo Tubes: 4×21in (submerged, beam)
Armour: 12–10in belt; 14–8in turrets; 12in CT

Machinery: 2-shaft vertical triple-expansion, 28,100hp = 21knots; 14 Babcock boilers (8 with super-heaters)
Coal Capacity: 1990/2870tons
Oil Capacity: 400tons
Endurance: 8000miles at 10knots
Complement: 864
Cost: £1,240,500 ($4,962,000) average, excluding guns

	Laid Down	Launched	Completed	Built/Engined
BB34 New York	11 Sept 1911	30 Oct 1912	Apr 1914	Brooklyn NY
BB35 Texas	17 Apr 1911	18 May 1912	Mar 1914	Newport News

This pair of ships continued the tendency of American battleships towards heavier armament and beamier hulls. When the development schedule of the new 14in gun appeared to be delayed even further the Bureau of Ships decided to arm them with fifteen 12in guns in triple turrets, but as the guns were ready in time they reverted to ten 14in guns in a modified *Florida* layout.

The recurrent problems with American turbine designs came to a head when tenders were requested for the *New York* class. While the *Delaware* class were a compromise, this time the manufacturers simply refused to accept the machinery specifications laid down by the Bureau of Ships. After a lengthy wrangle the Bureau took the unique step of going back to reciprocating machinery in order to show the manufacturers that the U.S. Navy would not be blackmailed into accepting standards below its military requirements. The solution may have seemed drastic, and possibly not justifiable in view of the international situation, but in the long run no harm came of the temporary reversion to triple-expansion engines, and the U.S. Navy ultimately took the lead in warship machinery.

Armament: The error of positioning 5in guns in exposed embrasures was repeated in this class, and five had to be removed in 1917–18 when war experience showed them to be useless. Two 3in anti-aircraft guns were added at the same time, positioned on the crowns of the stump-masts supporting the cranes.

Careers

New York: Serving with Battle Squadron 6, in the U.S. Atlantic Fleet when war broke out in April 1917; flying the flag of Rear-Admiral Rodman, she and the remainder of Battle Squadron 6 sailed to join the British Grand Fleet in November 1917; arrived 7 December and became Flagship, 6th Battle Squadron; at surrender of German High Seas Fleet she and her squadron were the third in line; flagship of squadron which met and escorted President Wilson to Brest in December 1918, after which she returned to U.S.A.; after peacetime service in the Atlantic and Pacific served in World War II, and was expended as a target 9 July 1948.

Texas: Serving with Battle Squadron 6 in April 1917, based on York River, Virginia; on training duties, and grounded off Block Island 28 September 1917; after three days she was refloated and repaired at New York Navy Yard; refitted for foreign service January 1918 and sailed to join 6th Battle Squadron, Grand Fleet; arrived Scapa Flow 11 February; with the remainder of the Squadron was present at surrender of High Seas Fleet and escorted President Wilson to Brest before returning to U.S.A. in December 1918; served in World War II, and was handed over in 1948 to the State of Texas for preservation as a war memorial; she lies in a permanent berth dredged out of the San Jacinto battlefield.

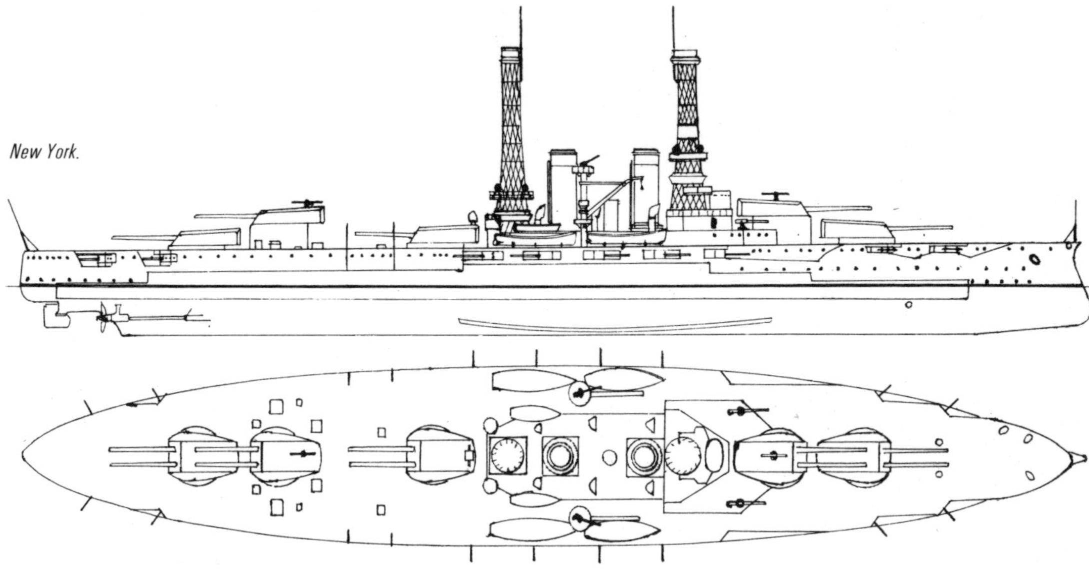

***Left,** three views of New York in British waters – probably the Firth of Forth – in 1918. Note the partial camouflage scheme on the bows and the tapering flush deck (all IWM). Below, New York or Texas photographed from a kite balloon (IWM).*

New York.

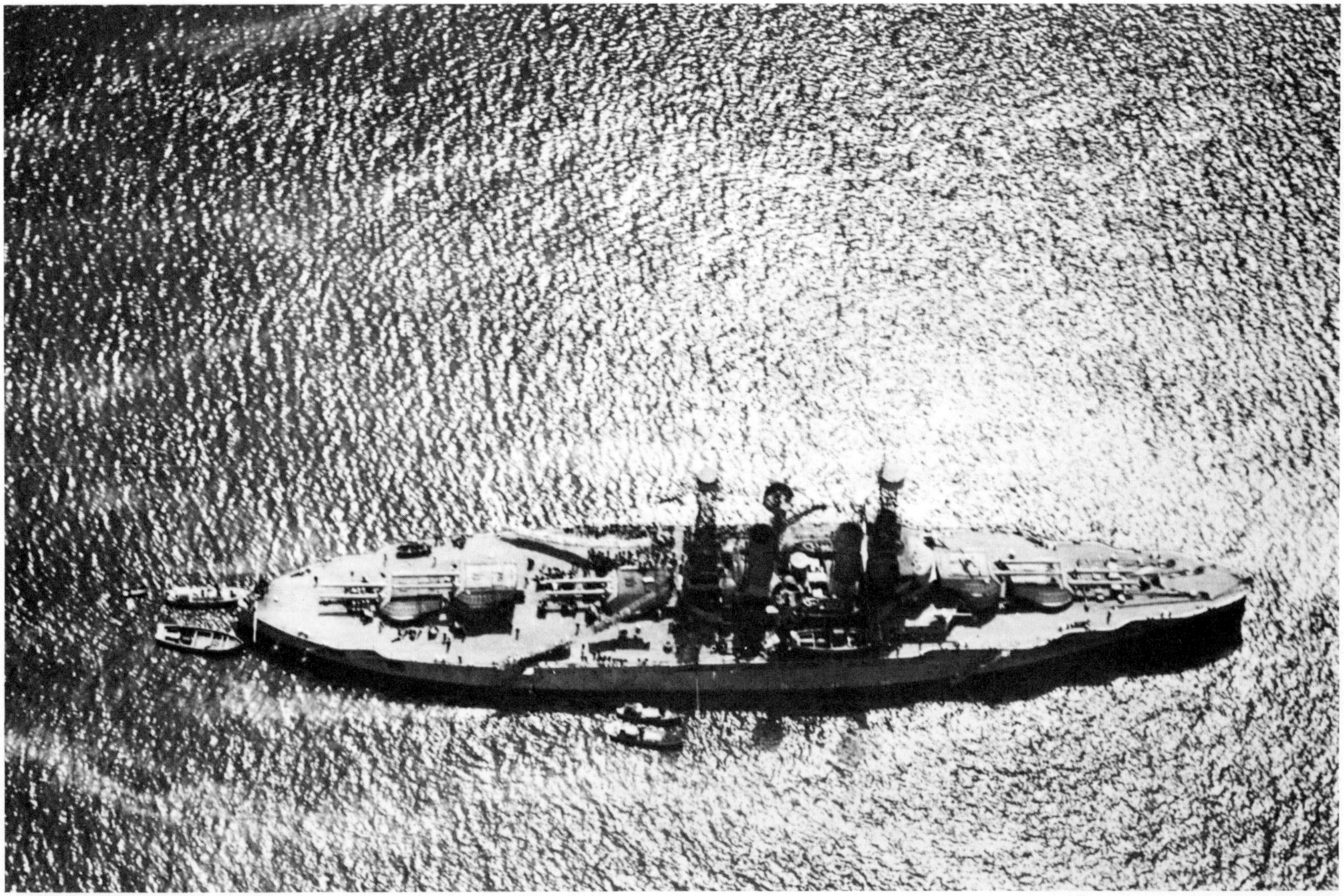

Right, Oklahoma as she appeared at
the end of the war with aircraft
platforms and deflection scales on No. 2
and No. 3 turrets (IWM).

Right, Oklahoma running trials in
1916 (IWM).

Right, Nevada as she appeared in
1919 with wartime modifications,
including aircraft platforms on No. 2
and No. 3 turrets, deflection scales and
range clocks and the forward 5in guns
removed (IWM).

Nevada class

Displacement: 27,500tons (normal):
28,900tons (load condition)
Dimensions: 575ft (wl)×95ft 3in×
28ft 6in
Guns: 10×14in 45cal (2×3, 2×2)
21×5in 51cal (21×1); reduced to
12×5in in 1917
2×3in A.A. (2×1) added in 1917
Torpedo Tubes: 4×21in (submerged,
beam)
Armour: 13½–8in belt; 18–9in
turrets; 16in CT
Machinery: Nevada: 2-shaft Curtis
geared turbines, 26,500hp = 20½knots;
12 Yarrow boilers
Oklahoma: 2-shaft vertical triple-
expansion, 24,800hp = 20½knots;
12 Babcock boilers
Coal Capacity: Nil
Oil Capacity: 1330/2037tons
Endurance: 10,000miles at 10knots
Complement: 864
Cost: £1,705,670 ($6,822,680)
average, excluding guns

	Laid Down	Launched	Completed	Built/Engined
BB36 Nevada	4 Nov 1912	11 July 1914	Mar 1916	Fore River S.B. Co.
BB37 Oklahoma	26 Oct 1912	23 Mar 1914	May 1916	New York S.B. Co.

The two *Nevada* class were the first 'superdreadnoughts' laid down for the U.S. Navy and they marked a radical departure from established practice. For the first time belt armour was concentrated in a citadel to protect the most vital parts of the ship—magazines and machinery; other parts of the ship were protected by internal bulkheads and decks. The chief advantage was the saving in weight which could be devoted to the heaviest belt armour possible, as opposed to thinner armour spread over a wide area of hull. This 'all-or-nothing' system of armouring was universally adopted in other navies after World War I.

The *Nevadas* were also the first American battleships to adopt oil fuel, and triple turrets. They were the first single-funnelled battleships since the old *Texas* (1892).

Gunnery: The 14in guns were mounted in new pattern turrets, which were unique in that all the guns were mounted in a single sleeve, and had to be elevated and depressed together. This made salvo-firing awkward, but as the U.S. Navy was still using the 'follow-the-pointer' system and had not yet adopted the director system, the disadvantage was not immediately obvious. As in the previous class, many of the 5in guns were badly positioned and nine were suppressed in 1917.

Protection: At normal load draught the armour extended from 9ft 6in above the waterline to 8ft 6in below, and was arranged in a single strake, with plates laid vertically. The ends of the ship were left totally unprotected on the waterline, and the 5in guns were similarly unarmoured. The funnel uptakes were given a conical mantle of 12in armour.

Appearance: They were distinguished from earlier dreadnoughts by the single funnel and widely spaced 'basket' masts. From 1917 the forward and after embrasures for 5in guns in the hull were plated over. In 1918 *Oklahoma* was dazzle-painted, and both ships had the normal range clocks and deflection scales added.

Careers

Nevada: Based on Guantanamo Bay, Cuba when war broke out; returned to Norfolk, Virginia to train destroyer crews and gun crews for armed merchantmen; as temporary flagship of Rear-Admiral Rodgers left Hampton Roads 13 August 1918 in company with *Oklahoma* for Bantry Bay, Ireland; arrived 23 August and proceeded to Scapa Flow to join 6th Battle Squadron, Grand Fleet; with other ships escorted President Wilson to Brest in December 1918; heavily damaged by Japanese aerial torpedo at Pearl Harbor 7 December 1941, but repaired and served with distinction during the remainder of World War II; used as target ship at Bikini and sunk 31 July 1948.

Oklahoma: Serving with Battleship Division 6, U.S. Atlantic Fleet in April 1917; stationed at Norfolk and New York until August 1918, when she and *Nevada* were sent to Berehaven, Bantry Bay to join the British Grand Fleet; escorted President Wilson to Brest and then returned to New York; after peacetime service on various stations she was part of the U.S. Pacific Fleet at Pearl Harbor on 7 December 1941; during the Japanese attack she was hit in the magazines by bombs and blew up.

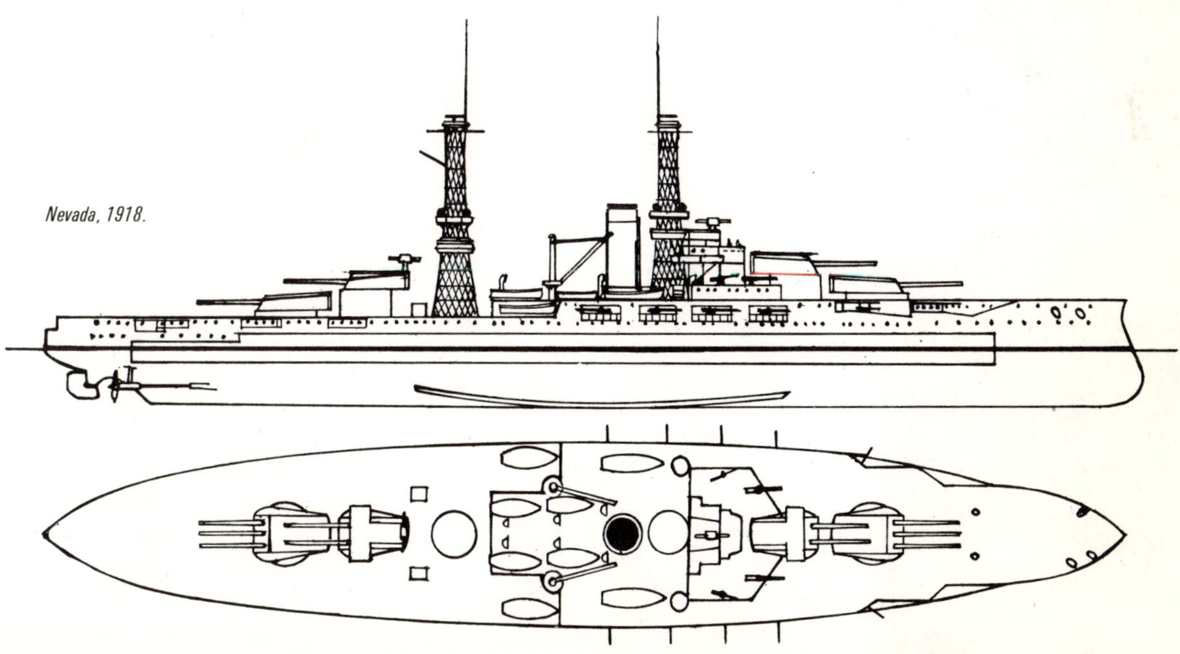
Nevada, 1918.

Right, Arizona as she appeared on
completion at the end of 1916. The 5in
gun positions stand out particularly
clearly having been screened with white
canvas (IWM).

Right, Pennsylvania's aftermost triple
14in gun turrets (IWM).

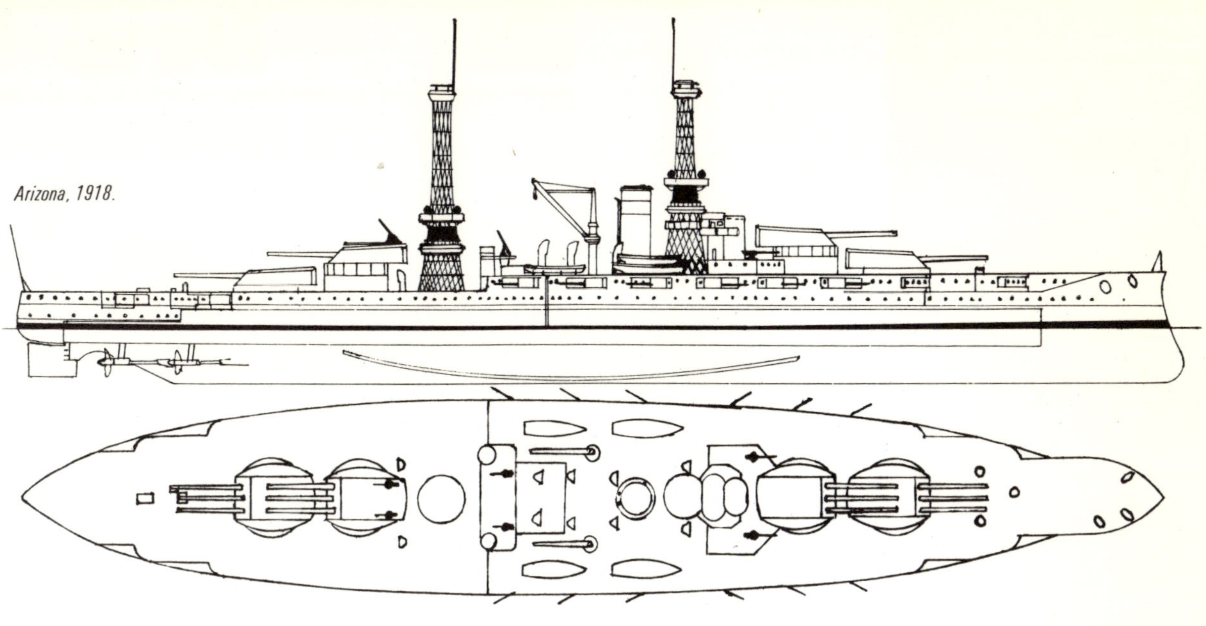

Arizona, 1918.

Pennsylvania class

Displacement: 31,400tons (normal): 33,000 (load condition)
Dimensions: 600ft (wl)×97ft×28ft 9in
Guns: 12×14in 45cal (4×3) 22×5in 51cal (22×1); reduced to 14×5in in 1918
2×3in A.A. (2×1) added in 1918
Torpedo Tubes: 2×21in (submerged, beam)
Armour: 14–8in belt; 18–9in turret; 16in CT

Machinery: Arizona: 4-shaft Parsons turbines, 34,000hp = 21knots; 12 Babcock boilers
Pennsylvania: 4-shaft Curtis turbines, 31,500hp = 21knots; 12 Babcock boilers
Oil Capacity: 1500/2322tons
Endurance: 10,000miles at 10knots
Complement: 915
Cost: £1,485,000 ($5,940,000) excluding guns

	Laid Down	Launched	Completed	Built/Engined
BB38 Pennsylvania	27 Oct 1913	16 Mar 1915	June 1916	Newport News
BB39 Arizona	16 Mar 1914	19 June 1915	Oct 1916	Brooklyn NY

This class marks a fuller development of the revolutionary ideas tested in the *Nevada class*. The adoption of four triple turrets gave 20 per cent more gunpowder without any increase in displacement, and the opportunity was taken to re-arrange the secondary armament.

Although the *Pennsylvania* was in theory the most advanced design afloat, there were disadvantages to offset many of her qualities. The triple 14in guns did not prove superior in practice to British and German twin mountings, being cramped and cumbersome. Again the secondary guns were mounted too far forward and aft, making them virtually useless in anything but calm weather. This was tacitly admitted when eight 5in guns were suppressed in 1917-18.

Machinery: In order to improve fuel consumption at cruising speeds *Pennsylvania* was fitted with gearing to her cruising turbines.

Appearance: They were similar to the *Nevada* class, but could be distinguished by a shorter and wider funnel. In 1917–18 the 5in guns at the bow and stern (eight in all) were removed, and aircraft-platforms similar to the British pattern were mounted on turrets 2 and 3.

Arizona: Had just joined Battleship Division 8 after her shake-down cruise, when war broke out; remained at Norfolk throughout 1917 and most of 1918 as gunnery training ship; joined U.S. 6th Battle Squadron in European waters towards the end of November 1918, and escorted President Wilson to Brest for Peace Conference; repatriated U.S. soldiers from Brest in December; after twenty years of various peacetime duties she was serving in U.S. Pacific Fleet at Pearl Harbor on 7 December 1941; struck by Japanese aerial torpedo and eight bombs, and blew up with the loss of 1100 men.

Pennsylvania: Returned to Yorktown, Virginia from courtesy visit to Haiti on day war broke out; remained on East Coast as Flagship, C-in-C U.S. Atlantic Fleet until December 1918; escorted liner *George Washington* carrying President Wilson from New York to Brest; returned to U.S.A. the same month; after twenty years of service on various stations she was a unit of the U.S. Pacific Fleet at Pearl Harbor in 1941; on 7 December she was slightly damaged while in dry dock; repaired and modernised for service in Pacific; used as target for atomic bombs at Bikini and subsequently sunk as a target 10 February 1948.

New Mexico cl...

	Laid Down	Launched	Completed	Built/Engined
BB40 New Mexico	14 Oct 1915	23 Apr 1917	May 1918	New York NY
(ex-California)				
BB41 Mississippi	5 Apr 1915	25 Jan 1917	Dec 1917	Newport News
BB42 Idaho	20 Jan 1915	30 June 1917	Mar 1919	New York NY

Displacement: 32,000tons (normal);
33,500tons (load condition)
Dimensions: 600ft (wl)×97ft 6in×30ft
Guns: 12×14in 50cal (4×3)
22×5in 51cal (22×1); reduced to 14 in
1918
2×3in A.A. (2×1)
Armour: 14–8in belt; 18–9in
turrets; 16in CT
Machinery: New Mexico: 4-shaft
turbo-electric drive, 27,500hp =
21knots; 9 Babcock boilers
Idaho and Mississippi: 4-shaft geared
turbines, 32,000hp = 21knots;
9 Babcock boilers
Oil Capacity: 2200/3277tons
Endurance: 10,000miles at 10knots
Complement: 1080
Cost: £1,485,000 ($5,940,000)
excluding guns

A class of two ships was authorised in 1914 and a third unit was financed out of the money from the sale of the original *Idaho* and *Mississippi* to Greece—a striking example of how the cost of battleships was rising.

Structurally the *New Mexicos* were only slightly improved *Pennsylvanias*. For the first time the weakness of exposed positions for the 5in guns was realised, and only eight hull positions were provided for secondary guns. These were plated over before completion and as the remaining guns were mounted a complete deck higher no problems were encountered.

The most interesting feature of the class was the introduction of prototype turbo-electric drive in the *New Mexico* herself. This was a highly novel arrangement of steam turbines driving generators, which in turn provided current for four-shaft electric motors. At the time electric drive was hailed as a great technical achievement, but after a decade of service the *New Mexico* and later ships were reengined with conventional geared turbines.

The Panama Canal had been opened in 1914, and had been made wide enough for the dreadnoughts then envisaged. However, in this class the beam was already only thirteen feet narrower than the canal locks, which shows how rapidly dreadnoughts were growing in size.

Appearance: They were similar to *Pennsylvania* in appearance, but with only two gun-ports on each side, under the forecastle and abaft turrets No.3 and No.4; other secondary guns were mounted higher. For the first time a distinctive 'clipper' bow was adopted.

Careers

Only *Mississippi* and *New Mexico* were completed before the end of hostilities, but they survived to play a major role in the Pacific in World War II, and were sold in 1947–56.

Mississippi: Commissioned for U.S. Atlantic Fleet, and did not see service outside American waters until after the Armistice; reconstructed and served in Pacific in World War II; in 1946 altered as weapon trials ship to replace *Wyoming*; fired the world's first anti-aircraft guided missiles in 1952, and finally sold 28 November 1956 to Bethlehem Steel for breaking up.

New Mexico: Joined 4th Squadron, Atlantic Fleet, and remained in American waters until the Armistice; scrapped 1947.

Mississippi, 1918.

Above, *New Mexico seen at Brest in February 1919. Note the distinctive clipper bow and that the gun positions under the forecastle have been plated up (IWM).*

Tennessee class

Displacement: 32,300tons (normal): 34,000tons (load condition)
Dimensions: 600ft (wl)×97ft 3in× 30ft 3in
Guns: 12×14in (4×3)
14×5in (14×1)
4×3in A.A. (4×1)
Torpedo Tubes: 2×21in (submerged, beam)
Armour: 14–8in belt; 18–9in turrets; 16in CT
Machinery: 4-shaft turbo-electric drive, 26,800hp (California 28,500hp) = 21knots; 8 Babcock boilers (Bureau Express in California)
Oil Capacity: 2200/4656tons
Endurance: 10,000miles at 10knots
Complement: 1083
Cost: Not published, but exceeded £1,500,000 ($6,000,000)

	Laid Down	Launched	Completed	Built/Engined
BB43 Tennessee	14 May 1917	30 Apr 1919	June 1920	New York NY
BB44 California	25 Oct 1916	20 Nov 1919	Oct 1921	Mare Island NY

Virtually repeat *New Mexicos*, these dispensed for the first time with all gun-ports in the hull. Neither ship was completed in time to see service in the war, but both survived heavy damage at Pearl Harbor to be completely rebuilt for service in World War II. Scrapped in 1959–60 at Baltimore.

With the completion of this class the U.S. Navy planned to have seven 'superdreadnoughts' (including the *Pennsylvanias* and *New Mexicos*) with a common armament, speed and handling characteristics. With this class we can say that pre1914 American ideas of battleship design reached their peak.

Appearance: Both ships resembled the *New Mexico* class closely, both in the design stage and as completed.

Colorado class

Displacement: 32,600tons (normal): 33,590tons (load condition)
Dimensions: 600ft (wl)×97ft 6in× 30ft 6in
Guns: 8×16in 45cal (4×2)
12×5in 51cal (12×1)
4×3in A.A. (4×1)
Torpedo Tubes: 2×21in (submerged, beam)
Armour: 16–8in belt; 18–9in turrets; 16in CT
Machinery: 4-shaft turbo-electric drive, 28,900hp = 21knots; 8 Babcock boilers
Oil Capacity: 2200/4570tons
Endurance: 10,000miles at 10knots
Complement: 1080
Cost: £1,383,000 ($5,532,000) excluding guns

	Laid Down	Launched	Completed	Built/Engined
BB45 Colorado	29 May 1919	22 Mar 1921	Aug 1923	New York S.B.
BB46 Maryland	24 Apr 1917	20 Mar 1920	July 1921	Newport News
BB47 Washington	30 June 1919	1 Sept 1921	—	New York S.B.
BB48 West Virginia	12 Apr 1920	19 Nov 1921	Dec 1923	Newport News

In 1916 Congress authorised the laying down of the first ships in what was to be a gigantic new fleet of the most powerful battleships in the world. Although the preceding ships of the *New Mexico* and *Tennessee* classes had been laid down since 1914, their design had been approved before the appearance of the newest British ships, the 15in gunned *Queen Elizabeth* class. In order to outclass the British ships the Americans pushed gun calibre up from 14in to 16in, but in order to keep size within reasonable bounds the triple turret was sacrificed in favour of eight 16in guns in a *Queen Elizabeth* layout.

The four *Colorados* were only the first of a projected series of sixteen capital ships, but they were so delayed that only the *Maryland* had been begun by the end of 1918. One, the *Washington*, was cancelled in 1922 under the terms of the Washington Disarmament Treaty, but the others survived to see service in World War II. The hull of the *Washington* was sunk as a gunnery and aircraft target on 25 November 1924 and the others were scrapped on the west coast of the United States between 1959 and 1961.

Appearance: As completed, they had the clipper bow, two broadly spaced thin funnels, and the usual 'basket' masts. The bridgework was more extensive than in previous classes.

South Dakota class

Displacement: 43,200tons (normal): 47,000tons (load condition)
Dimensions: 660ft (wl)×104ft 9in× 33ft
Guns: 12×16in 50cal (4×3)
16×6in 53cal (16×1)
4×3in A.A. (4×1)
Torpedo Tubes: 2×21in (submerged, beam)
Armour: 13½–6in belt; 18–9in turrets; 16in CT
Machinery: 4-shaft turbo-electric drive, 60,000hp = 23knots; 16 Babcock boilers
Oil Capacity: Not known
Endurance: Probably 10,000miles at 10knots
Complement: Approximately 1200
Cost: Not known

	Laid Down	Launched	Completed	Built/Engined
BB48 South Dakota	15 Mar 1920	—	—	New York NY
BB50 Indiana	1 Aug 1920	—	—	New York NY
BB51 Montana	1 Sept 1920	—	—	Mare Island NY
BB52 North Carolina	12 Jan 1920	—	—	Norfolk NY
BB53 Iowa	17 May 1920	—	—	Newport News
BB54 Massachusetts	4 Apr 1921	—	—	Bethlehem Quincy

This class of six ships was the second part of the big programme of naval expansion begun in 1916. When first authorised in 1917 they were the largest capital ships in the world and had the heaviest armament. The design was a logical development from the *Colorado* class, but with triple 16in replacing the twin turrets. However, the main belt armour was thinner and horsepower was increased in order to add two knots' speed.

Appearance: The published sketch designs show the *South Dakotas* to have been among the most outlandish looking battleships ever conceived, as they were to have had four funnels arranged in a square, but trunked into one pyramidal casing. The hull was basically similar to the *Colorado*'s, but the secondary guns were arranged in an unusual series of double-storey casemates. The class also marked the return of the 6in gun to American battleships, a step which was not to be repeated in any capital ship completed for the U.S. Navy.

None of the class was laid down until 1920, by which time public agitation against the new programme was growing. When it was learned that both the Japanese and British had taken the first steps towards building ships which would be individually superior to the American ships, and that a new naval arms race was looming, the U.S. Government wisely chose to call a halt. The result was the Washington Naval Disarmament Conference, following the ratification of which, the six *South Dakotas* were cancelled on 8 February 1922, along with the British and Japanese ships. The hulls were broken up in 1923 to clear the slipways.

Although the most powerful American ships of the period, and the most powerful in the world when laid down, the *South Dakotas* do not display the same blend of defensive and offensive power seen in the *Colorados*. The relatively thin belt and the idiosyncratic layout of secondary guns certainly do not compare with the simplicity and strength of the earlier class. Looking at them in retrospect one feels that they were conceived more to boost national prestige than to fulfil any pressing tactical fleet requirement.

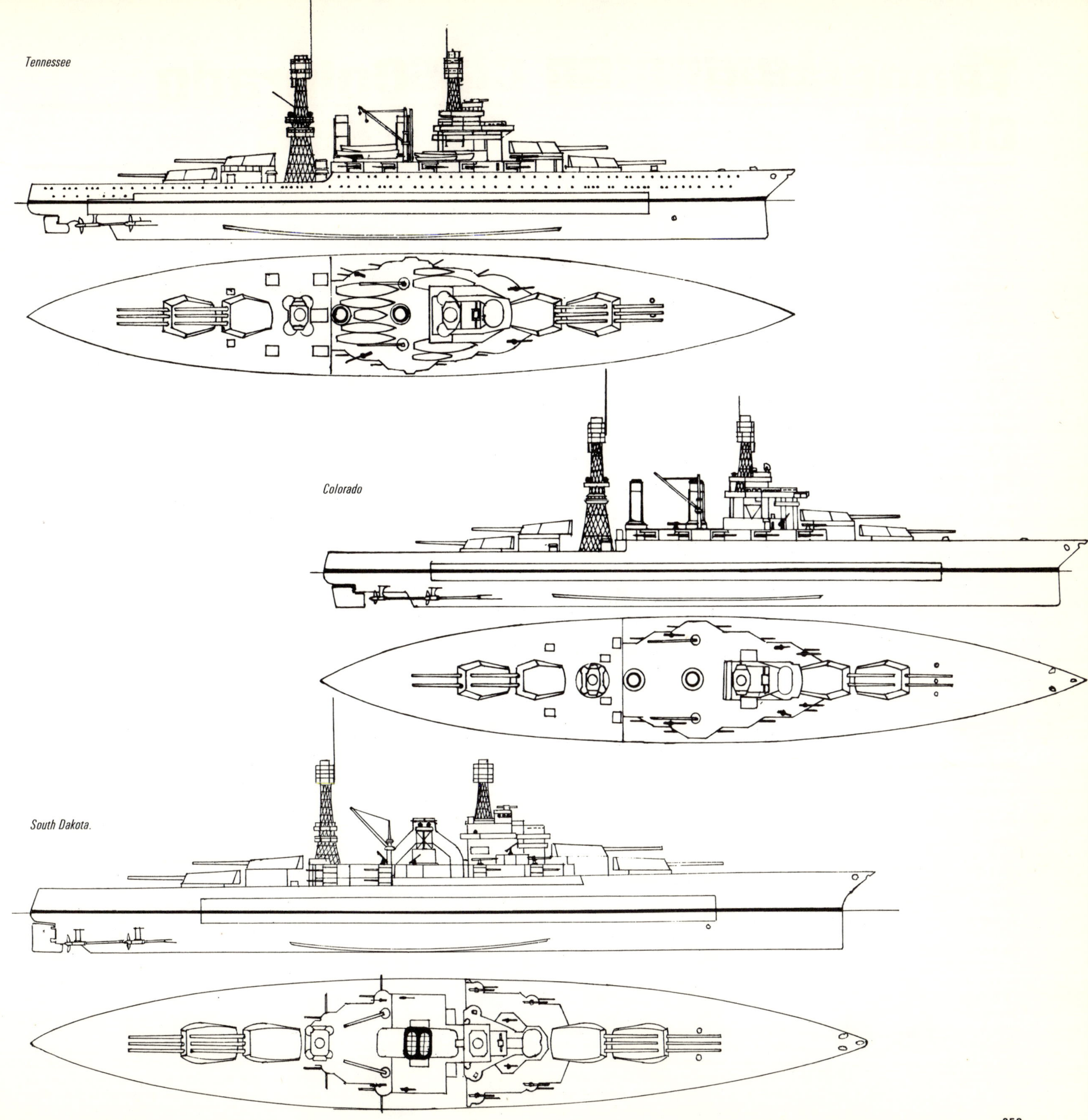

Tennessee
Colorado
South Dakota.

Lexington class

Displacement: 43,500tons (normal, for final design)

Dimensions: 850ft (wl)×105ft 6in× 31ft 3in

Guns: Original design: 10×14in (2×3, 2×2)
20×5in (20×1)
Second design: 8×16in (4×2)
14×6in (14×1)
Final design: 8×16in 50cal (4×2)
16×6in 53cal (16×1)
6×3in A.A. (6×1)

Torpedo Tubes: 4×21in (above water, beam at stern)

Armour: 7½in belt; 11–5in turrets; 12in CT

Machinery: 4-shaft turbo-electric drive, 180,000hp = 33¼knots; 16 Yarrow or Babcock boilers

Oil Capacity: Not known

Endurance: Not known, but probably lower than South Dakota class

Complement: 1315

Cost: Not known

	Laid Down	Launched	Completed	Built/Engined
CC1 Lexington (ex-Constitution)	8 Jan 1921	—	—	Bethlehem, Quincy
CC2 Constellation	18 Aug 1920	—	—	Newport News S.B.
CC3 Saratoga	23 Sept 1920	—	—	New York NY
CC4 Ranger (ex-Lexington)	23 June 1921	—	—	Newport News S.B.
CC5 Constitution (ex-Ranger)	25 Sept 1920	—	—	Philadelphia NY
CC6 United States	25 Sept 1920	—	—	Philadelphia NY

These six battle cruisers were the only vessels of this type to be ordered for the U.S. Navy, and they were the final instalment of the 1916 programme of naval expansion. When the changes in design are studied, it is clear that the Bureau of Ships' designers were under pressure to meet some unreasonable requirements.

The original design called for 14in guns disposed as in the *Nevadas*, but with 24 boilers and seven funnels. These funnels were to have been disposed in two groups of two abreast, and three more on the centreline. Then, when it was decided to give the new ships an armament of 16in guns on a par with the *Colorados*, four boilers were dropped, and with them two of the centreline funnels. Eventually a more rational layout of two large centreline funnels was adopted for the final design, with only sixteen boilers.

The armour arrangements as originally proposed were dangerously inadequate, and as half the boilers were placed above the armour (the engine-room consisting of a double-storey arrangement) these huge ships would have been vulnerable to being disabled by a 6in shell in action. They represent not only a departure from American practice but a departure from even the dubious logic of Fisher's battle cruisers, considering that the design was revised to incorporate lessons from Jutland.

Work on all six was suspended on 2 August 1922 to conform with the Washington Treaty and four were cancelled outright in August 1923. The *Lexington* and *Saratoga* were redesigned as aircraft-carriers (CV1 and CV2) and completed in 1927. In this role they proved highly successful, and acted as the backbone of American naval air power. *Lexington* was sunk by Japanese carrier planes in the Battle of the Coral Sea, 8 May 1942; *Saratoga* survived heavy war damage and was expended as a target for the atom bomb at Bikini in July 1946.

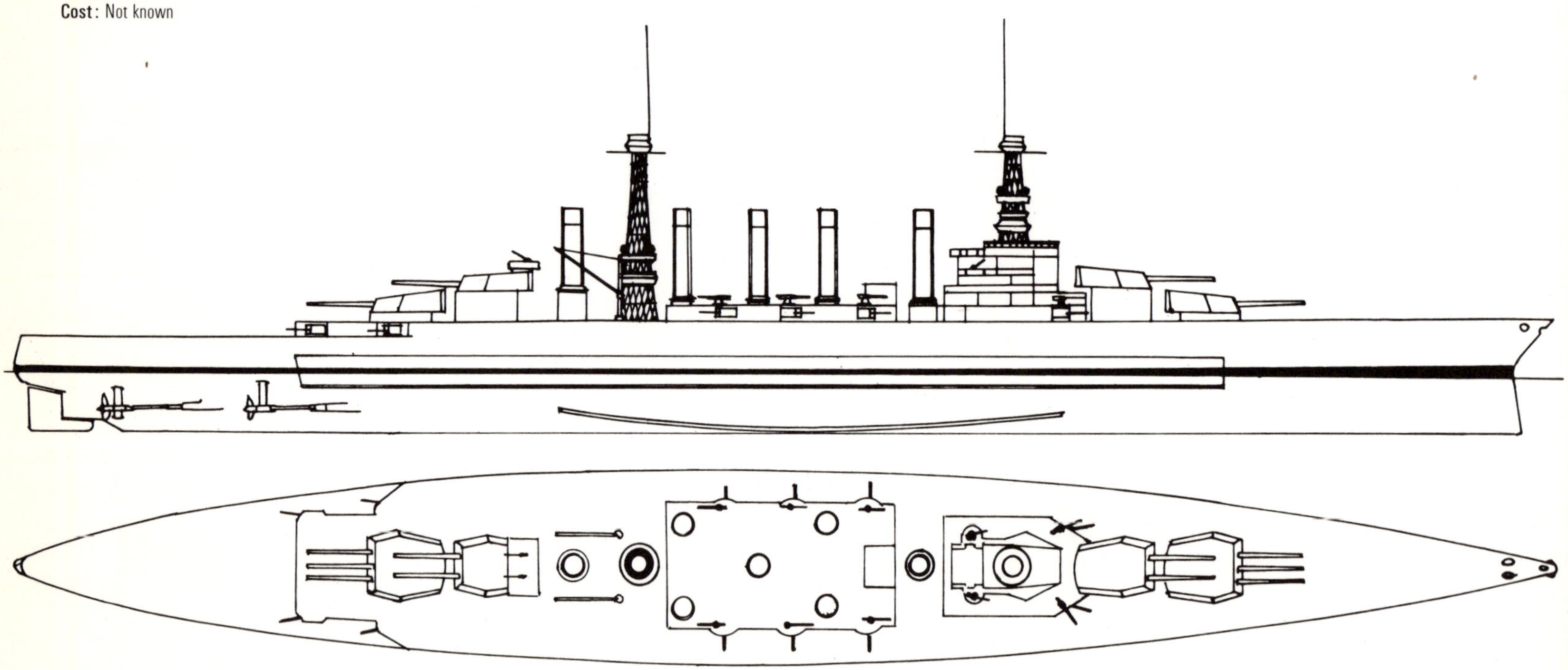

Appendices

Below, the Argentine dreadnought Moreno as she appeared between the wars (NMM)

Neutral Navies

All the major navies were involved in the war by 1917, leaving seven neutral navies whose fleets contained battleships. Of these only Argentina and Spain possessed dreadnoughts, the remainder having nothing larger than coast-defence ships.

Argentina

The Armada Republica Argentina was largely obsolescent, but in 1910 friction between Argentina, Brazil and Chile had resulted in the ordering of two dreadnought battleships. The remaining ships were all old and worn out.

Moreno; Rivadavia: 12×12in, 12×6in guns; built 1910–14 in U.S.A.

Independencia; Libertad: 2×9·4in, 4×4·7in guns; built 1890–2 in Great Britain.

Almirante Brown: 10×6in, 4×4·7in guns; built in Great Britain 1880 and modernised 1897.

Chile

The Chileans had two very powerful dreadnoughts under construction in British shipyards in 1914, but both these were pre-empted in August 1914. In 1917 other warships were transferred to compensate Chile for this, and in 1920 one of the ships, the *Almirante Latorre*, returned to Chilean ownership. The Chilean Navy was by far the most efficient of South American navies, and had recently begun a rearmament programme to replace obsolete tonnage.

Almirante Cochrane; Almirante Latorre: See *Canada* and *Eagle* under British section; *Eagle* became an aircraft carrier, but *Canada* was completed for British service.

Captain Prat: 4×9·4in, 8×4·7in guns; built in France 1888–93 and modernised 1909–10.

Denmark

The Royal Danish Navy was small but efficient, and relied on a home-based shipbuilding industry. Although placed in a dangerous position, with British and German warships likely to infringe her territorial waters, Denmark was not drawn into the conflict.

Nils Juel: 10×5·9in guns; built 1914–23 at Copenhagen.

Peder Skram: 2×9·4in, 4×5·9in guns; built 1905–9 at Copenhagen.

Skjold: 1×9·4in, 3×4·7in guns; built 1893–6 at Copenhagen.

Olfert Fischer: 2×9·4in, 4×5·9in guns; built 1900–4 at Copenhagen.

Herluf Trolle: 2×9·4in, 4×5·9in guns; built 1896–1900 at Copenhagen.

Iver Hvitfeldt: 2×10·25in, 8×57mm guns; built 1884–7 at Copenhagen and modernised 1907.

Netherlands

The Royal Netherlands Navy's heavy units were deployed to protect the Dutch colonial possessions, while home defence was entrusted to torpedo-craft. There was a strong home-based shipbuilding industry but guns came from Germany.

Konigin Regentes; De Ruyter; Hertog Henrik: 2×9·4in, 4×5·9in guns; built 1898–1904 at Amsterdam.

Marten Harpertszoon Tromp: 2×9·4in, 4×5·9in guns; built 1903–6 at Amsterdam.

Jacob Van Heemskerck: 2×9·4in, 6×5·9in guns; built 1904–8 at Amsterdam.

De Zeven Provincien: 2×11in, 4×5·9in guns; built 1908–12 at Amsterdam.

Norway

Like the other Scandinavian navies the Royal Norwegian Navy could use its rugged indented coastline to aid defence. Large battleships were too expensive and unwieldy for local defence, and for this purpose the Norwegians relied on small well-protected ships.

Harald Haarfagre; Tordenskjold: 2×8·2in, 6×4·7in guns; built 1896–8 in England.

Norge; Eidsvold: 2×8·2in, 6×6in guns; built 1899–1901 in England.

Bjørgvin; Nidaros: See *Gorgon* and *Glatton* under British section; taken over while under construction for conversion to monitors.

Spain

Spain had suffered the destruction of a large part of her navy at the hands of the United States in 1898, and so three dreadnought battleships were ordered in 1908 as part of a programme of replacement. Although built in Spain with Spanish labour, material and technical assistance were provided by a British syndicate.

Pelayo: 2×12·6in, 2×11in guns; built 1885–90 in France, and modernised 1897–8.

Alfonso XIII: 8×12in, 20×4in guns; built 1910–15 at Ferrol.

España: Guns as *Alfonso XIII*; built 1909–14 at Ferrol.

Jaime I: Guns as *Alfonso XIII*; built 1912–21 at Ferrol.

Sweden

It is not inappropriate that the first Swedish ironclads were copies of the famous turret-ships built for the United States by a Swedish engineer, John Ericsson. Unlike Norway, Sweden was able to meet all her naval requirements from her own shipbuilding resources, and by 1914 she had a flourishing armament industry as well.

Svea; Göta; Thule: 1×8·2in, 7×6in guns; built 1884–93 at Gothenburg (*Svea* and *Göta*) and Stockholm, and modernised 1901–4.

Oden; Njord; Thor: 2×10in, 4×4·7in guns; built 1894–9 in Sweden and modernised 1914–17.

Dristigheten: 2×8·2in, 6×6in guns; built 1898–1901 at Gothenburg.

Aran; Wasa; Tapperheten; Manligheten: 2×8·2in, 6×6in guns; built 1899–1904 in Sweden.

Oscar II: 2×8·2in, 8×6in guns; built 1903–7 at Gothenburg.

Sverige: 4×11in, 8×6in guns; built 1912–17 at Gothenburg.

Drottning Victoria: Guns as *Sverige*; built 1914–21 at Gothenburg.

Gustav V: Guns as *Sverige*; built 1914–22 at Malmö.

Above, the Danish Olfert Fischer (Author's collection).

Above, the Swedish Aran (Author's collection).

Above, the Swedish Gustav V (Author's collection).

Bibliography

Breyer, S. — **Schlachtschiffe und Schlachtkreuzer 1905–1970**
Munich, 1970

Churchill, W. S. — **The World Crisis**
London and New York, 1923–31. In six volumes

Colledge, J. J. — **Ships of the Royal Navy**
Newton Abbot and East Orange, New Jersey, 1969–70. In two volumes

Corbett, J., and Newbolt, H. — **Naval Operations**
London, 1920–31; reprinted in New York, 1970. In five volumes

Forstmeier, F. — **Deutsche Grosskampfschiffe 1915–1918**
Munich, 1970

Fraccaroli, A. — **Italian Warships of W.W.1**
London, 1969

Frost, Commander H. — **The Battle of Jutland**
London, 1936; reprinted in Annapolis, Maryland, 1970

Giorgerini, G., and Nani, A. — **Le Navi di Linea Italiane**
Rome, 1966

Gogg, K. — **Osterreichs Kriegsmarine 1848–1915**
Salzburg, 1967

Greger, R. — **Die Russische Flotte in Ersten Weltkrieg**
Munich, 1970

Gröner, Dr E. — **Die Deutschen Kriegsschiffe 1815–1936**
Munich, 1937

Hough, R. — **Dreadnought**
London and New York, 1964

Hough, R. — **The Big Battleship**
London, 1966, and New York, 1967

Hough, R. — **Admiral of the Fleet**
London, 1969, and New York, 1970. A biography of Lord Fisher

Hovgaard, W. — **Modern History of Warships**
London, 1920; Reprinted in London, 1970, and in Annapolis, 1971

Jane, F. T. — **The Imperial Russian Navy**
London, 1904

Jane, F. T. — **The Imperial Japanese Navy**
London, 1904

Jane, F. T. — **The British Battle Fleet**
London, 1915. In two volumes

Jane, F. T. (Ed) — **Jane's Fighting Ships**
for various years, but especially those for 1914–19

Jellicoe, J. R., 1st Viscount — **The Grand Fleet, 1914–1916**
London, 1919

Jellicoe, J. R., 1st Viscount — **The Crisis of the Naval War**
London, 1920

Jentschura, H. G., Jung, D., and Mickel, P. — **Die Japanischen Kriegsschiffe 1869–1945**
Munich, 1970

Kroschel, G., and Evers, A. L. — **Die Deutsche Flotte 1848–1945**
Wilhelmshaven, 1962

Kriegsmarine – Ministerium — **Der Krieg zur See**
Berlin, 1914–22. Seven sets by various authors

Le Fleming, H. M. — **Warships of World War 1**
London, 1962. Published in several parts and as a combined volume

Leyland, J. (Ed) — **Brassey's Naval Annual**
For various years, especially in the period 1914–19

Marder, A. J. — **British Naval Policy, 1880–1905**
London, 1940, and Newcastle-upon-Tyne, 1964

Marder, A. J. — **From the Dreadnought to Scapa Flow – The Royal Navy in the Fisher Era**
Oxford and New York, 1961–70. In five volumes

Parkes, Dr O. — **British Battleships**
London, 1956; reprinted in London, 1971

Pater, A. F. — **United States Battleships, The History of America's Greatest Fighting Fleet**
Beverly Hills, California, 1968

Rehder, J. — **Die Verluste der Kriegsflotten 1914–1918**
Munich, 1968

Silverstone, P. — **U.S. Warships of World War 1**
London and Garden City, New York, 1970

Sokol, Prof, A.   **The Imperial and Royal Austro-Hungarian Navy**
Annapolis, Maryland, 1969

Taylor, J. C.   **German Warships of World War 1**
London and Garden City, New York, 1969

Tirpitz, Admiral A. von   **My Memoirs**
London, 1919

Tomitch, V. M.   **Warships of the Imperial Russian Navy**
1968

Watts, A. J., and Gordon, B. G.   **Imperial Japanese Navy**
London, 1971

Wilson, H. W.   **Battleships in Action**
London, 1896. Reprinted in Michigan, 1968

Young, Filson   **With the Battle Cruisers**
London, 1921

Austro-Hungarian dreadnought
Viribus Unitis

1. Bow Torpedo Tube
2. No. 1 Barbette
3. Magazines
4. No. 2 Barbette
5. Armoured Tube
6. Conning Tower
7. Boilers
8. Boiler Uptakes
9. Main Machinery
10. After Conning Tower
11. No. 3 Barbette
12. No. 4 Barbette
13. Emergency Steering

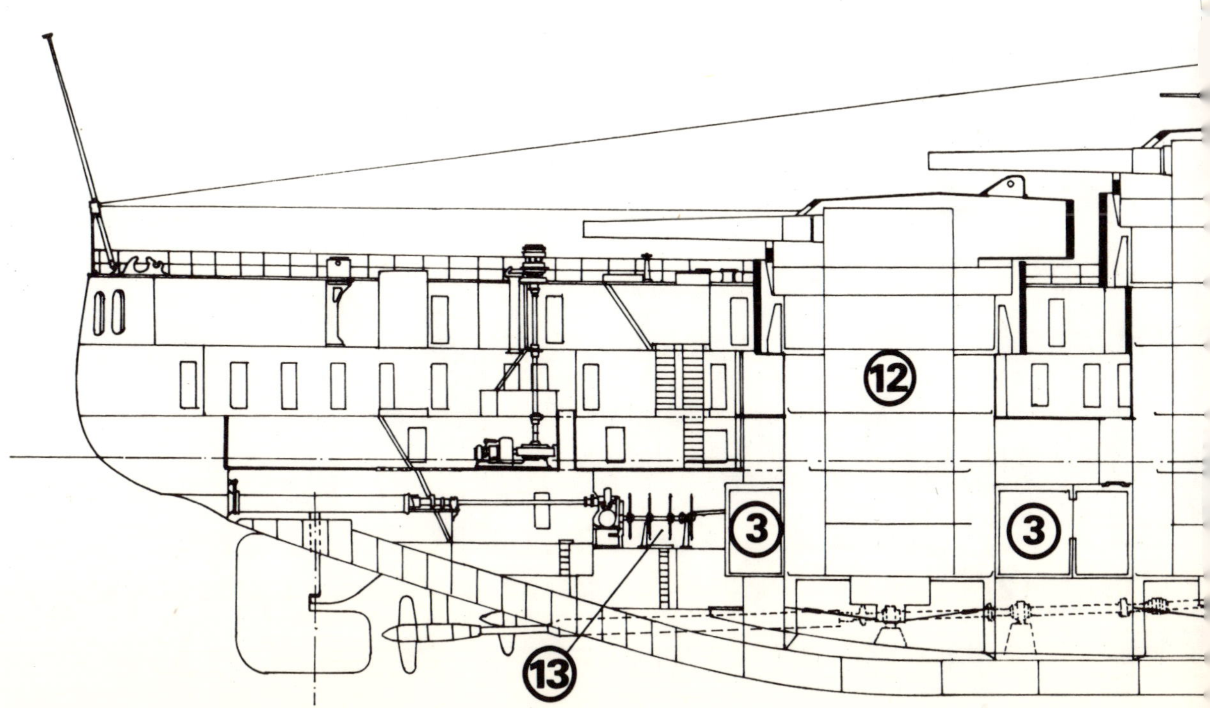

British battle cruiser Australia

1. No. 1 Barbette
2. Magazines
3. Armoured Tube to Conning Tower
4. Conning Tower
5. Boilers
6. Boiler Uptakes
7. No. 2 Barbette
8. No. 3 Barbette
9. Main Machinery
10. No. 4 Barbette
11. Emergency Steering

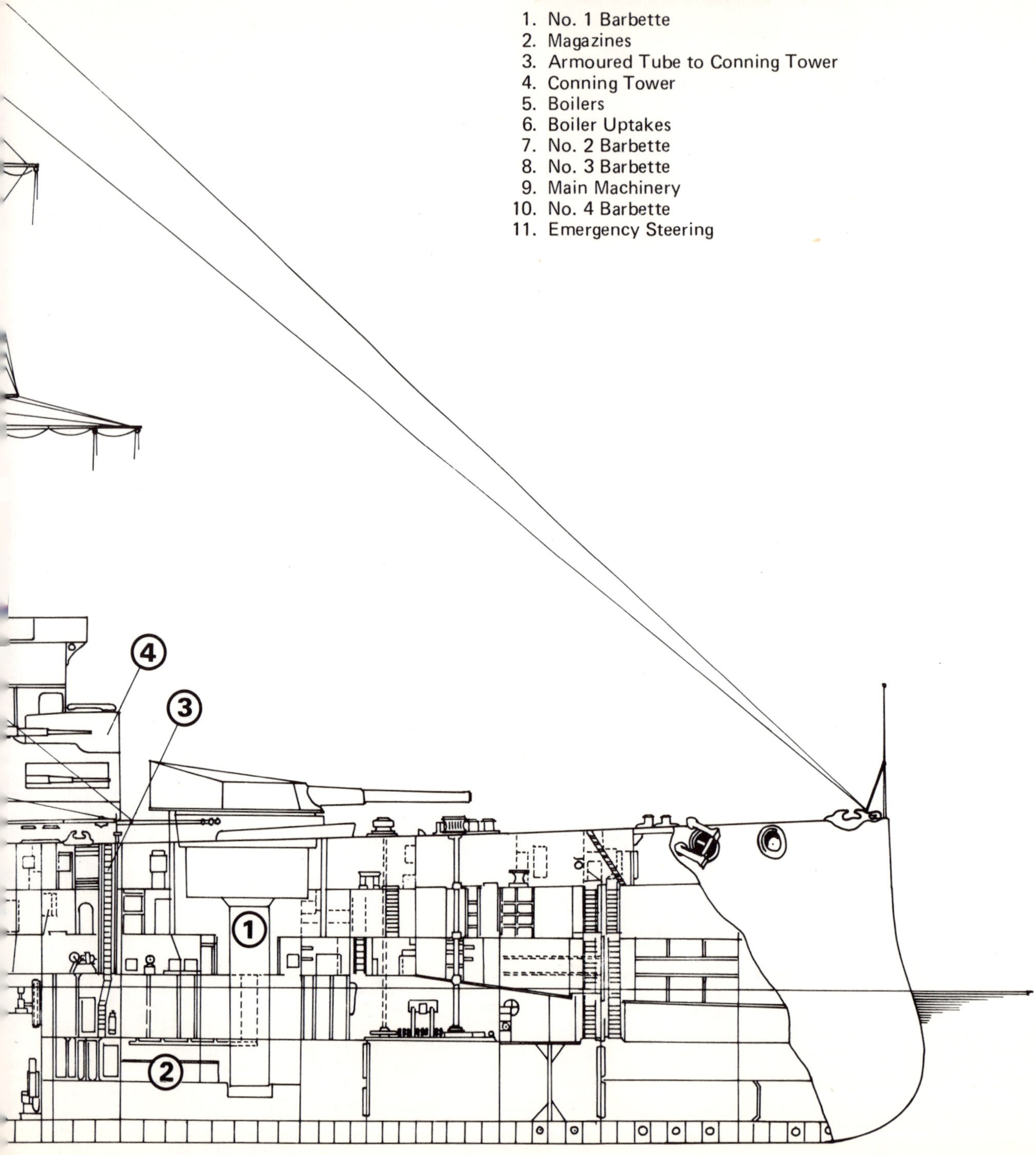

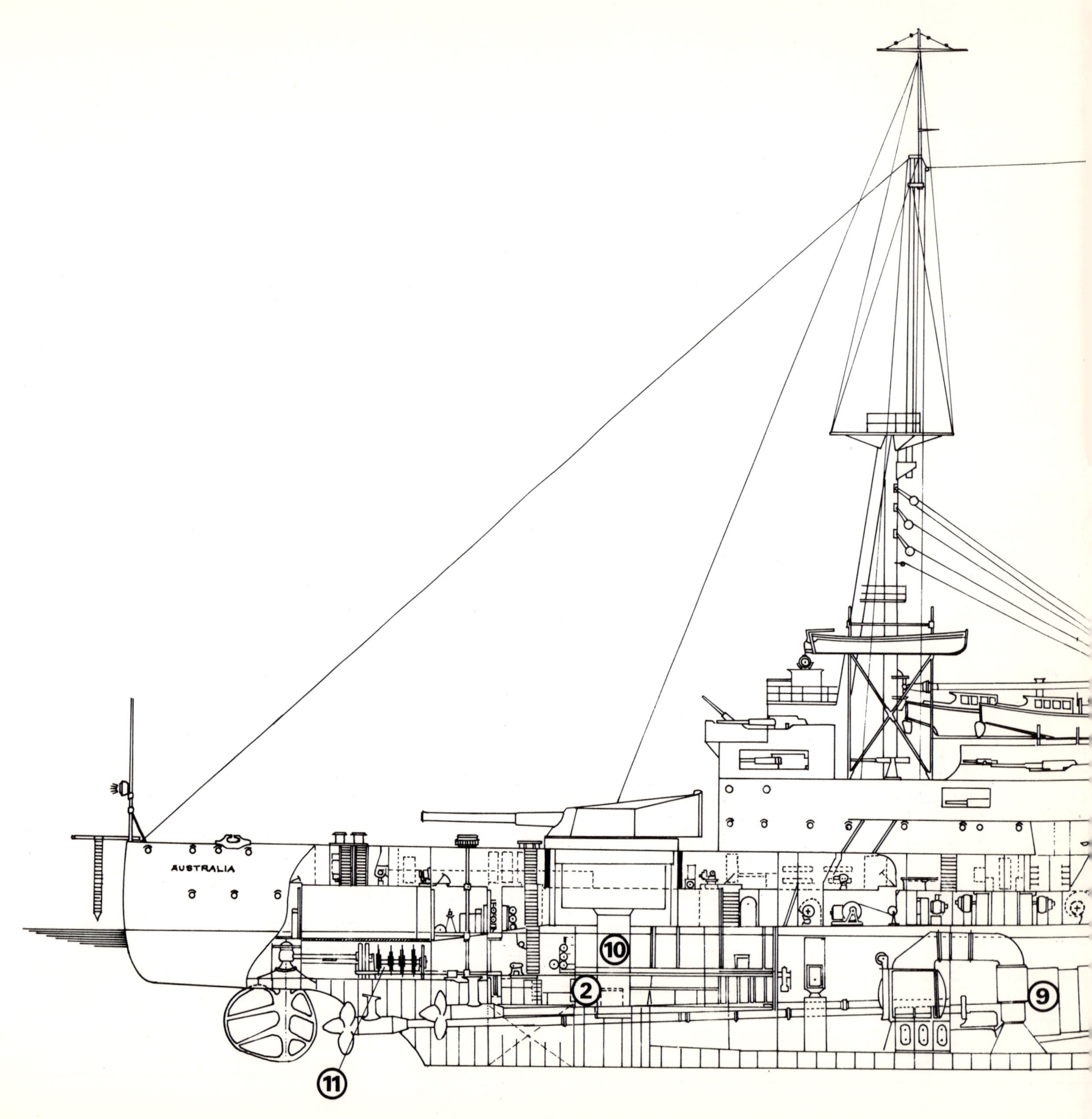

AUSTRALIA
10
2
9
11

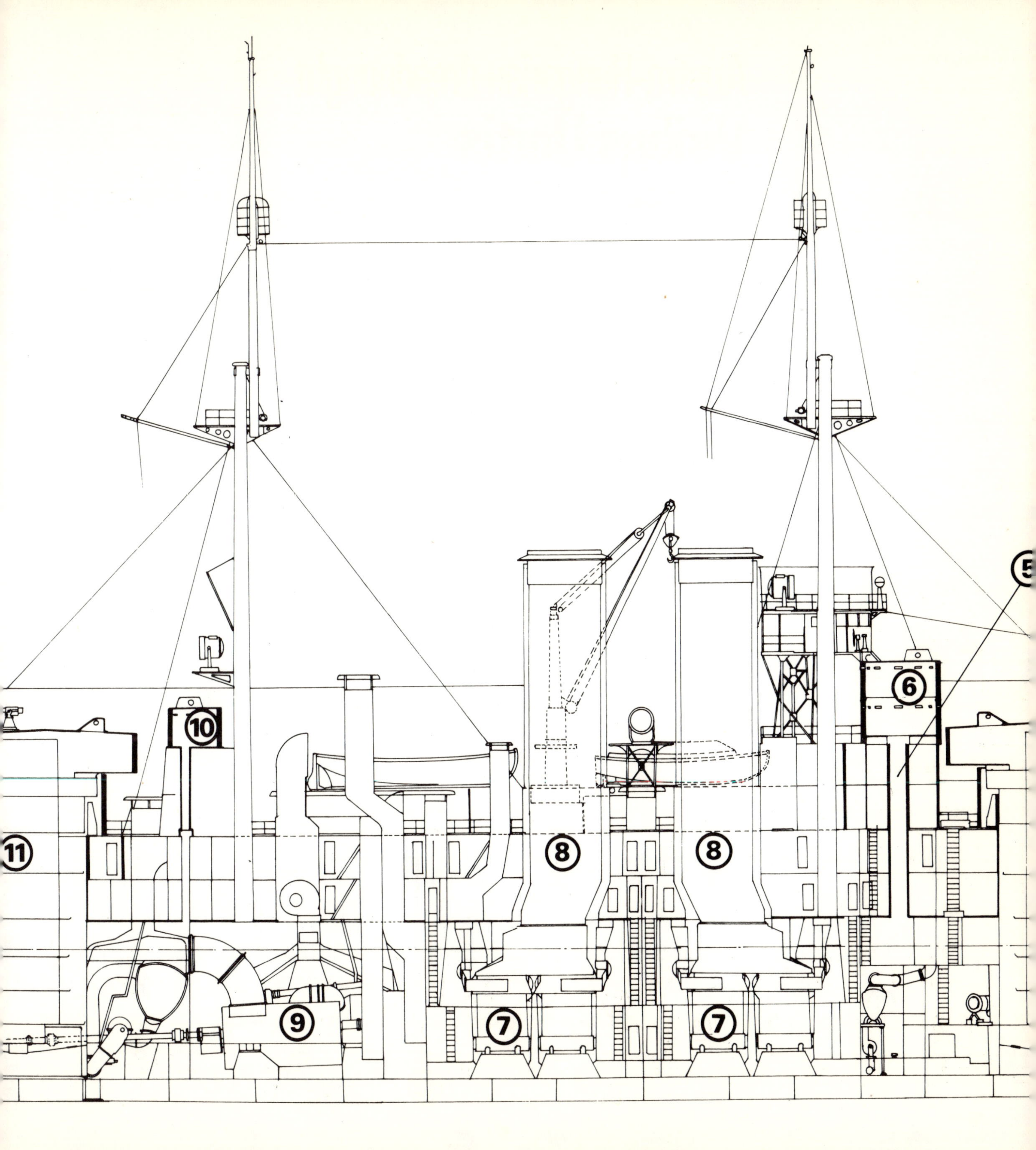

11
10
9
8
8
7
7
6
5

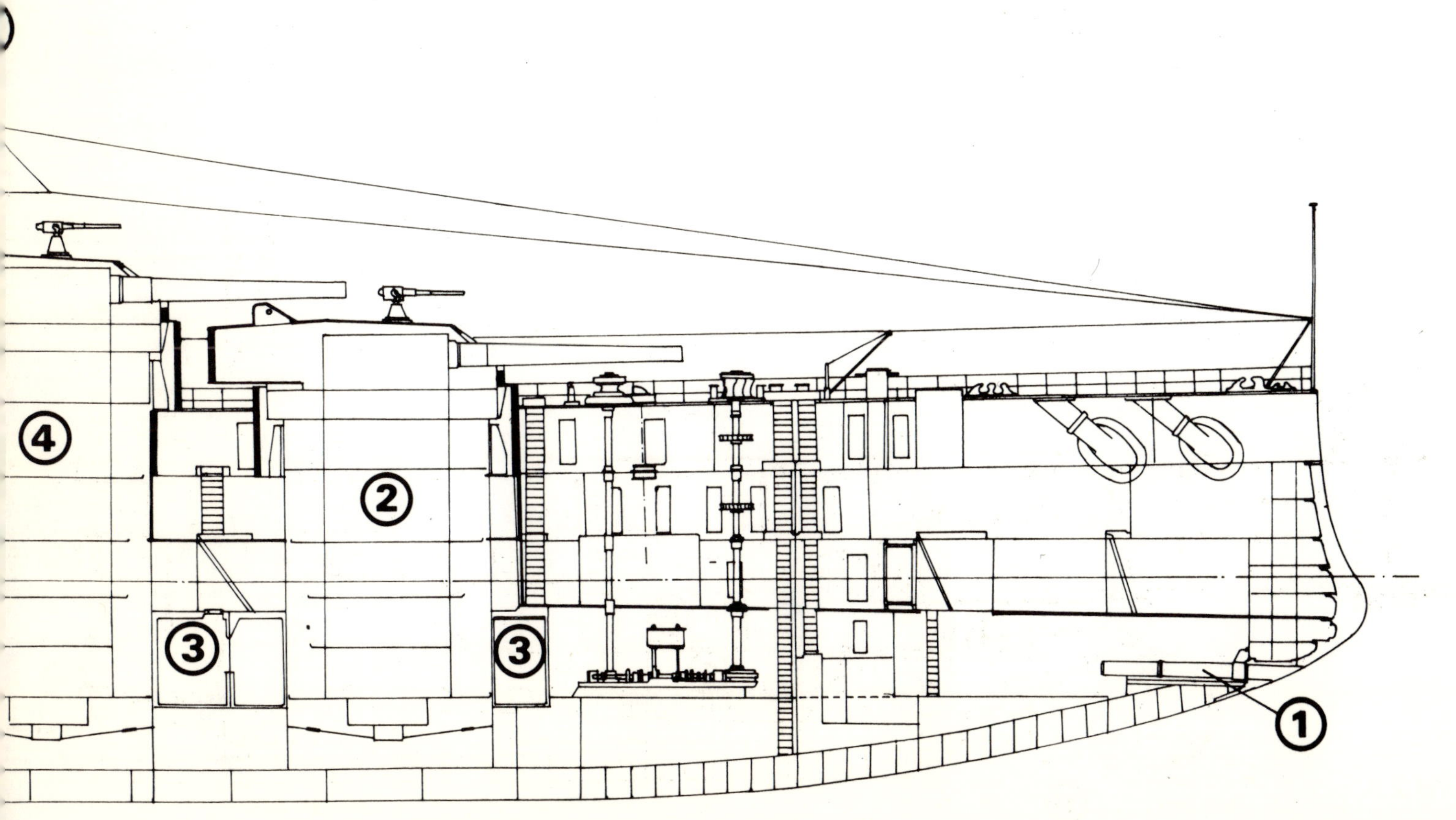

4
2
3
3
1

Index of ship names